Religious Leaders
of the World

MACMILLAN
PROFILES

Religious Leaders of the World

Macmillan Reference USA

an imprint of the Gale Group

Detroit • New York • San Francisco • London • Boston • Woodbridge, CT

Cover design by Berrian Design

Front cover, clockwise from top: Desmond Tutu (AP/Wide World); Stephen Wise (AP/Wide World); Dalai Lama (CORBIS); Pope John Paul II (CORBIS)

Contents

Preface

Macmillan Profiles: *Religious Leaders of the World* is a unique reference featuring over 150 profiles of significant spiritual leaders worldwide, from ancient times to the present. Macmillan Reference USA recognizes the need for reliable, accurate, and accessible biographies of notable figures in world and American history. The **Macmillan Profile** series can help meet that need by providing new collections of articles that were carefully selected to complement the middle and high school history curriculum. Macmillan Reference USA has published a wide array of award-winning reference materials for libraries across the world. It is likely that several of the encyclopedias on the shelves in this library were published by Macmillan Reference or Charles Scribner's Sons. All biographies in **Macmillan Profiles** have been recast and tailored for a younger audience by a team of experienced writers and editors. New biographies were commissioned to supplement entries from original sources.

Few people have had a greater impact on world history and culture than religious leaders. Since ancient times their teachings have shaped the way people think, live, and interact. The goal of *Religious Leaders of the World* is to present an inspiring introduction to the life and times of these influential men and women. Biographies include the founders and forebears of all the world's major religions and religious movements, including Buddhism, Christianity, Confucianism, Hinduism, Islam, Judaism, Taoism, and Zoroastrianism. *Religious Leaders of the World* crosses the continents and the centuries to describe medieval martyrs, wandering ascetics, scriptural scholars, colonial puritans, and nativistic prophets. It also highlights the contemporary evangelists who tap the powers of the modern media to spread their message, modern scientists who work to reconcile traditional religious belief with new scientific discoveries, and much more.

The article list was based on the following criteria: relevance to the curriculum, importance to history, name recognition for students, and representation of as broad a cultural range as possible. The result is a balanced, curriculum-related work that brings these historical figures to life.

FEATURES

Religious Leaders of the World is part of Macmillan's **Profiles Series.** To add visual appeal and enhance the usefulness of the volume, the page format was designed to include the following helpful features:

- Time Lines: Found throughout the text in the margins, time lines provide a quick reference source for dates and important events in the life and times of these important men and women.

- Notable Quotations: Found throughout the text in the margins, these thought-provoking quotations are drawn from interviews, speeches, and writings of the person covered in the article, or from documents relating to their history. Such quotations give readers a special insight into the distinctive personalities of these great religious leaders.

- Definitions and Glossary: Brief definitions of important terms in the main text can be found in the margins. A glossary at the end of the book provides students an even broader list of definitions.

- Sidebars: Appearing in shaded boxes throughout the volume, these provocative asides relate to and amplify topics.

- Pull Quotes: Found throughout the text in the margin, pull quotes highlight essential facts about a leader.

- Additional Resources: An extensive list of books, articles, web sites, and films about the men and women covered in the volume will help students who want to do further research.

- Index: A thorough index provides thousands of additional points of entry into the work.

Macmillan Reference USA

Muhammad Abduh

1849–1905 ● MUSLIM

Muhammad Abduh was an Egyptian intellectual regarded as the architect of Islamic modernism and one of the most prominent Islamic reformers of the nineteenth and twentieth centuries. He was born into a well-to-do family in a village of the Nile Delta. At the age of 13 he went to study at the Ahmadi Mosque in Tanta and continued his education at al-Azhar, the renowned university in Cairo, where he studied logic, philosophy, and mysticism. For a time he came under the influence of the pan-Islamic reformer Jamal al-Din al-Afghani and became involved in the Urabi revolt against the British (1881–1882). Exiled for six years after the revolt was put down, he worked in Lebanon to establish an Islamic school system and collaborated with al-Afghani in Paris on a number of activities, including the publication of a popular journal called The Firmest Bond. The tone of the paper was radical and agitational, reflecting the revolutionary spirit of Afghani rather than the reformist one of Abduh. Although it was naturally banned in Islamic countries under British occupation, its 18 issues were smuggled in and widely followed by Muslim intellectuals. The two men also established an association under the same name working for Muslim unity and social reform. In the course of these activities, Abduh traveled to Britain and Tunis and reportedly entered Egypt in disguise.

During his career Abduh held a number of important positions. In 1889 he was appointed judge and ten years later, he

Muhammad Abduh was an Egyptian intellectual regarded as the architect of Islamic modernism.

1

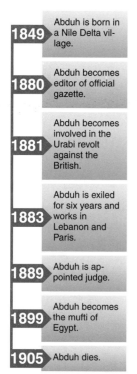

mufti: Arabic word signifying an individual recognized as the highest authority in the interpretation of Muslim law

sunnah: Arabic word which represents the traditions of the Prophet

became the ***mufti*** of Egypt, the highest authority on the interpretation of Muslim law. As mufti he initiated reform of the religious courts and the administration of *awqaf* (religious endowments).

Abduh considered Islam the cornerstone of private and public life. Yet he was struck by the decay of Islamic societies, which he saw as the main problem that all Muslim thinkers had to face. He sought to regenerate the religion and purify it of what he believed were alien accretions from the past. The aim of his life, as he defined it, was to free the minds of Muslims from the shackles of *taqlid* (blind acceptance of tradition) and to demonstrate the compatibility of Islam with modernity. For him, the cure for the ills of Muslim societies lay in a return to true Islam through the recovery of its essentials in the Koran and ***sunnah*** (traditions of the Prophet) and the interpretation of these texts in the light of modern times.

The best method to achieve these goals, Abduh believed, was through the exercise of individual judgment and the establishment of links between certain traditional concepts and the ideas of the modern age. He maintained that there was no incompatibility between Islam and reason or between revelation and science. Islam encouraged reason, condemned blind imitation, attacked fatalism, and affirmed the exercise of free will. He argued that Islam was in harmony with and tolerant of all rational inquiry and science. Thus, the scientific achievements of the West, to which the Muslims had contributed in their classical age, should be adopted without fear or hesitation. Failure to do so would lead either to stagnation and further underdevelopment, or to the indiscriminate importation of Western ideas, resulting in a loss of Islamic values.

Concrete reform and social change were Abduh's primary concerns. Like other reformers of his time, he addressed himself primarily to political issues rather than the rethinking of basic religious positions. He believed that the legal system was a crucial factor in the prosperity of countries and that laws should change according to circumstances. Stressing the need for social and political reform, he underlined the importance of education and attacked despotic rulers; for him the true Muslim leader was one bound by law and obliged to consult with the people.

The essence of Abduh's legacy, then, is his attempt to conduct a dialogue between Islam and the modern world; by so doing, he, perhaps more than any other Muslim thinker, contributed to the development of modernist and reformist trends in Islam, especially in the Arab countries and Indonesia. Ultimately Abduh owes his prominence to his search for an indigenous Islamic philosophy for modern times. He developed criteria by which the impact of Western civilization could be differentiated and controlled, and elaborated a synthesis of Islam and modernity with which Muslims could remain committed to their religion while actively engaged in modern society. His synthesis was subject to criticism, but the approach has left a marked impact on modern Islamic thought and society. ◆

Abernathy, Ralph David

1926–1990 ● BAPTIST

Ralph David Abernathy, was an American minister, civil rights leader, and confidant of the Reverend Martin Luther King, Jr. One of 12 children, Abernathy was the son of William L. Abernathy and Louivery Valentine Bell, farmers in Marengo County, Alabama. His parents were Baptists, and his father was active in the local black community. Abernathy attended high school at Linden Academy.

Abernathy joined the U.S. Army in 1944 and served in France and Germany, achieving the rank of platoon sergeant. After the war he completed the high school equivalency examination and, although he had no formal training for the ministry, was ordained a Baptist preacher in 1948. He received a B.S. degree in mathematics from Alabama State University in 1950. He then studied at Atlanta University, where he received an M.A. degree in sociology in 1951. While in Atlanta he met Martin Luther King, Jr., who was a guest preacher at the Ebenezer Baptist Church.

1926 Abernathy is born into an Alabama family.

1944 Abernathy joins the army.

1948 Abernathy is ordained a Baptist preacher.

1951 Abernathy receives an M.A. in sociology and becomes a pastor.

1952 Abernathy marries Juanita Odessa Jones.

1955 Abernathy becomes prominent during the Rosa Parks bus boycott.

1957 Abernathy cofounds the Southern Christian Leadership Conference.

1968 Abernathy delivers the eulogy at funeral of Martin Luther King.

1980 Abernathy endorses Republican Ronald Reagan for President.

1989 Abernathy publishes his autobiography.

1990 Abernathy dies.

In 1951 Abernathy became pastor of the First Baptist Church in Montgomery, Alabama. In August 1952 he married Juanita Odessa Jones; they had five children. In the meantime King became pastor of the Dexter Avenue Baptist Church in Montgomery. As respected religious leaders of Montgomery's black community, Abernathy and King rose to prominence during the Montgomery bus boycott, sparked by the refusal in December 1955 of Rosa Parks to relinquish her seat on a bus to a white man and move to the rear seats. Abernathy became King's assistant and ally.

In January 1957 Abernathy and King founded the Southern Christian Leadership Conference (SCLC). King assumed the presidency of the SCLC and Abernathy was secretary-treasurer. The SCLC advocated direct action based on Christian nonviolence to promote civil rights for black Americans. Abernathy's high profile in the founding of the SCLC catapulted him into national prominence. He was an outspoken leader, calling for "frontal attacks" on segregation. Not only did he and King shape SCLC's overarching strategy of civil disobedience, but the two of them shared the same southern jails 17 times in such cities as Selma, Alabama, and Albany, Georgia.

At the urging of King, Abernathy resigned as pastor of the First Baptist Church of Montgomery and accepted a position as pastor of the West Hunter Baptist Church in Atlanta in 1961. The move placed Abernathy near the headquarters of the SCLC in Atlanta. In 1965 Abernathy assumed the newly created position of vice president at large of the SCLC, a move that indicated that he was King's "heir apparent." In the mid-1960s Abernathy and King came under attack from the more radical Black Power movement, which rejected integration in favor of separation. To partially blunt the strident attacks of these Young Turks, Abernathy sought to mold old-line civil rights policies into a new strategy of demanding immediate economic opportunity and gain for America's black dispossessed, and in 1967 he began formulating plans for a massive march of poor people on Washington, D.C. The assassination of King in Memphis, Tennessee, on 4 April 1968 temporarily placed Abernathy's Washington protest on hold. Abernathy delivered the eulogy at King's funeral. In his remarks, he recalled their long friendship and sacrifices in the cause of human rights. Abernathy ended his eulogy with a magnanimous statement about how proud yet never envious he had been to spend 15 active years in the shadow of King.

Abernathy then assumed the presidency of the SCLC. With approval of its board, he pursued the Memphis strike of sanitation workers as a tribute to King. Within days the Memphis workers had won concessions from the city, and Abernathy became America's most visible civil rights leader. In characteristic fashion, he chose not to dwell on the Memphis victory but rather to fast and pray for new guidance in the cause of civil rights. He emerged from this period of abstinence by announcing a new commitment to social activism and a renewed pledge to complete the Poor People's Campaign.

Dressed in the traditional bib overalls of a southern field hand, Abernathy presided over the inauguration of the Poor People's Campaign in Washington on 13 May 1968. At that time he secured a pledge from the National Park Service to allow a shanty town to be built in park grounds near the Lincoln Memorial. This village of the poor, which Abernathy dubbed Resurrection City, U.S.A., eventually attracted some 50,000 protesters to Washington, but when Abernathy failed to dismantle Resurrection City as he had agreed with the Park Service, the police moved in on 24 June 1968 and forced the people to leave. Abernathy's refusal to acquiesce in this action led to his arrest and eventual 20-day jail sentence. His incarceration simply punctuated the failure of his Poor People's Campaign to ignite public opinion and mass support nationally in the wake of King's death.

Abernathy returned to Atlanta and for a brief time directed the SCLC's Operation Breadbasket in an attempt to bring pressure to hire and promote black employees on companies that discriminated against blacks. Through 1977 he concentrated his efforts on the SCLC's economic thrust and on his own ministry in Atlanta. Also in 1977 he resigned his unpaid, full-time position at the SCLC, ostensibly to run for a congressional seat from Atlanta, which he lost in the Democratic primary to Wyche Fowler. Rumors persisted, however, that he was forced out of the SCLC position because he had become an ineffectual leader and had led the organization into serious indebtedness. After his defeat Abernathy returned to his pastorship at West Hunter Street Baptist Church.

In 1980 Abernathy estranged himself from the black community when he endorsed the Republican candidate, Ronald Reagan, for president. Later, he conceded that he had no special, even limited, entree into the Reagan White House, and many of his longtime associates and supporters distanced them-

> "We are not going to let the white man put us down anymore. It's not white power, and I'll give you some news, it's not black power, either. It's poor power and we're going to use it."
> Ralph Abernathy, 1968

selves from him. In 1983 Abernathy suffered the first of two debilitating strokes and subsequently contracted glaucoma.

In 1989 Abernathy published *And the Walls Came Tumbling Down,* his autobiography and personal reminiscences of the civil rights movement. Although a moving account of his years in the civil rights movement, the book's references to King's marital infidelity caused a controversy. Abernathy reacted to the criticism of such black leaders as Joseph Lowery, his successor as president of the SCLC, by stating in *Time* magazine, "I am not a Judas. I have written nothing in malice and omitted nothing out of cowardice." Abernathy died of cardiac arrest at Crawford W. Long Hospital at Emory University and was buried at Lincoln Cemetery in Atlanta.

Abernathy was one of the nation's best recognized civil rights leaders, who was willing to speak out and take stands regardless of their unpopularity. ◆

Abu Bakr

c. 573–634 ● Muslim

Abu Bakr was the father-in-law of Muhammad and the first Muslim caliph. Born Uthman ibn Abdullah in Mecca, he was a successful merchant who also gained a reputation as a judge, interpreter of dreams, and local historian. Uthman met Muhammad the prophet in 610 and became the first male convert to Islam the following year. He was originally called Abd al-Kaaba, Arabic for "servant of the temple," but received the name Abu Bakr, meaning, "father of the virgin," when Muhammad married his daughter Aishah. Abu Bakr was also called Abd Allah (servant of God) and al-Siddik (the righteous one) because of his devotion to Muhammad.

Abu Bakr was a close friend and adviser to Muhammad and was the only person to accompany him on the *hegira,* Muhammad's migration from Mecca to Medina in 622 to escape persecution by the local authorities. During the next ten years, as the new religion spread, Abu Bakr remained in the background, often counseling Muhammad on Arab intrigues. He was already an elderly man with a stooping gait and a white beard dyed red. Although he was a far from imposing figure,

hegira: Arabic word for the Islamic prophet Muhammad's migration from Mecca to Medina in 622

The Koran

The Koran, or Qur'an, is the sacred text of Islam. From around 610 to 632 the prophet Muhammed recorded the chapters (or suras) that believers regard as the word of Allah himself. Muhammed, then about 40 years old, had a vision of the angel Gabriel, calling him to "recite." Once Muhammed overcame his initial resistance to the angel's command, he recorded what has become, alongside the Bible, one of the most widely-read and influential books in human history.

The Koran is a remarkable sacred text for several reasons. First, it was recorded by one person alone. Second, because it was written over the period of several years, it helps us learn about the ongoing concerns of the earliest followers of Islam. Third, it portrays itself not as replacing Jewish and Christian scriptures, but correcting them and bringing their prophetic message to fulfillment.

For most non-Muslim readers, however, the most striking feature of the Koran is the beauty of its language. The book did not simply take an existing language and apply it to religious questions; it reinvented and expanded the boundaries of the Arabic language itself. The beauty of the text extends far beyond the printed page. Because Islam forbids any visual representation of Allah, Islamic artists have turned to Allah's word for their subject matter, producing ornate calligraphy and illumination both in books and on the walls of mosques and other buildings. Some believers also show their devotion to the text by memorizing it entirely and reciting it. These recitations, as well as the constant recitation of the Koran in public spaces and media, marks a continuation of the call to "recite" that first led Muhammed to record the beautiful and stirring revelations.

Abu Bakr was well loved for his charity and for his nearness to the prophet.

Before his death Muhammad expressed his desire that Abu Bakr should succeed him by having him offer prayers for the people. When Muhammad died in 632, Abu Bakr went to the balcony of Muhammad's palace, which overlooked the anxious crowds waiting for news of the prophet, and declared, "Oh you believers! Know that the Prophet Muhammad is dead. But you who have faith in God, know that God is alive and can never die." Despite the protestations of Muhammad's son-in-law Ali, Abu Bakr was appointed caliph, an Arabic term for deputy. He himself defined the title by saying, "Call me not the Caliph of the Lord. I am but the Caliph of the Prophet of the Lord."

Although Abu Bakr reigned for only two years and three months, the period was important in Islamic history. Muhammad's death shook the new religion and many adherents sought to shake off the strict yoke of Muhammad's authority. The people of Nejd revolted against the tribute they were forced to pay; the people of the Hejaz sought to discard the new religion entirely. Even the city of Medina, capital of the caliphate, was threatened by religious upheaval. Abu Bakr suppressed these revolts in just two years and encouraged the campaign of Khalid, in which Iraq and Syria were attacked and overcome. The spread of Islam to Byzantium and Persia began during his reign.

Abu Bakr was instrumental in organizing Islam as a religion. At the urging of Omar, Abu Bakr wrote down the sayings of Muhammad and deposited them with the Prophet's widow, Hafsa. These writings later became the basis for the Koran, the Islamic scripture. Abu Bakr died in 634; it was rumored that he had been poisoned. Although he had had access to the wealth of his country, he died possessing only the clothes he was wearing, a servant, and a camel. ◆

Akiva ben Joseph

c. 50–c. 135 B.C.E. ● JEWISH

> "Rabbi Akiba, illiterate at forty, saw one day a stone's perforation where water fell from a spring, and having heard people say, "Waters wear stones," he thought, "if soft water can bore through a rock, surely iron-clad Torah should, be sheer persistence, penetrate a tender mind," and he turned to study."
>
> Talmud, Abot de Rabbi Nathan

Akiva ben Joseph, also known as Akiba or Aqiva ben Yosef, was an influential rabbi and Biblical scholar. He lived during the time of the transformation of Palestinian Judaism from a religion centered on the Temple of Jerusalem to one focused on the study of Torah, the totality of God's revelation to Moses and the Jewish people. 'Aqiva' was born shortly before the destruction of the Temple in 70 C.E. and died during the Bar Kokhba Revolt (132–135), the Jews' last attempt to wrest freedom from the Romans. Described as a poor shepherd, 'Aqiva', encouraged by his wife, supposedly began his rabbinic studies at the age of 40 and learned the alphabet together with his young son.

The influence of 'Aqiva' touched all areas of rabbinic thought and all levels of rabbinic lore. The major sages after 'Aqiva' traced their intellectual heritage back to him. Even the patriarch Gamliel of Yavneh acquiesced to the knowledge of 'Aqiva' and the greatest patriarch, Yehudah ha-Nasi, studied with the five major pupils of 'Aqiva'. Even Moses is said to have asked God why he revealed the Torah through him if he had such a one as 'Aqiva'.

Akira is said to have followed an imaginative and creative form of biblical exegesis and to have derived his comments

The Wailing Wall and Dome of the Rock

The Wailing Wall, also called the Western Wall, in Jerusalem, is part of the retaining wall of the Temple of Solomon or Second Temple, the holiest site in Judaism. The part of the Wall still visible today is about 160 feet long and 60 feet high and is made of stone blocks. It was built by the Romans in 20 and 19 B.C.E. as part of a reconstruction of the Wall and of the sixth-century B.C.E. Temple itself. Beginning about two centuries after the destruction of the Temple by the Romans in 70 C.E., Jews began making pilgrimages to the Wall to lament the Temple's destruction. Access to Jews was limited under many centuries of Muslim rule, but restrictions were removed after the state of Israel captured control of the area in 1967. The Wailing Wall stands near the Dome of the Rock, which was built by Arab Muslims from 687 to 691 C.E. The first great Islamic monument, it was built on the platform where the Second Temple had stood, above the Western Wall. The Dome's renowned features include its golden cupola, the octagon-shaped hall on which it rests, its mosaic tiles, and its marble panels. In the center of the hall stands the Holy Rock, from which the Prophet Muhammad is believed to have risen to heaven.

from every aspect of the biblical text, including the shapes of the letters and the peculiarities of biblical Hebrew, such as the repetition of words and phrases and the appearance of certain prepositions, conjunctions, and adverbs.

The rabbinic tradition assigns 'Aqiva' a prominent place in the compilations of the legal and exegetical collections, as well as a pivotal role in the formation of the mystical texts of Judaism. He is included, along with Ben Azzai, Elisha ben Avuyah, and Ben Zoma, among those "who entered the garden," which is taken as a reference to mystical teachings, and he alone is said to have "left in peace". His importance in the mystical tradition is seen in the attribution of sayings to him in the Heikhalot literature (collections of visions of those who traveled through God's palace).

'Aqiva' did not limit himself to the sphere of the intellect. He was pictured as being actively involved in the Bar Kokhba

Revolt. In fact, 'Aqiva' is normally said to have claimed that Bar Kokhba was the Messiah and to have been the major rabbinical supporter of the uprising. The rabbinic texts claim that he suffered a martyr's death at the hands of the Romans during the revolt.

Although recent scholarship has challenged many of the details regarding the life of 'Aqiva' that are found in rabbinic texts, it does not detract from the impression he made on his contemporaries and on subsequent generations. The picture we find in the documents of ancient Judaism is one of an extraordinary talent. He is described as affecting every aspect of rabbinic thought—legal, exegetical, mystical, and even philosophical. "Man has free will," 'Aqiva' is reported to have said, "but all is foreseen by God". His rise from poverty to greatness must have been an inspiration to many—so much so that he was placed at the center of the important historical and intellectual events of his time. ◆

Alexy II

1929– ● RUSSIAN ORTHODOX CHURCH

> "Peace about which the Apostle spoke cannot be attained through social, political or economic transformations. It cannot be established by a decree or order of even most authoritative leaders. . . . It has been brought to the earth by the Savior, and the eternal Kingdom of Heaven shines through it in the souls of all people."
>
> Alexy II, 1998

Patriarch Alexy II of Moscow and all Russia became only the 15th primate of the Russian Orthodox Church since that office was established in 1589. The Russian Orthodox Church is the largest religious denomination in Russia. It forms part of the Eastern Orthodox religion that grew from a split which occurred in the Christian church in 1054. The position of patriarch is similar to that of bishop in the Roman Catholic Church, and the ecumenical patriarch, based in Turkey, is regarded as the earthly head of the Eastern Orthodox Church.

Alexy was born Aleksey Mikhailovich Ridiger on February 23, 1929, in Tallinn, the capital of what is now Estonia. His father, Mikhail Aleksandrovich Ridiger, studied law and theology and was ordained a deacon and later a priest. Deacons are the first of the three main orders of Orthodox clergy, followed by priests and bishops. Although married men may become priests, bishops are only elected from among celibate or widowed clergy. For 16 years, Ridiger was rector of the Church of the Nativity of the Theotokos in Tallinn. Alexy's father and mother, Yelena Iosifovna Pisareva, took him on annual pilgrimages to a convent and a monastery.

From early childhood, Alexy served in the church, first under the guidance of his spiritual father, an archpriest. From 1944 to 1947, Alexy was a senior sub-deacon. He studied at a Russian secondary school in Tallinn. He entered the Leningrad (now St. Petersburg) Seminary in 1947 and graduated from it with honors in 1949. During his first year at the St. Petersburg Academy, Alexy was ordained deacon and priest in April 1950 and was appointed rector of the Church of the Epiphany at the town of Jyhvi. Father Alexy graduated from the theological academy with distinction and became a candidate for a theology degree.

In 1957, Alexy was appointed rector of the Cathedral of the Dormition in Tartu, Estonia's second largest city, and dean of the Tartu church district. In 1958, he was elevated to the rank of archpriest and in 1961, he took monastic vows. In September 1961, Alexy was consecrated Bishop of Tallinn and Estonia. Each Orthodox church is governed by its own head bishop. (The head bishops of the churches may be called patriarch, metropolitan, or archbishop.)

In 1964, Alexy was elevated to the rank of archbishop. In December 1964, he was appointed chancellor of the Moscow Patriarchate, a post he occupied until 1986. Alexy earned his Doctor of Theology degree from the St. Petersburg Theological Academy in 1984. In June 1986, Archbishop Alexy was appointed Metropolitan of Leningrad (now St. Petersburg) and Novgorod and administrator of the diocese of Tallinn. During the 1980s, Patriarch Alexy worked for the adoption of new laws restoring freedom for religious organizations in Russia. As a result, the Church regained the right to teach religion and to carry out charitable work in hospitals, houses for the elderly, and penitentiaries.

On June 7, 1990, the Local Council of the Russian Orthodox Church elected Alexy to the Patriarchal See of Moscow. His enthronement took place on June 10, 1990. For over 25 years, Alexy participated in the Conference of European Churches (CEC), serving as president starting in 1964 and ending as moderator in 1992. Alexy worked actively in international and Russian peace organizations. From 1963, he was member of the Soviet Peace Fund Board, and was a delegate to the World Christian Conference, "Life and Peace," in Sweden in 1982.

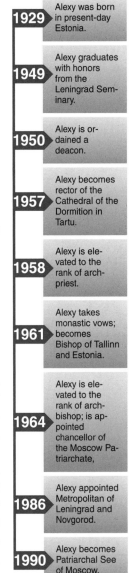

1929 Alexy was born in present-day Estonia.

1949 Alexy graduates with honors from the Leningrad Seminary.

1950 Alexy is ordained a deacon.

1957 Alexy becomes rector of the Cathedral of the Dormition in Tartu.

1958 Alexy is elevated to the rank of archpriest.

1961 Alexy takes monastic vows; becomes Bishop of Tallinn and Estonia.

1964 Alexy is elevated to the rank of archbishop; is appointed chancellor of the Moscow Patriarchate,

1986 Alexy appointed Metropolitan of Leningrad and Novgorod.

1990 Alexy becomes Patriarchal See of Moscow.

Patriarch Alexy worked for the preservation of church monuments in Russia and signed several agreements with the Russian Ministry of Culture in order to protect historically significant monasteries. Patriarch Alexy repeatedly reminded his people of the need to revive spirituality in Russia and to overcome barriers between religious and non-religious groups and between science and religion.

Patriarch Alexy took on a peacemaker role when political passions burst into a serious crisis in Russia in autumn 1993, threatening to grow into a civil war. He invited the clashing parties to negotiations and acted as mediator between them. The Patriarch also offered numerous peace initiatives in response to the wars in the republics of the former Yugoslavia as well as the conflict in the Russian Republic of Chechnya. ◆

Alinesitoue

c. 1920–1943 ● Traditional African

Alinesitoue transformed an exclusively male tradition of prophetic leadership into a predominantly female one during the period of French colonial rule.

Alinesitoue Diatta was an important West African prophet who led a major religious movement among the Diola ethnic group in Senegal, Gambia, and Portuguese Guinea from 1941 until 1943. Although she was not the first Diola to claim direct revelation from the Diola supreme being, Emitai, Alinesitoue and some less-known contemporaries transformed an exclusively male tradition of prophetic leadership into a predominantly female one during the period of French colonial rule.

Alinesitoue's visions began during a particularly repressive period of French rule in Senegal. An understaffed Vichy regime sought to obtain large quantities of Diola rice to supply the urban areas with food (at a time when drought had shrunk Diola grain reserves) and encouraged vigorous campaigns of Christian and Muslim proselytization in Diola communities. By building on earlier traditions of male prophetic revelation, Alinesitoue was able to introduce a series of new cults and to reform Diola religious practice in such a way as to provide access to religious authority for women and young adults. Furthermore, she challenged French colonial development plans that were based on the introduction of a new cash crop, peanuts, in the region. Among the northern Diola, men had already abandoned the primarily subsistence crop of rice to women so as to concentrate on peanuts. This interfered with a family mode of production and placed the entire burden of rice cultivation on women. She challenged these development schemes, asserting that the new cash crop of peanuts disrupted a covenantal relationship between the Diola and Emitai, in which Emitai provided rain for rice cultivation and Diola women and men provided labor. She taught that peanuts were not spiritually situated within a Diola ecology and that they fostered both a dependence on the French and infertility of the land, while eroding the economic importance of women.

As pilgrims flocked to Alinesitoue's village in 1942. Vichy officials worried about her potential to lead a revolt against an already weakened colonial authority. In 1943 French officials arrested her and many of her followers. She was exiled to Tombouctou, where she died of starvation. Since her exile there have been 28 other prophets, most of them women, all of whom claim to be following in her tradition of revelation from the supreme being and of opening up the tradition to previously marginalized groups. A separatist movement in Senegal's southern region of Casamance has also embraced the legacy of Alinesitoue, claiming her as the Joan of Arc of Casamance. ◆

Vichy officials worried about Alinesitoue's potential to lead a revolt against an already weakened colonial authority.

Allen, Richard

1760–1831 ● AFRICAN METHODIST EPISCOPAL

Richard Allen was an American minister and community leader. As a reformer and institution builder in the post-Revolutionary period, Richard Allen was matched in achievements by few of his white contemporaries. At age 20, only a few months after buying his freedom in Kent County, Delaware, Allen was preaching to mostly white audiences and converting many of his hearers to Methodism. At 27, he was a cofounder of the Free African Society of Philadelphia, probably the first autonomous organization of free blacks in the United States. Before he was 35, he had become the minister of what would be Philadelphia's largest black congregation—Bethel African Methodist Episcopal Church. Over a long lifetime, he

founded, presided over, or served as officer in a large number of other organizations designed to improve the condition of life and expand the sphere of liberty for African Americans. Although he received no formal education, he became an accomplished writer, penning and publishing sermons, tracts, addresses, and remonstrances; compiling a hymnal for black Methodists; and drafting articles of organization and governance for various organizations.

Enslaved at birth in the family of the prominent Philadelphia lawyer and officeholder Benjamin Chew, Allen was sold with his family to Stokely Sturgis, a small farmer near Dover, Delaware, in about 1768. It was here, in 1777, that Allen experienced a religious conversion, shortly after most of his family had been sold away from Dover, at the hands of the itinerant Methodist Freeborn Garretson. Three years later he and his brother contracted with their master to purchase their freedom.

For a short time, Allen drove a wagon carrying salt for the Revolutionary army. He also supported himself as a woodchopper, brickyard laborer, and shoemaker as he carried out a six-year religious sojourn as an itinerant Methodist preacher. In something akin to a biblical journey into the wilderness, Allen tested his mettle and proved his faith, traveling by foot over thousands of miles, from North Carolina to New York, and preaching the word to black and white audiences in dozens of villages, crossroads, and forest clearings. During this period of his life, it seems, Allen developed the essential attributes that would serve him the rest of his career: resilience, toughness, cosmopolitanism, an ability to confront rapidly changing circumstances, and skill in dealing with a wide variety of people and temperaments.

Allen's itinerant preaching brought him to the attention of white Methodist leaders, who in 1786 called him to Philadel-

"We will never separate ourselves voluntarily from the slave population in this country; they are our brethren by the trees of consanguinity, of suffering and of wrong; and we feel there is more virtue in suffering privations with them than fancied advantage for a season."

Richard Allen, 1887

phia to preach to black members of the Methodist flock that worshiped at Saint George's Methodist Church, a rude, dirt-floored building in the German part of the city. Allen would spend the rest of his life there.

In Philadelphia, Allen's career was marked by his founding of Mother Bethel, the black Methodist church that opened its doors in 1794, and by the subsequent creation, in 1816, of the independent African Methodist Episcopal (AME Church). Soon after his arrival in 1786, he began pressing for an independent black church. His fervent Methodism brought him into contention with other emerging black leaders who wished for a nondenominational or "union" church, and thus within a few years two black churches took form. Both were guided by the idea that African Americans needed "to worship God under our own vine and fig tree," as Allen put it in his autobiographical memoir. This was, in essence, a desire to stand apart from white society, avoiding both the paternalistic benevolence of its racially liberal members and the animosity of its racially intolerant members. Allen's Bethel church, after opening its doors in a converted blacksmith's shop in 1794, grew into a congregation of more than 500 members by 1800.

Bethel's rise to the status of Philadelphia's largest black church was accomplished amid a 20-year struggle with white Methodist leaders. White Methodists were determined to make the popular Allen knuckle under to their authority, and this ran directly counter to Allen's determination to lead a church in which black Methodists, while subscribing to the general doctrines of Methodism, were free to pursue their churchly affairs autonomously. The struggle even involved the ownership of the church building itself. The attempts of white Methodists to rein in Allen and his black parishioners reached a climax in 1815 that was resolved when the Pennsylvania Supreme Court ruled on January 1, 1816, that Bethel was legally an independent church. Just a few months later, African-American ministers from across the mid-Atlantic region gathered in Philadelphia to confederate their congregations into the African Methodist Episcopal Church, which was to spread across the United States and abroad in the nineteenth and twentieth centuries.

Allen's epic 20-year battle with white Methodist authorities represents a vital phase of the African-American struggle in the North to get out from under the controlling hand of

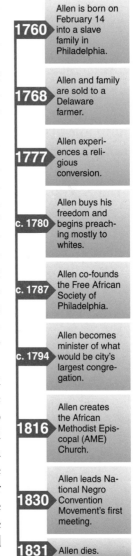

1760 Allen is born on February 14 into a slave family in Philadelphia.

1768 Allen and family are sold to a Delaware farmer.

1777 Allen experiences a religious conversion.

c. 1780 Allen buys his freedom and begins preaching mostly to whites.

c. 1787 Allen co-founds the Free African Society of Philadelphia.

c. 1794 Allen becomes minister of what would be city's largest congregation.

1816 Allen creates the African Methodist Episcopal (AME) Church.

1830 Allen leads National Negro Convention Movement's first meeting.

1831 Allen dies.

The AME Church, with Allen as its first bishop, quickly became the most important of the autonomous institutions created by black Americans.

white religionists. The AME Church, with Allen as its first bishop, quickly became the most important of the autonomous institutions created by black Americans that allowed former slaves to forge an Afro-Christianity that spoke in the language and answered the needs of a growing number of northern—and, later, southern—blacks. For decades, the AME helped to heal the disabling scars of slavery and facilitated the adjustment of black southern migrants to life as citizens in the North. Allen's success at Bethel had much to do with the warmth, simplicity, and evangelical fervor of Methodism, which resonated with a special vibrancy among the manumitted and fugitive southern slaves reaching Philadelphia in the early nineteenth century.

Between the founding of Bethel in 1794 and the organization of the AME Church, Allen founded schools for black youths and mutual aid societies that would allow black Philadelphians to quash the idea that they were dependent upon white charity. A successful businessman and a considerable property owner, Allen also wrote pamphlets and sermons attacking the slave trade, slavery, and white racism. The most notable of them, coauthored with Absalom Jones in 1794, was *A Narrative of the Proceedings of the Black People, During the Late Awful Calamity in Philadelphia, in the year 1793*. In this pamphlet, Allen and Jones defended the work of black citizens who aided the sick and dying during the horrendous yellow fever epidemic of 1793, but they went on to condemn the oppression of African Americans, both enslaved and free. In the first quarter of the nineteenth century, almost every African-American institution formed in Philadelphia included Allen's name and benefitted from his energy and vision.

In the later years of his life, Allen was drawn to the idea of colonization—to Africa, Haiti, and Canada—as an answer to the needs of African Americans who as freed persons faced discrimination and exploitation. His son, John Allen, was one of the leaders of the Haitian immigrants in 1824. The capstone of Allen's career came six years later, when he presided over the first meeting of the National Negro Convention Movement, an umbrella organization that launched a coordinated reform movement among black Americans and provided an institutional structure for black abolitionism. When death came to Allen shortly thereafter, his funeral was attended by a vast concourse of black and white Philadelphians. ◆

Ambedkar, B. R.

1891–1956 ● Buddhist

B. R. Ambedkar was a statesman, writer, reformer, and creator of a new Buddhist movement in India. Affectionately known as Babasaheb, Ambedkar was born in Mhow (now Mahu), India, where his father was headmaster of an army normal school. A member of the untouchable caste of *mahars* of Maharashtra, who traditionally worked as village menials, Ambedkar lived at a time when his outstanding personal capabilities, in conjunction with a strong sentiment for reform then emerging among Hindus and the beginnings of a movement for rights within his own caste, could effect extraordinary progress and change in the status of untouchables. In his early years he suffered prejudice in school, but was also aided in his education by Hindu reformers. K. A. Keluskar encouraged him in his studies when the family moved to Bombay, and gave him a copy of his book on the life of the Buddha. Two princes, the Gaikwad of Baroda and Shahu Chhatrapati of Kolhapur, helped finance his education, which eventually included a Ph.D. from Columbia University in New York, a degree from the University of London, and the title of barrister from Grey's Inn in London.

In 1917 Ambedkar returned to Bombay for a three-year period in the midst of his education abroad. During this time he participated in two conferences for the Depressed Classes, testified to the Government Franchise Commission on the rights of untouchables, and began a newspaper entitled *The Voice of the Mute*. All three activities—conferences to organize and inspire, attempts to use the parliamentary

1891 Ambedkar is born in India to the untouchable caste of mahars.

1917 Ambedkar returns to Bombay from his studies abroad.

1923 Ambedkar returns permanently to India.

1930 Ambedkar is a representative to London Round Table conferences.

1935 Ambedkar declares untouchables can be free only if not Hindu.

1942 Ambedkar founds the Scheduled Castes Federation.

1945 Ambedkar publishes book indicting Gandian form of paternalism.

1956 Ambedkar founds the Republican Party and converts to Buddhism; Ambedkar dies.

process for political and social rights, and educational work—were to become hallmarks of his lifelong efforts at reform.

Upon his return permanently to India in 1923, Ambedkar earned a living from teaching and law but spent a major part of his energies on building a movement among untouchables and creating political and social opportunities for them, chiefly through pressure on government. He made efforts to secure religious rights such as participation in public festivals, temple entry, wedding rituals, and the wearing of the sacred thread, but these ended in 1935 when he declared that although he was born a Hindu he would not die a Hindu, and that untouchables could be free only outside the Hindu religion. Earlier, at a conference called at Mahad, a small town south of Bombay, he had burned those portions of the classic Hindu law book, the *Manusmrti*, that condoned untouchability.

His unshakable faith in parliamentary democracy led Ambedkar to testify at every opportunity before the commissions that investigated the furthering of democratization in British India. The prominence he gained in these lengthy and sophisticated statements resulted in his being named a representative at the Round Table conferences in London in 1930 and 1931. Faced there with the demands of Muslims, Sikhs, and other minorities for separate electorates, he began to advocate separate electorates for untouchables also. This led him into direct opposition with Mohandas K. Gandhi, who fasted in prison in Poona against such separation of untouchables from the main Hindu body of voters. Although the Poona Pact of 1932 brought about a compromise with Gandhi consisting of an exchange of separate electorates for more reserved seats for the Depressed Classes, Ambedkar continued to regard as a deterrent to real change Gandhi's belief in a "change of heart," rather than legal measures as a cure for untouchability. His 1945 book, *What Congress and Gandhi Have Done to the Untouchables*, indicted the Gandhian form of paternalism.

During the British governmental reforms of the mid-1930s, Ambedkar founded the Independent Labour Party in opposition to the Indian National Congress. The year 1937 brought 11 Scheduled Castes (so called because the government placed untouchable castes on a schedule to receive representation in parliamentary bodies and government employment) into the Bombay Legislative Assembly. Although Ambedkar was to found two other political parties, the Scheduled Castes Federation in 1942 and the Republican Party in 1956, he never again achieved such a large number of seats.

Ambedkar himself was able to effect legislation guaranteeing rights for untouchables as well as measures affecting all India in the appointed positions of Labour member in the viceroy's executive council (1942–1946) and as minister for law in India's first independent ministry (1947–1951). He was also chairman of the Drafting Committee of the Constitution (1947–1948), hailed as the "modern Manu." Among the tenets of the Indian constitution is one outlawing the practice of untouchability, a tribute to the work of both Ambedkar and Gandhi.

Underlying Ambedkar's social and political work was a constant effort to educate his people. The newspapers *Excluded India People,* and *Awakened India* succeeded *The Voice of the Mute* and were widely circulated in spite of an extremely low literacy rate among the Depressed Classes. A modest beginning of building hostels so that untouchable children could attend government schools in towns culminated in the People's Education Society, which opened Siddharth College in Bombay in 1946 and Milind College in Aurangabad in 1951. The society runs two dozen institutions today and in 1982 laid the foundation stone for Dr. Ambedkar College in Poona.

Although Ambedkar's interest in Buddhism was evident all his life, he did not convert until 14 October 1956, less than two months before his death on 6 December. The ceremony, held at Nagpur, was witnessed by over half a million people, and in the conversion movement that followed, almost four million people, most of them from former untouchable castes, declared themselves Buddhists. In his talks and in his book *The Buddha* and *His Dhamma*, Ambedkar stressed a rational, humanitarian, egalitarian Buddhism drawn chiefly from Pali texts. Hindu beliefs and practices and any supernatural Buddhist ideas were eliminated from the Buddhism propounded by Ambedkar. He himself, however, was regarded as the savior of the untouchables and came to be held by many as a *bodhisattva*. In the years since his death, dozens of Buddhist **vihars** (temple compounds) have been built across the face of the state of Maharashtra, and hundreds of books have been written on Buddhist faith and practice, chiefly in Marathi. The Buddhist Society of India, founded by Ambedkar in 1951, is now headed by Prakash Ambedkar, his grandson. ◆

Underlying Ambedkar's social and political work was a constant effort to educate his people.

vihars: Buddhist temple compounds

Anandamayi Ma

1896–1982 ● HINDU

Anandamayi Ma (Ananda Ma) was a Hindu spiritual teacher and mystic from Bengal now Bangladesh). Born Nirmala Sundari ("Flawlessly Beautiful") Bhattacharya to Vaisnava brahmin parents in the village of Kheora, she received very little formal education but is remembered by tradition to have exhibited kindness, obedience, and an affinity for devotional songs (*kirtana*) and the chanting of God's name (*namajapa*). Just before age 13 she was joined by arranged marriage to Ramani Mohan Chakravarti (Bholanath) and went to live in his brother's household for the first five years of their marriage, while Bholanath traveled in search of work. Tradition says that their marriage was never physically consummated: when they set up house together in 1914. Nirmala began the conscious intent (*kheyala*) to enter into spiritual discipline (*sadhana*) as a mature realization of her childhood spirituality.

After 1918 she began to enter into lengthy meditations and *namajapas*, culminating in her initiation, on 3 August 1922, in which she experienced the identification of the seemingly disparate realities of master (guru), sacred words of initiation (mantra), initiate (sisya), and Lord (ista). Her realization led to her teaching that everything is One (*advaita*, nonduality), and that all apparent distinctions are due to the *lila* (divine play) of God. Gradually disciples began to come to her in her new home in Dhaka to attend her frequent entrance into *samadhi*, or state of intensive contemplation, and her regular performances of *kirtana*.

From 1926 until her death, Anandamayi Ma undertook spontaneous pilgrimages throughout Bengal and across northern India, stopping at ashrams her disciples had established, such as the main ashram at Asi Gha in Banaras. She came to be understood in many ways—as the embodiment of Bliss (*anandamayi*), as a healer, and as an incarnation of the goddess Kali; some say she gave Indira Gandhi a *mala* (sacred beads) in 1977 that helped return her to the prime ministership in 1980. Her disciples are active in India today. ◆

Anderson, H. George

1932– ● LUTHERAN

Hugh George Anderson was born on March 10, 1932, in Los Angeles, California. His birth parents put him up for adoption, and he was adopted by Rueben Leroy and Frances Nielsen Anderson, and baptized on May 1 of that year. At the age of 13, he was confirmed at Grace Lutheran Church in Alhambra, California. Robert Marshall, the pastor of that congregation, was known for taking seriously the task of giving youth a solid grounding in the Lutheran faith.

As a young student Anderson showed great academic promise, and after graduating from Alhambra High School in 1949, he went to Yale University for his undergraduate work. Though he was considering majoring in and pursuing a career in science, his life experiences would soon lead him in a different direction. He had volunteered to do service work in West Virginia. Because of the failing health of the pastor who had ministerial responsibility for the area, Anderson was enlisted as a kind of constant companion for the minister, assisting him as he went about his daily duties.

This experience left a deep impression on Anderson, who, while continuing his involvement in the Christian religious life at Yale outside the classroom, began taking a greater academic interest in theology and religion. After graduating Phi Beta Kappa from Yale in 1953, he attended the Lutheran Theological Seminary in Philadelphia, Pennsylvania. His leadership abilities were already evident when he was elected student body president at the Seminary. Anderson was ordained in the year of his graduation (B.D., 1956), at his Alhambra congregation, by Carl V. Tambert. Thereafter Anderson accepted a teaching fellow position at the Seminary, and meanwhile earned a Ph.D. from the University of Pennsylvania (1962). He continued his teaching service at Lutheran Theological Southern Seminary in Columbia, South Carolina. There he made his mark as an administrator (serving as director of graduate studies) and scholar, producing English translations and essays for lay and scholarly audiences alike. He also demonstrated a deep

"Time no longer holds humanity captive, locking us into a few decades of existence. Time has been pushed aside and now swings open to reveal an eternity beyond. This is a new world we live in, full of endless promise and hope."

H. George Anderson, 1999

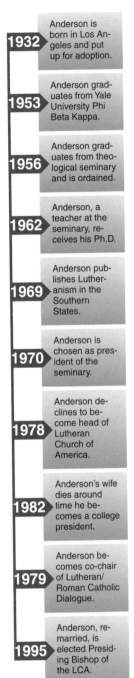

1932 Anderson is born in Los Angeles and put up for adoption.

1953 Anderson graduates from Yale University Phi Beta Kappa.

1956 Anderson graduates from theological seminary and is ordained.

1962 Anderson, a teacher at the seminary, receives his Ph.D.

1969 Anderson publishes Lutheranism in the Southern States.

1970 Anderson is chosen as president of the seminary.

1978 Anderson declines to become head of Lutheran Church of America.

1982 Anderson's wife dies around time he becomes a college president.

1979 Anderson becomes co-chair of Lutheran/Roman Catholic Dialogue.

1995 Anderson, remarried, is elected Presiding Bishop of the LCA.

love for religious topics of local interest, producing *Lutheranism in the Southern States* (1969). On the strength of his personal rectitude and energetic service to the community, he was chosen as president of the seminary in 1970, a position he would hold for 11 years.

During this time, he continued his prodigious output of scholarly and lay writings on theology, church history, and the Lutheran faith. As important as his writings and his administrative duties, however, was the way he strove to avoid factionalism in his dealings inside and outside the Lutheran Church in America. During the 1970s a sister denomination, the Lutheran Church-Missouri Synod, was undergoing great upheaval, as traditionalists attempted to rein in what they saw as the excessively liberal stances of many seminary faculty members. The LCA was not unaffected by these debates, nor by the tensions caused by ecumenical discussions between the LCA, the American Lutheran Church, and Association of Evangelical Lutheran Churches (with whom the LCA would merge some years later, forming the Evangelical Lutheran Church in America, ELCA). As the LCA struggled to redefine its own identity, Anderson successfully led the Seminary and continued to add his distinctive voice to the conversation, including serving on the Committee on Lutheran Unity (1974–1982).

His efforts did not go unnoticed. In 1978, Anderson was the favorite of delegates to succeed Robert Marshall, his former pastor in Alhambra, as president of the LCA. He felt a lack of calling, however, and declined. Not long thereafter, his wife was diagnosed with cancer. She died in 1982, soon after the deaths of his father and mother and just as he was assuming the presidency of Luther College in Decatur, Illinois. In the period of depression that followed, his faith was tested and enriched by the community where he worshiped.

Anderson continued to write prolifically and serve as an effective administrator to the Seminary; he also became more directly involved in interfaith dialogue, serving as co-chair of the Lutheran/Roman Catholic Dialogue from 1979–1990. He married Jutta Fischer, a former student, and adopted her two children, who joined the two children from his first marriage. In 1995, Anderson was elected Presiding Bishop of the LCA, a denomination of over five million members. ◆

Saint Anthony

c. 251–356 ● CHRISTIAN

Saint Anthony, also called Antony of Egypt, was an Egyptian anchorite credited with founding monasticism. The son of a wealthy Christian family, he hated school, never learned Greek, and was reliant on Coptic translations of religious texts throughout his career. Orphaned at 20, he began frequenting religious services and soon felt that the texts read were directed at him personally. He was particularly struck by the verse: "If you want to be perfect, go, sell what you have and give to the poor" (Matthew 19:21). After sending his younger sister to a convent, he joined a group of **ascetics** living in a cemetery.

Anthony lived in a tomb for 15 years, learning the life of a hermit before setting out across the desert to an abandoned fortress at Pispir, overlooking the Nile. For 20 years he lived there, seeing no one. Food was thrown to him over the fortress walls; visitors seeking his advice were turned away. As his reputation spread, an entire community of anchorites developed around the fortress. Although they had no contact with the saint, the anchorites were inspired by his holy solitude. Legends grew according to which Anthony was constantly besieged by demons, often disguised as wild beasts, enticing and provoking him to forgo his seclusion.

When Anthony finally joined his followers, they expected to see an emaciated individual crawl from behind the walls, but were astounded to see that he was as youthful and vigorous as on the day he began his seclusion. Anthony remained with his followers for five

ascetics: group of people practicing strict austerity measures in relation to their religious faith

c. 251 Anthony is born into a wealthy Christian family.

c. 271 Anthony becomes an orphan and joins a group of ascetics.

c. 310 Anthony begins a second retreat, this time into the desert.

311 Anthony visits Alexandria to lend support to Christian martyrs.

c. 350 Anthony visits Alexandria to preach against the Arian heresy.

356 Anthony dies at the age of 105.

years, teaching the principles of a monastic life under rule (an innovation) before abandoning them for a second retreat into the desert (c.310). For the next forty-five years he lived at a remote spot between the Nile and the Red Sea. The rule he now imposed upon himself allowed him to see visitors and he occasionally visited the anchorite community at Pispir. He is known to have visited Alexandria on two occasions: in 311, to lend support to Christian martyrs, and about 350 to preach against the Arian heresy. Among his visitors at the monastery was Egyptian church leader Athanasius, who sought shelter there from rival bishops. Athanasius's gripping biography of the saint as a simple yet heroic Christian submitting to his destiny persuaded many Christians throughout history to emulate Anthony by joining monastic orders.

Anthony died at the age of 105; the site of his grave was kept secret to avoid its becoming a place of veneration. At the site of his final retreat, a monastery, Mar Antonius, was founded.

Anthony was not the first Christian ascetic. His importance lies in his emphasis on seclusion and in his initiating retreat into remote regions. Because of his fondness for desert expanses, Saint Anthony is the patron saint of herdsmen. His feast is celebrated on January 17. The temptation of Saint Antony became a popular theme of art and literature. ◆

Armstrong, Herbert W.

1892–1986 ● WORLDWIDE CHURCH OF GOD

Herbert W. Armstrong was the founder of the Worldwide Church of God, whose Pasadena, California, headquarters continues to oversee hundreds of churches around the world.

Armstrong was born in Des Moines, Iowa, in 1892, the first of four children of Quakers Horace Elon Armstrong, a businessman, and Eva (Wright) Armstrong. As a youth he showed little interest in religion. He attended North High School in Des Moines. Ambitious and intellectually aggressive, he sold display ads for the *Des Moines Daily Capital* and the *Merchants Trade Journal*. In January 1917 he met Loma Dillon, and they were married the following July; they had four children. Ac-

cording to official church writings, shortly after their marriage, Loma had a dream of three angels, one of whom embraced the Armstrongs and told them Christ was coming shortly and had "important work for them to do in preparing for His coming." Armstrong reportedly dismissed the dream as insignificant.

The Armstrongs settled in Salem, Oregon. In 1926 a friend convinced Loma Armstrong, a Methodist, that Christians should observe the Sabbath on Saturday instead of Sunday. Herbert Armstrong, alarmed at what appeared to be religious fanaticism and gullibility, vowed to study the issue to set his wife straight. Exhaustive research in primary sources, however, convinced him of the legitimacy of observance of the Sabbath on Saturday. The Armstrongs thereafter affiliated themselves with the Sabbatarian Church of God, headquartered in Stanberry, Missouri. As a layman, Armstrong studied the Scriptures assiduously between 1926 and 1931, developing understandings that would become the foundational doctrines of the church he would eventually found.

1892 Armstrong is born in Iowa to a Quaker couple.

1917 Armstrong marries Loma Dillon.

1926 Armstrong changes his belief to holding the sabbath on Saturday.

1928 Armstrong preaches his first sermon.

1931 Armstrong is ordained a minister of the Church of God.

1933 Armstrong establishes the Radio Church of God.

1937 Armstrong's radio broadcasts now reach across U.S. into Canada.

1947 Armstrong founds Ambassador College to train church leaders.

1968 Armstrong renames his religion The Worldwide Church of God.

1986 Armstrong dies in his sleep in Pasadena, California.

With the encouragement of the Oregon Conference of the Church of God, Armstrong preached his first sermon in 1928 near Jefferson, Oregon, and by June 1931 he was an ordained minister of the church. Preaching tours in tent meetings that year established his reputation as a pulpiteer. When the Church of God suffered an internal organizational schism in 1933, Armstrong established his own Radio Church of God.

Armstrong started broadcasting a Sunday morning radio program over tiny 100-watt radio station KORE in Eugene, Oregon, a program that cost $2.50 in broadcasting fees at a time when Armstrong's salary as a minister was only $3.00 a week. The success of his Radio Church of God encouraged him to add stations in Portland (KXL) and Salem (KSLM) in 1936. He stepped up to a more powerful broadcaster, KWJJ, in 1937, thus establishing a broadcasting network that soon carried his message across the United States and into Canada and Alaska. In his program, "The World Tomorrow," he avoided overt preaching, offering instead news analysis with religious comment. At its peak the program aired over 374 radio stations and 165 television stations worldwide; in 1968 the organization was renamed the Worldwide Church of God.

Always the gifted advertising salesman with a love of the printed page, Armstrong initiated a church bulletin in April 1933. This quickly grew into a weekly magazine titled the *Plain Truth*, distributed worldwide with a peak printing run of 7.5 million in 1985. By 1946 the church had relocated to Pasadena, California, was operating its own printing plant, and was broadcasting internationally in prime-time radio slots. In 1947 Armstrong founded Ambassador College to train leaders for the church. (The college became Ambassador Center, located at Azusa Pacific University, and provides Worldwide Church of God men and women with an accredited Christian education.) Meanwhile, he was writing and publishing prolifically and crisscrossing the country on baptizing tours. Self-appointed the pastor general, he and the Worldwide Church of God became a phenomenon on the American religious scene, preaching a message that was, in his words, "radically different from what mainstream Christianity teaches."

According to Armstrong, the Worldwide Church of God restored 18 essential truths that Christianity had either lost or ignored, including the church's proper name, Sabbath keeping, baptism by immersion, faith healing, three levels of tithing, the ministry of angels, the adoption of Jewish feast days, and the indissolubility of marriage. Armstrong accepted the divinity of Christ but rejected Trinitarian language. He condemned any reliance on medical science, revised the commonly accepted understanding of the Passion Week calendar, and declared that British- Israelism—the theory that Anglo-Saxons are the descendants of the "lost" ten northern tribes of Israel—was the key to understanding biblical prophecy.

In the 1970s, scandal rocked the church. The former wife of a church executive won a $1.26 million libel suit, claiming that Armstrong and other church leaders had tried to smear her reputation after her divorce in 1976. When several former church members charged that Armstrong and other leaders had diverted millions of dollars in church money for their own use, the California attorney general placed the church's finances under control of a court-appointed receiver. The state eventually dropped the charges, but not before nationwide press coverage brought the church and Armstrong unwanted publicity. In 1977, ten years after the death of his wife, Armstrong married Ramona Martin. Their marriage ended in an acrimonious divorce in 1984. Armstrong's son Garner accused his father of violating the doctrine of the indissolubility of marriage. Armstrong died in his sleep in Pasadena and was buried at Mountain View Cemetery in Altadena, California.

Armstrong's handpicked successor, Joseph Tkach, gradually led the church away from most of the unique doctrinal and operational positions that were originally a part of Armstrong's message, so that relatively little remains of "Armstrongism" in the Worldwide Church of God. ◆

According to Armstrong, the Worldwide Church of God restored 18 essential truths that Christianity had either lost or ignored, including the church's proper name.

Asbury, Francis

1745–1816 ● METHODIST

Francis Asbury, was the chief architect of American Methodism. Raised on the fringes of Birmingham in England's "Black Country," where the industrial revolu-

tion was beginning, Asbury became a lay preacher at 18, eager "to live to God, and to bring others to do so." In 1766 he was admitted as one of John Wesley's itinerant preachers, and in 1771 he was chosen as one of the second pair of volunteers to serve in America. Asbury proved a tough and dedicated pioneer, a stable and influential leader in the manner of Wesley, whose writings saturated his mind. During the Revolutionary War he endeared himself to native-born Methodists by his refusal to return to England, and he restrained those who wanted to break away from Wesley. In 1784 Wesley named the absent Asbury a member of the "legal hundred" to administer British Methodism after Wesley's death, and he also appointed him to receive ordination as "superintendent," or bishop without pomp, at the hands of Thomas Coke. Asbury refused such ordination without the summoning of a conference of his colleagues, who thereupon elected him to that office.

At first Asbury and Coke jointly administered the new Methodist Episcopal Church, but Coke's frequent absences from America increasingly left authority in the hands of Asbury, who was in any case much more fully identified with the American preachers and laity. Asbury was noteworthy for his own tireless travels, both in settled areas and along the expanding frontiers, and his constant recruiting and nurturing of native preachers. He maintained that Methodism would succeed in its mission only through the retention of a disciplined itinerant system and an authoritative but sacrificial episcopacy such as his own. His preachers accepted his discipline because they recognized in him the true marks of the apostle of American Methodism. ◆

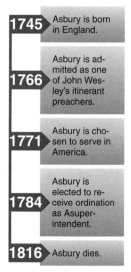

1745 ▷ Asbury is born in England.

1766 ▷ Asbury is admitted as one of John Wesley's itinerant preachers.

1771 ▷ Asbury is chosen to serve in America.

1784 ▷ Asbury is elected to receive ordination as Asuperintendent.

1816 ▷ Asbury dies.

Saint Augustine

354–430 ● CHRISTIAN

Saint Augustine, also known as Augustine of Hippo, was the bishop of Hippo (now in Algeria) and an early Christian church father. The volume of his writing exceeded that of any other ancient author and he exerted a profound influence on his contemporaries and succeeding generations. His adoption of Platonic philosophy as a basis for his own religious and political thought made it the dominant philosophical system in western Europe. His view of the Christian religion as an organic system of faith influenced ecclesiastical organization in the Middle Ages as well as relations between church and lay society. His political ideas, as represented in *The City of God*, were at the foundation of the medieval Christian state, which sought to realize the ideal theocratic regime, with the church leading the way to salvation.

He was born in Roman North Africa to Patricius, a pagan who later converted to Christianity, and Monica, a devout Christian who was later canonized by the church. His early life is described in his autobiographical *Confessions*. Written from the viewpoint of his conversion to Christianity, they are severely critical of his past life—he called it "his misspent youth"—including the years during which he lived with a mistress, by whom he had a son named Adeodatus.

He read extensively and Plato exerted a strong influence on him. After studying at Carthage he began teaching rhetoric. Cicero's *Hortensius* led him to become interested in philosophy and he experimented with several philosophical systems. Augustine spent nine years as a Manichaean because its fundamental principles of conflict between good and evil seemed at the time the most plausible basis for a philosophical and ethical system. It was also relatively lenient with novices which, judging from his petition, "Lord make me pure and chaste—but not just yet," must have suited him at the time. Eventually disillusioned, he turned to skepticism, then to Neoplatonism, and finally to Christianity. One day, according to his own account, he heard a voice saying, "Take and read." He opened the Scrip-

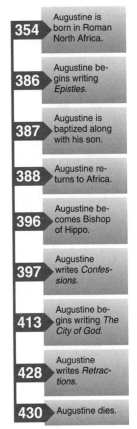

354 Augustine is born in Roman North Africa.

386 Augustine begins writing *Epistles*.

387 Augustine is baptized along with his son.

388 Augustine returns to Africa.

396 Augustine becomes Bishop of Hippo.

397 Augustine writes *Confessions*.

413 Augustine begins writing *The City of God*.

428 Augustine writes *Retractions*.

430 Augustine dies.

Saint Augustine

tures and read the first passage he saw, which was, "Not in riot-ing and drunkenness, not in chambering and impurities, not in contention and envy, but put ye on the Lord Jesus Christ, and make not provision for the flesh in its concupiscence" (Romans 13:13–14). He immediately embraced Christianity and was baptized in 387 along with his son, much to the joy of his mother. The following year he returned to Africa where he was to become bishop of Hippo in 355. Finding in himself a bent and a desire for Christian exegesis, he began a lifelong career in justifying and interpreting the Christian faith.

Augustine was primarily a religious thinker who desired to know and represent God and the human soul. "I desire to have knowledge of God and the soul. Of nothing else? No of nothing else whatsoever," and, "O God always one and the same, if I know myself, I shall know Thee." Philosophy was but a means to that end, a body of knowledge from which he could draw illustrations and explanations. He saw Christianity as an organic system of faith that could create conditions for salvation through the knowledge of God and the correct behavior of the faithful within the church. He taught that the only true church was characterized by unity, holiness, catholicity, and apostolicity, and became so convinced of this truth that he eventually believed it was justifiable to coerce the intractable to join the church.

His political program, which suggested the identification of the state with Christian society, implied the exclusion of non-Christians from the political body. Although pagans were treated severely, Jews were tolerated and barred only from public office and land tenancy. In order to prevent propagation of heresy, the church had to investigate and punish heretics—this goal was at the root of the Inquisition at the end of the twelfth century.

Augustine was a persuasive writer, excellent stylist, and prolific author. Aside from his famous *Confessions* (397), he wrote *The City of God* (413–426), in which he is represented as a divided man, one part embodying ancient culture, the other the new Gospel; but as the book clearly illustrates, Christianity is ascendant. Ten of its 22 books are concerned with refuting the pagan notion that worshiping the gods brings prosperity in this life or the life to come, while the other 12 discuss the history, progress, and destiny of the city of God and its eventual triumph over the city of this world. Other works include *Retractations* (428), *Epistles* (386–429), and numerous treatises. ◆

"Who can unravel that twisted and tangled knottiness? It is foul. I hate to reflect on it. I hate to look on it. But thee do I long for, O righteousness and innocency, fair and comely to all virtuous eyes, and of a satisfaction that never palls! With thee is perfect rest, and life unchanging."
Augustine, *Confessions*, Book II

Aurobindo Ghose

1872–1950 ● Hindu

Aurobindo Ghose was a yogin, nationalist, poet, and spiritual leader of India. Born in Calcutta, Aurobindo was educated in England from the age of seven to age

1872 ▸ Aurobindo is born in Calcutta.

c. 1879 ▸ Aurobindo travels to England for his education.

1893 ▸ Aurobindo returns to India after college.

1906 ▸ Aurobindo becomes a prominent voice in the Nationalist party.

1908 ▸ Aurobindo, in prison before an acquittal, deepens his interest in yoga.

1910 ▸ Aurobindo moves to French India.

1950 ▸ Aurobindo dies.

21 at the insistence of his father, Dr. Krishnadhan Ghose, who had been one of the first Indians educated in England. Having grown up ignorant of Indian culture and religion, Aurobindo neither discovered nor appreciated Indian languages, literature, or history until he returned to India after college, in 1893. He served for a time as a teacher of French and English and as vice principal and acting principal of Baroda College. In 1906 Aurobindo joined the political movement of Indian resistance to British colonial rule and became a prominent voice of the Nationalist party, arguing for complete independence from Britain. Through his writings, Aurobindo nourished a revolutionary consciousness among Indians by addressing the issues of self-rule and boycott. He was open to the use of armed revolt as well as nonviolent means for achieving independence. In this he was flexible and pragmatic: the means of social change were selected on the basis of circumstances, not adherence to an absolute ethical principle.

In 1908 Aurobindo was arrested in connection with an unsuccessful bombing episode against a British district judge. Although he was ultimately acquitted, he spent a year in the Alipore jail during the investigation and trial. During this imprisonment his interest in yoga deepened. In 1910, following "a sudden command from above," Aurobindo moved to French India. He spent the next 40 years of his life in Pondicherry, formulating his vision of spiritual evolution and Integral Yoga, and refusing to pursue direct involvement in political events.

"Spiritual evolution," or the evolution of consciousness, is the central framework for understanding Aurobindo's thought. *Consciousness* is a rich and complex term for Aurobindo. Consciousness is inherent in all things, in seemingly inert matter as well as plant, animal, human, and suprahuman life. It participates in the various levels of being in various ways. *Sachchidananda*, literally the highest level of "being, consciousness, and bliss," is also known as the Absolute. The Supermind mediates *sachchidananda* to the multiplicity of the world. The Overmind serves as delegate of the Supermind. Intuitive Mind is a kind of consciousness of the heart that discerns the truth in momentary flashes rather than in a comprehensive grasp. Illumined Mind communicates consciousness by vision, Higher Mind through conceptual thought. Mind generally integrates reality through cognitive, intellectual, and mental perceptions rather than through direct vision, yet mind is also open to the higher levels of consciousness, for it is basically oriented to Supermind, in which it participates in a derivative way. The Psyche is the conscious form of the soul that makes possible the evolution from ignorance to light. Life is cosmic energy through which the divine is received and made manifest. Matter, the lowest level in Aurobindo's hierarchy of consciousness manifestation, is not reducible to mere material substance, but is an expression of *sachchidananda* in diminished form.

This hierarchical view of consciousness or spirit must also be seen in a process perspective in which the supreme is seen as continuously being and becoming manifest in these many levels of being. Consciousness liberates itself through an inner law that directs evolution. Spiritual evolution is also seen as a series of ascents from material, physical existence up to supramental existence, in which we are able to reach our true being and fulfillment.

Yoga is a means by which this evolutionary thrust can be consciously assisted. Whereas evolution proceeds slowly and indirectly, yoga functions more quickly and directly. Evolution seeks the divine through nature, while yoga reaches out for the divine as transcendent to nature.

Aurobindo's Integral Yoga is so named because it seeks to incorporate the essence and processes of the old yogas, blending their methods and fruits into one system. It is integral also insofar as it seeks an integral and total change of consciousness and nature, not for the individual alone but for all of humanity and the entire cosmos. Unlike some yogas of the past, Integral Yoga does not seek release from the cycle of birth and death but seeks a transformation of life and existence, by, for, and through the divine. In most yogas, ascent to the divine is emphasized. In Integral Yoga, ascent to the divine is but the first step; the real goal is descent of the new consciousness that has been attained by the ascent.

Disciples, admirers, and advocates of Aurobindo's vision of spiritual evolution and system of Integral Yoga gather in communities throughout the world. Best known are those who have begun construction of Auroville, a city near Pondicherry designed to embody Aurobindo's ideal for a transformed humanity, and the ashram at Pondicherry where Aurobindo himself lived for 40 years. ◆

"The Godhead is infinitely greater than any natural manifestation can be. By his very infinity, by his absolute freedom, he exists beyond all possibility of integral formulation in any scheme of worlds or extension of cosmic Nature, however wide, complex, endlessly varied this and every world may seem to us."
Ghose Aurobindo, *Essays on the Gita,* 1920

The Bab

1819/20–1850 ● BABISM (BAHA'I)

The Bab, a Persian religious reformer and leader, was the founder of Babism, the precursor of the Baha'i religion. A descendant of the prophet Muhammad, the Bab was born into the traditional Shiite Muslim community. Shiites had religious leaders, *imams*, who ruled over them in the distant past. The last imam was said to have died in 819; he was followed by a series of "Hidden Imams," whose identity was unknown. As the millennium of the last imam's death approached, Muslim mystics foretold the birth of a new imam who would revolutionize the faith. The Bab, whose birth coincided with the 1000th anniversary of the death of the last imam, was considered a fulfillment of the prophecy.

The Bab was born Mirza Ali Muhammad in Shiraz, Persia; his father, a cloth merchant, died when he was three so Ali Muhammad was raised by an uncle. He was an intelligent child, given to religious speculation and meditation. At 17 he entered the family business, but spent a year in Iraq visiting Shiite shrines. At Karbala, Haj Sayyid Kazin, head of the Shaykhi movement, introduced him to the mystic rituals and beliefs of that sect. The meeting of the two men had a marked influence on Ali Muhammad. Although he returned to Shiraz and married in 1842, he frequently visited the neighboring forests to meditate and pray. In 1844 he declared himself the Bab, or Gate.

> "Know thou that first and foremost in religion is the knowledge of God."
>
> Bab, *The Seven Proofs*

1819 ▸ Bab is born and considered the new imam by the Shiite Muslims.

c. 1836 ▸ Bab enters his uncle's business.

1842 ▸ Bab marries.

1844 ▸ Bab declares himself the Bab; makes pilgrimage to Mecca.

1847 ▸ Bab is imprisoned after the death of the governor.

1850 ▸ Bab is executed; a disciple later forms the Baha'i faith.

"It is better to guide one soul than to possess all that is on earth, for as long as that guided soul is under the shadow of the Tree of Divine Unity, he and the one who hath guided him will both be recipients of God's tender mercy, whereas possession of earthly things will cease at the time of death."

Bab, *Persian Bayán*

This declaration has been given two interpretations: he believed himself to be the precursor of the Hidden Imam whose arrival was imminent; he regarded himself as that Hidden Imam, a belief which developed throughout his career until, in prison, he declared himself a manifestation of God.

The first person to whom the Bab declared himself was Mullah Hussayn, who was convinced of the Bab's transcendental knowledge and was staggered by the intensity of a book, the *Kittab-al-Awwal* (The First Book), that the Bab had written. Whereas many ridiculed the Bab, Mullah Hussayn remained an impassioned disciple and had the title, Babu'l-Bab (Gate to the Gate) conferred on him. The two gathered a significant following led by 18 foremost disciples. Adherents of the growing sect became known as Babis. That same year the Bab made a pilgrimage to Mecca. Before going, he wrote to the Sharif of Mecca, declaring himself to be the *Mahdi*, or Muslim messiah.

Both the government and the clergy regarded the Bab as a threat to civil order. Many Babis claimed that since his appearance, the laws of the Koran were no longer valid. Women abandoned the veil and other symbols of male dominance, claiming that they were now equal with male adherents. The Bab was arrested and brought to Shiraz, where he denied his claim to being the precursor of the Hidden Imam. He later explained his repudiation in a letter, saying that he was not the Gate to the Hidden Imam but to God Himself.

The Bab escaped to Isfahan, where the Christian governor, a known opponent of the regime, offered him sanctuary and even an army to defend himself; while he accepted asylum, he refused military assistance. At the same time, he did not dissuade his followers from bearing arms in self-defense. In Isfahan, the Bab established his religious ascendancy by claiming that he could, in just three hours, write 1000 sentences on any topic and produced a brilliant commentary on a particularly obscure portion of the Koran as proof.

Following the death of the governor in 1847, the Bab was imprisoned. According to Shiite tradition he finally recanted his claim to be the Mahdi in a letter, which is still preserved in the Iranian Parliament. This letter has not, however, been authenticated and its contents, even if genuine, might still reflect the Bab's earlier uses of double-talk to save his life.

The Babis were not shaken by the imprisonment of their leader; many violent clashes with the government ensued in which thousands of Babis met their death. The Persian government finally concluded that only the Bab's death would end the uprisings which threatened the regime's stability. In Tabriz the Bab was sentenced to death for **apostasy.** That night, his followers congregated around him in his cell. One follower, Mirza Muhammad Ali, begged the Bab to be allowed to share in his martyrdom; his request was granted.

apostasy: abandonment or renunciation of a religious faith

The next day the two men were dragged through the streets of Tabriz. First, Mirza Muhammad Ali was suspended from a parapet with ropes and shot by a firing squad. The Bab was then suspended but when the smoke cleared, the ropes had been cut and the Bab was nowhere to be seen. After a careful search, he was found in a nearby barracks, unscathed. Again he was taken for execution, and his bullet-ridden body was cast outside the city walls. His followers bribed local officials to have the body removed for secret burial. Some years later the Bab was re-interred on Mount Carmel in Palestine. In Haifa, a magnificent shrine today stands over the tomb. A disciple of the Bab, the Baha'ullah, later combined the teachings of the Bab with his own beliefs to form the Baha'i faith. This claims to incorporate the best of all religions, teaching the unity of all mankind, without regard to race, color, or creed. W. M. Miller, *The Bahai Faith: Its History and Teachings*, 1974. ◆

Baha' ullah

1817–1892 ● BAHA'I

Baha' ullah was the founder of the Baha' i religion. Baha' ullah, whose real name was Mirza Husayn 'Ali Nuri was, born in Iran into a noble Tehran family that had given several ministers to the Persian court. According to Baha'i tradition and his own writings, he never attended school. He was a profoundly religious personality and soon began following the teachings of the Persian religious reformer known as the Bab, although he never met the Bab personally. From his writings it appears that he never read the Bab holy book, the *Bayan* (Declaration), but nevertheless knew it by heart.

In the wave of repression against Babis in 1852, he was thrown into the Tehran prison known as "Black Hole", where he had the mystical experience that Baha'is consider to be the

Baha'i House of Worship

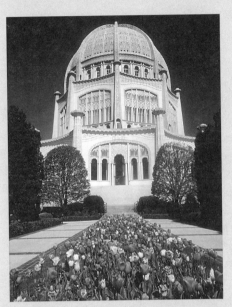

The Baha'i House of Worship in Wilmette, Illinois, is a striking landmark set near the shore of Lake Michigan and visible from many miles around. It is a gleaming white, nearly 200-foot-high dome of intricate filigree created from reinforced concrete made of bits of quartz in white cement. The interior of the dome is glass, with the concrete providing its outer covering. The bell-shaped temple has nine sides, a number with special significance to Baha'is. Visitors enter the temple through one of nine doors. Lovely gardens spread out from each side and surround nine circular pools. The gardens add to the goal of designer Louis Bourgeois to create "a place of meditation and prayer for people from all backgrounds." The temple, dedicated in 1953, took more than 30 years to build. Temple members raised the more than $3-million cost.

Inside, the temple contains no images, pews, or altars, in keeping with Baha'i simplicity. Drapes hang against the walls, and rows of chairs provide seating. Over each of the entries is an inscription from the writings of Baha'u'llah, the Prophet-Founder of the Baha'i Faith. The faith began in Iran in the mid-1800s and emphasizes the oneness of mankind. Devotional services are short, usually including brief readings from the Bible, Torah, Koran, and other spiritual writings.

first intimation of his future mission. As he describes this experience in *Epistle of the Son of the Wolf,* he heard a voice crying, "Verily we will succor you by means of yourself and your pen. Be not afraid...you are in security. And soon God will raise up the treasuries of the heart, namely those men who shall succor you for love of you and your name, by which God will bring to life the hearts of the sages." At other times he felt that a great torrent of water was running from the top of his head to his chest "like a powerful river pouring itself out on the earth from the summit of a lofty mountain."

Upon his release from prison in January 1853, his possessions were confiscated and he was banished with his family to Baghdad. There he exerted increasing spiritual influence on the Babi exiles, while that of his half brother, Mirza Yahya (known as Subh-i Azal, "dawn of eternity") declined. In 1854 Baha' ullah went to Kurdistan, where he lived as a nomadic dervish near Sulaymaniyah. When he returned to Baghdad two years later, his influence upon the Babi exiles and numerous Persian visitors was such that the Persian consul asked the Ottoman authorities to remove him to Istanbul. Shortly before his departure, on 21 April 1863, in the garden of Najib Pasha near Baghdad. Baha' ullah declared himself to be "he whom God shall manifest" as promised by the Bab.

After some months in Istanbul, the exiles were sent to Edirne, and there Baha' ullah openly declared his prophetic mission, sending letters (known as *alwah*, "tablets") to various sovereigns, including Pope Pius IX, to invite support for his cause. The majority of the Babis accepted him and came to be known as Baha'is. A minority provoked incidents that impelled the Ottomans to banish the Baha' is to Palestine and Cyprus. Baha' ullah arrived in Acre (in present-day Israel) with his family in August 1868, and for this reason the Baha'is consider Palestine as the Holy Land.

For nine years Baha' ullah was imprisoned in the fortress at Acre but was then allowed to move to a country house he had rented at Mazra'ah. Between 1877 and 1884 he occupied himself with writing his fundamental work, *The Most Holy Book*. About 1880 he was allowed to go to Bahji, near Haifa, where he died 12 years later after a short illness. According to his will, his eldest son, 'Abbas Effendi (1844–1921), who had faithfully accompanied his father in his travels and his exile, became the infallible interpreter of his father's books and writings and the "center of the covenant". He was known thereafter as 'Abd al-Baha' ("servant of the glory [of God]"). Baha' ullah's will was contested by his other son, Muhammad 'Ali, who set up a rival organization and tried with all his means to compromise his brother in the eyes of the already hostile Ottoman authorities. 'Abd al-Baha' was formally released from prison in 1908 under the amnesty granted by the new government of the Young Turks. In 1910 he began his three missionary journeys to the West: to Egypt (1910), to Europe (1911), and to America and Europe (1912–1913); he returned to Palestine in 1913.

The first Baha'i group in America was formed as early as 1894, and in December 1898, the first American pilgrims arrived in Acre. Although one of the objects of 'Abd al-Baha's trips was to counter the propaganda of his brother's supporters, he also formed Baha'i groups in the countries he visited. In

1817 Baha'ullah is born into a noble Tehran family.

1852 Baha'ullah is put in prison and has a mystical experience.

1853 Baha'ullah is released from prison and banished with his family to Baghdad.

1854 Baha'ullah goes to Kurdistan and lives as a nomadic dervish.

1863 Baha'ullah declares himself to be "he whom God shall manifest."

1868 Baha'ullah arrives in present-day Israel.

1877 Baha'ullah is released from prison and begins work on a holy book.

1880 Baha'ullah is allowed to go to Bahji near Haifa.

1892 Baha'ullah dies after a short illness.

1920 he was knighted by the British government; he died the following year and was buried near the Bab in the great shrine on Mount Carmel. In his will he appointed Shoghi Effendi Rabbani (1899–1957), the eldest son of his eldest daughter, as "guardian of the cause of God" and infallible interpreter of his writings and those of his father. ◆

Barbour, Ian G.

1923– ● SCIENTIST AND THEOLOGIAN

> "We hear of debates between atheistic scientists and biblical literalists. One side believes in evolution but not God, the other believes in God but not evolution. But between these two extremes are many people who believe in both God and evolution, or see evolution as God's way of creating."
>
> Ian Barbour, 1999

Ian G. Barbour is a physicist and theologian whose landmark book, *Issues in Science and Religion*, is credited with launching today's interdisciplinary study of science and religion. He is also widely known as an influential advocate for ethics in technology. For his years of effort in fostering dialogue between theologians and scientists, Barbour was awarded the 1999 Templeton Prize, the world's largest monetary prize.

Barbour was born in 1923 in what is now Beijing, China, the son of George and Dorothy Dickinson Barbour, both teachers at Yenching University. His father was Scottish and his mother was an American. Barbour grew up in both Beijing and England, and at the age of 14 he moved with his family to the United States.

In 1943 Barbour graduated from Swarthmore College in Pennsylvania with a degree in physics. He completed his M.A. in physics at Duke University in 1946. At the university he met Deane Kern, and they were wed in 1947. Throughout his studies, Barbour devoted time to various humanitarian and civic efforts, including leading an international student group in clearing rubble from bombed-out buildings in Germany in 1948.

In 1949 Barbour completed his Ph.D. in physics at the University of Chicago, where he had worked as a teaching assistant under the renowned physicist and Nobel laureate Enrico Fermi. After graduation, he began teaching physics at Kalamazoo College in Michigan, and he became the physics department chair in 1951. In 1955 he enrolled at Yale Divinity School to study theology, philosophy, and ethics. At the time ethical concerns about nuclear research were being hotly debated at universities, but Barbour's decision to pursue religious studies was purely personal. In 1955 Barbour began teaching physics and religion at Carleton College in Northfield, Minnesota, and he soon became chair of the religion department. He became a U.S. citizen in 1955 and completed his divinity degree the following year.

The year 1965 became a pivotal point in his career with the publication of his seminal work, *Issues in Science and Religion*. The book explored religion's relation to the history, methods, and theories of science. It garnered Barbour international recognition and became the most widely used text in the field of science and religion.

Barbour's subsequent academic career was studded with awards and fellowships. In 1986, he became professor emeritus at Carleton, but his publications and activities in the field of science and religion continued. Barbour's extensive publications include books and articles that discuss the ethical issues that have surfaced with the advance of such technology as genetic engineering and artificial intelligence. He has also written on the religious implications of Creation and the Big Bang and the ways in which traditional concepts of God are compatible with the evolutionary theory. Barbour is a longtime advocate of dialogue between scientists and theologians, feeling that they have much to gain from working with each other.

In May 1999, Barbour received the Templeton Prize for Progress in Religion. The prize goes each year to a living person who has shown exceptional originality in advancing the public understanding of God and spirituality. In 1999 the prize amounted to about $1.24 million. Barbour announced that he would give $1 million to The Center for Theology and the Natural Sciences in Berkeley, California, to establish an endowment for scholarships. ◆

1923 Barbour is born to a Scottish and American couple in China.

1937 Barbour moves with his parents to the US.

1943 Barbour graduates from Swarthmore College with a physics degree.

1946 Barbour receives his master's degree in physics.

1949 Barbour earns his Ph.D. in physics from the University of Chicago.

1951 Barbour becomes chair of physics department at Kalamazoo College.

1956 Barbour completes his divinity degree.

1965 Barbour publishes his seminal work *Issues in Science and Religion*.

1999 Barbour receives Templeton Prize for Progress in Religion.

Barth, Karl

1886–1968 ● PROTESTANT

Karl Barth was a Swiss Reformed theologian, described by Pope Pius XII as the greatest theologian since Thomas Aquinas, and certainly the most influential of the twentieth century. Barth stands as a prophetic voice calling the Christian church back to the Bible and to its foundation in

Jesus Christ. This message sounded forth powerfully in his first book, *Romans* (especially in the largely rewritten second edition of 1921), which drew widespread attention. Barth later said that in writing this book he was like a man in a dark church tower who accidentally trips, catches hold of the bell rope to steady himself, and alarms the whole countryside. As a result, he was called to university chairs in Gottingen (1921), in Munster (1925), and in Bonn (1930). From this latter post he was dismissed in 1935 because of his refusal to take an oath of loyalty to Nazi dictator Adolf Hitler and because of his leading role in the struggle against the Nazi attempt to control the German Evangelical church. He returned to his native Switzerland to a professorship in Basel, where he taught for the rest of his long life until his death in 1968, drawing students from all over the world to his classrooms and publishing his lectures in his massive *Church Dogmatics*.

> "Conscience is the perfect interpreter of life."
>
> Karl Barth,
> *The Word of God and the Word of Man,* 1957

Barth was born in Basel on 10 May 1886, the son of Fritz Barth, a professor of church history and New Testament in Bern. In Bern, Barth received his earliest education, and there, on the eve of his confirmation, he "boldly resolved to become a theologian" out of an early eagerness to understand his faith and see its relevance for the twentieth century. He commenced his university studies in Bern, where, while receiving a solid grounding in Reformed theology, he began to study theoretical and practical philosophy.

Barth soon expressed a desire to study at Marburg with Wilhelm Herrmann (1846–1922), a leading theologian in Europe. However, under his father's influence, he went first to Berlin to spend a semester under Adolf von Harnack, the most outstanding church historian and liberal theologian of the day, before returning to complete a third year in Bern. In 1907 he enrolled in Tubingen to study under the conservative New Testament theologian Adolf Schlatter, before spending a final year in Marburg.

Throughout his life Barth endeavored to interpret the gospel and examine the church's message in the context of society, the state, war, revolution, totalitarianism, and democracy, over against the pretensions of man to solve the problems of his own destiny, without the judgment of the message of the cross and the resurrection of Jesus Christ. Toward the end of his life he could write, "I decided for theology, because I felt a need to find a better basis for my social action." The fundamental question was how to relate what the Word of God in the Bible says about the sovereignty and transcendence of God, grace, the coming of the Kingdom, the forgiveness of sins, and the resurrection of the dead with human problems. Barth voiced his concern over the bankruptcy of much contemporary religion and theology in his commentary on *Romans* (1919). In this book, which was described by a Roman Catholic theologian as "a bombshell in the playground of the theologians," Barth seeks to summon the church back to the living God of the Bible, before whom are exposed the pretensions of human religion or piety, the proud sinful attempts to assert oneself without God. Salvation is God's gift, and the Kingdom must break in "vertically from above," summoning humankind to radical response and decision, that God's righteous purposes might be fulfilled in the world.

There were distinctive stages in Barth's theological development, in each of which he wrestled with the polarities of God and man. Nineteenth-century liberal thought too readily presupposed an inward continuity between the divine and the "highest" and "best" in human culture, positing that knowledge of God is given in the depths of the human spirit in human self-understanding and inward religious experience. Barth rejected this view early in his ministry, saying that we do not talk about God by "talking about man in a loud voice." At first he identified conscience with the voice of God, but increasingly he argued that the voice of God is heard only in scripture, in encounter with Christ, the living Word. God meets us in the moment of crisis and decision, creating his own point of contact and summoning us to radical obedience.

The chasm between God and man can be bridged by God alone, and not by man. The Word of the cross means that God says no to our human sin and pride and pretensions, while in grace God says yes to his own good creatures in a word of forgiveness. If in this early period Barth, like the early Marten Luther, stressed God's "no" (God's righteousness as God), his

1886 Barth is born in Switzerland, son of a professor of church history.

1907 Barth begins studies under a conservative New Testament theologian.

1927 Barth begins writing *Christian Dogmatics*.

1932 Barth begins writing *Church Dogmatics*.

1934 Barth and others publish the *Barmen Declaration*, which deprives him of a university chair.

1968 Barth dies.

> "God will not be alone in eternity, but with the creature. He will allow it to partake of His own eternal life. And in this way the creature will continue to be, in its limitation."
>
> Karl Barth, *Church Dogmatics*, 1962

later message, like that of the later Luther, became more powerfully a "yes": God's righteousness as a triumph of grace through the vicarious humanity of Jesus Christ. In the manner of the great medieval theologians, Barth saw that there are elements of negation and affirmation in all human knowledge of God, leading him to see an analogy of "relation," but not of "being," between God and man grounded in grace.

In 1927 Barth began writing *Christian Dogmatics*, intending to expound all the main Christian doctrines, by grounding all he had to say on God's self-revelation in Jesus Christ. The first volume was entitled *Christian Doctrine in Outline, Volume I: The Doctrine of the Word of God, Prolegomena to Christian Dogmatics*. In it he argues that possibility of Christian knowledge of God is grounded on the actuality of the revelation in Jesus, as he makes himself known to faith by the Holy Spirit.

Within this self-revelation of God we can distinguish three forms of the one Word of God: the eternal Word incarnate in Jesus Christ, the written Word in the witness of the Bible to that primary Word, and the Word of God as proclaimed in the church. The task of Christian dogmatics is to be faithful to this Word, and therefore to examine the content of the church's preaching by tracing it back to its source in God, by the standard of holy scripture, and under the guidance of its creeds and confessions.

The reviewers of this first volume criticized Barth for so casting the gospel into the language of an immediate timeless encounter with God that he was in danger of dehistoricizing the gospel and transposing theology into a new philosophical mold. Barth took this criticism seriously and gave himself to examining the question of method in theology. In 1931 he published his results in *Faith Seeking Understanding*. He had learned that the Word of God has its own rational content in God. The polarity of God and man must be interpreted, not so much in the language of an existential encounter between God and man in the crisis of faith, but primarily in terms of the given unity of God and man in Jesus Christ, the incarnate Lord, in whom God has come not simply *in* a man, but *as* a man—in a once and for all reconciling act in which we are called to participate through the Holy Spirit.

Barth's approach in the future was to build all theology on the reality of the Word of God in Jesus Christ. This led him to turn from his *Christian Dogmatics* to a new work entitled *Church Dogmatics*, which he began in 1932 and which occupied him for the rest of his life (resulting in 13 part-volumes). In *Church Dogmatics* he argues that all we know and say about God and about humankind is controlled by our knowledge of Jesus Christ as "true God and true man."

Barth was concerned with unpacking the implications of this Christ-centered perspective in every area of life. It proved highly significant in his outspoken opposition to Hitler, to the persecution of the Jews, and to the so-called German Christians who sought to justify National Socialism and its racist policies by an appeal to the natural orders of creation. Barth felt that this was a betrayal of the Christian understanding of grace by its appeal to sources of revelation other than that given to us in Jesus Christ. God's election of Israel for a vicarious role among the nations finds its fulfillment in Jesus Christ, the Jew in whom God has broken down the barriers between the Jews and all other ethnic groups (the gentiles). Christ as Lord is head over church and state, and to him alone we owe supreme loyalty in both spheres. The state must be interpreted not just in terms of the orders of creation and preservation (as he had earlier thought), but in terms of the orders of redemption. This found explicit formulation in the *Barmen Declaration* of 1934, largely written by Barth. For this stand he was deprived of his university chair in Bonn, but his theological insights and interpretation of the political scene gained him enormous prestige. Barth saw himself standing in the tradition of the ancient fathers of the church and of the Protestant reformers like Luther and Calvin, engaging in life-long dialogue with liberal Protestantism on the left and Roman Catholicism on the right, both of which he felt weakened the emphasis of the Bible that God accepts us by grace alone in Jesus Christ. ◆

> Barth saw himself standing in the tradition of the ancient fathers of the church and of the Protestant reformers like Luther and Calvin.

Bartholomew

1940– ● EASTERN ORTHODOX CHRISTIAN

When Ecumenical Patriarch Bartholomew became the spiritual leader of 300 million Eastern Orthodox Christians worldwide on November 2, 1991, he took over a church struggling to survive a difficult century. As the prominent Christian church in Russia, Eastern Europe, and western Asia, the Orthodox religion had withstood years of repression by communist governments.

The Eastern Orthodox religion is a federation of churches. These churches are usually called by their national names, such as the Greek Orthodox Church or the Russian Orthodox Church. The Orthodox religion grew from a split within the Christian church that occurred in 1054. After the split, the patriarch of Constantinople (now Istanbul, Turkey) became known as the ecumenical patriarch. The position of patriarch is similar to that of bishop in the Roman Catholic Church and the role of ecumenical patriarch became the top position, similar to that of the pope.

Bartholomew was born February 29, 1940, in the village of Aghioi Theodoroi, on the island of Imvros, Turkey, to Christos and Meropi Archontonis, who christened him Demetrios. His father worked as a barber and owned a coffee shop. Following his studies at Imvros and Istanbul, Demetrios enrolled at the Theological School of Halki, graduating with high honors in 1961. He was immediately ordained a deacon and given the name Bartholomew. Deacons are the first of the three main orders of Orthodox clergy, followed by priests and bishops. Although married men may become priests, bishops are elected from among celibate or widowed clergy. Bartholomew fulfilled his military obligation as an officer in the Turkish army reserve from 1961 through 1963.

Bartholomew pursued postgraduate studies on a scholarship at the Gregorian University in Rome from 1963 to 1968, receiving a doctorate in Canon Law, the legal system developed by the Catholic church. He pursued further studies at the Ecumenical Institute in Bossey, Switzerland, and the University of Munich, Germany, specializing in church law. Bartholomew became fluent in seven languages—Greek, English, Turkish, Italian, Latin, French, and German. Returning to Istanbul in 1968, he was appointed assistant dean of the Sacred Theological School of Halki.

On October 19, 1969, Bartholomew was ordained a priest. On Christmas Day 1973, Father Bartholomew was consecrated a bishop and named Metropolitan of Philadelphia (a region in Asia Minor). Each Orthodox church is governed by its own head bishop. The head bishops of the churches may be called patriarch, metropolitan, or archbishop. On January 14, 1990, Bartholomew was enthroned as the Metropolitan of Chalcedon.

Hagia Sophia Cathedral

Hagia Sophia, also known as the Church of the Holy Wisdom, in Constantinople (now Istanbul, Turkey), was the most important church of the East Roman Empire. It served as the seat of the patriarch, the spiritual leader of the Eastern Orthodox Church, from the sixth to the fifteenth century. Built between 532 and 537 c.e. by Emperor Justinian I, it represents one of today's greatest examples of Byzantine architecture. The cathedral is known architecturally for its massive dome and large, open, square interior. The dome, which measures more than 100 feet (30 meters) in diameter, soars 185 feet (56 meters) above the floor and is ringed at the bottom by 40 arched windows. Beautiful marbles, granite, and mosaics decorate the interior of the building. Mosaics depicting religious figures were first added to the building in the ninth century. In 1453, Mehmet II, Sultan of the Ottoman Empire, captured Constantinople and subsequently converted the Hagia Sophia into a mosque. The Muslim Turks plastered over the Christian images, hanging great round shields with Arabic quotations from the Koran to the building's interior and erecting minarets at the four outside corners of the building. The Turks also constructed a large sultan's box near what once served as the sanctuary and replaced the cross on the dome with a crescent, a symbol of Islam. In 1935, Mustafa Kemal Atatürk, the founder of modern Turkey, made Hagia Sophia into a museum. Many of the original mosaics have since been uncovered.

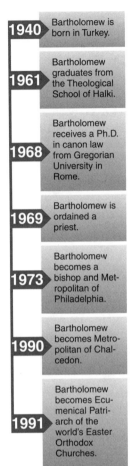

1940 Bartholomew is born in Turkey.

1961 Bartholomew graduates from the Theological School of Halki.

1968 Bartholomew receives a Ph.D. in canon law from Gregorian University in Rome.

1969 Bartholomew is ordained a priest.

1973 Bartholomew becomes a bishop and Metropolitan of Philadelphia.

1990 Bartholomew becomes Metropolitan of Chalcedon.

1991 Bartholomew becomes Ecumenical Patriarch of the world's Easter Orthodox Churches.

For many years, Bartholomew was active in the World Council of Churches (WCC) and held the position of vice president for eight years. The WCC works to promote unity among all the churches of the world. In January 1991, Metropolitan Bartholomew headed the Orthodox delegation at the Seventh General Assembly of the WCC in Canberra, Australia. At that meeting, he helped avoid a rift between the WCC and Orthodox members who objected that the WCC was moving away from essential Orthodox beliefs. Bartholomew remained a strong advocate of working for unity among churches.

For 19 years, Bartholomew worked with Ecumenical Patriarch Dimitrios as one of his closest confidants. After Dimitrios died on October 2, 1991, Bartholomew was unanimously elected Ecumenical Patriarch on October 22 and was installed on November 2.

After completing his first year on the Ecumenical Throne, His All Holiness, as he is called, began an extensive round of official visits abroad. He visited the Patriarchates of Russia, Serbia, and Romania as well as the Orthodox Archdiocese of Sweden and Scandinavia and the Orthodox Archdiocese of Germany. During 1995, Bartholomew visited the patriarch of the Ethiopian Church and the Orthodox Church of Jerusalem, where he met with the political figures of Israel as well as Palestinian leader Yasser Arafat. In June 1995, Bartholomew visited Pope John Paul II and declared his intent to continue dialogue and cooperation with the Catholic church.

Bartholomew has led his people into the end of a difficult century for Orthodox Christians. Following the Russian Revolution of 1917, the church was violently persecuted by the Communist government in the Soviet Union and severely restricted in other Communist nations of Eastern Europe. As Communist rule became less repressive and finally broke up in the late 1980s and early 1990s, the Orthodox religion regained its strength. Bartholomew took an active role in post-Communist Eastern Europe by strengthening relations with various Orthodox national churches and through his visits to Orthodox nations. By the late 1990s, the Orthodox religion proclaimed itself as a growing faith, gaining members around the world.

As a citizen of Turkey, a nation unique for its position between the Christian and Muslim worlds, Bartholomew made a priority of reconciling Catholic, Muslim, Jewish, and Orthodox communities in the Middle East and around the world. In addition, Bartholomew earned the nickname the "Green Patriarch," for expressing the religious importance of protecting the environment. He initiated seminars and dialogues to discuss the need to achieve harmony between humanity and nature, and he co-sponsored a conference on the environment at the Theological School of Halki. ◆

Becket, Thomas

c. 1118–1170 ● CHRISTIAN

Saint Thomas Becket (Thomas a Becket; was the archbishop of Canterbury. Born in London to a Norman merchant family, Thomas Becket's pious mother—the only woman who ever had a place in Becket's life—strongly influenced her son. He grew up in an England divided among powerful lords and torn apart by civil wars between the weak rival claimants to the throne of Henry I. The clergy ruled England during that period, insofar as it was ruled at all.

Physically attractive, brilliant, and verbally adept, Becket came to the attention of the foremost prelate in England, the archbishop of Canterbury, Theobald, who sent him to Italy to study law. At 25 he became one of the eager and ambitious young clerks surrounding Theobald. With the prudent use of tact, charm, and an astute judgment of character, he set out to become indispensable to Theobald and succeeded, rapidly becoming Theobald's favorite as well as being generally respected.

In 1154 Henry II became king of England, ending almost 20 years of civil war. Faced with the enormous task of restoring order to a war-ravaged country, he needed men with loyalty and administrative skills. Theobald, wishing to have the position filled by an ally who could be depended on to protect the church's interests, suggested Becket, then 36, for the position of high chancellor.

A man of action, skilled in administration, organization, diplomacy, debate, and war, Becket was a superb chancellor, becoming almost as wealthy and powerful as the king. Known for his lavish hospitality, he lived in opulent luxury. He was on excellent terms with Henry II throughout his seven years as chancellor. Friends as well as colleagues, they hunted, ate, and drank together.

> "Then, with another blow received on the head, he remained firm. But with the third the stricken martyr bent his knees and elbows, offering himself as a living sacrifice, saying in a low voice, "For the name of Jesus and the protection of the church I am ready to embrace death."
>
> Edward Grim, describing Becket's murder in *Vita S. Thomae, Cantuariensis Archepiscopi et Martyris*, late 12th century.

Henry was determined to unite England under a strong central monarchy. Fighting to break the barons, he appointed Becket the new archbishop of Canterbury in 1162, believing that Becket would support him in his efforts to bring the church under his control. Until this time Becket had merely been a lay person associated with the church; he did not want to become archbishop of Canterbury but eventually yielded to pressure from all sides, including the papal legate, who wanted a strong archbishop to defend the church's prerogatives.

Becket changed his way of life completely on becoming archbishop. He resigned as chancellor (despite Henry's opposition) and abandoned his wealthy, luxurious way of life. Determined to live a physically stern and austere life, he wore coarse clothing, with a haircloth next to his skin, scourged himself frequently, gave much charity, and washed the feet of 13 beggars every night. As chancellor he had worked tirelessly for the crown. As archbishop his first loyalty was to the church and he became the unyielding defender of all the church's rights and privileges, even against the throne. Becket's relationship with the king changed, too. As archbishop, Becket felt that he was the king's spiritual mentor, but Henry could not relate to his old hunting and drinking companion that way; their bitter quarrels killed Henry's love for Becket.

The core of their dispute was whether the church in England would be independent, with ties to Rome, or subordinate to the king. The surface cause of their conflict was the king's desire to establish a uniform system of justice for all as opposed to the church's wish to maintain the clergy's right to be tried in an ecclesiastical (where their crimes often went unpunished) rather than civil court. The Constitution of Clarendon (1164) was designed to put an end to many clerical immunities. Becket refused to sign the constitution (which was promulgated nonetheless) and Henry tried him for feudal disobedience at the royal court. When his own bishops found him guilty, he fled England for France.

Believing that only excommunication and interdiction could move Henry, Becket turned to the pope, submitting his resignation. Pope Alexander III defended Becket, publicly recognizing him as the church's champion, but as he himself was plagued by rival popes backed by Frederick I, he was not in a strong enough position to oppose Henry fully, and sent Becket to live for a time as a simple monk.

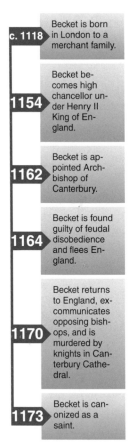

c. 1118 Becket is born in London to a merchant family.

1154 Becket becomes high chancellor under Henry II King of England.

1162 Becket is appointed Archbishop of Canterbury.

1164 Becket is found guilty of feudal disobedience and flees England.

1170 Becket returns to England, excommunicates opposing bishops, and is murdered by knights in Canterbury Cathedral.

1173 Becket is canonized as a saint.

OPPOSITE:
Saint Thomas Becket

Canterbury Cathedral

Canterbury Cathedral is the seat of the archbishop of Canterbury, the foremost clergyman of the Church of England. It is located in Canterbury, in the county of Kent, some 53 miles east southeast of London. The archbishopric was established in 597, and the original cathedral may have been an old Roman building. A year after the Norman conquest of England in 1066, the cathedral burned down. A new church was erected in the Romanesque style starting in 1070. On December 29, 1170, Archbishop Thomas Becket was murdered in the cathedral by four barons for resisting the authority of King Henry II. For the remainder of the Middle Ages, large numbers of pilgrims—immortalized in Geoffrey Chaucer's late-fourteenth-century *Canterbury Tales*—traveled to the cathedral to visit the shrine for the canonized martyr. After Canterbury Cathedral was badly damaged by a fire in 1174, rebuilding was done in the Gothic style. The stained glass of the choir and sanctuary, considered the best in England, dates back to the early thirteenth century. In the fourteenth century the nave was reconstructed in a late Gothic style known as English Perpendicular. The tower over the transept, known as Bell Harry, was built in that style during the late fifteenth century.

Becket remained in exile for six years. Attempts to effect a reconciliation with Henry were always bogged down by the intransigence of one or the other, Becket having abandoned tactful charm for unyielding, righteous stubbornness. Henry only yielded when the pope finally threatened him with interdiction if he refused to restore Becket to his see.

Becket returned to England in triumph in 1170 and immediately excommunicated the bishops who had opposed him. Henry was furious when he heard of this, exclaiming, "What! Shall a man who has eaten my bread...insult the King and all the kingdom, and not one of the lazy servants whom I nourish at my table does me right for such an affront?" Four knights heard his words and, apparently without Henry's knowledge, went to Canterbury where they murdered Becket at the altar of the cathedral, just four weeks after his return to England.

Becket dead succeeded where Becket living had not. Horrified, Christendom responded to his murder by declaring him a saint and excommunicating Henry for his part in the assassination. Henry declared his innocence to the pope, ordered the apprehension of the assassins, and restored all the rights and properties of the church. Finally, he came to Canterbury as a penitent, barefoot, wearing a hair shirt, begging the monks to whip him for his part in Becket's death. Becket was canonized in 1173 and his tomb became the most popular shrine in England. The drama of the conflict between the king and the "turbulent priest" is the subject of modern plays by T. S. Eliot (*Murder in the Cathedral* 1935) and Jean Anouilh (*Becket ou l'honneur de Dieu*, 1959, *Becket or the Honor of God*, 1961). ◆

Saint Benedict

c. 480–547 ● CHRISTIAN

Saint Benedict was an early Christian anchorite and the father of Western monasticism. Little is known about his life; the hagiography in the *Dialogues* of Gregory the Great allows for some sifting of fact from legend, while his character can be construed from the Rule of Saint Benedict. Born in Nursia, Italy, Benedict apparently received a classical education in Rome. He was surrounded by wanton companions but at the age of around 20 rejected the debauchery of Rome in favor of a simple, religious life. Benedict did not originally plan to become a hermit. At first he was accompanied by his nurse, who attended to his physical needs while he studied and prayed.

One day the nurse was sifting flour when the sieve broke. Benedict miraculously restored the sifter in what was his first miracle. After this event he retreated to a cave to pursue a hermit's life. Initially only Romanus, a local monk who provided him with food and a coarse monk's habit, was allowed in his company, but as Benedict's reputation grew he attracted a considerable following. Monks from Vicovaro invited Benedict to be their abbot, little anticipating that he would not only try to revitalize their religious life but would even interfere in their temporal existence

> "The vice of personal ownership must by all means be cut out in the monastery by the very root, so that no one may presume to give or receive anything without the command of the Abbot; nor to have anything whatever as his own, neither a book, nor a writing tablet, nor a pen, nor anything else whatsoever, since monks are allowed to have neither their bodies nor their wills in their own power."
>
> *Rule of St. Benedict,* Chapter XXXIII, c. 530

by becoming a self-proclaimed law-giver. In the growing tension, an attempt was made to poison Benedict's food; he fled the monastery accompanied by a small group of followers willing to accept his authority. Benedict organized his disciples into 12 monasteries of 12 monks and an abbot; he was abbot of a thirteenth monastery. The monasteries flourished until a jealous local priest forced him to flee. Benedict reestablished himself at Monte Cassino and lived there until the end of his life.

To run his monastery, Benedict composed the Rule. Its 73 chapters became the basis of later European monastic tradition. Beginning with an exhortation to identify with Christ, Benedict stressed the role of the abbot, not only as a teacher but as an authoritative father figure. The rule calls on monks to practice obedience, silence, and humility, and explains how these traits can best be acquired. Benedict was not a radical anchorite (a person living alone for religious reasons): he encouraged his monks to perform community services as cenobites (people living together in a religious community) before isolating themselves from the world. Nor did he deny the pleasures of the material world; unlike other orders, which insisted on austere regimentation, Benedict contended that monks should receive adequate physical comforts. His recommended menu included one pound of bread per day, meat once a day, and at least two cooked dishes at each meal. Wine, though not encouraged, was not proscribed. Benedict also insisted that his monks sleep six to eight hours each night and allowed for an additional siesta in the summer months. Monks were to be provided with adequate blankets and pillows and with warm clothing in the winter. The popular Benedictine Rule spread throughout the region and was adopted by Benedict's twin sister, Scholastica, for her own convent located nearby.

Benedict achieved renown for his miracles (he is usually depicted with a serpent and a raven, commemorating two of his miracles) and his prophetic powers. Even the Gothic king Totila, then at war with the Byzantine Empire, sought his advice. To test Benedict, Totila first sent an officer dressed in royal attire pretending to be the king, but Benedict detected the impersonation and asked to see the real king. Benedict told Totila that he would conquer Rome, cross the seas, and rule for nine years; the prophecy was fulfilled exactly as Benedict had said. Benedict also foretold the exact hour of his own death. When the time came, the ailing abbot was brought to the chapel. He received communion and died, and was buried in

Monte Cassino in the same grave as his sister, Saint Scholastica.

It appears that the Benedictine Rule fell into disuse for some time before being restored throughout Europe by Charlemagne. Today Saint Benedict is credited with founding and encouraging the liberal Western monasticism that eventually prevailed in Europe. In 1964 Pope Paul VI declared Benedict patron saint of all Europe. His feast is celebrated in the West on July 11. ◆

Saint Bernard

1090–1153 ● CHRISTIAN

Saint Bernard of Clairvaux, was a French monastic reformer and ecclesiastical writer. Born to a noble family at the Chateau of Fontaines near Dijon in Burgundy, he was destined for an ecclesiastical career and as a child was sent to be educated for this purpose. Shy and reserved, showing no special vocation for the religious life, he nevertheless displayed a talent for writing, particularly ribald verses.

It was following his mother's death when he was 17 that he became conscious that his "weak character needed a strong medicine," as he himself declared. He entered the monastery of Citeaux in 1112 despite the protestations of family and friends at his choice of such an austere way of life. Bernard undertook to persuade them to change their way of life instead; the timid young man succeeded in imparting his enthusiasm and inducing 30 members of his family to follow his example.

In 1115 he was given the task by his abbot, Stephen Harding, of founding an abbey of the Cistercian order. Bernard founded the abbey in a deserted valley in Champagne, naming the area *Clara vallis* (the Clear Valley). He soon became one

> "If an opportunity for prayer in solitude offered itself, he seized it; but in any case, whether by himself or with companions, he preserved a solitude in his heart, and thus was everywhere alone."
>
> William of St. Thierry, *Life of St. Bernard*, c. 1140

> "The knight of Christ, I say, may strike with confidence and die yet more confidently, for he serves Christ when he strikes, and serves himself when he falls. Neither does he bear the sword in vain, for he is God's minister, for the punishment of evildoers and for the praise of the good."
>
> Bernard of Clairvaux, early 12th century

of the most active formulators of church policy, establishing his reputation as the leader of monastic reform of his age. He was at loggerheads with the king, Louis VI, whom he accused of opposing the reform, and with Peter the Venerable, abbot of Cluny, who was both his friend and rival. Already enjoying great prestige, in 1128 Bernard was asked by the Knights Templar at the Council of Troyes to write their code of discipline, which was approved by the council. In one of his most important treatises. *In Praise of the New Knighthood*, he attacked secular chivalry while praising the idealism of religious knights, who sacrifice their private interests to fight against the infidels.

A champion of orthodoxy, he was to become the virtual dictator of Christendom in western Europe. He criticized the rationalism of Peter Abelard and had him condemned at the Council of Sens in 1140. He also attacked the Parisian scholars on the grounds that they constituted a new "Babylon." From 1141 to 1143 Bernard opposed Louis VII's government but after a reconciliation between the two, Bernard was able to influence Louis's decision to lead the Second Crusade. When one of his pupils was elected pope in 1143, Bernard of Clairvaux's influence increased substantially.

He wrote a treatise, *Five Books on Consideration*, for the new pope, Eugenius III, in which he argued for a theocracy, claiming that the rule of the Christian world is the prerogative of the pope alone, while it was the king's and nobles' duty to fight the infidels. He was the spiritual leader of the Second Crusade, preaching for the fulfillment of the duty to protect the Holy Land and the Holy Sepulcher in Jerusalem. While the pope advocated the crusade on both religious and political grounds, Bernard saw it solely as a religious expedition whose intent was the salvation of souls. Moreover, his spiritual concepts were at variance with the lay manners of the Crusaders. Bernard opposed the crusade's anti-Jewish manifestations and his intervention saved the Jews of the Rhineland from persecution.

Under Bernard's administration the Abbey of Clairvaux experienced a period of prosperity and was considered one of the most prestigious monasteries of western Europe, so much so that Alphonso I, king of Portugal declared his kingdom as vassal of the abbey and undertook to pay an annual tribute.

Toward the end of his life Bernard of Clairvaux was already regarded as a saint, his pupils attributing his activities to the Divine Spirit and considering them as miracles. He was canonized 20 years after his death. ◆

Bernardin, Joseph

1928–1996 ● Catholic

Joseph Louis Cardinal Bernardin became one of the most beloved and respected leaders of the Roman Catholic Church in the United States. He gained a reputation for his gentleness and for his role as peacemaker. Whether among high officials or regular churchgoers, he often introduced himself simply as "Joe Bernardin."

Bernardin was born in Columbia, S.C., on April 2, 1928, to Joseph "Bepi" and Maria M. Simion Bernardin. Bepi, a stonecutter, had emigrated from the small mountain town of Tonadico in northern Italy. After finding work in North Carolina, he returned to marry Maria in 1927 and bring her to America. Bepi struggled for two years with a recurrence of cancer before dying in 1934, leaving Maria, Joseph, age six, and his sister Elaine, age two. Maria earned their living as a seamstress, and Joseph helped out at home.

After Bernardin attended both public and Catholic schools, he earned a scholarship to the University of South Carolina where he planned to study medicine. However, a group of priest friends convinced Bernardin that he would make a good priest, and he decided to become one. Bernardin studied at Saint Mary's College in Kentucky then at Saint Mary's Seminary in Baltimore, where he received a Bachelor of Arts degree in philosophy. In 1951, he received a Master of Arts degree in education from the Catholic University of America in Washington, D.C.

Bernardin was ordained a priest on April 26, 1952, at the age of 24. He served in the Diocese of Charleston, South Carolina, for 14 years, moving up into several administrative positions. At age 38, Bernardin became the youngest bishop in the nation when Pope Paul VI appointed him the Auxiliary Bishop of Atlanta in March 1966. Bernardin served a four-year term as General Secretary of the National Conference of Catholic Bishops starting in 1968, and in 1972, he was elected to the three-year position of president of the conference. He became a spokesman for opposing the nuclear arms race and racial injustice, and sought greater economic justice and health care for the poor. In November 1972, Pope Paul VI appointed Bernardin Archbishop of Cincinnati, where he served for nearly ten years.

"People look to priests to be authentic witnesses to God's active role in the world, to his love. They don't want us to be politicians or business managers; they are not interested in the petty conflicts that may show up in parish or diocesan life. Instead, people simply want us to be with them in the joys and sorrows of their lives."

Cardinal Bernardin, *The Gift of Peace,* 1997

1928 — Bernardin is born in South Carolina.

1951 — Bernardin earns an M.A. in education from Catholic University.

1952 — Bernardin is ordained a priest.

1966 — Bernardin becomes Auxiliary Bishop of Atlanta.

1972 — Bernardin becomes Archbishop of Cincinnati.

1982 — Bernardin becomes Archbishop of Chicago.

1983 — Bernardin is elevated to the rank of Cardinal.

1995 — Bernardin makes a pilgrimage to the Holy Land.

1996 — Bernardin dies from cancer.

Bernardin was installed as the Archbishop of Chicago on August 25, 1982, heading one of the nation's dioceses, with more than 2 million Catholics. Pope John Paul II appointed Bernardin as cardinal in 1983, making him the senior church leader in the United States and a leading candidate for successor to the pope. During the 1980's, Bernardin emerged as a key mediator between American Catholics and the more conservative leadership in Rome.

One of the greatest challenges of Bernardin's career came in November 1993, when a man named Steven Cook filed a lawsuit charging that when he was a seminarian nearly 20 years earlier, Bernardin had forced him to submit to a sexual act. Bernardin felt shocked and humiliated by the accusation, but after the story made national headlines, Bernardin faced reporters calmly and stated, "I have always lived a chaste and celibate life." Within months, Cook's story fell apart and in February 1994, he dropped the charges. Bernardin felt pity for Cook's suffering and, with his permission, Bernardin flew to Philadelphia to meet Cook. In a deep and touching encounter, Cook apologized to Bernardin and the cardinal forgave and blessed him. Within a year, Cook died of AIDS.

Relieved of that strain, Bernardin happily attacked his many projects. In March 1995, he made his first pilgrimage to the Holy Land, leading a delegation of Catholic and Jewish leaders from Chicago to meet with top Middle Eastern leaders. Bernardin regretted not having enough time to visit places where Jesus had lived, and he vowed to return some day.

But that was not to be. In June 1995, doctors discovered a deadly form of cancer in Bernardin's pancreas, and he underwent surgery, chemotherapy, and radiation treatments. Throughout his courageous ordeal, Bernardin shared his experience with the public and comforted many other cancer patients.

On April 2, 1996, Bernardin celebrated a cancer-free 68th birthday. However, he announced on August 30 that his cancer had returned. Ten days later, President Clinton presented Bernardin with the Medal of Freedom at the White House. As his life slipped rapidly away, Bernardin wrote *The Gift of Peace* (1997), to share his reflections on the spiritual journey of death. On November 14, 1996, he died. Admirers around the world mourned and thousands of people viewed or attended the cardinal's funeral rites, which ended with a two-hour, 100-car procession through Chicago area neighborhoods to his burial site in Hillside, Illinois. ◆

Besant, Annie

1847–1933 ● THEOSOPHIST

Annie Besant was a British theosophist and social reformer. She was born Annie Wood in England into a devout Christian family. She married the Reverend Frank Besant, but growing doubts about the basic tenets of the Christian faith led her, in 1873, to leave her husband and to break with the church. She then joined the National Secular Movement, and in that organization she discovered her remarkable gift for oratory. In 1885 she joined the influential, socialist Fabian Society. Feminist, socialist, and political agitator, Besant is especially noted for her role during this period as a strike leader and union organizer. Throughout her life she remained devoted to social and educational reform.

In 1889, Besant was asked to review H. P. Blavatsky's *The Secret Doctrine,* and she subsequently met the author. Besant then joined the Theosophical Society, of which Blavatsky had been a founder, and resigned from the Fabian Society, to the great shock of her colleagues. In 1891 Blavatsky died in Besant's home in London while Besant was on a lecture tour of the United States. Besant succeeded her as head of the "inner school" of the society.

In 1893, Besant first traveled to India (she always described her arrival there as "coming home"), where she enjoyed great success. At this time, she met C. W. Leadbeater, an Anglican clergyman who purportedly had great psychic powers, and she began to develop her own latent psychic abilities.

Besant was elected president of the Theosophical Society in 1907. Shortly thereafter, she and Leadbeater met a small, frail boy in Adyar (near Madras). Believing this boy, Jiddu Krishnamurti, to have the potential to be a great spiritual teacher, she adopted him and had him educated in England. She lectured widely, proclaiming Krishnamurti a "world teacher."

Besant spent years promoting home rule for India, and in 1917 she was elected the first woman president of the Indian National Congress. Later, she lost her political influence because she differed with Mohandas Gandhi's ideas, believing that India should be free but remain part of the British Commonwealth. Her long interest in Indian education led her to found Central Hindu College (now Banaras University) and

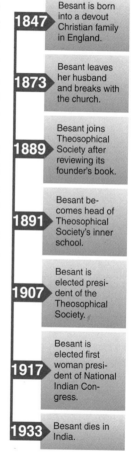

1847 Besant is born into a devout Christian family in England.

1873 Besant leaves her husband and breaks with the church.

1889 Besant joins Theosophical Society after reviewing its founder's book.

1891 Besant becomes head of Theosophical Society's inner school.

1907 Besant is elected president of the Theosophical Society.

1917 Besant is elected first woman president of National Indian Congress.

1933 Besant dies in India.

several other schools in India, and her contributions to India's education and political independence are still appreciated by the Indian people. Besant died in India in 1933.

Annie Besant was the most effective speaker in the Theosophical Society's history, and during the 26 years of her presidency the society grew and flourished. She was the author of numerous works on theosophy, writings that are characterized by the combination of Western occultism with Indian (chiefly Hindu) philosophies. Thus, her theory of human life in three worlds—the physical world, the world of desire, and the mental world—correlates elements of Hindu philosophy. The themes of reincarnation and of clairvoyance and spiritual evolution are central to her thought.

In her autobiography, Besant claims an experiential knowledge of the soul as the true self and of the soul's power to seek spiritual knowledge beyond the body. Rejecting the materialist beliefs that she had earlier held, she came to regard man as "Spiritual Intelligence, a fragment of Divinity clothed in matte." ◆

Besht

1700–1760 ● JEWISH

Besht is an abbreviation for the title Ba'al Shem Tov (Hebrew for "master of the good name"), identifying the founder of the Hasidic movement in eastern Europe. There are few historically authentic sources that describe the life of the Besht; most information must be gleaned from nineteenth-century hagiography, especially the collection of more than 300 stories about him, known as *Shivhei ha-Besht* (In Praise of the Besht; first printed in 1815), and the works of later Hasidic writers.

Born in the small town of Okopy in southern Ukraine, Israel ben Eliezer, is said to have begun preaching around 1738, after a long period of seclusion in the Carpathian Mountains with his wife. According to other accounts, he served throughout his life as a popular healer, writer of **amulets,** and exorcist of demons from houses and bodies, which were the traditional roles of a *ba'al shem* ("master of the name")—in other words,

amulets: charms that were believed to ward off evil such as disease or witchcraft

the master of the name that empowered him to perform what he wished.

In his wanderings around many Jewish communities, the Besht came into contact with various circles of **pietists.** In some cases he was criticized by the rabbis, but his powers as a preacher and magician attracted disciples. The Besht is regarded by scholars as the founder of the great eastern European Hasidic movement, even though knowledge of his organizational work is scanty and even though the first Hasidic center was established only after his death by Dov Ber, who became the leader of the movement.

pietist: a person displaying overly emotional or exaggerated religious devotion

Although he was not a scholar in Jewish law, the Besht was well versed in Kabbalah and in popular Jewish ethical tradition, on which he relied when delivering his sermons and formulating his theories. He saw the supreme goal of religious life as *devequt* ("cleaving"), spiritual communion with God; this state can be achieved not only during prayers but also in the course of everyday activities. In his view, there is no barrier between the holy and the profane, and worship of God can be the inner content of any deed, even the most mundane one. His teachings also included the theory that evil can be transformed into goodness by a mystical process of returning it to its original source in the divine world and redirecting it into good spiritual power; this idea was further developed by his followers.

The Besht believed that he was in constant contact with the divine powers and saw his mission as that of correcting and leading his generation. The Besht claimed to practice '*aliyyat neshamah,* or the uplifting of the soul. In this way, he explained, he communicated with celestial powers who revealed their secrets to him. According to the document, these included the Messiah, who told him that redemption would come when his teachings were spread all over the world (which the Besht interpreted as "in a long, long time").

> The Besht believed that he was in constant contact with the divine powers and saw his mission as that of correcting and leading his generation.

The Besht was convinced that his prayer carried special weight in the celestial realm and that it could open heavenly gates for the prayers of the people as a whole. His insistence that there are righteous people in every generation who, like himself, carry special mystical responsibilities for their communities laid the foundations for the later Hasidic theory of the function of the *tsaddiq,* or leader, a theory that created a new type of charismatic leadership in the Jewish communities of eastern Europe. ◆

Bhave, Vinoba

1895–1982 ● HINDU

Vinoba Bhave, was an Indian social and religious reformer. Vinayak Narhari Bhave was closely associated with Mohandas Gandhi, who bestowed upon him the affectionate epithet Vinoba ("brother Vino"). He is generally acclaimed in India as the one who "stepped into Gandhi's shoes." As a young man Bhave studied Sanskrit and the Hindu religious tradition in Varanasi. It was here that he read accounts of Gandhi's patriotic speeches. Attracted by Gandhi's ideas, Bhave joined Gandhi as his disciple in 1916 and soon became one of his close associates.

In 1921 Gandhi had Bhave move to a new ashram (retreat center) in Wardha in the state of Maharashtra. Here he began experimenting with many Gandhian ideas designed to implement self-rule for India. His main goal was to engage in village service for the benefit of the Indian masses. As a result, he

became a skillful farmer, spinner, weaver, and scavenger. Many of these activities were later incorporated into several of his plans for the moral and spiritual uplift of all humanity. Impressed with his political and religious dedication, his spiritual way of life, and his belief in nonviolent methods of social action, Gandhi chose him in 1940 as the first *satyagrah* (one who uses nonviolent means to bring the opponent to the point of seeing the truth) in a protest against British rule.

After India's independence Bhave emerged from the shadow of his teacher as he began his *pad yatr* ("journey on foot") to meet the people of India. The famous Bhoodan ("land gift") movement was born when on one such journey he sought a donation of land in order to distribute it among the landless poor. Later he designed a program to collect 50 million acres of land for the landless. For the rest of his life, he tirelessly worked for *gram swaraj* ("village self-rule") to free the people from the rich and the powerful. He retreated to his ashram in Paunar, near Wardha, in 1970 and died there in 1982.

Bhave's influence was greatest in his promotion of Gandhian principles. He became the chief exponent of the Sarvodaya ("welfare of all") movement and executed Gandhi's nonviolent philosophy through a series of activities known as "constructive works." These included such programs as promotion self-spun cloth, new education, woman power, cow protection, and peace brigade. He created the Sarva Seva Sangha ("society for the service of all") in order to carry out the work of Sarvodaya, and served as its spiritual adviser. Bhave also launched a series of movements connected with the Land Gift movement in order to tackle the problem of exploitation of the farmers by their landlords.

Bhave organized village councils to oversee the village development program. His aim was not only to bring self-sufficiency to the villages but also to establish a nonviolent society based on religious ideals. Through the constructive programs of Sarvodaya, Bhave sought to create a moral force in Indian society. The aim of his movement was not to promote the greatest good for the greatest number, but the greatest good for all people. The goal of Sarvodaya philosophy can be summarized as follows: in the social realm it advocates a casteless society, in politics it shares a democratic vision of the power of the people, in economics it promotes the belief that "small is beautiful," and in religion it asks for tolerance for all faiths. Its final goal is to promote peace for all mankind.

The failure of many of Bhave's plans to come to fruition ultimately led to dissension in the Sarvodaya. In the 1960s Jai Prakash Narayan, a Marxist-turned-Gandhian activist and an associate of Bhave, sought to steer the Sarvodaya movement in other directions. The controversy arose over the issue of whether Sarvodaya workers should participate in politics in order to initiate change in Indian society. Disenchanted with Bhave's nonpartisan religious approach and the slow moving program of *gram swaraj*, Narayan began taking an active part in contemporary politics. By the 1970s this led to a serious split within the organization of the Sarva Seva Sangha (the work agency of Sarvodaya) and the parting of ways of these two gi-

1895	Bhave is born in India.
1916	Bhave becomes a disciple of Mohandas Gandhi.
1921	Bhave moves to a new ashram and becomes a farmer.
1940	Bhave is chosen by Gandhi as the first satyagrahi.
1970	Bhave retreats to his ashram; his life is described in *Vinoba: His Life and Works*.
1982	Bhave dies in his ashram.

"There is no true joy for the man whose life is cut off from the heavens above and the world of Nature around. This means that the task before education is to change the whole system of values and the way of life that is current in our cities. How this is to be done is not a question for you and me alone, but for the whole humanity."

Vinoba Bhave, quoted in *Selections from Vinoba*, Vishwanath Tandon, ed., 1981

ants of the Gandhian movement. The conflict brought into focus various ideological differences that existed within the Sarvodaya movement. However, Bhave's supporters continued to maintain that his was a movement to "change the hearts of the people" through moral force and nonpartisan alliances. Since Bhave's death, many programs for social reform are still being carried out within the Sarvodaya movement by the *lok sevaks* ("servants of the people") whom he inspired. ◆

Black Elk

1863–1950 ● NATIVE AMERICAN

Black Elk was a Sioux spiritual leader, known in Lakota as Hehaka Sapa. Few American Indian spiritual leaders have gained greater national and indeed international recognition than this Oglala Lakota of the western American plains. Although Nickolas Black Elk was well known by his own people as a holy person, it was the poetic interpretation given to his life and sacred experiences in *Black Elk Speaks* (1932) by John G. Neihardt that first caught the attention and imagination of a much wider public. A second book, on the seven rites of the Lakota, was dictated at Black Elk's request to Joseph Epes Brown. This work, *The Sacred Pipe* (1963), further stimulated interest in the man and his message, both of which became, especially during the 1960s, meaningful symbols for a generation seeking alternate values. In his introduction to the 1979 edition of *Black Elk Speaks*, the Dakota writer Vine Deloria, Jr., referred to these books as the "Black Elk theological tradition" and predicted that they will become "the central core of a North American Indian theological canon which will someday chal-

lenge the Eastern and Western traditions as a way of looking at the world."

Of the Big Road band of Lakota, Black Elk was born in December 1863 on the Little Powder River within the borders of present-day Wyoming. In those early nomadic days following their adoption of the horse, his people hunted west of the Black Hills until 1877, when they were forced to move east to the area of their present reservation at Pine Ridge in South Dakota. At the age of 13 Black Elk was present at General Custer's defeat at the Battle of the Little Bighorn. He remembered the murder at Fort Robinson of his relative, the great warrior and spiritual leader Crazy Horse, and recalled the years during which his people sought refuge with Sitting Bull's band in Canada. He was also present at the tragic massacre at Wounded Knee (1890), which ended the revivalistic Ghost Dance movement.

Against that background of traumatic historical events, Black Elk at the age of nine involuntarily received the first of a long series of sacred visionary experiences that set him upon a lifelong quest to find the means by which his people could mend "the broken hoop" of their lives, could find their sacred center where "the flowering tree" of their traditions could bloom again. This first of many vision experiences was of terrifying thunder beings, the powers of the West; whoever received their power was obliged to become a *heyoka*, or sacred clown. Shaken by his experience, Black Elk could not bring himself to reveal the vision until the age of 17. Then he confided it to the holy man Black Road, who instructed Black Elk in the spring of 1881 to enact part of his visionary experience, the Great Horse Dance, so that the people might share in the power of his vision.

It was in part his mission to find a means for helping his people that led Black Elk to join Buffalo Bill's Wild West Show in 1886. He appeared in New York and then in England in 1887–1888 for the Golden Jubilee of Queen Victoria, whom he apparently met. He subsequently joined another "western" show and toured France, Germany, and Italy, finally returning to South Dakota in 1889. There, under the influence of Roman Catholic missionaries, and still seeking a way for his people, Black Elk turned to Christianity and even became a catechist for the church. A devout Christian, he nevertheless was able to accommodate both religious traditions without inner conflict. Like many American Indians through

1863 Black Elk is born in present-day Wyoming.

c. 1870 Black Elk has his first visionary experience at the age of nine.

1881 Black Elk is instructed to enact part of his visionary experience.

1886 Black Elk joins Buffalo Bill's Wild West Show.

1889 Black Elk finishes touring, returns to US, and becomes a Christian.

1932 John Niehardt published *Black Elk Speaks*.

1950 Black Elk dies holding a Christian rosary and a Lakota sacred pipe.

history who have had to adapt and borrow selectively in order to survive, Black Elk could be neither traditional Indian nor complete convert, for he had realized the truth of both religions. When he died on 19 August 1950, in his log cabin at Manderson, South Dakota, there was for him no contradiction in the fact that he was holding a Christian rosary as well as a Lakota sacred pipe, which he had never given up smoking in the ceremonial manner.

Although Black Elk may have died feeling he had failed to revive his people's culture, the question of his success remains for history to answer. Black Elk knew something of the power of the printed word. He was thus willing to give through two books details of his visions with their force of mission, as well as accounts of the rites and metaphysics of his people. The widespread popularity of these two books, among both Indians and non-Indians, and the subsequent revitalization of traditional ceremonies across the reservations by younger tribespeople attest that Black Elk still speaks. ◆

Blake, Eugene

1906–1985 ● PRESBYTERIAN

Eugene Carson Blake, was an American Presbyterian ecumenical leader best known for social activism and efforts toward Christian unity in the 1960s.

Blake was born in St. Louis, Missouri, in 1906, the youngest of three children of Lulu Carson and Orville Prescott Blake. He grew up in a devout Presbyterian home where his father was a steel company salesman and his mother a housewife and active church-woman. Six feet tall, broad-shouldered, and affable, Blake was educated at the Lawrenceville School in Lawrenceville, New Jersey; Princeton University (A.B., 1928), where he played on the varsity football team; New College in Edinburgh; and Princeton Theological Seminary (D.M., 1932).

Blake married Valina Gillespie on 12 September 1929, following a short period of missionary service in British India. They had no children. In 1932 they moved to New York City, where Blake began his career as assistant pastor of the Collegiate Church of St. Nicholas (Reformed Church in America). In 1935 he was called to become senior minister of the First

Presbyterian Church of Albany New York, and in 1940 he moved to southern California to assume leadership of the Pasadena Presbyterian Church. During his ten years there, the Pasadena church grew to be the third largest Presbyterian congregation in the United States, with about 4,500 members.

In Pasadena, Blake emerged as an outstanding preacher and denominational leader whose theology was greatly influenced by the ideas of Reinhold Niebuhr and the neo-orthodox movement. Revealing the strong interests in social activism that would mark his later national and international career, Blake spoke out from his pulpit against racial segregation, substandard housing, and the violation of civil liberties by "loyalty" investigations.

On 29 May 1951, Blake was elected by the General Assembly of the Presbyterian Church in the U.S.A. to the office of stated clerk, the highest executive position in that denomination. During his nearly 15 years in that post, Blake, based in Philadelphia, expanded the range of its power and influence, and he became the dominant spokesman for American Presbyterians as well as a highly visible leader of mainline Protestantism in general. Disturbed by the excesses of anticommunism in the McCarthy era, in 1953 he and John McKay, president of the Princeton Seminary, issued a "Letter to Presbyterians" denouncing allegations of communist sympathies that had been made against Protestant clergymen. They defended the right and duty of ministers to speak out on controversial social issues. In a 1954 *Look* magazine article, Blake warned of uncritical patriotism in the post-World War II religious upsurge, and in 1960 he joined other Protestant leaders in condemning attacks on the Roman Catholic background of presidential candidate John F. Kennedy.

Unquestionably the two most famous events of Blake's entire career were his proposal for Protestant church union in 1960 and his arrest during a civil rights demonstration in 1963. Accepting an invitation from Episcopal bishop James A. Pike to preach at Grace (Protestant Episcopal) Cathedral in San Francisco on 4 December 1960, Blake proposed the merger of the Presbyterian, Episcopal, Methodist, and United Church of Christ denominations as the first step in a process of reuniting the fragmented elements of Christianity in the United States. He spoke out of his already extensive ecumenical experience in the National Council of Churches of Christ in the U.S.A. (he had been its president in the years 1954–1955), and he be-

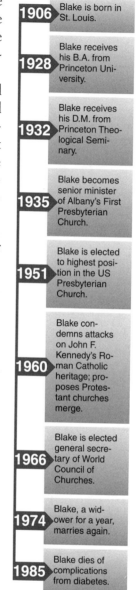

1906 Blake is born in St. Louis.

1928 Blake receives his B.A. from Princeton University.

1932 Blake receives his D.M. from Princeton Theological Seminary.

1935 Blake becomes senior minister of Albany's First Presbyterian Church.

1951 Blake is elected to highest position in the US Presbyterian Church.

1960 Blake condemns attacks on John F. Kennedy's Roman Catholic heritage; proposes Protestant churches merge.

1966 Blake is elected general secretary of World Council of Churches.

1974 Blake, a widower for a year, marries again.

1985 Blake dies of complications from diabetes.

lieved that these four denominations possessed sufficiently common historical and theological traditions to overcome their differences in liturgy and church governance.

The Blake-Pike proposal, as it was called (although almost entirely the work of Blake alone), generated much public attention. It led directly to the formation in 1962 of the Consultation on Church Union (COCU), which eventually grew to include ten Protestant denominations. For a few years hopes were high that obstacles to organizational unity could be overcome, but in 1966 COCU failed to adopt a timetable for full church union. Thereafter, Blake's vision of organic merger gradually faded.

Blake's commitment to racial justice also became more focused and active in the 1960s. Throughout the previous decade he had urged Presbyterians to denounce segregation and discrimination verbally, but the sight of the brutal treatment of civil rights demonstrators in Birmingham, Alabama, in May 1963 compelled him to take direct, personal action. On 4 July 1963 Blake joined a racially mixed group seeking to enter the segregated (whites-only) Gwynn Oak Amusement Park in Baltimore. He was arrested for violating Maryland's criminal trespass law, taken to a police station to be fingerprinted, and then released on bond. He pleaded not guilty and the charges were ultimately dropped, but the incident reverberated widely, because Blake was the first national Protestant executive to take such action.

Although some Presbyterians denounced him for "disgracing" their church, Blake became a hero to the many clergy who were active in the social causes of the 1960s.

Although some Presbyterians denounced him for "disgracing" their church, Blake became a hero to the many clergy who were active in the social causes of the 1960s. In a speech he gave at the historic March on Washington for civil rights on 28 August 1963, Blake lamented that white Christians had been too slow to participate in the struggle for racial justice, stating: "We come, and late we come." He worked to overcome that hesitancy by laboring intensively for passage of the Civil Rights Act of 1964 and committing Presbyterians to establish and fund an ongoing agency for racial reconciliation.

On 11 February 1966 Blake was elected general secretary of the World Council of Churches in Geneva, Switzerland, a position he held until his retirement in August 1972. During those years religious leaders from Asia, Africa, and Latin

America challenged the traditional European and North American dominance in ecumenism. The World Council, made up of Protestant and Orthodox churches, also began to engage more intensively with Roman Catholics on matters of common theological and social concern. These new developments were widely manifest at the Uppsala (Sweden) Assembly of the World Council in July 1968. Blake sought to bridge the racial, economic, and generational divides with more emphasis on programs to deal with poverty, racism, and international conflict, and to open more dialogue with other world religions.

The council's Program to Combat Racism became controversial in the early 1970s, when charges were made that its funds were going to armed guerrilla movements in several African countries. Blake denied the accusations and strongly defended the concept of "secular ecumenism." Another historic moment during Blake's tenure was the visit of Pope Paul VI in June 1969, the first visit to Geneva by a Catholic pontiff in more than 400 years.

Blake returned to the United States upon his retirement in 1972 and, following the death of his wife Valina in 1973, married Jean Ware Hoyt of Stamford, Connecticut, on 14 June 1974. He lived in retirement in Stamford and became active in Bread for the World, an ecumenical organization concerned with world hunger and poverty. He enjoyed swimming, golf, and watching sports. He died of complications from diabetes.

Blake's ecclesiastical career was entirely in the service of liberal, denominational, and ecumenical Protestant Christianity. The high points of his service coincided with two significant periods, the growth in popular religious interest and activity in the United States in the two decades after World War II, and the social activism and ecumenical enthusiasm of the mainline churches in the 1960s. Blake remained convinced that the institutional church was the best setting for religious life and work, but came to believe that the various denominations needed to find ways to make their expressions of faith serve common goals and purposes. From a later perspective the settings in which Blake worked came to seem overly bureaucratic, hierarchical, and male-dominated. Blake was, however, in the context of his time, an advocate and an example of openness to change that was rooted in historic Christian belief. ◆

Blake sought to bridge the racial, economic, and generational divides with more emphasis on programs to deal with poverty, racism, and international conflict.

Blavatsky, H. P.

1831–1891 ● THEOSOPHICAL

> "If there were such a thing as void, a vacuum in Nature, one would find it produced, according to a physical law, in the minds of helpless admirers of the 'lights' of science, who pass their time in mutually destroying their teachings."
>
> H. P. Blavatsky,
> *The Secret Doctrine*, 1888

Helen Petrova Blavatsky was the principal founder of the modern theosophical movement. Blavatsky, nee Hahn-Hahn, was born in Ekaterinoslav (present-day Dnepropetrovsk), Russia, of noble parentage. From earliest childhood she displayed remarkable paranormal powers, and these, coupled with her tempestuous personality and unconventional behavior, made her the controversial figure she remains to this day—attacked and vilified by some, honored and respected by others.

Married at 17, Blavatsky soon left home and husband. The very figure of an emancipated woman, she spent years traveling alone in Europe, the Americas, Egypt, and India, fighting with Giuseppe Garibaldi in Italy and even reaching Tibet, where she at last met the personage she claimed was the "master" who had long appeared to her in dreams.

Although she had little formal education, Blavatsky wrote encyclopedically, ranging over ancient as well as living religious traditions, drawing upon the sciences of her day, and quoting extensively from scholarly sources. This last aspect of her works led to charges of plagiarism, but she defended herself by saying that she was merely the transmitter, not the originator, of theosophical doctrines, which she traced to ancient Greek as well as Asian origins. She maintained that the real authors of her works were those she called her "masters," enlightened guardians of an ancient mystery tradition that lies at the heart of all religions and unifies them.

Restlessly seeking the work she felt appointed to do, Blavatsky reached New York in 1873 and quickly became involved in the spiritualist movement, which she saw as a force for penetrating the defenses of both scientific materialism and religious orthodoxy. She openly criticized spiritualist practices, however, thereby attracting the attention of inquirers interested in the philosophical aspects of the subject. Most notable among these inquirers was Colonel Henry S. Olcott, who joined with Blavatsky and others in forming the Theosophical Society in New York City on 17 November 1875.

Two years later Blavatsky published *Isis Unveiled*, in which she introduced the Eastern and Western esoteric teachings that she later developed more fully. *The Secret Doctrine* (1888), her major work, expatiates upon three fundamental propositions: (1) that there is an omnipresent, eternal, boundless, and immutable Reality, of which spirit and matter are complementary aspects; (2) that there is a universal law of periodicity, or evolution through cyclic change; and (3) that all souls are identical with the universal Oversoul, which is itself an aspect of the unknown Reality.

In 1878, Blavatsky and Olcott left for India, where they founded *The Theosophist*, a journal dedicated to uniting Eastern spirituality with Western advances in thought. Blavatsky's increasing renown brought her into contact with many prominent people, and the Theosophical Society grew rapidly. But her outspoken criticism of Anglo-Indian attitudes toward Hindus and Hinduism, as well as the striking phenomena her followers claimed she produced, aroused the hostility of missionaries and other establishment figures, who tried to discredit her and her teachings. Often accused of being an impostor and even a Russian spy, she was, in the "Hodgson Report" (1885) that was issued by the London Society for Psychical Research, denounced as a fraud who had forged the letters she claimed to have received from her Tibetan mahatmas—a charge that was finally retracted in 1963. These allegations were vigorously protested by her many supporters as being false to Blavatsky's character and purpose, but the atmosphere of suspicion aggravated her already poor health, and she decided to leave India in 1885.

The remaining years of Blavatsky's life were spent in England and Europe. In spite of her increasing illness, she founded a new journal, *Lucifer*, wrote two works (*The Voice of the Silence* and *The Key to Theosophy*, both 1889), and completed *The Secret Doctrine*, which was published two and a half years before her death on 8 May 1891, a date still commemorated by members of the Theosophical Society as White Lotus Day. ◆

1831 Blavatsky is born in what is now Dnepropetrovsk, Russia.

1873 Blavatsky became involved in spiritualist movement in New York.

1875 Blavatsky forms the Theosophical Society.

1877 Blavatsky publishes *Isis Unveiled*.

1878 Blavatsky co-founds the journal *The Theosophist* in India.

1888 Blavatsky publishes her major work, *The Secret Doctrine*.

1889 Blavatsky publishes *The Voice of the Silence* and *The Key to Theosophy*.

1891 Blavatsky dies.

Bonhoeffer, Dietrich

1906–1945 ● LUTHERAN

Dietrich Bonhoeffer was a Lutheran pastor, theologian, and martyr. The sixth of eight children, Bonhoeffer was raised in Berlin, Germany, in the upper-middle-class family of a leading neurologist. He received his doctorate in theology from the University of Berlin, where he was deeply influenced by the writings of the Swiss Protestant Karl Barth. From 1930 to 1931, Bonhoeffer studied at Union Theological Seminary in New York with Reinhold Niebuhr. He then returned to Berlin, teaching theology and becoming student chaplain and youth secretary in the ecumenical movement.

As early as 1933 Bonhoeffer was struggling against the Nazification of the churches and against the persecution of the Jews. Disappointed by the churches' non-action against Nazism, he accepted a pastorate for Germans in London. However, when the Confessing church (made up of Christians who resisted Nazi domination) founded its own seminaries, he returned to Germany to prepare candidates for ordination, a task he considered the most fulfilling of his life. As a result of this work, he was forbidden to teach at the University of Berlin. In 1939, after conflicts with the Gestapo, he accepted an invitation to the United States, again to Union Theological Seminary. After four weeks, however, he returned to Germany, convinced he would be ineffectual in the eventual renewal of his nation were he to live elsewhere during its most fateful crisis. He then became an active member of the conspiracy against Nazi dictator Adolf Hitler. On 5 April 1943 Bonhoeffer was imprisoned on suspicion. After the plot to assassinate Hitler failed, Bonhoeffer was hanged (on 9 April 1945), along with 5,000 others (including three other members of his family) accused of participating in the resistance.

Bonhoeffer's writings have been widely translated. His early work reflects his search for a concrete theology of revelation. In 1937, Bonhoeffer published his controversial *The Cost of Discipleship*. Asserting that "cheap grace is the deadly enemy of our Church," this work, which is based on the Sermon on the Mount, critiques a Reformation heritage that breaks faith and obedience asunder. In *Life Together* Bonhoeffer's most widely read book, the author considers experiments to renew a kind of monastic life for serving the world. In 1939 Bonhoeffer began to write a theological ethics, the work he intended to be his lifework, but he only completed fragments of it.

The most influential of Bonhoeffer's posthumous publications has become *Letters and Papers from Prison*. Among his daily observations was a vision of a future Christianity ready for "messianic suffering" with Christ in a "nonreligious world." To Bonhoeffer "religion" was a province separated from the whole of life—providing cheap escapism for the individual—and a tool in the hands of the powers that be for continuing domination of dependent subjects. Bonhoeffer was critical of Western Christianity because of its complicity with the Holocaust; his letters reveal his conviction that a life with Christ means "to exist for others." It was his belief in a "religionless Christianity"—that is, a praying church that responds to Christ out of the modern (not sinless) strength of human beings and their decisions—that enabled Bonhoeffer to begin to write a revised theology of "Jesus, the man for others," and to participate in the conspiratorial counteraction against the deadly forces of Hitler.

Bonhoeffer's thought emerged from his cultural heritage of German liberalism. He suffered when he experienced its weakness in the face of Nazism. He rethought this heritage within a Christ centered theology, thus becoming a radical critic of his contemporary church and of contemporary theology because they seemed to him to touch only the insignificant corners of life.

Bonhoeffer's words and deeds teach that each generation must discern its own particular means to express its contribution to faith and action. In areas where developments press toward a "confessing church," Bonhoeffer challenges Christians to analyze and to resist ideological syncretism with any Zeitgeist, whether the result is a Greek, a Teutonic, or an American Christ.

Bonhoeffer's influence is worldwide for two reasons. First, his life as theologian and thinker was sealed by martyrdom. Second, Bonhoeffer's legacy has stimulated ecumenism beyond his own national, spiritual, and institutional borders, including influence among Roman Catholics and Jews who see in him a Christian theologian who never cheaply evaded controversial issues. ◆

1906 Bonhoeffer is born into a middle class family in Germany.

1930 Bonhoeffer begins studying at Union Theological Seminary.

1933 Bonhoeffer struggles against the nazification of German churches.

1937 Bonhoeffer publishes his controversial *Cost of Discipleship*.

1939 Bonhoeffer travels to the US after conflicts with the Gestapo; returns to Germany to fight against Hitler.

1943 Bonhoeffer is imprisoned.

1945 Bonhoeffer is hanged after the plot to assassinate Hitler fails.

1976 Bonhoeffer's *Letters and Papers from Prison* is published.

Booth, William

1829–1912 ● EVANGELICAL CHRISTIAN

William Booth was an English evangelist and founder of the Salvation Army. Booth was born on 10 April 1829 in Nottingham, England, the only son of the

four surviving children of Samuel and Mary Moss Booth. The elder Booth, an unsuccessful building contractor, and his wife were no more than conventionally religious, but William, intelligent, ambitious, zealous, and introspective, was earnest about Christianity from an early age. He was converted at the age of 15 and two years later gave himself entirely to the service of God as the result of the preaching of James Caughey, a visiting American Methodist revivalist.

From the age of thirteen until he was 22 Booth worked as a pawnbroker's assistant, first in Nottingham and, after 1849, in London. His zeal and compassion for the poor among whom he passed his youth drove him to preach in the streets and, in 1852, to become a licensed Methodist minister. Although Booth had been forced by his father's financial ruin to withdraw from a good grammar school at age thirteen, he read avidly, sought instruction from older ministers, and developed an effective style in speech and writing. In 1855 he married Catherine Mumford, a woman of original and independent intelligence and great moral courage, who had a strong influence on him. They had eight children.

In 1861 Booth began to travel as an independent and successful evangelist, sometimes appearing with Catherine, who publicly advocated an equal role for women in the pulpit. In 1865 the couple established a permanent preaching mission among the poor in the East End of London, in a place where Booth had conducted an especially effective series of meetings. This new endeavor, which soon included small-scale charitable activities for the poor, was known for several years as the Christian Mission. In 1878 the mission was renamed the Salvation Army.

The military structure suggested by the new name appealed to the Booths and to the co-workers they had attracted to their work. Booth remained an orthodox Methodist in doctrine, preaching the necessity of repentance and the promise of holiness—a voluntary submission to God that opened to the believer a life of love for God and for humankind. As an evangelist, Booth was convinced that the fastest way to complete the work of soul winning that would herald the return of Christ was to establish flying squads of enthusiasts who would spread out over the country at his command. The General, as Booth was called, saw evangelism as warfare against Satan over the souls of men; the militant tone of scripture and hymn were not figurative to Booth and his officers, but literal reality. The autocracy of military command was well suited to Booth's decisive and uncompromising personality; and it appealed both to his close associates, who were devoted to him and who sought his counsel on every matter, and to his more distant followers, the "soldiers" recently saved from sin, most of them uneducated, new to religion, and eager to fit themselves into the great scheme.

William and Catherine were convinced from the beginning of their work in London that it was their destiny to carry the gospel to those untouched by existing religious efforts; to them this meant the urban poor. Their sympathy for these people led them to supplement their evangelism by immediate and practical relief. They launched campaigns to awaken the public to the worst aspects of the life of the poor, such as child prostitution and dangerous and ill-paid piecework in neighborhood match factories. Soup kitchens, men's hostels, and "rescue homes" for converted prostitutes and unwed mothers became essential parts of the Army's program.

In 1890 William Booth published *In Darkest England and the Way Out*, which contained a full-fledged program to uplift and regenerate the "submerged tenth" of urban society. The heart of the scheme was a sequence of "city colonies" (urban missions for the unemployed), "land colonies" (where rest would be combined with retraining in agricultural skills), and "overseas colonies" (assisted emigration to America or one of Britain's colonies). The book also explained existing programs like the rescue homes and promised many new schemes in addition to the colonies: the "poor man's lawyer," the "poor man's bank," clinics, industrial schools for poor children, missing-persons inquiries, a "matrimonial bureau," and a poor-man's seaside resort, "Whitechapel-by-the-Sea." The *Darkest England* scheme, which was widely endorsed, represents an important turning point in public support for the Army.

Booth would not have claimed to be a saint in any conventional sense, and there are certainly controversial aspects to his

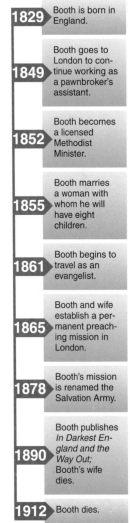

1829 Booth is born in England.

1849 Booth goes to London to continue working as a pawnbroker's assistant.

1852 Booth becomes a licensed Methodist Minister.

1855 Booth marries a woman with whom he will have eight children.

1861 Booth begins to travel as an evangelist.

1865 Booth and wife establish a permanent preaching mission in London.

1878 Booth's mission is renamed the Salvation Army.

1890 Booth publishes *In Darkest England and the Way Out*; Booth's wife dies.

1912 Booth dies.

> "As Christ came to call not the saints but sinners to repentance, so the New Message of Temporal Salvation, of salvation from pinching poverty, from rags and misery, must be offered to all."
>
> William Booth, *In Darkest England and The Way Out,*

life and work. Always overworked and chronically unwell, he often had strained relationships with his close associates, especially after the death of Catherine in 1890. Many of his statements about the Army overlooked the fact that much of its program was not original. He offered no criticism of the basic social and political structure that surrounded him, and his confidence in the desirability of transferring the urban unemployed to the more healthful and "natural" environment of the country was romantic and impractical. Yet the fact remains that Booth combined old and new techniques of evangelism and social relief in an immensely effective and appealing program. He displayed great flexibility in adapting measures to the needs of the moment, altering or eliminating any program, however dear to him, if it had ceased to function. He abandoned anything in the way of theology (like sacraments) or social theory (like the then still popular distinction between the "worthy" and "unworthy" poor) that might confuse his followers or dampen their zeal for soul winning and good works.

Guileless and unsentimental, Booth showed a rare and genuine single-mindedness in the cause of evangelism. His last public message, delivered three months before his death on 20 August 1912, is still cherished by the Army that is his most fitting memorial. The concluding words of the message were these: "While there yet remains one dark soul without the light of God, I'll fight—I'll fight to the very end!" ◆

Bowman, Thea

1937–1990 ● CATHOLIC

Thea Bertha Bowman ("Sister Thea") was the only black member of the Franciscan Sisters of Perpetual Adoration, who urged the Catholic church to embrace African-American culture.

Bowman was born in 1937 in Yangoo City, Mississippi, the only child of Theon Edward Bowman, a physician, and Mary Esther (Coleman) Bowman, a homemaker. Her Protestant parents sent her to a Catholic school, Holy Child Jesus, in Canton, Mississippi, because it offered the best education available to an African-American child in that part of Mississippi. The school was administered by the Franciscan Sisters of Perpetual

Adoration, an order of nuns based in La Crosse, Wisconsin. Bowman converted to Catholicism when she was 12.

Feeling called to religious life, she entered the novitiate in La Crosse in 1956, taking the name Sister Thea (she took her final vows in 1963). She studied at Viterbo College in La Crosse, where she received a B.A. degree in English literature in 1960. The next year she returned to Mississippi to teach at the Holy Child Jesus High School in Canton. Beginning in 1968 she studied English literature at the Catholic University of America in Washington. D.C., focusing on William Faulkner and on African-American literature. She received an M.A. degree in 1970 and a Ph.D. in 1972.

Sister Thea then returned to Viterbo College, where from 1972 to 1978 she taught African-American literature and was chair of the English Department. She also founded and directed the Hallelujah Singers. Known for its singing of spirituals, the group performed regularly throughout the United States.

In 1978 Sister Thea returned to Canton to help care for her sick and aging parents. She also became the head of the Office for Inter-Cultural Awareness for the Diocese of Jackson. In this position, she created programs that allowed Catholics of different cultural backgrounds to share their cultural traditions and to use them in worship. She encouraged African-American children to learn about their history and traditions and worked to make those traditions an integral part of the Catholic church.

Sister Thea also taught at Xavier University in New Orleans, where she was on the faculty of the Black Catholic Studies Institute. Her essay "Black History and Culture" was published in the *U.S. Catholic Historian* in 1988; in it she argues that "where Black culture is alive in our Churches, its vitality spills over into our communities." She thought that black culture could revitalize both the churches and poor urban or rural communities. During the 1980s Sister Thea participated in the National Black Catholic Congress, where she gave speeches and helped to formulate the group's national agenda. She explained that "when we understand our history and culture, then we can develop the ritual, the music, and the devotional expression that satisfy us in the Church." With this goal in mind she published a collection of black spirituals called *Songs of My People* (1989), in which she explicated each spiritual, tying its biblical themes to African-American history as

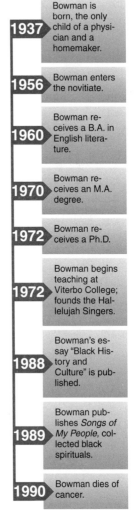

1937 Bowman is born, the only child of a physician and a homemaker.

1956 Bowman enters the novitiate.

1960 Bowman receives a B.A. in English literature.

1970 Bowman receives an M.A. degree.

1972 Bowman receives a Ph.D.

1972 Bowman begins teaching at Viterbo College; founds the Hallelujah Singers.

1988 Bowman's essay "Black History and Culture" is published.

1989 Bowman publishes *Songs of My People*, collected black spirituals.

1990 Bowman dies of cancer.

> "Sick people can teach the world an appreciation for health and movement and life. The sick can share insight into what it means to live, what it means to suffer, what it means to face death"
>
> Thea Bowman

well as spirituality. In the article "Let the Church Say 'Amen!'" (*Extension*. March/April 1987), Sister Thea highlighted a particularly vital African-American congregation, the Holy Ghost Parish in Opelousas, Louisiana. As the largest and most active black parish in the nation, she presented it as a model for incorporating black spirituality into the Catholic church. A typical Sunday mass at the church was attended by some 3,000 people, and the congregation, led by the choir, readers, servers, and celebrant, sang and "moved in rhythms held sacred for generations." She argued that this type of physical and psychological engagement with religion was a gift and a lesson that could be imparted by African Americans to the wider Catholic community in America.

Sister Thea wore African-style gowns and wore her long hair in elaborate braids. She asked the church to adapt itself culturally to other peoples in order to retain its vitality and grow. In 1984 she began a six-year struggle with cancer. Despite chemotherapy, constant illness, and confinement to a wheelchair, she continued to be a spokeswoman for intercultural and interracial awareness. She battled her debilitating disease with grace and courage, asking only "Lord, let me live until I die."

Sister Thea Bowman gained a national reputation among Catholic leaders, convincing many to make their religious services reflect different cultural styles of music and worship. The innovations at the Holy Ghost Parish in Opelousas, Louisiana, and in Jackson, Mississippi, which Sister Thea lauded, have been adopted by other Catholic parishes whose revitalization is tied to building up new membership and generating commitment among African Americans. ◆

Braide, Garrick Sokari

1882?–1918 ● ANGLICAN

Garrick Sokari Braide was a Nigerian missionary and prophet. Braide was born in the village of Obonoma in Kalabar, in the Niger Delta. Obonoma was a stronghold of traditional religious worship, being a center of pilgrimage to the titular deity, Ogu. Some accounts speak of the young Braide being initiated into the Ogun cult at Obonoma by his mother.

Braide grew up in Bakana, where his father had settled. His parents were too poor to send him to school; consequently, he came of age somewhat on the periphery of Christianity, which had penetrated the area. However, Christianity would become familiar to him from the practice of open-air meetings that were held in Bakana from about 1886 onward. Such public meetings seem to have had an influence on him; in the 1890s he had become an Anglican inquirer and had joined the St. Andrew's Sunday School in Bakana. While there he came under the instruction of the Reverend Moses Kemmer of Brass. All the instruction was in the Igbo (Ibo) language, which Braide undertook to learn. It was a long apprenticeship; he finally completed his catechetical course and was baptized on 23 January 1910, at age 28. In 1912, at age 30, he was confirmed by Bishop James Johnson, the eminent Yoruba clergyman.

Braide's mature years increased his sense of personal urgency about the role he would play in his newly adopted religion. He embarked on intense religious exercises at this time, slipping into St. Andrew's Church on weekdays for personal devotions. These devotions comprised prayers for forgiveness of sin and attention to the personal mediation of Jesus.

It is difficult to resist the interpretation that Braide was seeking an outlet for the untested energies of young adulthood, and that his childhood initiation into Ogun found coalescence with the parallel rites of Christian baptism and confirmation to give center to his life and fix his mind. He spoke of his confirmation in the language of a divine commissioning. He said a thrill came over him in the course of it, and an unusual degree of self-awareness. He testified to being agitated in his mind, finding himself in a state of emotional unrest so acute that he suffered insomnia on account of it. This reached a climax with his being challenged to accept the charge of preacher and missionary.

Braide soon became a prominent figure in the Niger Delta Pastorate Church, noted for his charismatic gifts of prayer, prophecy, and healing. He used these gifts to advance his claim to authority. Thus, on one occasion he is reputed to have caused a heavy storm as punishment for those who defied his orders to observe Sunday as a day of rest and prayer. On another occasion he successfully prayed for rain to spoil plans for a local dance that he deemed offensive to religion. His reputation for thaumaturgy was gaining widespread recognition,

c. 1882 Braide is born in Nigeria.

c. 1893 Braide becomes an Anglican inquirer and goes to Sunday School.

1909 Briade begins preaching.

1910 Braide is baptized.

1912 Braide is confirmed.

1916 Braide is arrested and tried for economic sabotage and false teaching.

1918 Braide dies in an accident shortly after his release from prison.

which makes it difficult to say which was the more powerful motivator for him—Ogun or Christianity.

As if to clear up that ambiguity, Braide launched a campaign against the symbols of African religion, demanding that devotees abandon their charms, confess their sins, and make trust in God their supreme rule in life. Braide seemed driven to deal with the reality of the old spirits and would not rest till he had subdued his rivals. Yet his method deepened the paradox that Christianity would provide answers to questions about which the old spirits had at long last exhausted themselves. Into that contested frame of reference Braide would assert Christianity, or his form of it. In any case, his gratitude to Christianity could not have been more genuine than his keen sense of Ogun's power.

If the cult of Ogun adapted without incident to the new Christian teaching, it was a different matter with the colonial administration. Braide was as effective in preaching against alcohol consumption as he had been in his campaign against indigenous gods. Drunkenness and alcoholism had wreaked havoc on the populations of the Delta towns and villages. Some three million gallons of gin and rum were consumed there every year, a level of consumption that produced steady income to fill the coffers of the colonial administration with dues from the excise tax. Consequently, Braide's temperance drive threatened the excise revenue and turned him into a major public threat. By 1916, at the height of Braide's movement, the government was showing a massive loss of revenue, some 576,000 pounds in excise taxes. Meanwhile, the French in Cote d'Ivoire had at about the same time been closely watching the actions of another charismatic figure, Prophet William Wade Harris, which prompted the British to take up a similar surveillance of Braide's activities. As a self-declared prophet, Braide had become a lightning rod for local discontent, and he could not be ignored. Besides, the events of World War I had by then also produced deep anxiety in official circles: Germany, the common enemy of the French and the British, was entrenched in the nearby Kamerun colony (present-day Cameroon). Braide was arrested in March 1916 and tried for economic sabotage and false teaching. He was found guilty and sent to prison. He died in an accident in November 1918, some months after his release.

Two general consequences of Braide's life and work may be considered in conclusion. His preaching had a burgeoning ef-

> Braide seemed driven to deal with the reality of the old spirits and would not rest till he had subdued his rivals.

fect on the membership rolls of the churches in the Niger Delta, Protestant, Catholic, and Independent alike. In 1909, when Braide began preaching, there were only 900 baptized Christians on the membership rolls of all the churches. By 1918 that number had increased to some 11,700. The increase for Catholics in the period between 1912 and 1917 was 500 percent, and this growth was due largely to Braide's work.

Such numbers could not be contained within the historic mission churches, and so a large group of followers constituted themselves as a separate body in 1916, taking the name Christ Army Church. The church in effect became a rival to the Niger Delta Pastorate Church presided over by Bishop James Johnson. In 1917 the Christ Army Church applied for affiliation to the World Evangelical Alliance in London, a necessary insurance policy for an indigenous movement without much educated leadership and caught in the web of global forces.

The second general consequence was Braide's adoption by nationalist opinion as an agent of African autonomy. The *Lagos Weekly Standard* espoused his cause in editorials and other leader articles. The *Standard* claimed that Braide was anointed by "the God of the Negro" as an instrument to achieve the liberation of Africa. Braide was defended against the attacks of Bishop James Johnson and other leaders of the Niger Delta Pastorate Church. The *Standard* applauded Braide's career as demonstrating that colonial and episcopal structures and hierarchies were irrelevant to the special conditions of Africa, affirming that he should be endorsed by all genuine patriots. Braide, according to this opinion, had offered an African cultural alternative to the Western forms of Christianity, and had relied on people at the grass roots to lead in the church. His accomplishment was revealing about Africa's potential for independence. ◆

> Braide offered an African cultural alternative to the Western forms of Christianity, and relied on people at the grass roots to lead in the church.

Buddha, Gautama

C. 563– C. 483 B.C.E. ● BUDDHIST

Gautama Buddha was an Indian philosopher and founder of Buddhism. A man of noble character, intense vision, compassion, and profundity, he established a great new religion which continues to influence millions of lives across

"Reflecting his right understanding, the great hermit arose before the world as Buddha, the Englightened One. He found self nowhere, as the fire whose fuel has been exhausted. Then he conceived the Eightfold Path, the straightest and safest path for the attainment of this end."

Ashvaghosha, Buddhacarita 14

the world. As accounts of his life and teachings were written by devoted followers, however, and only many years after his death, it is difficult to extricate fact from legend and myth. Thus a reconstruction of his personal history can only be taken as a general outline.

Although it is not certain exactly when he lived, it is known that he died at about the age of 80. He was born in Kapilavastu, India, near the border with present-day Nepal, to Queen Maha Maya and King Suddhodana of the Sakya warrior caste, and was originally named Prince Siddhartha. He later acquired many other names, including Sakyamuni ("sage of the Sakya tribe"), Bhagavat ("he who possesses happiness"), Tathagata ("he who has succeeded"), Jina ("the victorious"), and Buddha ("enlightened one").

According to the legends and many paintings of the scene. Buddha entered his mother's womb in the guise of a small elephant and was assisted into the world by a god while his mother supported herself with a fig tree. His mother died shortly after his birth and his father, who feared he would choose the life of an ascetic over that of a warrior and ruler, strove to eradicate any such tendencies by keeping him in the palace and removing any cause of unhappiness or sight of suffering from his life. Educated, intelligent, every material want satisfied, he married when he came of age and seemed to have everything. Yet one day in 533 B.C.E., according to legend, something drew him away from the carefree, self-indulgent life of the palace and into the streets outside, where he encountered an old man, a sick man, and a corpse being carried away for burning. Thus, suddenly introduced to the knowledge that none can escape suffering, he became extremely troubled. As he returned to the palace he met a monk and determined to adopt a similar lifestyle. That night he bade his wife and newborn son a silent farewell and rode into the forest, replacing his royal attire with the simple clothes of an ascetic. This decision is known as the Great Renunciation.

He wandered all over northern India seeking an answer to the problem of suffering and finally elected to study with two Brahman teachers. Unsatisfied, he eventually left them and for the next six years maintained an extremely austere lifestyle, along with five followers, in an attempt to pit mind against body. When he decided to abandon asceticism, his followers left him. Having failed to understand the problem of

Dharma

Dharma is a term with a wide range of meanings that has grown out of the Hindu tradition. In general it is the moral and religious laws of Hindus and Buddhists. The word comes from the Sanskrit term *dhar,* which means *to uphold.*

In Buddhism, the dharma is a guide for rules of behavior. These rules came from the Buddha, the founder of Buddhism, who taught that life is a continuous cycle of death and rebirth. According to Buddhism, if one follows the dharma, one can overcome the suffering that accompanies the cycle death and rebirth, and achieve nirvana, the ultimate state of peace. The term *dharma* can also mean both the path to nirvana and the teachings of the Buddha that guide people on the path. The teachings of the Buddha are collected in writings called sutras. The most authoritative text of the Buddha's teachings is known as the *Tripitaka.*

The Hindu meaning of dharma differs slightly from the Buddhist version. In Hinduism dharma is the conduct that a person should follow to maintain the natural and moral order of the world. The term applies to religious rites and rituals, as well as to social conduct. According to Hindu tradition, people are born into a certain caste (social class), and each caste has a different dharma. Hindus believe that by following the dharma of their particular caste, they may be rewarded in the next life by being born into a higher caste. Dharmic behavior is codified in the ancient Sanskrit texts known as the dharmasastras and the dharmasustras. The most influential of the dharmasastras is the *Laws of Manu,* a code of law traditionally attributed to the mythological lawgiver Manu. The *Laws of Manu* contain 2,685 verses in 12 books. Scholars believe it was composed between about 200 B.C.E. and 300 C.E.

pain through meditation or self-mortification, he sat quietly one day under a Bodhi tree (tree of enlightenment), reflecting on the human plight, and suddenly experienced the Great Enlightenment, which revealed to him the way of salvation from suffering. A short time later he preached his first sermon in the Deer Park near Benares and established an order of monks. His five former disciples rejoined him there and began to accompany him throughout India to spread his word. He spoke in the vernacular, using language that everyone could understand, and acquired numerous followers, for he accepted everyone regardless of sex or caste. During the rainy seasons when travel was impossible, he would stop for meditation and the sites where he stopped later became permanent retreats. Although, as his fame grew, kings and other wealthy patrons began to donate parks and gardens for retreats. Buddha's life remained a simple one of meditation and teaching. He returned briefly to his hometown, where he converted members of his family to his beliefs, but for the next 45 years continued to wander through India teaching. He died in Nepal, apparently of food poisoning. His last words to his disciples, according to legend, exhorted them not to mourn his death: "And now, O *bhikkhus*, I take leave of you. All living elements are transitory. Work out your own salvation with diligence."

Buddha's rejection of metaphysical speculation in favor of logical thinking and his dismissal of Hindu hedonism, asceticism, spiritualism, and the caste system, revolutionized Oriental thinking. His doctrine opposed non-ego and impermanence to the basic concepts of Hinduism, i.e., the self and the permanence of Brahman, or Absolute Being. It also opposed a spirit of universal charity and sympathy to the exclusiveness of the caste system, thus attracting millions of followers. His teachings were an attempt to communicate the experience of awakening, a transformation of consciousness in which one is released from the confines of individual personality. He summarized his doctrine in a formula known as the Fourfold Noble Truths concerning suffering, the origin of suffering, the cessation of suffering, and the way to its cessation. The way to cessation is called the Eightfold Way and consists of eight "steps" (right views, right intention, right speech, right action, right livelihood, right effort, right mindfulness, and right concentration). Adoption of the Way leads to a state of peace, *nirvana*, in which all craving for material things ends, although the self is not annihilated.

> Buddha's teachings were an attempt to communicate the experience of awakening, a transformation of consciousness in which one is released from the confines of individual personality.

In the centuries after Buddha's death Buddhism diversified, probably as much as did Christianity, and spread across most of India to Ceylon, Turkestan, China, Korea, Japan, Burma, and Tibet. Although in India it eventually became virtually extinct, it exists throughout Asia in two main forms, the Hinayana in Ceylon (Sri Lanka), Siam (Thailand), Burma, and Indochina, and the Mahayana (the later form) in China, Korea, Tibet, and Mongolia.

The practice of Buddhism has acquired different rituals in different countries, although in popular Buddhism the tendency is to deify him. Buddha is generally recognized as a mortal who realized the ideal of what any man may become. ◆

Bukhari, Al-

810–870 ● Muslim

Al-Bukhari, more fully Muhammad ibn Isma'il al-Bukhari, was a great scholar of Islam who devoted his career to the collection, transmission, and classification of *hadith*. Hadith is the narrative record of the sayings & customs of the prophet Muhammad, as well as the collective body of traditions relating to Muhammad and his companions.

Al-Bukhari was an Iranian, born in Bukhara, an outstanding center of Islamic scholarship in Central Asia. His attraction to the study of *hadith* manifested itself early: from the age of ten he began to learn the reports of the life and words of the prophet Muhammad as transmitted by scholars in Bukhara. At 16 he made the pilgrimage to Mecca in Saudi Arabia with his mother and brother, and from then on he traveled extensively to Balkh, Baghdad, Mecca, Medina, Basra, Egypt, Damascus, Homs, and other localities in search of *hadith*. Before reaching maturity he had established a reputation for the thoroughness and exactitude with which he collected and learned *hadith*.

Upon the suggestion of an older colleague, Ibn Rahwayh of Nishapur (d. 853), al-Bukhari undertook to prepare a compendium of *hadith* carefully selected from the mass of material that he had at his disposal. This task is said to have taken 16 years, and the resulting collection constitutes the enduring monument to al-Bukhari's science. Entitled *Al-jami' al- sahih* (The Sound Epitome), it is the result of the compiler's rigorous sifting of a fund of *hadith* reported to have numbered 600,000.

The collection of al-Bukhari represents a major development in the science of *hadith* criticism. Where earlier compilers tended to include material from all possible sources, without regard for the degree of reliability of their chains of transmission, al-Bukhari designated the 2,602 different texts as authentic on the basis of the competence and integrity of their narrators. After many centuries of scrutiny by Muslim scholars, the authenticity of only 110 texts in his collection has been questioned, and *Al-jami' al-sahih* remains the most respected collection of *hadith* in the Islamic world.

> "There are two pleasures for the fasting person, one at the time of breaking his fast, and the other at the time when he will meet his Lord; then he will be pleased because of his fasting."
>
> Al-Bukhari, Hadith on Fasting, c. 870

Al-Bukhari considered his collection to be a work of religious devotion, and it is said that he never included a text in the compilation without first bathing and engaging in prayer. It was also intended to be a tool for the study of jurisprudence, with many of the texts arranged according to the categories of Islamic law; the headings of the different sections reveal the compiler's competence in jurisprudence. Although all four schools of Sunni law consider him to be one of their basic sources, he never identified with any particular school. Al-Bukhari's work also contains much material on Koran interpretation, morals and religious life, and the early history of Islam. Because many texts are repeated under several subject headings, the total number of *hadith* including repetitions, is 9,082.

In his later life al-Bukhari returned to his home city but was not able to stay because of a dispute with the local governor. He died in the village of Khartank, near Samarkand. ◆

Cabrini, Frances Xavier

1850–1917 ● Catholic

Frances Xavier Cabrini, the first American citizen canonized a Roman Catholic saint, founded the Institute of the Missionary Sisters of the Sacred Heart of Jesus. The tenth of 11 brothers and sisters, of whom only four survived to adulthood, Maria Francesca Cabrini was born in Lombardy, Italy. Her consistently poor health never stopped her from working strenuously to fulfill her desire to be a missionary. After initial difficulties she was allowed in 1880 to organize her religious institute. Her interests were channeled by Pope Leo XIII in 1889 to missionary work not in Cabrini's intended destination, China, but to the United States, where she would assist the growing community of Italian immigrants in New York.

In the wake of the great Italian immigrations in the late nineteenth and early twentieth centuries, Mother Cabrini expanded her ministries to both North and South America and the activities of the Missionary Sisters to Spain, France, England, and Italy. She exhibited tireless perseverance and independence as she personally established a network of convents, schools, parishes, orphanages, and hospitals among the Italian immigrant communities. In the United States, she worked in New York, New Orleans, Chicago, Philadelphia, Denver, Seattle, and Los Angeles among other locations. Though not fluent in English herself, she stressed ability in the language as a necessity for living in the United States. She also favored main-

1850 Cabrini is born in Lombardy, Italy, the 10th of 11 children.

1880 Cabrini is allowed to organize her religious institute.

1889 Cabrini begins helping the Italian immigrant community in New York.

1890 Cabrini begins keeping travel diaries.

1917 Cabrini dies.

1946 Cabrini is canonized as a Roman Catholic saint.

1950 Cabrini is declared "Patroness of Immigrants" by Pope Pius XII.

taining Italian language and culture within the immigrant community.

Despite her fear of travel over water, she sailed to Central and South America, leaving sisters and new institutions in Nicaragua, Panama, Argentina, and Brazil to assist Italian immigrants, especially women and children. Her letters to her sisters, in the form of travel diaries, which she began in 1890, and her personal spiritual notes written when on retreat are especially helpful in understanding her spirituality. She was canonized on 7 July 1946. In 1950, Pope Pius XII declared her "Patroness of Immigrants." ◆

Calvin, John

1509–1564 ● PROTESTANT

John Calvin was a French theologian and ecclesiastical statesman. Born in Noyon, Picardy, the son of middle-class parents, Calvin was educated with the local bishop's sons at the College de Montaigu in Paris, where Desiderius Erasmus had also studied. He pursued advanced law studies and later studied under the outstanding Greek scholar of his era, Guillaume Bude. The next year he published his first book, a study of Seneca's *Concerning Clemency*, which demonstrated his excellent command of Latin, his considerable erudition in matters of ancient history and literature, and his kinship with the humanism of Erasmus and Bude.

The precise reason for Calvin's conversion to Protestantism remains a matter of conjecture. He may have been influenced by the reforming humanist beliefs of his tutors and friends in Paris, while the treatment meted out to his family by the Catholic authorities—his brother Charles's body was publicly hung after his death as a result of his heterodoxy and his father died excommunicate—also contributed to his decision. He broke with the church in 1533 after a religious experience in which he believed he had received a charge to restore the church to its pristine purity. In 1534 Calvin moved to Basle, Switzerland, where he devoted himself to theological study.

The fruit of these studies was Calvin's *Institutes of the Christian Religion*. First published in 1536, it has been described as the masterpiece of Protestant theology. Written in Latin and designed as a defense of Protestantism to the king of France, it constituted a manual of spirituality and molded the doctrines of the Protestant movement into a logical system based on the Augustinian premise that man was created for communion with God and remains unfulfilled as long as this need is not satisfied.

Calvin was to expand, revise, and translate this work in many subsequent editions; the definitive French edition appeared in 1560, although as early as 1552 the city council in Geneva was declaring that the book represented a holy doctrine which no man might speak against. It remained the single most influential religious manual produced during the Reformation, immediately enjoying widespread circulation, and assuring Calvin's reputation as a key Reform spokesman.

Calvin visited Geneva in 1536 and was persuaded to remain there by Guillaume Farel, the inflammatory preacher who had incited the city's population to anti-Catholic rebellion. Beginning as a public lecturer, Calvin went on to write *Instruction in Faith* to educate the Genevan citizens in the Reformed faith. However, both he and Farel were forced to leave Geneva by a city council alarmed by the austerity of their proposed regulations.

Calvin took refuge in Lutheran Strasbourg. There he gained valuable practical experience in the administration of a parish, and he was able to become personally acquainted with prominent Lutheran theologians (though he never met Martin Luther himself). The failure of attempts at reconciliation between Rome and the Reformers left Calvin convinced of the futility of such negotiations; thereafter he was to promote complete conversion to the new Gospel as the only feasible means to end conflict.

In 1541, three years after his expulsion and a year after his marriage to Idelette de Bure, Calvin made a triumphant return

> "Do not men pay to images and statues the very same reverence which they pay to God? It is an error to suppose that there is any difference between this madness and that of the heathen. For God forbids us not only to worship images, but to regard them as the residence of his divinity, and worship it: as residing in them."
>
> John Calvin,
> *The Necessity of Reforming the Church*, 1543

1509 Calvin is born in France to middle class parents.

1533 Calvin breaks with the church after a religious experience.

1534 Calvin moves to Switzerland to study theology.

1536 Calvin publishes his *Institutes of the Christian Religion;* visits Geneva.

1541 Calvin returns to Geneva and becomes its guiding light.

1552 Calvin's book is declared "a holy doctrine" by Geneva's city council.

1555 Calvin begins propagating his creed in other countries, especially France.

1564 Calvin dies.

to Geneva to save the city from imminent administrative collapse. The ecclesiastical ordinances he established have formed the constitution of the church of Geneva ever since, as well as serving as a model for other Reformed churches and communities. Four ministering orders (doctors, pastors, elders, and deacons) became responsible for the spiritual and social welfare of the community, while the threat of excommunication by the Consistory (a court constituted by the pastors and elders) ensured strict conformity to moral and religious norms.

Although Calvin's only official position in Geneva was that of moderator of the company of pastors, he was the city's guiding light and de facto dictator. His preaching and rigorous Biblical exegesis drew religious refugees from all parts of Europe. Dissent was not tolerated, however, and could be brutally punished. Nevertheless, there was a considerable degree of elective representation in Geneva; thus, as Calvinism spread, its influence on Western democratic institutions was great.

After 1555, the ascendancy of his doctrines within Geneva firmly assured, Calvin concentrated his energies on propagating his creed in other countries, especially France. He displayed his considerable political acumen by enlisting the support of powerful French aristocrats on the side of the Reform Protestants. Similar support was offered to fledgling Reformed movements in other countries. A tireless correspondent, administrator, legislator, and diplomat, Calvin successfully paved the way for the continued growth of the church he had founded, especially through the institutional network he developed, which was copied wherever Calvinism took root. During his lifetime, Geneva could, with some justification, be called a Protestant Rome; after his death, Calvinism played a crucial role in shaping the societies of Western Europe and North America. ◆

Campbell, Alexander

1788–1866 ● Disciples of Christ

Alexander Campbell was one of the founders and the foremost early leader of the Disciples of Christ. Campbell was born in County Antrim, Northern Ireland, the son of a Presbyterian minister, Thomas Campbell. He immigrated to America in 1809, joining his father, who had come two years earlier. When he arrived, Campbell discovered that his father had broken with the Presbyterian church and had begun a small, non-sectarian "Christian association." Young Campbell embraced his father's reform and quickly became the most prominent leader of the new movement. For a time the Campbells were Baptists, and from 1823 to 1830 Alexander edited the *Christian Baptist*, a periodical that attracted many supporters in the West and South. Beginning in the 1830s Campbell and his "Reforming Baptist" supporters separated into independent churches. Campbell preferred the name Disciples of Christ, but local churches frequently were called Christian Church or Church of Christ. In 1832 the church nearly doubled in

size through a union with the Christian movement led by Barton Stone of Kentucky; Campbell quickly became the dominant figure in the united denomination.

From 1830 until 1864, Campbell edited a journal called the *Millennial Harbinger*, which became a mirror of his maturing thought. The heart of Campbell's plea was an appeal for Christian union through the "restoration of the ancient order of things," that is, by restoring New Testament Christianity. Prior to 1830 Campbell was extremely iconoclastic in his attacks on the popular churches, ridiculing the clergy and seeming to attack all cooperative societies. After 1830 he became a more constructive builder and seemed confident that the millennium was about to begin, initiated by the restoration movement. In 1849 a group of Disciples leaders established the young church's first national organization, the American Christian Missionary Society, and, although he was not present at the meeting, Campbell accepted the presidency of the society.

Campbell's formal college training consisted of less than one year at Glasgow University, but he was a man of considerable erudition. He established a national reputation as a debater, especially as a result of widely publicized debates with the renowned Scottish socialist and atheist Robert Owen, in 1829, and with the Roman Catholic archbishop of Cincinnati, John B. Purcell, in 1837. Campbell became financially independent as a result of his marriage to Margaret Brown in 1811, and he spent the remainder of his life living near his wife's home in Brooke County in western Virginia. He became a moderately wealthy man, and in 1829, in his only venture into politics, he was elected a delegate to the Virginia Constitutional Convention.

In 1841, Campbell established Bethany College near his home. Until his death he served as president and professor of moral sciences at the college and trained a generation of leaders for Disciples churches. Campbell traveled and preached widely throughout the United States, as well as in England and Scotland. The aging reformer was discouraged by the sectional tension caused by the slavery debate and the Civil War. He counseled moderation and believed that the restoration movement could survive the tragedy, but by the time of his death his millennial hopes had given way to pessimism. ◆

Campbell, Joan Brown

1931– ● DISCIPLES OF CHRIST/BAPTIST

> "As I see it, ecumenism lives in your heart, is acted out in your life and shapes how you organize. In short, being ecumenical is a way of being Christian."
> Joan Brown Campbell, quoted in *The Christian Century,* 1995

The Reverend Joan Brown Campbell became the first woman to serve as the head of the National Council of the Churches of Christ (NCC), the nation's leading ecumenical organization, in 1991. The ecumenical movement works for unity among Christian groups. The NCC also works toward justice and peace in the United States and the world.

A Youngstown, Ohio, native, Campbell was born in 1931, the granddaughter of a Presbyterian minister. She earned her Bachelor of Arts and Master of Arts degrees from the University of Michigan. She later completed the Graduate Clergy Internship program at Case Western Reserve School of Social Work in Cleveland, Ohio, and studied at Bossey Ecumenical Institute, in Geneva, Switzerland. From 1954 to 1967, Campbell worked as a homemaker, mother of three, and community volunteer. She then held several executive positions in Cleveland: Community United Headstart (1967–69), Welfare Action Coalition (1969–71), Action Training Network of

Ohio (1971–73), and Action for Change Program of the Catholic Diocese (1973).

Campbell was ordained as a minister in both the Christian Church (Disciples of Christ) and the American Baptist Church. From 1973 to 1979, she was Associate Director of the Greater Cleveland Interchurch Council, serving also as pastor of Euclid Baptist Church for several years.

Campbell became closely involved with the NCC when she joined its Governing Board in 1972. She then joined their staff as an Assistant General Secretary from 1979 to 1985. In that position, she worked to strengthen a national network of 750 ecumenical organizations. She directed the NCC office from 1985 until she became General Secretary in 1991.

The NCC was formed in 1950 in Cleveland, Ohio, by the merger of 12 ecumenical agencies, and grew into the largest ecumenical body in the United States. The NCC's 35 member communions include Protestant, Orthodox, and Anglican churches, making up more than 52 million Christians that belong to member churches. In addition to promoting Christian unity, the NCC offers disaster relief and refugee assistance overseas. Headquartered in New York City, the council stands for social justice, theological dialogue, and interfaith relations.

Campbell often used her high-profile position as General Secretary to speak out on such issues as racial and cultural diversity, poverty, the environment, women's rights, religious persecution, and education. She was invited to give sermons and speeches at regional, national, and international gatherings. Many of these talks as well as her articles and academic lectures have been published in magazines and books. She served on a number of important boards of educational institutions and governmental policy committees.

In November 1994, President Bill Clinton invited Campbell to join a group of U.S. religious leaders attending the signing of a historic peace agreement between Jordan and Israel.

"One of the reasons ecumenical bodies have been controversial is that they have often placed at their table issues that the churches themselves find very difficult to deal with."
Joan Brown Campbell, quoted in *The Christian Century*, 1995

1931 Campbell is born Ohio.

1967 Campbell becomes head of Cleveland Community Headstart program.

1972 Campbell joins the governing board of the National Council of Churches.

1979 Campbell becomes the NCC's Assistant General Secretary.

1991 Campbell becomes General Secretary of the NCC.

1994 Campbell and other U.S. religious leaders attend the signing of a peace agreement between Jordan and Israel.

1999 Campbell and Jesse Jackson travel to Yugoslavia to secure the release of three American soldiers.

Clinton said Campbell's participation witnessed to the churches' strong belief in continued movement toward peace.

In 1995 and 1996, Campbell and the NCC addressed the problem of about 50 arson burnings of black churches that occurred mainly in the South. Campbell organized a meeting of black ministers in Washington, D.C. and a two-day series of events to draw national attention to the church burning. Many churches around the nation organized to help rebuild some of the burned churches.

In May 1999, Campbell joined the Reverend Jesse Jackson in a 15-member interfaith delegation to the warring nation of Yugoslavia to secure the release of three American soldiers. Their highly publicized and risky trip, made independently of the U.S. government, became a dramatic success. The delegation conferred with the president of Yugoslavia, Slobodan Milosevic, and he ordered the release of the soldiers. Campbell wrote later of being invited by religious leaders from Yugoslavia, saying, "By going, by putting ourselves ever so briefly under the same bombing they endure night after night, we believe we helped to strengthen their witness for peace." Upon returning to Washington, Campbell, Jackson, and the others met with Clinton and other top officials to report on their journey. They urged the president to negotiate an end to the war.

Joan Campbell has three grown children and seven grandchildren. She is a member and elder at Park Avenue Christian Church in New York City. She enjoys listening to classical music and reading. Campbell wrote the introduction to the well-received *How to Be a Perfect Stranger, Vol. 2: A Guide to Etiquette in Other People's Religious Ceremonies: More Faiths in the US* (1996). She has also received a number of prestigious awards for her achievements. ◆

Channing, William Ellergy

1780–1842 ● Unitarian

William Ellergy Channing was an American Unitarian minister. He was born on 7 April 1780 in Newport, Rhode Island, to a distinguished family. He entered

Harvard College in 1794, graduated in 1798, and was elected a regent of Harvard in 1801. He then began his lifelong ministry at Boston's Federal Street Congregational Church in 1803. Channing defended the liberal Congregationalist ministers in 1815 against an attack in the journal *The Panoplist* by Jedidiah Morse, who accused them of covertly holding the views of the English Unitarian Thomas Belsham, who held that Christ was strictly human in nature, with human imperfections. Channing replied that the liberals were Arians and hence believed that Christ's character included intellectual, ethical, and emotional perfection. Thrust into prominence by this defense, Channing was asked to prepare a manifesto for the liberals, which he did in "Unitarian Chris-

tianity," his 1819 ordination sermon for Jared Sparks in Baltimore. This sermon unified the liberals around Channing's leadership; yet when the American Unitarian Association was organized in 1825, he refused the office of president, because he did not want Unitarianism to become a sect.

Channing was the outstanding representative of early American Unitarian theology in the period prior to the Transcendentalist controversy. He emphasized the authority of reason and revelation, the unique and infallible authority of Jesus, human educability to a Christlike perfection, and human essential similarity to God.

The influence of English philosopher John Locke is present in Channing's arguments for the rational character of revealed religion and his emphases on miracles and fulfilled prophecies as evidences for the truth of Christianity. In his 1819 sermon "Unitarian Christianity," he called for a careful use of reason in interpreting scripture. Channing held that reason judges even the claim of a revelation to authority. Reason approves the claim of the Christian scriptures to authority. Rationally interpreted, these scriptures yield the doctrines of the unipersonality and moral perfection of God.

Channing viewed Christ as morally perfect. He based this view on scriptural evidences of Christ's perfection and his own belief in the freedom of the will. Christ exemplified the perfection to which others can attain. In order to account for Christ's flawless moral perfection, Channing inferred from it Christ's preexistence; yet he maintained that others should aspire to, and can achieve, a similar perfection.

Channing advocated prison reform and opposed alcoholism and other social evils, but he was reluctant to speak out openly against slavery. He acknowledged the fairness of rebukes for his silence. In 1835 he published *Slavery*, which had a marked effect in arousing public opinion against the slave system; thereafter his outspoken opposition to slavery cost him friends and support. His writings during this period show that his optimism and his rejection of the doctrine of depravity in no way blinded him to the reality of sin.

Channing's essays made him famous on both sides of the Atlantic Ocean. These, along with his sermons, lectures, and *Slavery*, were translated into German, French, Hungarian, and other languages. Channing became ill on a vacation trip and died at Bennington, Vermont, on 2 October 1842. ◆

Confucius

551–479 B.C.E. ● CONFUCISM

Confucius was a Chinese philosopher and teacher; China's supreme sage and foremost teacher, whose thought has defined and shaped Chinese culture. Born in the state of Lu, in what is now Shantung province, to an impoverished noble family named K'ung, Confucius was named Ch'iu, meaning hill, due to a prominent bump on his head. He was later to use the appellation Chung-ni as his literary name. However, he was most commonly and famously referred to as K'ung Fu-tzu, "Venerable Master K'ung," by the Latinized form of which, Confucius, he became familiar in the West.

Confucius's father died when he was three, so he was brought up by his loving and devoted mother, who was his father's second wife. Nicknamed "long fellow" by his playmates

"If you govern the people legalistically and control them by punishment, they will avoid crime, but have no personal sense of shame. If you govern them by means of virtue and control them with propriety, they will gain their own sense of shame, and thus correct themselves."
Analects of Confucius, c. 5th century B.C.E.

Confucius

due to his unusual height, he early evinced a liking for practicing many of the rituals that were an integral part of traditional Chinese life and manners. Family circumstances dictated that he had to work from an early age, which he did with diligence, earning praise from the employer who hired him to attend the granaries and flocks of a rich noble.

The boy enjoyed little formal education, but such was his thirst for knowledge and his determination that he became the

"There are three things of which the superior man stand in awe. He stands in awe of the ordinances of Heaven. He stands in awe of great men. He stands in awe of the words of the sages. The mean man does not know the ordinances of Heaven, and consequently does not stand in awe of them. He is disrespectful to great men. He makes sport of the words of the sages."
Analects of Confucius, c. 5th century B.C.E.

most learned man of his day. He was later to reflect on his lifetime quest for wisdom: "At 15, I set my heart on learning. At 30, I was firmly established. At 40, I had no more doubts. At 50, I knew the will of Heaven. At 60, I was ready to listen to it. At 70, I could follow my heart's desire without transgressing what was right."

At this time, China was in a state of turmoil and decline. The Chou dynasty had lost power and the empire had disintegrated into a number of warring feudal states. Political dislocations were accompanied by a degeneration in the observance of the time-honored mores, codes of conduct, and ceremonies that gave Chinese society its stability and coherence. Confucius saw these trends as reflections of a deeper moral and spiritual disorder infecting the body politic: its alienation from the natural law that he regarded as the true foundation of successful human relations. He regarded the pursuit of knowledge as the path to wisdom and a better life for the individual and society. He quickly achieved a reputation as a teacher of outstanding ability, and people from all walks of life came to study under him.

Throughout his life Confucius sought an administrative position that would enable him to disseminate his ideas effectively. He was eventually appointed a high-ranking minister in the state of Lu, but was unable to achieve the reform he promoted due to the jealousy and intrigue of fellow-administrators and neighboring states. He resigned in disgust at the age of 54, and then embarked on a thirteen-year period of traveling and teaching in various states in China. He was received with respect wherever he went, as befitted his reputation as a sage, but was not entrusted with the sort of government post he considered commensurate with his abilities. At the age of 67 he was welcomed back to Lu at the intercession of one of his disciples who was a minister there, and spent his remaining years editing the classical Chinese religio-philosophical texts and continuing his teaching.

Defending the way of the ancients at a time when the old religious imperatives and rituals which regulated all social and political intercourse had lost their force, Confucius invested them with a new moral justification. His way presupposed that the hierarchical structure of the old society corresponded to a natural moral order. It was therefore necessary for each individual to play his proper part and fulfill the moral obligations inherent in his position as, say, son, father, subject, or ruler. This accounts for the stress Confucius placed on the six traditional

The Analects of Confucius

The *Analects* is a collection of the conversations and sayings of Confucius, the world's most famous and respected Chinese teacher. It forms the basis of the Confucian philosophy and is regarded as one of the most influential texts in human history. The *Analects* presents the principal teachings of Confucius in the form of a dialogue between the teacher and his disciples. In general the teachings espouse such values as benevolence to others and loyalty to the family. They also emphasize the importance of ritual in conserving the past and upholding social order, and the necessity of moral and exemplary leadership in government. In addition the *Analects* gives great insight into Confucius as a person by forming a portrait of his disposition and personal ethics.

The *Analects* was compiled into a collection of twenty books by the disciples of Confucius more than 2,000 years ago. Much of it comes in the form of questions and answers between Confucius and his disciples. The writings are short with little background or extensive discussion of a subject. Along with several other texts, some of which Confucius is said to have edited and others of which were based on his teachings, it forms a body of work known as the Confucian Classics. For hundreds of years the ideas found in the classics served as the basis of civil service examinations for Chinese government officials. Some scholars believe that Confucius's teachings on humanity and righteousness continue to be relevant in today's society.

arts of rituals, music, archery, charioteering, literature, and mathematics: only through a return to the decorum and formality that had underscored the great days of the past could society heal itself. Tradition relates that of his 3,000 pupils, 72 had mastered the six arts.

Despite his emphasis on tradition and manners, Confucius was by no means a conservative. He taught that government must be reformed to make its objective the happiness of its subjects rather than the gratification of the whims of the rulers. Thus he instanced war, often engaged in as a diverting pastime by the ruling class, as a pursuit that rendered the life of the subject onerous and should therefore be avoided if at all possible. He was also in favor of decreasing the severity of punishments for all but the most serious crimes. The key to good government, he believed, was self-rectification on the part of the ruler. Once this had been undertaken and achieved, the state would naturally return to a state of order in harmony with the dictates of nature, and people would be attracted to such a kingdom as a center of peace and justice. Hereditary rulers should have the common sense to delegate all power to ministers selected for their talent and virtue.

Confucius's teaching was not directed solely at the influential and powerful, although many of his pupils were young gentlemen whom he was preparing for government office. An egalitarian who believed that everyone was equally entitled to education, he pursued an open door policy, with enthusiasm and ability rather than wealth or social standing the criteria that mattered: fees were graded, with students paying according to their financial means. Instruction took place through small group discussions conducted in an informal atmosphere. Such an approach was revolutionary; moreover, prior to Confucius, education had been the prerogative of the nobility, with instructors drawn from a caste of petty nobles who were government officials; he was the first private teacher in China, and the first to regard teaching as a vehicle for reform as well as a livelihood.

jen: Confucian virtue translated as humanity and benevolence; a moral and social philosophy

The cardinal virtue of Confucius's moral and social philosophy was **jen,** usually translated as humanity, "benevolence," or "human-heartedness," and a homophone of the Chinese for "man". *Jen* embraced all the moral qualities of the true man: loyalty, reciprocity, courtesy, friendship, filial and fraternal affection, and dutifulness. Since he held that man had an innate predisposition to goodness, Confucius regarded *jen* as a fundamental human quality, to be developed or revealed rather than learnt.

chun-tzu: Confucian term meaning "noble man"

Confucius appropriated the idea of the **chun-tzu,** or "noble man," to illustrate the ideal type of personality. The word previously had the literal meaning, "son of a prince;" Confucius used it for the individual who was a prince among men, regardless of his nominal social status: virtue was not the exclusive preserve of the high-born. Such a person is characterized by effortless adherence to the virtuous path, rooted in a profound understanding of and sympathy with the dictates of the law that informs creation: he is kind, patient, humble, learned, and generous.

The only reliable source for Confucius's teaching is the *Lun-yu* (Analects), a collection of brief dialogues and sayings recorded by his disciples. As one of the *Four Books*, texts traditionally regarded as written by him or his disciples, it has provided the syllabus for Chinese education at the primary level; secondary-level education in China has long been based on the *Five Classics*, classical texts edited with commentary by Confucius.

Many of his disciples achieved positions of influence in government, so Confucius's ideas took firm root and grew in significance after his death; developed and modified by others, they came to dominate Chinese thought and manners. ◆

Thomas Cranmer

1535–1556 ● PROTESTANT

Thomas Cranmer was the archbishop of Canterbury (1533–1556) and a principle figure in the reformation of the Church of England. Born of a gentry family in Nottinghamshire, Cranmer entered Jesus College, Cambridge, at the age of 14. After taking his B.A. (1511) and M.A. (1515), he became a fellow of the college. His marriage to a gentlewoman named Joan cost him the fellowship, but it was restored when Joan, with her baby, died in childbirth.

After his ordination (before 1520), he was appointed one of 12 university preachers and a university examiner in divinity. Cranmer kept aloof from other Cambridge scholars who met frequently to discuss Martin Luther's writings. Instead, he privately tested these writings by his own independent study of the Bible and early church fathers.

Cranmer left Cambridge in 1529 to serve the cause of King Henry VIII's annulment of his marriage to Queen Catherine. During an embassy to Emperor Charles V in 1532 he became acquainted with several Lutheran leaders, among them Andreas Oslander at Nuremberg, whose niece Margaret he secretly married. She bore him a daughter and a son. Few were privy to this marriage until the next reign.

When Archbishop William Warham died in 1532, Henry decided that Cranmer would succeed him at Canterbury. The king was convinced that Cranmer would be dutiful not for any personal convenience, much less ambition, but from his sincere (and somewhat extreme) belief that scripture taught obedience to the divine right of kings and princes. This conviction explains many compromises and vacillations in Cranmer's life. Privately he would advise and admonish Henry and plead for mercy for the king's victims, but he would never openly disobey him.

In January 1533, Henry's secret marriage to Anne Boleyn, already pregnant, made the annulment issue urgent. Although

> "And so her Grace, sustained on each side with two bishops, the bishop of Lincoln and the bishop of Winchester, came forth in procession unto the Church of Westminster…and so entered up into the high altar, where diverse ceremonies used about her, I did set the crown on her head, and then was sung Te Deum."
>
> Thomas Cranmer, describing the coronation of Anne Boleyn, 1533

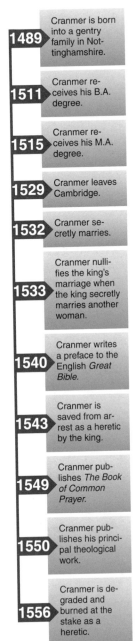

1489 ▶ Cranmer is born into a gentry family in Nottinghamshire.

1511 ▶ Cranmer receives his B.A. degree.

1515 ▶ Cranmer receives his M.A. degree.

1529 ▶ Cranmer leaves Cambridge.

1532 ▶ Cranmer secretly marries.

1533 ▶ Cranmer nullifies the king's marriage when the king secretly marries another woman.

1540 ▶ Cranmer writes a preface to the English *Great Bible.*

1543 ▶ Cranmer is saved from arrest as a heretic by the king.

1549 ▶ Cranmer publishes *The Book of Common Prayer.*

1550 ▶ Cranmer publishes his principal theological work.

1556 ▶ Cranmer is degraded and burned at the stake as a heretic.

Pope Clement VII suspected Henry's intentions, he consented to Cranmer's consecration, which took place on 30 March. Both before and twice during the rite Cranmer read a protestation that his oath of obedience to the pope did not bind him if it was against the law of God, the laws and prerogatives of the Crown, or the reformation of the church.

Within a few weeks, Cranmer pronounced the marriage to Catherine null and that to Anne valid. In July the pope issued but did not publish excommunications of Henry, Anne, and Cranmer. Any hope of reconciliation ended when the Act of Supremacy (1534) declared the king and his successors "the only supreme head in earth of the Church of England."

Cranmer supported but did not initiate the major reforms of Henry's reign: the dissolution of all monastic and religious houses between 1536 and 1539 (carried out more because of the Crown's greed for their vast properties than for the sake of any principle) and the official authorization in 1539 of the English "Great Bible," for which Cranmer wrote a notable preface in 1540.

The stringent Act of Six Articles (1539) closed the door to any reforms in doctrine or practice. Cranmer spoke against it in the House of Lords, but he voted for it because the king willed it. By now Cranmer was commonly believed to be a Lutheran. In 1543 the privy council voted to arrest him as a heretic, but Henry intervened and saved him. Until Henry's death, Cranmer worked quietly on projects of liturgical reform, but of these only the *English Litany* of 1544 was authorized.

Reformers dominated the privy council of King Edward VI (y1547–1553), Henry's precocious young son who was educated by Protestant tutors. Among the councillors committed to religious reform were the young king's uncle the duke of Somerset and Lord Protector, and Cranmer, his godfather. Cranmer soon published a *Book of Homilies,* one part to be read every Sunday, and translated a Lutheran catechism by Justus Jonas. Clerical celibacy was abolished. Communion including both bread and wine was ordered, for which Cranmer prepared *The Order of the Communion* (1548), a vernacular devotion for the people's Communion at Mass.

At Pentecost 1549, *The Book of Common Prayer* came into use under an act of uniformity. The book's reforming principles were derived from Lutheran sources; but its Catholic heritage was preserved by Cranmer's skillful adaptation and translation of liturgical forms and prayers from Latin service books. The daily offices were reduced to two, **matins** and **evensong,** with one chapter from both the Old and New Testaments read at each. The Holy Communion eliminated all sacrificial references except "praise and thanksgiving" and forbade any elevation of the consecrated elements. The prayer book was not popular, however, with either conservatives or radical reformers.

matin: relating to the early morning
Evensong: an evening prayer

After Somerset's fall from power, the duke of Northumberland became Lord Protector. He was more interested in the church properties he acquired than in the radical reforms he promoted. In 1550 Cranmer published *The Form and Manner* for ordaining bishops, priests, and deacons, based on the Latin *Pontifical* and a work of Martin Bucer, and also his principal theological work, *A Defence of the True and Catholike Doctrine of the Sacrament of the Body and Blood of Our Saviour Christ.*

A revised prayer book was issued in 1552 under an act of uniformity. Most of the old vestments and ceremonies were abolished, and the Communion service was rearranged and conformed to the Swiss reformers' doctrine. All images, crosses, **rood screens** and other ornaments were smashed, removed, or sold; and a wooden "holy Table" replaced all altars.

rood: a cross or crucifix symbolic of the cross on which Jesus Christ is said to have died

While Edward lay dying, Northumberland plotted to place his cousin Lady Jane Grey (granddaughter of King Henry VII) on the throne. Cranmer strongly opposed this until Edward commanded him to submit. But the coup was short-lived. Mary I, the elder daughter of Henry VIII, was acclaimed queen. Many reformers fled to the continent, and Cranmer sent his family back to Germany.

An ardent Roman Catholic, Mary persuaded Parliament to revoke all reforms of Edward's reign. Cranmer was arrested, tried, and condemned as a traitor; but Mary had other plans. When Cardinal Reginald Pole, papal legate and archbishop-designate of Canterbury arrived in 1554, he absolved the kingdom and restored papal authority. The burning of heretics then began.

Under pressure, Cranmer wrote several recantations, but to no avail. On the day of his degradation and burning, 21 March 1556, he publicly recanted all his recantations, hastened to the stake, thrust his fist into the fire crying "This hand has offended," and soon collapsed. His monument lives in *The Book of Common Prayer,* often amended and enriched, which is used in the worship of all churches of the Anglican communion. ◆

Crowther, Samuel Ajayi

1806?–1891 ● ANGLICAN

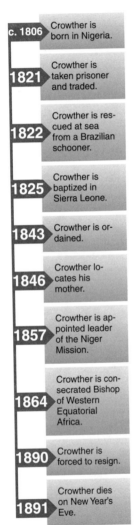

c. 1806 Crowther is born in Nigeria.

1821 Crowther is taken prisoner and traded.

1822 Crowther is rescued at sea from a Brazilian schooner.

1825 Crowther is baptized in Sierra Leone.

1843 Crowther is ordained.

1846 Crowther locates his mother.

1857 Crowther is appointed leader of the Niger Mission.

1864 Crowther is consecrated Bishop of Western Equatorial Africa.

1890 Crowther is forced to resign.

1891 Crowther dies on New Year's Eve.

Samuel Ajayi Crowther was a Nigerian missionary, traveler, translator, and the first African Anglican bishop. Born in Osogun, near Eruwa in Oyo State of Nigeria, he was taken prisoner and enslaved there in early 1821 and then traded down to the coast, to Lagos, during 1821–1822. He was loaded onto a Brazilian schooner on 7 April 1822, rescued at sea the same day by British antislavery activists, and taken to Freetown, Sierra Leone, where he was baptized in 1825 and educated by the Christian Missionary Society (CMS). Crowther was taken to visit London in 1826. The next year he became a foundation student at the CMS's Fourah Bay College in Freetown. He began to study Yoruba, among other languages, and to preach in it. Crowther joined the 1841 Niger Expedition. He was ordained in 1843. He served as a pioneering member of the CMS Yoruba Mission to Badagry in 1844 and, in 1846, to Abeokuta, where he found his mother. Crowther was a principal figure in the translation of the Bible into Yoruba, a most remarkable linguistic and literary feat. A well-known traveler, he joined the 1854 Niger Expedition, exploring the Benue River up to Ibi; in 1857 he accompanied the expedition up to Jebba. Twice, in 1859 and 1871, when the expedition ship ran aground at Jebba, he traveled down to Lagos on foot through Ogbomosho, Oyo, and Ibadan.

Crowther was appointed leader of the Niger Mission in 1857 and subsequently opened mission stations at Akassa, Onitsha, Lokoja, and Idah. In 1864 he was consecrated Bishop of Western Equatorial Africa in Regions beyond the Queen's Dominions with his seat in Lagos; he had no jurisdiction in the Yoruba country where European missionaries operated, but he did supervise Episcopalian church missions in Liberia and Rio Pongas, among other places. He opened another mission in Bonny for the Niger Delta. The Niger Mission was dependent on the operation of the mail steamer that attracted small-scale traders from Freetown and Lagos. The irregular schedule of the steamer made the work of supervising the mission very difficult; problems with the steamer were also why the staff of both the Niger and the Niger Delta missions in the 1860s and 1870s were exclusively Africans (recruited mostly from Freetown), who did not need to go on leaves abroad regularly. The missionaries cooperated with the traders from Freetown and Lagos to open up the Lower Niger Valley to European trade. The mission was hailed as a great success in the 1870s but, with the rising tide of imperialism, Sir George Goldie and other major British traders came to see African traders as rivals and African missionaries as obstacles.

From the 1850s on, Crowther was the acknowledged leader of the up-and-coming African educated elite not only in Nigeria but throughout western Africa. European missionaries very critical of Crowther's administration entered the Niger Mission, and in 1890 Crowther was forced to resign. Before he died on New Year's Eve 1891, in Lagos, he made plans to reconstitute the Niger Delta Mission as an autonomous pastorate under his son, Archdeacon Dandeson Crowther. Eventually, in 1898, this pastorate was reconciled with the CMS. ◆

Dalai Lama

1935– ● BUDDHIST

The 14th Dalai Lama is the religious and political leader of the Tibetan people. He is a renowned Buddhist scholar and a man of peace who is widely respected for his humanity, his compassion, and his qualities of leadership. Since 1959 he has led a campaign to end China's domination of Tibet through nonviolent means, and for this effort he won the 1989 Nobel Peace Prize.

On July 6, 1935, the Dalai Lama was born to a humble farming family in the small village of Taktser in northeastern Tibet. He was named Lhamo Thondup. In 1938, a delegation of monks recognized him as the reincarnated Dalai Lama, who is the leader of the Yellow Hat order, the chief Buddhist sect of Tibet. The monks then brought him to Lhasa to raise him according to the monastic tradition. He began his monastic education at the age of six and completed his Doctorate of Buddhist Philosophy when he was 25.

In 1950 Communist Chinese troops poured over the Tibetan border with the intention of "liberating" Tibet from imperialist rule. The Chinese invasion frightened the Tibetan people and they turned to their spiritual leader for guidance. In response to their appeals for political leadership, the Dalai Lama was made head of the state of Tibet at the age of 15, three years short of the typical ascension to political power.

In order to avoid a confrontation with the advancing army, the Tibetan government sent a delegation to the Chinese capi-

"No matter what part of the world we come from, we are all basically the same human beings. We all seek happiness and try to avoid suffering. We have the same basic human needs and concerns. All of us human beings want freedom and the right to determine our own destiny as individuals and as peoples."

Dalai Lama, 1989

"The preservation of our cultural identity is a primary concern for all Tibetans. Growing international support for Tibet is a source of much encouragement to us. Still, the situation inside Tibet remains extremely grave."

Dalai Lama, 1999

tal of Peking to negotiate with the Communist authorities and make it clear that Tibet did not require liberation. The result of the negotiations was a document called the Seventeen Point Agreement, which provided that the Tibetan people would become a part of the People's Republic of China and that the Chinese would assume control of foreign affairs and military responsibilities in Tibet. In return the Tibetans would be assured religious and political freedom. The young Dalai Lama was alarmed by the terms of the agreement that surrendered the sovereignty of Tibet to the Chinese government, and he felt it must have been coerced out of the delegates. But rather than face the massive Chinese army with force, which seemed futile and was also against his Buddhist nature, the Dalai Lama decided to maintain further negotiations with the Chinese.

In 1954 the Dalai Lama traveled to China, where he met with Mao Zedong, China's ruler, and Zhou Enlai, the premier of China. He found the Chinese leaders cordial but oblivious to the importance of Buddhism to himself and the Tibetan people. While traveling, he eagerly learned about the Chinese advances made in industry and science. He felt that Tibet was in dire need of reform in certain areas—including education, communications, the judicial system—and he was open-minded to the Chinese approaches in these areas.

Through the mid-1950s tension between the Chinese authorities and Tibetans increased and resistance to Communist authority was met with beatings and executions. In early 1959 thousands gathered on the streets of Lhasa in protest of Chinese rule and out of concern for what they perceived as a threat to the life of the Dalai Lama. In a show of authority, the Chinese sent armed troops to crush the demonstration. At the urging of his family and ministers, who were convinced that the loss of his life would mean the end of Tibetan life, the Dalai Lama fled with an entourage across the Himalayas to seek political assistance for his country in India. Several hours after his departure, the Chinese began an attack on the Tibetan demonstrators. The crackdown continued into 1960, and by 1961 more than 80,000 Tibetans had been killed.

Once in India, the Dalai Lama was granted political asylum. In 1960 he established a government-in-exile in Dharamsala in northern India with military protection from the Indian government. From Dharamsala he devoted himself to supporting the increasing numbers of Tibetans refugees seeking exile in India and to preserving Tibetan culture against adverse odds. He also worked tirelessly on building international support for Tibetan autonomy. Throughout these campaigns he continued to conduct his life as a monk, meditating four hours a day and spending several hours more daily studying and writing on Buddhist texts.

In the meantime China continued to increase its control over Tibet and repress Tibetan culture. It placed restrictions on religious practice and the economy and installed Chinese as local government administrators and teachers. It began agricultural reforms that required peasants to sell a fixed amount of grain to the government and forced them to grow wheat rather than barley, their traditional crop. Aggressive farming methods also rapidly eroded the thin layer of topsoil on the Tibetan plains, and led to crop failure and years of famine. Communications and road systems were built, but China remained in control of the local media and travel for Tibetans was restricted in the early years. During the Cultural Revolution of the 1960s, formal religion was banned, and Chinese soldiers looted and destroyed all but about 10 of Tibet's 6,000 monasteries. Many

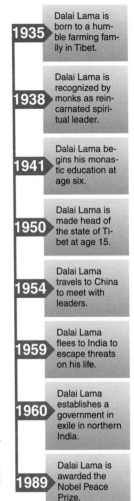

1935 Dalai Lama is born to a humble farming family in Tibet.

1938 Dalai Lama is recognized by monks as reincarnated spiritual leader.

1941 Dalai Lama begins his monastic education at age six.

1950 Dalai Lama is made head of the state of Tibet at age 15.

1954 Dalai Lama travels to China to meet with leaders.

1959 Dalai Lama flees to India to escape threats on his life.

1960 Dalai Lama establishes a government in exile in northern India.

1989 Dalai Lama is awarded the Nobel Peace Prize.

The Potala Palace

The Potala Palace in Lhasa, Tibet, was formerly the seat of the Tibetan government and a residence of the Dalai Lama, the spiritual leader of Tibet and its former head of state. Made up of about 1,000 rooms and rising 13 stories, it is the greatest monumental structure in all of Tibet. The palace is perched on a rocky outcrop called the Red Hill, overlooking Lhasa. It once included the private chambers of the Dalai Lama, meditation halls, a monastery and assembly hall for monks, the jewel-encrusted tombs of eight Dalai Lamas, numerous chapels and shrines, and government offices for the conduct of state affairs. It also served as a warehouse for ancient, illuminated scriptures and other cultural treasures. The Potala was originally built in the seventh century by King Songsten Gampo. Most of what now makes up the Potala was built during the seventeenth century after the Fifth Dalai Lama began expanding the palace in 1645. In 1959, the Fourteenth Dalai Lama fled the Chinese Communist regime in Tibet and has remained in exile in India ever since. Today, the palace today serves as a museum, but it also stands as a symbol of Tibetan Buddhism and it attracts thousands of pilgrims to Lhasa each year.

thousands of Tibetans were killed and many others were thrown in prison to face starvation. Though the Chinese government began to relax some restrictions on the Tibetan economy, religious practice, and culture in the 1980s, restrictions were renewed after a riot in Lhasa against the slow pace of reform and the continued discrimination in Tibet.

In an effort to aid his people the Dalai Lama traveled around the world to talk about the disregard for human rights in Tibet and the destruction of the indigenous culture there. He met political, religious, and human rights leaders around the world, and formed large groups in support of his cause. And despite criticisms from some exiled Tibetans for his insistence on nonviolence, the Dalai Lama has continued to advocate peaceful solutions to the Tibetan problem based upon tolerance and mutual respect with the Chinese people.

For his leadership in the pursuit of freedom and peace and for his distinguished writings in Buddhist philosophy the Dalai Lama has received numerous honors around the world. In 1989 he won the Nobel Peace Prize for his consistent opposition to the use of violence in his struggle for human rights in Tibet.

The Dalai Lama describes himself as a simple monk who spends at least four hours daily in meditation and much of the rest of his day tending Tibetan affairs of state and studying Buddhist texts. In the 1990s he began to speak out on the need for better understanding and respect among the different faiths of the world. ◆

> The Dalai Lama describes himself as a simple monk who spends at least four hours daily in meditation.

Dan Fodio, Usuman

1754/5–1817 ● Muslim

Usuman Dan Fodio was a renowned Islamic teacher and political leader. Usuman was born in the Hausa kingdom of Gobir, in the north of the present-day state of Sokoto, Nigeria. He came from a line of Muslim scholars of the Fulbe clan Torodbe that had been established in the area since about 1450. They worked as scribes, teachers, and in other literate roles and contributed over several generations to the dissemination of Sunni Islam among the inhabitants of Gobir. As a result, the Gobir royals were superficially won over to Islam. Nonetheless, authority in Gobir still rested on customary norms, not the Islamic law, at the end of the eighteenth century c.e.. This caused mounting frustration among these Muslim literates and resulted in the emergence of an Islamic reform movement that reached its peak at that time. Usuman became widely accepted in Gobir and neighboring kingdoms as its leader.

Usuman spent his early manhood as a teacher and preacher of Islam in Gobir and the nearby kingdoms of Zamfara, Katsina, and Kebbi. He appears to have had no initial intention of pursuing reform by force, but the prolonged resistance of the Gobir chiefs and courtiers to demands for stricter adherence to Islam built up tension. After several violent incidents, organized warfare broke out between the Gobir forces and Usuman's followers in 1804. For the Muslim reformers this was *jihad,* war against unbelievers.

The campaigns in Gobir ended in 1808, when the Gobir dynasty collapsed and was replaced by a polity organized along Islamic lines. Usuman remained its titular head until his death in 1817, when he was succeeded by his son, Muhammadu Bello. Elsewhere in the Hausa kingdoms and even as far south as Yorubaland and the Nupe kingdom other *jihads,* led by Usuman's "flag bearers," or military commanders, continued until brought to a halt by the colonial occupations of the late nineteenth and early twentieth centuries.

Usuman was also a scholar and poet in the classical Arabic tradition. Best known among his verse works is his **panegyric** to the prophet Muhammad, *The Ode Rhyming in Dal,* that helped to spread the prophet's cult and was seminal to a genre of Hausa prophetic panegyric among the generations that followed him.

His Arabic prose works are numerous. Their main thrust is against all manifestations of indigenous, non-Islamic Hausa culture—song, music, ornate dress, architecture, social mores, and so on—and an insistence that these be replaced by Islamic alternatives. His works also influenced his society, and posterity, by disseminating the ideas of the Qadiri order of Sufis, to which he was deeply committed.

The immediate political consequences of the *jihad* were to overthrow the discrete Hausa principalities based on traditional, unwritten customary codes and to substitute a unified Islamic system of government. More long-term cultural and religious consequences were to displace, to some extent, indigenous African notions about cosmology and replace them with the Islamic celestial architecture, to challenge African cyclical explanations of life and death with the finality of the Islamic doctrine of divine punishment and reward, and to enhance the status of Arabic literacy in Hausa society.

Usuman is still a much revered personality among Hausa Muslims, having become something of a symbol of Hausa Muslim nationalism. ◆

jihad: Arabic word for holy war against non-believers on behalf of Islam

panegyric: formal and oftentimes elaborate religious praise

Day, Dorothy

1897–1980 ● CATHOLIC

Dorothy Day was a Catholic reformer, journalist, and lecturer. Between 1933, when she brought out the first penny-a-copy issue of the monthly newspaper *Catholic Worker*, and 1980, when she died, Dorothy Day became, in the opinion of many, America's foremost Roman Catholic voice calling for peace and a profound change in the major institutional forms of the contemporary world. She opposed what she regarded as the enslaving colossus of the modern state and the technological giantism to which it was a partner. Fundamental to her ideas of social reordering was her insistence on the personal transformation of value based on the primary reality of spirit rather than the spirit of acquisitiveness. For her, this meant taking her directions from church tradition, the papal encyclicals, and her literal reading of the Gospels. She used these sources to justify her absolute pacifism and her communitarian ideas on social reconstruction.

For Day, the ultimate and transfiguring value was love, a subject that was the theme of her best writing. The exercise of a sacrificial love was at the heart of her personalist revolt against the enlarging domain over life of institutional forms. The world would be renewed by persons who loved and not by state management. In her own case she chose to wage her revolution by establishing "houses of hospitality" in the destitute areas of lower Manhattan in New York City, by promoting communitarian farms, and by an immense writing and speaking regimen that left few Catholic parishes or schools untouched by her ideas by the time of her death.

Day was born the third in a family of five children in Brooklyn on 8 November 1897, the daughter

> "We believe further that the revolution that is to be pursued in ourselves and in society must be pacifist. Otherwise it will proceed by force and use means that are evil and which will never be outgrown.
> Dorothy Day, in *The Catholic Worker*, 1972

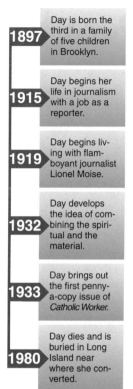

1897 Day is born the third in a family of five children in Brooklyn.

1915 Day begins her life in journalism with a job as a reporter.

1919 Day begins living with flamboyant journalist Lionel Moise.

1932 Day develops the idea of combining the spiritual and the material.

1933 Day brings out the first penny-a-copy issue of *Catholic Worker*.

1980 Day dies and is buried in Long Island near where she converted.

of Grace Satterlee and John Day. An opening in journalism for John Day took the family to San Francisco in 1903, but the earthquake there, three years later, forced a removal to Chicago. In 1915 the family moved to New York where Dorothy, having finished two years at the University of Illinois, began her own life in journalism as a reporter for the Socialist *Call*.

For the next five years she dabbled in radical causes, moving from one cheap flat to another, mostly in the lower New York area. In 1919 she left a hospital nurse's training program to live with a flamboyant journalist, Lionel Moise. The affair ended with her having an abortion, a circumstance that filled her with such grief that she was brought to the brink of suicide. Later, living in a fisherman's shack on Staten Island as the common-law wife of Forster Batterham, she bore a daughter, Tamar Therese. Out of gratitude for her daughter and a mystical rapture she felt in living on such close terms with nature, she turned to God and was subsequently baptized a Catholic. In 1932 she met the French itinerant philosopher, Peter Maurin, and after some months of tutelage she acquired from him the idea of "the correlation of the spiritual with the material." This was the beginning point of her vision of social recreation.

Her personality was remarkably forceful and engaging, but she could be given to moments of authoritarian harshness. After a series of retreats during World War II, the unremitting struggle of her life was to grow in sanctity. In her later years the impression she gave was of one who had achieved a rare level of holiness. She died on 29 November 1980 and was buried at Jamestown, Long Island, not far from the site of her conversion. ◆

Dayananda Sarasvati

1824–1883 ● HINDU

Dayananda Sarasvati (also spelled Sariswati or Sariswathi) was a leading 19th century Hindu reformer and founder of the Hindu sect Arya Samaj. What is known of Dayananda's early years comes from two autobiographical statements made after he founded the Arya Samaj in 1875. Although he refused to reveal his family and personal names or place of birth in order to preserve his freedom as a *samnyasin* ("renunciant"), these statements allow a reconstruction of his life before he became a public figure.

Dayananda claimed to have spent his childhood in a small town—from his description, most likely Tankara—in the princely state of Morvi in northern Kathiawar, now in Gujarat's Rajkot District in India. His father was a high-caste brahman landowner and revenue collector and a devout worshiper of the Hindu god Shiva (Siva). Dayananda began to study Sanskrit and the Vedas at age eight. Although his father preferred that he become a devotee of Shiva, an experience in the local Shiva temple undermined Dayananda's faith that the temple icon was God, and turned him away from ritual practice involving images. The deaths of a sister and a beloved uncle a few years later made him realize the instability of worldly life, and when, around 1845, he learned that his family had secretly arranged his marriage, he fled to become a homeless wanderer.

The young mendicant studied the philosophy of the Upanisads with several teachers before being initiated into an order of *samnyasins* with the religious name Dayananda Sarasvati in 1847. He lived as an itinerant yogin for the next thirteen years, but in 1860 he settled in Mathura to study with the Sanskrit grammarian Vrijananda (1779–1868). Vrijananda, whom Dayananda accepted as his guru, aided Dayananda in perfecting his Sanskrit and also convinced him that the only truthful texts were those composed by the *rsis* ("seers") before the Mahabharata (a sacred Hindu poem), since, he taught, all later works contained false sectarian doctrines. Dayananda committed himself to spreading this message when he left his guru in 1863, though it took him most of his life to decide which individual texts were true and which were false.

Between 1863 and 1873, Dayananda spent most of his time in small towns along the Ganges River in what is now western Uttar Pradesh meeting representatives of various Hindu communities and debating sectarian pandits. These experiences confirmed his early doubts about image worship and led him to reject all of the Hindu sectarian traditions. He argued with growing conviction for a united Hinduism based on the monotheism and morality of the Vedas.

Throughout this period Dayananda continued to dress as a yogin in loincloth and ashes and debated only in Sanskrit; thus his message was restricted mainly to those orthodox upper-caste Hindus who were most solidly opposed to his views. Early

1824 Dayananda is born.

1845 Dayananda becomes a wanderer to escape an arranged marriage.

1847 Dayananda is initiated into a religious order.

1860 Dayananda begins studying with a Sanskrit grammarian.

1863 Dayananda leaves his guru to spread his message.

1873 Dayananda spends time with leader Debendranath Tagore.

1875 Dayananda founds the Arya Samaj (society of honorable ones).

1883 Dayananda dies soon after revising his major doctrinal statement.

The Vedas

As a young man, Dayananda Sarasvati studied the Upanishads, a group of philosophical writings included in sacred Hindu texts call Vedas. The Vedas are the world's oldest Hindu religious texts and the foundation of all contemporary Hindu beliefs. The Vedas include information on the nature of the soul, methods of prayer and meditation, the relationship between the mind and body, and on reincarnation; the belief that a person's soul survives after death and is reborn in another living being. The Vedas are believed to have been revealed to wise men and poets in a sacred revelation. The term *Veda* is an ancient Sanskrit word that means *knowledge.*

The sacred Vedas is comprised of four books written in Sanskrit that are known as the Samhitas. They include the Rig Veda, a collection of hymns; the Yajur Veda, a collection of sacrificial prayers; the Sama Veda, a collection of chants; and the Atharva Veda, a collection of hymns or magic charms used by priests in rituals. Each of these Vedas has four parts: mantras, Brahmanas, Aranyakas, and Upanishads. The mantras, which are devotional hymns or songs of praise, are the oldest portion of the Vedas. The earliest of them probably originated about 1400 B.C.E. The Brahmanas are commentary on the proper use of mantras and explanations of the mythic background of the verses. The Aranyakas ("forest books") are guidance books on secret rituals for sages and hermits who were known to seek the seclusion of forests for their religious practices. The Upanishads are esoteric philosophical texts on the nature of absolute reality and on the inner self. They are also referred to as the *Vedanta,* which means the *conclusion of the Veda.*

in 1873, however, he spent four months in Calcutta as the guest of the Hindu leader Debendranath Tagore, met the great Hindu spokesman Keshab Chandra Sen, and discussed religious issues with these and other westernized Hindu intellectuals. Dayananda, learned the value of educational programs, public lectures, and publications in effecting change, and accepted from Sen some valuable advice to improve his own reception: abandon the loincloth and the elitist Sanskrit in favor of street clothes and Hindi.

Dayananda left Calcutta with an unchanged message but a broader perspective and a new style, lecturing and writing in Hindi and seeking a receptive audience for his message. He found the first such audience in Bombay, where he founded the Arya Samaj ("society of honorable ones") on 10 April 1875. His major breakthrough, however, came two years later in the Punjab, where a rising class of merchants and professionals was seeking a defense of Hinduism against Christian missionary activity. A chapter of the Arya Samaj was founded in Lahore in

1877, and this soon became the headquarters for a rapidly expanding movement in the Punjab and western Uttar Pradesh.

Dayananda left control of the Arya Samaj in the hands of local chapters and spent his last years perfecting his message. He completed the revision of his major doctrinal statement, *Satyarth prakas*, shortly before his death on 30 October 1883. With final conviction, he declared that the Vedic hymns revealed to the *rsis* were the sole authority for truth, and he reaffirmed his faith in the one eternal God whose revelation thus made salvation possible for all the world. ◆

Demetrios

1928– ● GREEK ORTHODOX CHURCH

His Eminence Archbishop Demetrios, Primate of the Greek Orthodox Church of America, became the spiritual leader of about 1.5 million Greek Orthodox Christians when he was enthroned on September 18, 1999. The Greek Orthodox Church is part of the Eastern Orthodox religion, a federation of independent churches that grew from a split in the Christian church that occurred in 1054.

Demetrios Trakatellis was born in Thessaloniki, Greece, in 1928. From 1946 to 1950, he attended the University of Athens School of Theology, graduating with honors. Demetrios was ordained a deacon in 1960 and to the priesthood in 1964. Deacons are the first of the three main orders of Orthodox clergy, followed by priests and bishops. Although married men may become priests, bishops are elected only from among celibate or widowed clergy. In 1965, Demetrios enrolled at the Harvard Divinity School in Cambridge, Massachusetts, where he completed a Ph.D. in Philosophy with honors in 1972.

Demetrios was elected titular (figurehead) bishop of Vresthena, Greece, in 1967 and an auxiliary bishop to the Archbishop of Athens. In 1968, he was elected Metropolitan (a position similar to that of bishop) of Attika and Megaridos, but refused the post because he opposed the military junta ruling Greece at that time.

Demetrios received a doctorate in theology from the University of Athens 1977, and became an internationally known New Testament scholar and author. From 1983 to 1993, he

> "Let the living mutual love and the eagerness to transcend ourselves for the sake of the other who is in need, be the distinctive sign of our Orthodox ethos."
>
> Archbishop Demetrios, 1999

1928 ▶ Demetrios is born in Greece.

1950 ▶ Demetrios graduates from the University of Athens School of Theology.

1960 ▶ Demetrios is ordained a deacon.

1964 ▶ Demetrios is ordained a priest.

1968 ▶ Demetrios declines the office of Metropolitan of Attika and Megaridos.

1972 ▶ Demetrios completes a Ph.D. at Harvard.

1977 ▶ Demetrios earns a second Ph.D. from the University of Athens.

1999 ▶ Demetrios becomes Primate of the Greek Orthodox Church of America.

served as the Distinguished Professor of Biblical Studies and Christian Origins at Holy Cross Greek Orthodox School of Theology in Brookline, Massachusetts. He also taught at Harvard Divinity School as a Visiting Professor of the New Testament. Demetrios' experience in the United States included service as a parish priest in Pittsburgh, Pennsylvania.

When Demetrios was appointed Primate of the Greek Orthodox Church of America in 1999, he became the sixth Archbishop to be enthroned since that Archdiocese was established. In 1918, an archbishop of Greece had come to organize the Church in the New World, and the Ecumenical Patriarchate in Turkey officially proclaimed the Greek Orthodox Archdiocese of North and South America in 1922.

Demetrios succeeded Metropolitan Spyridon of Italy, who was appointed in 1996 but had resigned within three years due to heavy criticism of his governing style. Ecumenical Patriarch Bartholomew, known for stressing the importance of protecting the environment and for his ecumenical views, appointed Demetrios to his new position. The ecumenical patriarch, based in Turkey, holds the top role in the Eastern Orthodox Church, similar to the pope in the Catholic church. In the United States, the many separate ethnic communities within the Orthodox religion led to a very different structure than that of the Orthodox Church abroad. Some large American metropolitan areas have several Orthodox bishops and many Orthodox parishes of different ethnic groups.

The scholarly Demetrios can read several languages, including English, Coptic, Greek, German, Hebrew, and Latin. He is the author of three academic books on Orthodox Christian theology: *Authority and Passion* (1987), *The Transcendent God of Eugonostos* (1991), and *Christ, the Pre-existing God* (1992). His brother, Anthony Trakatellis, was a biochemistry professor in Greece and a member of the European Parliament. ◆

Saint Dominic

c. 1170–1221 ● Christian

Saint Dominic (Domingo de Guzman), was the Spanish founder of the Dominican order. Dominic, probably a scion of the patrician Guzman family, was born in

Calaruega in old Castile, Spain. Before his birth his mother dreamt that she would give birth to a dog bearing a torch that would set the world aflame. Her premonition was interpreted as accurate: Dominic revitalized the church in a critical period during which heretics exploited the unscrupulous behavior of clergymen to their advantage. His teachings and personal example made him the object of universal veneration during his lifetime. Like his two brothers, Dominic attended the college of Palencia, then staffed by the most eminent Spanish theologians. He was a diligent student, who at 14 already adopted an ascetic regimen, refusing wine and sleeping on the floor. Crowds flocked to the local church to hear him sing in the choir, but he was best known for his charitable endeavors. While he was twice prevented from selling himself to redeem Christians from Saracen slave dealers, he did sell his richly annotated books and donated the money to charity. Upon ordination in 1195 Dominic was appointed a canon of Osma, his native diocese, and rose rapidly in the church hierarchy.

With the appointment of Diego d'Azevedo as bishop in 1200, Dominic became his aide. In 1203 King Alphonso VIII of Castile sent Diego and Dominic to negotiate a marriage for his son. On their way north, the two spent some time in Toulouse, where Dominic first encountered the Albigensians, a heretical sect advocating fanatical asceticism culminating in suicide. Unlike his contemporaries, Dominic rejected force to counter the heretics. Although the clergy acted otherwise, he believed that asceticism was a fundamental tenet of the church and proposed himself as an example of true Christian asceticism. Donning shabby clothes he walked the streets barefoot, flailing himself with a heavy iron chain, yet all the time smiling and singing hymns. Doting crowds eagerly attended his debates with the Albigensians even though these sometimes lasted as long as eight days. Dominic's vast erudition and sparkling humor so unnerved the heretics that they twice threw his notes into a fire. Miraculously these survived the flames, further enhancing Dominic's reputation.

After Diego's death in 1207 Dominic was offered the bishopric. He declined, preferring to engage in missionary work. He grew a beard to disguise himself for a planned mission to Tartary, but because the problems faced by the church at home were no less troublesome the mission was canceled; however, Dominic kept the distinctive beard. He then planned to organize reconverted Albigensians and his rapidly growing following into a monastic order of preachers. While Simon de Montfort organized a brutal crusade against the Albigensians to avenge the murder of a papal legate by the count of Toulouse (they were eventually annihilated, as was the unique troubadour culture of Provence), Dominic favored compassion to draw dissenters back to the fold. Legend depicts him racing through the ravaged streets of Beziers, cross in hand, pleading with Simon's troops for the lives of the apostates.

Dominic's new order was first established in Toulouse and a convent for women was established in Prouille. To prepare his devotees for their mission, Dominic encouraged them to attend university; he also accumulated an extensive library. The Order of Friars Preacher, commonly known as the Dominicans, was officially recognized by Pope Honorius III in 1216. Not content with the narrow confines of Provence, Dominic aspired to extend his mission to the leading intellectual centers of Christendom. Only eight friars were kept in Toulouse; the majority were sent to establish missions in Paris, Bologna, and Spain, where they were similarly successful. In 1219 there were 30 brothers in Paris; by 1224 the number had increased to 120. In a short time Dominican missionaries had spread as far afield as Morocco, Norway, and, nine days after Dominic's death, Oxford. Dominic insisted that his order maintain its poverty, and often ripped up deeds of land bequeathed to it. Rather than have his friars touch money, he proposed the appointment of business managers for each monastery, but in keeping with the democratic spirit of the order, his proposal was rejected. The Dominicans, as zealous defenders of the church, were also prominent in staffing the Inquisition.

Even in his lifetime Dominic was the focus of cultic veneration; legends spread crediting him with numerous miracles, among them the resurrection of the dead. The devotion of the rosary was ascribed to a revelation of the Virgin Mary to him. Dominic was buried in Bologna; his tomb was later adorned by Michelangelo. At Dominic's canonization (1234), Pope Gregory IX declared that he doubted his saintliness no more than he doubted that of Peter and Paul. The feast of Saint Dominic is celebrated on August 4. ◆

> Dominic insisted that his order maintain its poverty, and often ripped up deeds of land bequeathed to it.

Eddy, Mary Baker

1821–1910 ● CHRISTIAN SCIENCE

Mary Baker Eddy was an American religious leader and the founder of Christian Science. Along with a growing interest in feminine spirituality within the Christian tradition, late- twentieth-century scholarship has begun to reassess the work and character of Mary Baker Eddy. Academic perceptions of her have generally been slow to catch up with insights provided by biographical studies. This is largely traceable to the persistence of one-sided portrayals, both negative and positive, going back to controversies generated in Eddy's own lifetime. Not only did she initiate a radical religious teaching that claimed to cut through centuries of orthodoxy to the living power of the gospel, but she also organized and led the Christian Science movement as a woman within a male-dominated society.

Eddy always remained a child of the American Puritan tradition in which she was raised in rural New Hampshire. There the influence of a deep-seated Puritan piety in the theological tradition of Jonathan Edwards prevailed over the liberalizing tendencies that were shaping so much of American religious life. The toughness and resilience reflected in her leadership of the Christian Science movement were expressions of the vein of "puritan iron" in her nature.

At the same time, the independence of Eddy's nature was observable in her youthful revolt against the stark Calvinistic view of God as foredooming a major portion of the human race to eternal damnation. Later, the same tendency toward revolt was to become apparent in her rejection of the view of God as permitting any human suffering whatever. Unable to abandon her thoroughly ingrained belief in God's sovereignty or her equally strong conviction of God's goodness and love, she was to advance in Christian Science a radical interpretation of the gospel through a new concept of God's relation to humanity.

Eddy's path to what she was to call the "discovery" of Christian Science led her through 20 years of personal loss and suffering, which included the deaths of several family members (including her husband), enforced separation from her only child, an unsuccessful second marriage, and bouts of increasing nervous debility and acute, if ill-defined, physical suffering.

Through the investigation of various healing methods in her search for health, Eddy came to believe that the cause of disease lay in the mind, a belief reinforced by her contact with a Maine healer named Phineas Quimby, to whom she appealed for aid in 1862. Eddy's own thinking, however, was not basically shaped by Quimby's views, which were rooted in mesmerism, but by the New Testament Christianity to which she had always clung. She saw the gospel in a new light after a healing following a severe accident in 1866, a cure that she attributed to a moment of profound illumination upon reading an account of one of Jesus' healings in *Matthew*. That experience marked a turning point in her life. It led to nine years of scriptural study, healing activity, and teaching, culminating in 1875 with the publication of *Science and Health with Key to the Scriptures*. Eddy considered that book to contain the statement of the "science" that underlay Jesus' works and of the method that make those works repeatable.

Eddy was, however, quickly disabused of what she was to call her "sanguine hope" that the Christian churches would readily accept Christian Science. The beginnings of her pioneering efforts in the mill towns of Massachusetts were bleak and inauspicious; she attracted only a few followers during her first decade of work. In 1877 Eddy married for the third time, and relied on her husband for moral support from this time until his death five years later.

In 1879 Eddy and a small band of followers founded the Church of Christ, Scientist, which began to take shape when she moved to Boston two years later. There she continued to write, teach, and preach, and to defend the movement against both internal schism and external attack, launching Christian Science as a significant movement in American religious life.

The strong opposition she encountered, as well as the defection of followers who found the discipline of Christian Science too severe, actually brought increased authority to her leadership. This increase in authority in turn aroused charges of authoritarianism and paranoia. She herself used the image of a "lioness robbed of her young" to describe her efforts in the 1880s to prevent Christian Science from being distorted beyond recognition by those who borrowed her language to promote what she saw as an essentially non-Christian form of "mind-cure." Eddy strongly disavowed that Christian Science healing was produced in any way by mental suggestion. She did, however, insistently warn that hatred projected through mental suggestion could have destructive effects—a view that intensified the controversy she aroused.

As Christian Science gradually became a widespread religious movement, Eddy found it necessary to devise an institution effective enough to protect and perpetuate her teachings. In 1889 she suspended the operations of existing national Christian Science organizations in order to thoroughly reorganize the church, which took its present form in 1892 as the First Church of Christ, Scientist, in Boston, the "mother" church of Christian Science branch churches throughout the world. Three years later she published *Manual of The Mother Church*, a slim body of rules for governing the denomination, rules that she continued to revise to the end of her life.

Eddy was often accorded somewhat backhanded praise for displaying an organizational genius more generally associated with men. Yet her struggles to institutionalize her teaching without becoming submerged in bureaucracy were severe and were accompanied in the last two decades of her life by episodes of intense physical suffering. Her recognition of the need

1821 Eddy is born into a Puritan family.

1862 Eddy appeals to a Maine healer for help.

1866 Eddy, healed of severe injuries, sees the gospel in a new light.

1875 Eddy publishes *Science and Health with Key to the Scriptures*.

1877 Eddy marries for the third time.

1879 Eddy founds the Church of Christ, Scientist.

1889 Eddy suspends operations of her organization in order to reorganize.

1892 Eddy's church is renamed the First Church of Christ, Scientist.

1895 Eddy publishes *Manual of the Mother Church*.

1908 Eddy founds *The Christian Science Monitor*.

to relate Christian Science more effectively to the world gave impetus to her last major achievement, the founding in 1908 of the widely respected newspaper *The Christian Science Monitor*.

By the time of her death, Eddy was commanding international attention. Her view that mortality was not part of God-centered reality, which is spiritual, put her thinking at variance with conventional theological formulations. This view and the healing practice that grew out of it have aroused sometimes bitter antagonism on the part of the clergy as well as the medical profession. Nonetheless, Mary Baker Eddy's significance in the stream of Christian thought and the appeal of Christian Science itself lie in the fact that they have offered a new basis for the credibility of Christian claims to truth and have provided a new religious alternative for many people. ◆

> "Disease is an experience of so-called mortal mind. It is fear made manifest on the body."
> Mary Baker Eddy, *Science and Health with Key to the Scriptures*, 1875

Edwards, Jonathan

1703–1758 ● PURITAN

Jonathan Edwards was one of the most important theologians, or religious thinkers, in the British colonies. By challenging some of the Puritans' practices, he played an important role in launching a religious revival known as the Great Awakening.

Born in East Windsor, Connecticut, Edwards was the son of a minister and the grandson of Solomon Stoddard, one of the most famous and powerful Puritan preachers in New England. Edwards entered Yale College when he was not quite 13 years old. After receiving his bachelor's and master's degrees, he had a deeply religious experience that prompted him to follow in the footsteps of his father and grandfather and become a minister.

Edwards served briefly as a pastor in New York City, then returned to Yale as a tutor. In 1726 he left to become his grandfather's assistant at a church in Northampton, Massachusetts, the most important Puritan church outside of Boston. When Solomon Stoddard died two years later, Edwards took over his ministry. In 1731, at the invitation of Puritan officials in Boston, the young minister delivered a forceful public sermon, which earned him almost immediate recognition as a commanding speaker and religious thinker.

> "There is no want of power in God to cast wicked men into hell at any moment. Men's hands cannot be strong when God rises up. The strongest have no power to resist him, nor can any deliver out of his hands."
> Jonathan Edwards, *Sinners in the Hands of an Angry God*, 1741

Edwards's emotional preaching helped bring about a brief but intense religious revival in the Connecticut River valley in the mid-1730s. Hundreds of colonists renewed their faith and restored their bonds to their churches. This revival, known as the "Little Awakening," was the first stage of the Great Awakening, a religious movement that swept through the British colonies in the early 1740s. Though not alone in launching this religious renewal, Edwards's fiery preaching contributed to its early success. In 1741 he delivered a sermon in Connecticut called "Sinners in the Hands of an Angry God"—perhaps the most famous sermon in American history. In it, Edwards used frightful images of fire and floods to emphasize the idea that sinners can be saved only through the grace of God's will, not by their own good deeds.

After the Great Awakening calmed down somewhat, Edwards continued to encourage highly emotional religious experiences. At the same time, he was a stern minister who demanded rigid orthodoxy of his followers. His relationship with his own congregation became strained, primarily because of his unyielding views on church membership. Edwards was opposed to allowing anyone who wanted salvation to join the church. He insisted that only the genuinely faithful, those chosen for salvation, could participate in Communion and other religious rituals. This view created great controversy in his congregation and led to his dismissal in 1750.

Edwards spent most of the remaining years of his life in western Massachusetts. In 1751 he accepted a position as minister of a frontier church in Stockbridge, Massachusetts, where he directed missionary work among the Indians. Despite the hardships of frontier life and the responsibilities of his ministry, Edwards wrote several important books during this time, including *A Careful and Strict Inquiry into . . . Freedom of Will* (1754). In 1757 Edwards became president of the College of New Jersey (now Princeton University), but he died only a few months after arriving at the college. Jonathan Edwards had tremendous influence on the religious thinking of colonial America. As the foremost theologian of his time, he combined traditional Puritan beliefs with the ideas of Enlightenment writers, who believed that the universe was governed by laws that could be explained by reason. Emphasizing personal religious experience, Edwards focused on such issues as original sin, free will, and the need for grace. ◆

"The wrath of God burns against them, their damnation does not slumber; the pit is prepared, the fire is made ready, the furnace is now hot, ready to receive them; the flames do now rage and glow. The glittering sword is whet, and held over them, and the pit hath opened its mouth under them."

Jonathan Edwards, *Sinners in the Hands of an Angry God*, 1741

Elaw, Zilpha

c. 1790–c. 1845 ● Methodist

Zilpha Elaw was an African-American Methodist preacher who wrote a moving autobiography, which remains the only known source of information about her life. She was born in Pennsylvania around 1790 to free parents and grew up in the area near Philadelphia. (Because she only referred to herself by her married name, Elaw, in her *Memoirs*, her original family name is unknown.) After her mother's death in 1802 Elaw went to live with the Mitchels, a Quaker family, as a servant. Distressed about their lack of outward religious expression, she underwent a conversion experience at age 14 in which, while she milked a cow, Christ appeared to her. She felt this to be a genuine experience because even the cow seemed to sense the vision. She later joined the Methodist Episcopal Church.

Upon leaving the Mitchels in 1808, Elaw continued to practice Methodism. In 1810 she married Joseph Elaw, a garment worker. About two years later she had a daughter. Although she tried to respect her husband's wishes, his lack of piety led to conflicts. He sought to curtail her religious activities and tried to induce her to go to a ballroom in Philadelphia, which she thought sinful. Despite these obstacles, in 1817 she went to a camp meeting. Here she found spiritual companionship with other women and African Americans as pious as she. As time went on, Elaw regularly felt God's presence in her life: she often had visions of angels giving her advice. At one point when she was very ill, Elaw had a vision of a spirit who told her to preach. She hesitated until she attended another camp meeting, when she was moved to preach. Although some of the white clergy encouraged her, the reaction of the black members of her church to the exhorting was less than enthusiastic. A congregation nevertheless grew up around her in Burlington, New Jersey. Elaw was forced to give up preaching when her husband died in 1823. At first she secured domestic positions for herself and her daughter, but the work proved harmful to her health. She then founded a school for black children in Burlington with the help of Quaker donations.

In 1828, feeling as if she were ignoring the will of God, Elaw resumed preaching. Without denominational or congre-

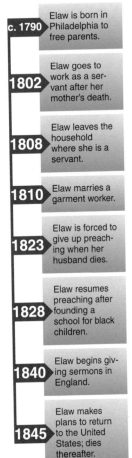

c. 1790 ▶ Elaw is born in Philadelphia to free parents.

1802 ▶ Elaw goes to work as a servant after her mother's death.

1808 ▶ Elaw leaves the household where she is a servant.

1810 ▶ Elaw marries a garment worker.

1823 ▶ Elaw is forced to give up preaching when her husband dies.

1828 ▶ Elaw resumes preaching after founding a school for black children.

1840 ▶ Elaw begins giving sermons in England.

1845 ▶ Elaw makes plans to return to the United States; dies thereafter.

gational support, she journeyed to the slave states, impressing a widely diverse group of white and black Southerners with her preaching abilities, despite the dangers accompanying her travels as a black woman. After her tour of the South she continued to preach in the Northeast until she responded to a call to preach in England. From 1840 to 1845, Elaw delivered over a thousand sermons in central England. In 1845 Elaw began to make plans to return to the United States. However, since her autobiography breaks off at this point, we have no further information about Elaw's life. Nevertheless, her *Memoirs* remain an exceptional document of African-American women's role in shaping American religion, particularly African-American Christianity. ◆

Essrog, Seymour

1933– ● JEWISH

Seymour Leo Essrog, a Conservative rabbi, was born in New York City on October 22, 1933, the son of Morris Essrog and Sadie Pluznick Essrog. In 1955 he received a bachelor of arts degree from Yeshiva University in New York City. In 1959 Essrog obtained a master of Hebrew letters degree at Yeshiva and was ordained a rabbi there the same year. Eight years later he was awarded a master of liberal arts degree from Johns Hopkins University.

Essrog is a rabbi in the Conservative movement. Like Reform Judaism, from which it split away in the late nineteenth century, Conservative Judaism regards the Jewish religion as an evolving one. But unlike Reform Jews, who place more stress on ethics than on traditional practices, Conservative Jews preserve most of those practices.

After his rabbinical ordination, Essrog served as U.S. Army chaplain at Fort Eustis, Virginia, from 1959 to 1961. He then became rabbi at the Beth Israel Congregation in Randallstown, Maryland, where he served for over 30 years. Since then, he has been rabbi at the Beth Shalom Congregation in Carroll County, Maryland.

Essrog has served as president of the Jewish Community Council in Baltimore, the Maryland Region of the Jewish National Fund, and the Baltimore Board of Rabbis. At the na-

1933 Essrog is born in New York City.

1955 Essrog receives a bachelor or arts degree from Yeshiva University.

1959 Essrog receives master of Hebrew letters degree and becomes a rabbi and U.S. Army chaplain.

1968 Essrog receives master of liberal arts degree.

1980 Essrog becomes a member of the Maryland Values Education Commission.

1990 Essrog becomes Rabbinical Assembly's international conventions chairman.

1998 Essrog becomes Rabbinical Assembly's 48th president.

tional level, he has served on the executive council of both the Rabbinic Cabinets of Israel Bonds and the United Jewish Appeal. Essrog is past chairman of the Community Council of Central Maryland Sudden Infant Death Syndrome Center of the University of Maryland Medical School. In 1980, Maryland governor Harry Hughes appointed Essrog to the Values Education Commission of the Maryland State Board of Education. Ten years later Essrog received the Harry Greenstein Memorial Award from the Board of Jewish Education of Baltimore for distinguished service in Jewish Education and Community Service.

Closely identifying with the state of Israel, Essrog has led more than two dozen trips to the Jewish state. The Israeli government's Tourist Office has presented to him the Shalom Award for his efforts to promote tourism to Israel. Essrog has also gone on fact-finding missions to Jewish communities in the former Soviet Union, Poland, Morocco, Turkey, Egypt, Romania, Hungary, and Czechoslovakia. Essrog is a vice president of MERCAZ USA, the Zionist organization of the Conservative movement.

Essrog has held many posts in the Rabbinical Assembly, the international association of Conservative rabbis, and in 1990 and 1991 he was chairman of its international conventions. In February 1998 he became its forty-eighth president. One of Essrog's major concerns in his new post is promoting Conservative Judaism in Israel, where the Orthodox rabbinate has fought to preserve its virtual monopoly on religious practice.

While president of the Rabbinical Assembly, Essrog has taken stands on social and political issues that can be described as liberal. In 1998 he urged Congress to sustain President Bill Clinton's veto of a bill to ban "partial-birth" abortions, arguing that abortion is a personal issue that women should be permitted to make without the interference of politicians. In January 1999 he called upon the Senate to censure President Clinton rather than remove him from office for perjury and obstruction of justice. ◆

Farrakhan, Louis

1933– ● MUSLIM

Louis Eugene Walcott was born in the Bronx, New York, but was raised in Boston by his West Indian mother. Deeply religious, Walcott faithfully attended the Episcopalian church in his neighborhood and became an altar boy. With the rigorous discipline provided by his mother and his church, he did fairly well academically and graduated with honors from the prestigious Boston English High School, where he also participated on the track team and played the violin in the school orchestra. In 1953, after two years at the Winston-Salem Teachers College in North Carolina, he dropped out to pursue his favorite avocation of music and made it his first career. An accomplished violinist, pianist, and vocalist, Walcott performed professionally on the Boston nightclub circuit as a singer of calypso and country songs. In 1955, at the age of 22, Louis Walcott was recruited by Malcolm X for the Nation of Islam. Following its custom, he dropped his surname and took an X, which meant "undetermined." However, it was not until he had met Elijah Muhammad, the supreme leader of the Nation of Islam, on a visit to the Chicago headquarters that Louis X converted and dedicated his life to building the Nation. After proving himself for ten years, Elijah Muhammad gave Louis his Muslim name, "Abdul Farrakhan," in May 1965. As a rising star within the Nation, Farrakhan also wrote the only song, the popular "A White Man's Heaven is a Black

> "We must accept the responsibility that God has put upon us, not only to be good husbands and fathers and builders of our community, but God is now calling upon the despised and the rejected to become the cornerstone and the builders of a new world."
>
> Louis Farrakhan, remarks at the Million Man March, Washington, D.C., 1995

129

1933 Farrakhan is born in the Bronx to a West Indian mother.

1953 Farrakhan drops out of college after two years to be a musician.

1955 Farrakhan is recruited by Malcolm X for the Nation of Islam.

1964 Farrakhan is appointed National Spokesman when Malcolm leaves.

1965 Farrakhan is given the Muslim name Abdul Farrakhan.

1975 Farrakhan leaves the New York Mosque.

1978 Farrakhan forms a new organization, also called Nation of Islam.

1979 Farrakhan begins printing editions of *Final Call.*

1984 Farrakhan supports Jesse Jackson's campaign for presidency.

Man's Hell," and the only dramatic play, *Orgena* ("A Negro" spelled backward), endorsed by Mr. Muhammad.

After a nine-month apprenticeship with Malcolm X at Temple No. 7 in Harlem, Minister Louis X was appointed as the head minister of the Boston Temple No. 11, which Malcolm founded. Later, after Malcolm X had split with the Nation, Farrakhan was awarded Malcolm's Temple No. 7, the most important pastorate in the Nation after the Chicago headquarters. He was also appointed National Spokesman or National Representative after Malcolm left the Nation in 1964 and began to introduce Elijah Muhammad at Savior Day rallies, a task that had once belonged to Malcolm. Like his predecessor, Farrakhan is a dynamic and charismatic leader and a powerful speaker with an ability to appeal to masses of black people.

In February 1975, when Elijah Muhammad died, the Nation of Islam experienced its largest schism. Wallace Dean Muhammad, the fifth of Elijah's six sons, was surprisingly chosen as supreme minister by the leadership hierarchy. In April 1975 Wallace, who later took the Muslim title and name of Imam Warith Deen Muhammad, made radical changes in the Nation of Islam, gradually moving the group toward orthodox Sunni Islam. In 1975 Farrakhan left the New York Mosque. Until 1978 Farrakhan, who had expected to be chosen as Elijah's successor, kept silent in public and traveled extensively in Muslim countries, where he found a need to recover the focus upon race and black nationalism that the Nation had emphasized. Other disaffected leaders and followers had already formed splinter Nation of Islam groups-Silas Muhammad in Atlanta, John Muhammad in Detroit, and Caliph in Baltimore. In 1978, Farrakhan formed a new organization, also called the Nation of Islam, resurrecting the teachings, ideology, and organizational structure of Elijah Muhammad, and he began to rebuild his base of followers by making extensive speaking tours in black communities. Farrakhan claimed it was his organization, not that of Wallace Muhammad, that was the legitimate successor to the old Nation of Islam.

In 1979, Farrakhan began printing editions of *The Final Call,* a name he resurrected from early copies of a newspaper that Elijah Muhammad had put out in Chicago in 1934. The "final call" was a call to black people to return to Allah as incarnated in Master Fard Muhammad or Master Fard and witnessed by his apostle Elijah Muhammad. For Farrakhan, the final call has an eschatological dimension; it is the last call, the last chance for black people to achieve their liberation.

Farrakhan became known to the American public via a series of controversies which were stirred when he first supported the Rev. Jesse Jackson's 1984 presidential campaign. His Fruit of Islam guards provided security for Jackson. After Jackson's offhand, seemingly anti-Semitic remarks about New York City as "Hymietown" became a campaign issue, Farrakhan threatened to ostracize *Washington Post* reporter Milton Coleman, who had released the story in the black community. Farrakhan has also become embroiled in a continuing controversy with the American Jewish community by making anti-Semitic statements. Farrakhan has argued that his statements were misconstrued. Furthermore, he contends that a distorted media focus on this issue has not adequately covered the achievements of his movement.

Farrakhan's Nation of Islam has been successful in getting rid of drug dealers in a number of public housing projects and private apartment buildings; a national private security agency for hire, manned by the Fruit of Islam, has been established. The Nation has been at the forefront of organizing a peace pact between gang members in Los Angeles and several other cities. They have established a clinic for the treatment of AIDS patients in Washington, D.C. A cosmetics company, Clean and Fresh, has marketed its products in the black community. Moreover, they have continued to reach out to reform black people with the Nation's traditional dual emphases: self-identity, to know yourself; and economic independence, to do for yourself. Under Farrakhan's leadership, the Nation has allowed its members to participate in electoral politics and to run for office, actions that were forbidden under Elijah Muhammad. He has also allowed women to become ministers and public leaders in the Nation, which places his group ahead of all the orthodox Muslim groups in giving women equality. Although the core of Farrakhan's Nation of Islam continues to be about 20,000 members, his influence is much greater, attracting crowds of 40,000 or more in speeches across the country. His group is the fastest growing of the various Muslim movements, largely through the influence of rap groups like Public Enemy and Prince Akeem. International branches have been formed in Ghana, London, and the Caribbean. In the United States throughout the 1990s, however, Farrakhan has remained an immensely controversial figure. ◆

> Farrakhan became known to the American public via a series of controversies which were stirred when he first supported the Rev. Jesse Jackson's 1984 presidential campaign.

Father Divine

c. 1880–1965 ● CHRISTIAN

Father Divine was a leading African American Christian preacher. Born George Baker to ex-slaves in Rockville, Maryland, he endured poverty and segregation as a child. At age 20 he moved to Baltimore, where he taught Sunday school and preached in storefront churches. In 1912, he began an itinerant ministry, focusing on the South. He attracted a small following and, pooling his disciples' earnings, moved north and purchased a home in 1919 in the exclusively white Long Island community of Sayville, New York. He opened his doors to the unemployed and homeless.

By 1931, thousands were flocking to worship services in his home, and his white neighbors grew hostile. In November they summoned police, who arrested him for disturbing the peace and maintaining a public nuisance. Found guilty, he received the maximum fine and a sentence of one year in jail. Four days later, the sentencing judge died.

The judge's sudden death catapulted Father Divine into the limelight. Some saw it as evidence of his great powers; others viewed it as sinister retribution. Although Father Divine denied responsibility for the death, the incident aroused curiosity, and throughout the 1930s the news media continued to report on his activities.

Father Divine's Peace Mission Movement grew, establishing extensions throughout the United States and in major cities abroad. He relocated his headquarters to Harlem, where he guided the movement, conducted worship services, and ran an employment agency. During the Great Depression, the movement opened businesses and sponsored a national network of relief shelters, furnishing thousands of poor people with food, clothes, and jobs.

Father Divine's appeal derived from his unique theology, a mixture of African-American folk religion, Methodism, Catholicism, Pentecostalism, and the ideology based on the power of positive thinking, New Thought. He encouraged followers to believe that he was God, to channel his spirit to generate health, prosperity, and salvation. He demanded they adhere to a strict moral code, abstaining from sexual intercourse and alcohol. Disciples cut family ties and assumed new names. His worship services included a banquet of endless courses, symbolizing his access to abundance. His mind-power theology attracted many, especially those suffering from racism and economic dislocation, giving disciples a sense of control over their destinies in a time filled with chaos and confusion.

His social programs also drew followers. Although rigid rules governed the movement's shelters, they were heavily patronized. An integrationist, Father Divine campaigned for civil rights, attracting both African-American and Euramerican disciples. Challenging American racism, he required followers to live and work in integrated pairs.

With economic recovery in the 1940s, Father Divine's message lost much of its appeal; membership in the movement declined and Peace Missions closed. In 1946 he made headlines with his marriage to a white disciple named Sweet Angel. He spent his declining years grooming her for leadership. Upon his death in 1965, she assumed control of the movement, contending that Father Divine had not died but had surrendered his body, preferring to exist as a spirit. The movement perseveres with a small number of followers and businesses in the Philadelphia area. ◆

> "Without a righteous judgment, mankind would start a revolutionary war, and would overthrow the different governments as they stand, but with the right concept and the recognition of God's presence, we will not overthrow them, but we will transform them."
>
> Father Divine, 1935

Fools Crow, Frank

c. 1890–1989 ● NATIVE AMERICAN

Frank Fools Crow was a Lakota Sioux Indian spiritual leader and medicine man. He became known for helping negotiate a peace during the occupation of Wounded Knee in 1973. He also became the first Native American holy man to lead the opening prayer for a session of the United States Senate in 1975.

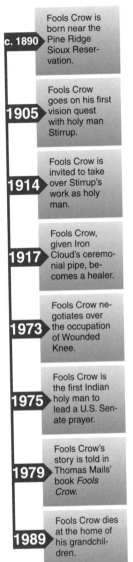

c. 1890 Fools Crow is born near the Pine Ridge Sioux Reservation.

1905 Fools Crow goes on his first vision quest with holy man Stirrup.

1914 Fools Crow is invited to take over Stirrup's work as holy man.

1917 Fools Crow, given Iron Cloud's ceremonial pipe, becomes a healer.

1973 Fools Crow negotiates over the occupation of Wounded Knee.

1975 Fools Crow is the first Indian holy man to lead a U.S. Senate prayer.

1979 Fools Crow's story is told in Thomas Mails' book *Fools Crow*.

1989 Fools Crow dies at the home of his grandchildren.

The exact date of Frank Fools Crow's birth is unknown, but it is believed to have been 1890 or 1891. He was born near the Pine Ridge Sioux Indian Reservation in South Dakota. Ten years earlier, his people suffered through one of the most notorious events in American Indian history, the massacre of up to 300 Lakota Sioux Indians by U.S. Army troops in 1890. The incident became known as the Massacre of Wounded Knee or the Battle of Wounded Knee.

The name Fools Crow came from Frank's paternal grandfather, Knife Chief, whose eldest son died by the hands of Crow Indians. Frank's father and his grandparents raised him in traditional Lakota ways. Frank did not attend school beyond the third grade, but two men gave him much of his education. One was his uncle Iron Cloud, a Lakota leader, and the other was a well-known holy man named Stirrup. At the age of 13, when Frank felt a strong urge to become a medicine man, his father took him to Stirrup, who became Frank's teacher. In 1905, Stirrup took Fools Crow on his first vision quest to receive his spiritual teachers. Vision quests are traditional Indian spiritual initiations in which a young person undergoes a ceremony to find a guardian spirit. They sometimes go without food and sleep or venture alone into the wilderness. Fools Crow found at this time that he possessed spiritual power. In 1914, Stirrup asked Frank's father to approve his choice of Frank to take over his work as a holy man.

A turning point in Fools Crow's life occurred in 1917, when Iron Cloud, who died several days later, gave him a ceremonial pipe. From that point, Fools Crow felt he was destined to heal people, and he began that work. He lived the life of a medicine man, which is supposed to be free of such behaviors as drinking, womanizing, or fighting. Although the Sun Dance of the Oglala Sioux had been outlawed by the U.S. government in 1881, Fools Crow acknowledged that it was secretly held nearly every year. The Sun Dance was a four-day ceremony in which young men dance around a pole, sometimes with a long pin inserted through cuts in the dancers' chest or back muscles. Leather ropes connected to the pins are attached to the pole or to buffalo skulls dragged behind the dancers. Dancers may have visions and gain sacred power. The Bureau of Indian Affairs had authorized some aspects of the ceremony, and in 1952, Fools Crow was allowed to pierce the young men if he assumed responsibility for negative consequences.

In the 1920s, Fools Crow participated in the Buffalo Bill Cody Wild West show and traveled throughout Europe and the United States. He appeared in a movie called *War Bonnet* and helped publicize Western movies.

Fools Crow took over leadership from his father of the Porcupine District of the Pine Ridge Reservation, which involved him in tribal politics. In 1973, about 200 armed Indians occupied Wounded Knee, a village on the reservation. The occupation resulted from a dispute over tribal leadership and was also a protest against the federal government's violation of treaties with Indians. During the occupation, Fools Crow negotiated with federal officials and with Native American protesters. He relayed a document from the federal officials outlining a settlement of the crisis. When both sides signed the agreement, the occupation ended. It had lasted 71 days and led to 2 deaths and over 300 arrests.

In September 1975, Fools Crow led a large group of Lakota to Washington, D.C., to discuss issues with government officials and with the president. While there, on September 5 he led the opening prayer for the U.S. Senate, the first Indian holy man to do so.

Fools Crow told his life story to Thomas E. Mails, who published *Fools Crow* in 1979. Fools Crow had five children. His first wife, Fannie Afraid, died in 1954, and his second wife, Kate, died in 1988. Fools Crow died November 28, 1989, at the home of his grandchildren. ◆

> In the 1920s, Fools Crow participated in the Buffalo Bill Cody Wild West show and traveled throughout Europe and the United States.

Forbes, James A.

1935– ● PROTESTANT

D r. James A. Forbes, senior minister of the Riverside Church in New York City, was born in the town of Burgaw, North Carolina, in 1935. He was raised in the Baptist Church, and early on he discovered that he had a calling to the ministry. Nonetheless, as a young man he initially pursued an education in science, earning his undergraduate degree in chemistry from Howard University in 1957. It was not long, however, before he responded to his lifelong calling. By 1960 he had taken up the role of minister, returning to North

1935 Forbes is born.

1957 Forbes receives his undergraduate degree in chemistry.

1960 Forbes begins serving as pastor in North Carolina.

1962 Forbes earns a Union Theological Seminary Master of Divinity.

1968 Forbes receives the Clinical Pastoral Education Certificate.

1975 Forbes earns his Doctor of Ministry degree.

1976 Forbes accepts a preaching professorship at UTS.

1983 Forbes receives the first of what will be 12 honorary degrees.

1985 Forbes is named UTS Professor of Preaching.

1989 Forbes becomes Senior Minister at Riverside Church.

1995 Forbes is named one of 12 most effective English-speaking preachers.

Carolina to serve as pastor at the Holy Trinity Church in Wilmington and at St. Paul's Holy Church in Roxboro. At the same time, he embarked upon formal religious training at Union Theological Seminary in New York City, where he earned the Master of Divinity in 1962.

It was during his pastorate in North Carolina that Forbes truly developed his skills as preacher and pastor, and where his charismatic style earned him respect within the religious community. In 1965 he left his position at Holy Trinity Church to assume pastoral duties at St. John's United Holy Church of America, in Richmond, Virginia, while continuing to serve his Roxboro, North Carolina, congregation. To these responsibilities he added a third, in 1968, when he took on the role of campus minister at Virginia Union University. In that same year he earned his third academic credential, the Clinical Pastoral Education Certificate, granted by the Medical College of Virginia in Richmond, Virginia.

By the end of the 1960s Forbes had already distinguished himself as a gifted preacher and pastor. He nonetheless felt it important to deepen his formal training in religion. To free up his schedule to accommodate a return to graduate school he left his pastorate at St. Paul's Holy Church in 1969 and resigned from the Virginia Union campus ministry in the following year so that he could devote himself to his studies at Colgate-Rochester Divinity School. In 1975 that school conferred upon him the Doctor of Ministry.

With his skills and training, it was only to be expected that Forbes would soon be called upon to teach, and in 1976 he accepted an appointment as the Brown and Sockman Associate Professor of Preaching at Union Theological Seminary, where he had earned his Masters degree. He so distinguished himself that in 1983 he received the first of his 12 honorary degrees—Dickinson College, in Carlisle, Pennsylvania, granted him an honorary Doctorate of Sacred Theology. In 1985 he was named the Joe R. Engle Professor of Preaching at Union Theological.

In addition to fulfilling his pastoral responsibilities and pursuing his education, Forbes has always been strongly ecumenical in his outlook. He has led workshops, retreats, and conferences for a broad spectrum of Christian organizations, including the National Council of Churches of Christ USA, the National Association of Campus Ministry, the American Baptist Churches, the United Church of Christ, the African Methodist Episcopal Church, the Christian Church (Disciples of Christ), the Episcopal Church, the United Methodist Church, the Presbyterian Church (USA), and the Roman Catholic Church.

Throughout the 1980s, Forbes continued to distinguish himself as an educator, preacher, and public speaker. In 1986 he was invited by Yale University to give a series of lectures (the Lyman Beecher Lecture) which were later published as *The Holy Spirit and Preaching* (1989). In that same year he received another honorary doctorate, this time from the Protestant Episcopal Theological Seminary. By this time he had earned the respect of both the national and international religious communities.

On June 1, 1989, Forbes took up his current position as Senior Minister at the Riverside Church, an interdenominational church established in 1927 with funds that were provided by John D. Rockefeller Jr. His background is uniquely suited to Riverside, which is committed to welcoming and celebrating diversity among its membership and to activism for the betterment of society. Throughout the next decades he continued to garner honors and honorary degrees. His reputation as a "preacher's preacher" continued to grow, and in 1995 he was named one of the 12 most effective preachers in the English-speaking world. He has committed himself to the cause of social justice for all, to education, and to the urban ministry. ◆

> "My work has been guided by the strong conviction that moral and religious revitalization is necessary if our great nation is to fulfill its destiny as a leader among nations in the next century. However, religious revitalization can only come from the people and from their religious institutions, not from government."
>
> James A. Forbes, Jr., 1995

Fox, George

1624–1691 ● QUAKER

George Fox was the English founder of the Society of Friends, or Quakers. The son of a Puritan weaver in Leicestershire, Fox was apprenticed to a cobbler who kept sheep. He lived in a time and place very preoccupied with religion; tending sheep gave him time to brood over religious matters. He felt that Christianity had failed if Christians could indulge in excesses, and left home to travel the country and seek answers to his spiritual doubts and questions.

Fox turned inward and had a religious revelation that gave him the answers he had been seeking; everyone has a divine light in his heart which will guide him if he but listens; no one

is holier than anyone else. Fox felt that his belief revived primitive Christianity after ages of apostasy, and that an individual's revelation from the divine light within is as sacred as the revelation that produced the Bible. He rejected prearranged form, external sacraments, and consecrated buildings.

His gospel of the brotherhood and equality of man led to Quakers becoming fervent social reformers. He advocated reform of the penal code and prison conditions, abolition of capital punishment, education for both men and women (women had equality with men in his organization), payment of a living wage, serving honestly, and treating slaves well. All people were ministers, for "to be bred at Oxford or Cambridge was not sufficient to fit a man to be a Minister of Christ."

Fox began to preach, traveling about on foot, and establishing small local congregations. At first (1648 - 1652), his followers were few and his attacks on established religious authority and ritual sometimes led to his being stoned and beaten. His insistence on addressing everyone as "thee" instead of using the plural pronoun "you" to people of high rank, his refusal to doff his hat (a gesture of reverence he reserved for God), or take oaths, offended people of authority and rank; they felt it showed a lack of respect, and such actions and omissions led to many beatings and imprisonments for Fox and his followers.

In 1649 Fox was imprisoned for the first time—he was imprisoned eight times between 1649 and 1673—when he interrupted the minister preaching in Nottingham Church. Fox was accused of blasphemy and imprisoned for a year (1650). For telling the magistrates to tremble at the name of the Lord he received the nickname "Quaker." His jailers were so impressed by his preaching and conduct that he was soon allowed to preach and to attend meetings outside his prison. In one such instance he so impressed a group of soldiers that they offered him a captaincy which he rejected on the grounds that war was evil and unlawful and that Jesus's servants do not fight—earning himself six months in the felons' dungeon. In 1652 he won over large groups in Westmoreland, including Margaret Fell, who became his faithful follower and friend. During the Commonwealth, under Oliver Cromwell, Fox traveled and preached all over England and Scotland, was imprisoned four times, and had several meetings with Cromwell. A powerful and eloquent speaker, he inspired many men and women to become preachers and set out with missionary zeal to convert others.

The Restoration (1660) led to severe persecutions of the Quakers, who were suspected of plotting against the king. Fox was imprisoned four times, including a sentence of two and one-half years in a cold damp cell that ruined his health. He organized a formal Quaker network of monthly, quarterly and yearly meetings to discuss problems and to meet their business and religious needs.

Fox married Margaret Fell (1669) but, each busy with work for the Quakers, they were seldom together. Worn out, he spent his last 15 years living with different friends around London, an honored elder who preached, wrote, and was consulted on practical matters, and was overjoyed when the Toleration Act of 1689 brought relief to the Quakers. ◆

1624	Fox is born, the son of a Puritan weaver.
1648	Fox begins preaching.
1649	Fox is imprisoned for what will be the first of eight times.
1650	Fox is accused of blasphemy and imprisoned for a year.
1652	Fox wins over large groups in Westmoreland.
1669	Fox marries Margaret Fell, who became his follower in 1652.
1689	Fox is overjoyed when the Toleration Act brings relief to the Quakers.
1691	Fox dies.

Saint Francis of Assisi

1182–1226 ● CHRISTIAN

Saint Francis of Assisi (Francesco di Pietro di Bernardone) was the Italian founder of the Franciscan order. Called the **seraphic** or angelic saint, Saint Francis of Assisi was a leading figure in the movement for church reform in the thirteenth century. He founded three Franciscan orders: the monastic friars for men, the Poor Clares women, and a lay order for those who wanted to follow his teachings while remaining worldly.

Francis's father was a rich textile merchant in Assisi, Italy, and his mother was of cultured French descent: he was educated to read and write in Latin and until age 20 he assisted his father in business. Francis aspired to a martial reputation, and

seraphic: angelic saint; another name ascribed to St. Francis of Assisi

"When I was in sin the sight of lepers was too bitter for me. And the Lord himself led me among them, and I pitied and helped them. And when I left them I discovered that what had seemed bitter to me was changed into sweetness in my soul and body."

St. Francis, *Testament*, c. 1226

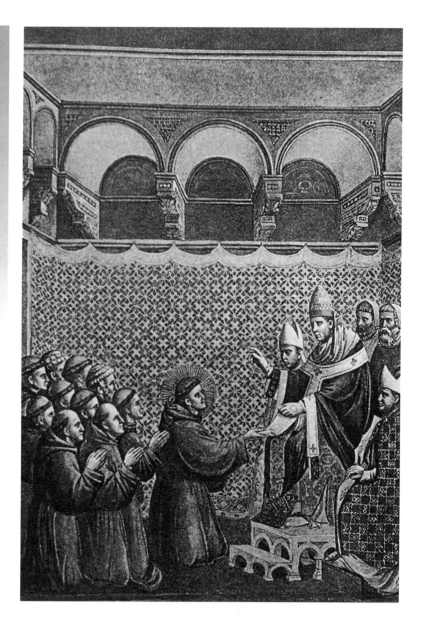

when Assisi entered into a dispute with neighboring Perugia in 1202 he joined the battle, but was captured and imprisoned by the Perugians for several months. After his release he fell seriously ill and this confinement brought him his first opportunity for deep spiritual self-examination.

A cluster of experiences resulting in Francis's conversion occurred at this time. On a pilgrimage to Rome he was moved to exchange clothes with a beggar and spend a day begging for alms. Theretofore disgusted by the lepers, he now gave them alms and kissed a leper's hand, expressing his feelings of universal humanity. Finally, he had a series of visions of Christ. In one of his visions Christ told Francis to "rebuild his house which is in ruins." Francis, who at that time was standing in the crumbling Chapel of Damiano outside Assisi, returned to his father's house. Collecting bolts of cloth, he loaded his father's horse and proceeded to another town, where he sold everything. He then returned to offer the money to the priest of the decrepit church. Francis's father tried to take him to the civil authorities but the youth would not obey. Proclaiming his only true father to be in heaven, Francis went off by himself to the wooded area around the city.

Having given up his possessions, Francis nevertheless managed to restore the Chapel of Damiano as well as two others around Assisi. Inspired by the surrender of property proclaimed by Christ to the Apostles, Francis committed himself to a life of poverty and began to preach as a layman to the people of his community. Soon a group of followers gathered around him, attracted by his character and kindness. In 1209 Francis, together with a dozen disciples, journeyed to Rome and received the verbal approval of Pope Innocent III to establish a new order.

Francis and his friars returned to the area of Assisi, basing themselves in Porziuncola and relying on the alms of the community for their survival. Their preaching followed the basic teachings of Christ and soon attracted many more adherents. Francis taught his followers to utterly deny the self, using whatever they were given to help others. He and his followers kept no possessions for themselves, even as communal property. In 1217 the order was organized by provinces, with supervising ministers.

Saint Francis's material poverty opened the way for a recognition of the common bond of every creature, all united in their dependence upon God. He spoke of every element and experience in creation as his brothers and sisters. Not only "brother sun" and "sister moon" but, toward the end of his life, suffering from a mortal sickness, he even wrote of "sister Death."

Francis set out for the Holy Land but was shipwrecked. During the next years he tried to reach the Moors in Spain in order to convert them but illness incapacitated him. In 1219 he went to Egypt on his way to the Holy Land and entered the camp of the Muslim Saracens. The sultan allowed him to pro-

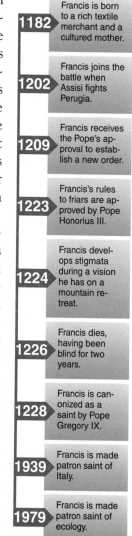

1182 Francis is born to a rich textile merchant and a cultured mother.

1202 Francis joins the battle when Assisi fights Perugia.

1209 Francis receives the Pope's approval to establish a new order.

1223 Francis's rules to friars are approved by Pope Honorius III.

1224 Francis develops stigmata during a vision he has on a mountain retreat.

1226 Francis dies, having been blind for two years.

1228 Francis is canonized as a saint by Pope Gregory IX.

1939 Francis is made patron saint of Italy.

1979 Francis is made patron saint of ecology.

The Basilica of St. Francis of Assisi

The Basilica of St. Francis of Assisi forms the religious heart of the town of Assisi in central Italy. Construction began on the basilica two years after St. Francis died. The structure consists of two churches, one above the other. The lower basilica was completed in 1230 in Romanesque style, and the body of Francis was entombed under its main altar. Many pilgrims traveled to visit the basilica, where they can view the saint's tunic and sandals. The upper basilica, built in Gothic style, was completed in 1236. Great Italian artists were asked to paint frescoes on its walls and ceilings. It is believed that artist Giotto painted the most important frescoes, portraying the life of Francis. Giotto was unique for his portrayal of lifelike figures through depth and shadowing.

In September 1997, an earthquake seriously damaged the basilica. Four people died when a huge segment of the painted ceiling crashed down. Although the upper church sustained serious damage, the lower level was less damaged and reopened two months later. Many volunteers worked to piece together more than 100,000 fresco fragments, but by mid-1999, less than 20 percent had been reassembled. Church authorities planned to reopen the upper basilica by 2000. It was uncertain whether the frescos would be reattached to the wall or if the fragments would be displayed in a museum.

ceed to Palestine, but when he reached the Holy Land he was forced to hurry home as word reached him that the friars in Italy, now numbering some 5,000, were locked in dispute over the direction the order was to take. The simplicity of Francis's rule of life had given but scanty guidance to the friars and he returned to Assisi to expand and clarify the rule of life laid down at the order's inception. This expanded rule was approved by Pope Honorius III in 1223, and with that Francis's involvement in the order waned progressively during the remainder of his life.

In the summer of 1224 Francis removed himself to a mountain retreat at La Verna near Assisi for the celebration of the Assumption of the Blessed Virgin Mary and in order to prepare himself for Saint Michael's Day. He planned a fast of 40 days, praying to know how best to serve God. As he prayed he was overwhelmed by a vision of Christ that inflamed his heart and left him with stigmata, wounds on his hands and feet similar to those of crucifixion. He suffered from these wounds for two years, hiding them from his followers, as well as being afflicted by near blindness until his death.

In 1228 he was canonized by Pope Gregory IX. In 1939 Saint Francis was made patron saint of Italy and in 1979 he became patron saint of ecology. ◆

Gandhi, Mohandas

1869–1948 ● Hindu

Mohandas Gandhi was a political leader, social reformer, and religious visionary of modern India. Although Gandhi initially achieved public notice as a leader of India's nationalist movement and as a champion of nonviolent techniques for resolving conflicts, he was also a religious innovator who did much to encourage the growth of a reformed, liberal Hinduism in India. In the West, Gandhi is venerated by many who seek an intercultural and socially conscious religion and see him as the representative of a universal faith.

Mohandas Karamchand Gandhi was born into a *bania* (merchant caste) family in a religiously pluralistic area of western India -the Kathiawar Peninsula in the state of Gujarat. His parents were Vaisnava Hindus who followed the tradition of loving devotion to Lord Krsna. His father, Karamchand Uttamchand, the chief administrative officer of a princely state, was not a very religious man, but his mother, Putalibai, became a follower of the region's popular Pranami cult. This group was founded in the eighteenth century by Mehraj Thakore, known as Prananath ("master of the life force"), and was influenced by Islam. Prananath rejected all images of God and, like the famous fifteenth-century Hindu saint Narsinh Mehta, who came from the same region, advocated a direct link with the divine, unmediated by priests and ritual. This Protestant form of Hinduism seems to have been accepted by Gandhi as normative throughout his life.

> "Nonviolence is the first article of my faith. It is also the last article of my creed."
> Mohandas Gandhi, 1922

Mohandas Gandhi

Other enduring religious influences from Gandhi's childhood came from the Jains and Muslims who frequented the family household. Gandhi's closest childhood friend, Mehtab, was a Muslim, and his spiritual mentor, Raychandbhai, was a Jain. Early contacts with Christian street evangelists in his home town of Porbandar, however, left Gandhi unimpressed.

When Gandhi went to London to study law at the age of 19 he encountered forms of Christianity of quite a different sort. Respecting vows made to his mother, Gandhi sought meatless fare at a vegetarian restaurant, where his fellow diners were a motley mix of Theosophists, Fabian Socialists, and Christian visionaries who were followers of Russian novelist Leo Tolstoy. These esoteric and socialist forms of Western spirituality made a deep impression on Gandhi and encouraged him to look for parallels in the Hindu tradition.

When, in 1893, Gandhi settled in South Africa as a lawyer (initially serving in a Muslim firm), he was impressed by a Trappist monastery he visited near Durban. He soon set up a series of ashrams (religious retreat centers) supported by Hermann Kallenbach, a South African architect of Jewish background, whom Gandhi had met through Theosophical circles. Gandhi named one of his communities Tolstoy Farm in honor of the Christian utopian with whom he had developed a lively correspondence. While in South Africa Gandhi first met C. F. Andrews, the Anglican missionary to India who had become an emissary of Indian nationalist leaders and who eventually became Gandhi's lifelong friend and confidant. It was through Andrews that Gandhi met the Indian poet Rabindranath Tagore in 1915, after Gandhi had returned to India to join the growing nationalist movement. Tagore, following the practice of Theosophists in South Africa, designated Gandhi a *mahatma*, or "great soul."

Although the influences on Gandhi's religious thought are varied—from the Sermon on the Mount to the *Bhagavadgita*—his ideas are surprisingly consistent. Gandhi considered them to be Hindu, and in fact, they are all firmly rooted in the Indian religious tradition. His main ideas include the following.

1. *Satya* ("truth"). Gandhi equated truth with God, implying that morality and spirituality are ultimately the same. This concept is the bedrock of Gandhi's approach to conflict, *satyagraha*, which requires a fighter to "hold firmly to truth."

2. *Ahimsa* ("nonviolence"). This ancient Indian concept prohibiting physical violence was broadened by Gandhi to include any form of coercion or denigration. For Gandhi, *ahimsa* was a moral stance involving love for and the affirmation of all life.

3. *Tapasya* ("renunciation"). Gandhi's asceticism was, worldly and not removed from social and political involvements. To Gandhi, *tapasya* meant not only the traditional requirements of simplicity and purity in personal habits but also the willingness of a fighter to shoulder the burden of suffering in a conflict.

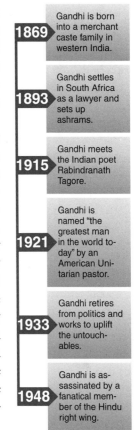

1869 Gandhi is born into a merchant caste family in western India.

1893 Gandhi settles in South Africa as a lawyer and sets up ashrams.

1915 Gandhi meets the Indian poet Rabindranath Tagore.

1921 Gandhi is named "the greatest man in the world today" by an American Unitarian pastor.

1933 Gandhi retires from politics and works to uplift the untouchables.

1948 Gandhi is assassinated by a fanatical member of the Hindu right wing.

> "I discovered in the earliest stages that pursuit of truth did not permit violence being inflicted on one's opponent, but that he must be weaned from error by patience and sympathy. For what appears truth to the one may appear to be error to the other. And patience means self-suffering."
>
> Mohandas Gandhi, 1922

4. *Swaraj* ("self-rule"). This term was often used during India's struggle for independence to signify freedom from the British, but Gandhi used it more broadly to refer to an ideal of personal integrity. He regarded *swaraj* as a worthy goal for the moral strivings of individuals and nations alike, linking it to the notion of finding one's inner self.

In addition to these concepts, Gandhi affirmed the traditional Hindu notions of *karman* and *dharma*. Even though Gandhi never systematized these ideas, when taken together they form a coherent theological position. Gandhi's copious writings are almost entirely in the form of letters and short essays in the newspapers and journals he published. These writings and the accounts of Gandhi's life show that he had very little interest in the colorful anthropomorphic deities and the rituals of traditional Hinduism.

It is not his rejection of these elements of Hindu culture that makes Gandhi innovative, however, for they are also omitted by the leaders of many other sects and movements in modern India. What is distinctive about Gandhi's Hinduism is his emphasis on social ethics as an integral part of the faith, a shift of emphasis that carries with it many conceptual changes as well. Gandhi's innovations include the use of the concept of truth as a basis for moral and political action, the equation of nonviolence with the Christian notion of selfless love, the redefinition of untouchability and the elevation of untouchables' tasks, and the hope for a more perfect world even in this present age of darkness.

Gandhi's religious practices, like his ideas, combined both social and spiritual elements. In addition to his daily prayers, consisting of a simple service of readings and silent contemplation, he regarded his daily practice of spinning cotton as a form of mediation and his campaigns for social reform as sacrifices more efficacious than those made by priests at the altar. After Gandhi retired from politics in 1933, he took as his central theme the campaign for the uplift of untouchables, whom he called *harijans* ("people of God"). Other concerns included the protection of cows, moral education, and the reconciliation of Hindus and Muslims. The latter was especially important to Gandhi during the turmoil precipitated by India's independence, when the subcontinent was divided along religious lines. It was opposition to Gandhi's cries for religious tolerance that led to his assassination, on 30 January 1948, by a fanatical member of the Hindu right wing.

The Bhagavad Gita

The Bhagavad Gita, or "Song of the Lord," is one of the greatest of the Hindu texts. It presents the Hindu god Krishna's teachings on the most effective way to be religious and portrays Krishna as a great god with whom people can have a trusting and loving relationship. The Gita is composed of 700 verses in the Sanskrit language. It forms Book VI of the Mahabharata, an epic poem of ancient India about a great battle in the royal Bharata family.

The Gita is written in the form of a dialogue between the warrior Prince Arjuna and Krishna, just before the epic battle is about to begin. It tells the story of how Arjuna faces a crisis on the battlefield when he finds that friends and family are among those in the opposing army. He wonders whether he should allow himself to be killed or whether he should kill his loved ones just for the sake of winning the battle. Krishna, who appears in human form as Arjuna's chariot driver, instructs him that it is his duty as a warrior to fight. Were he not to fight, he would disgrace himself and threaten the social order that is based on people carrying out the duties of their social class. Arjuna then questions whether it would be better to renounce his warrior status and assume the life of an ascetic. Krishna's response makes up the main part of the poem. He teaches Arjuna that the way to reach God is to follow one's duty without concern for personal gain and to do so with total devotion to God.

Since Gandhi's death, neither Indian society nor Hindu belief has been restructured along Gandhian lines, but the Gandhian approach has been kept alive in India through the Sarvodava movement, for which Vinoba Bhave has provided the spiritual leadership, and Jaya Prakash Narayan the political. Gandhi has provided the inspiration for religious and social activists in other parts of the world as well. These include Martin Luther King, Jr. in the United States, E. M. Schumacher in England, Danilo Dolci in Sicily, Albert Luthuli in South Africa, Lanza del Vasto in France, and A. T. Ariyaratna in Sri Lanka.

Over the years, the image of Gandhi has loomed larger than life, and he is popularly portrayed as an international saint. This canonization of Gandhi began in the West with the writings of an American Unitarian pastor, John Haynes Holmes, who in 1921 proclaimed Gandhi "the greatest man in the world today." It continues in an unabated flow of writings and films, including Richard Attenborough's *Gandhi* (1982.) At the core of this Gandhian hagiography lies the enduring and appealing image of a man who was able to achieve a significant religious goal: the ability to live simultaneously a life of moral action and spiritual fulfillment. For that reason Gandhi continues to serve as an inspiration for a humane and socially engaged form of religion in India and throughout the world. ◆

Ghazali, Abu Hamid al-

1058–1111 ● Muslim

> "To suppose that certitude can be only based upon formal arguments is to limit the boundless mercy of God."
>
> Abu Hamid Al-Ghazali, *Deliverance from Error,* c. 1100

Abu Hamid al-Ghazali, named Muhammad ibn Muhammad ibn Muhammad, was a distinguished Islamic jurist, theologian, and mystic who was given the honorific title Hujjat al Islam (Arabic for "the proof of Islam").

Al-Ghazali was born in the town of Tus, near modern Mashhad (eastern Iran), and received his early education there. When he was about 15 he went to the region of Gorgan (at the southeast corner of the Caspian Sea) to continue his studies. On the return journey, so the story goes, his notebooks were taken from him by robbers, and when he pleaded for their return they taunted him that he claimed to know what was in fact only in his notebooks; as a result of this incident he spent three years memorizing the material.

At the age of 19 he went to Nishapur (about 50 miles to the west) to study at the important Nizamiyah college under Imam al-Haramayn, one of the leading religious scholars of the period. Jurisprudence would be central in his studies, as in all Islamic higher education, but he was also initiated into theology and philosophy. He later helped with teaching and was recognized as a rising scholar.

In 1091, when he was about 33, he was appointed to the main professorship at the Nizamiyah college in Baghdad, one of the leading positions in the Sunni world. After just over four years, however, al-Ghazali abandoned his professorship and adopted the life of an ascetic and mystic.

We know something of al-Ghazali's personal history during these years in Baghdad from the autobiographical work he wrote when he was about 50, entitled *The Deliverer from Error*. This work is not conceived as an autobiography, however, but as a defense of his abandonment of the Baghdad professorship and of his subsequent return to teaching in Nishapur about a decade later. In it, he describes his intellectual journey after the earliest years as containing a period of skepticism lasting "almost two months," when he doubted the possibility of attaining truth. Once he ceased to be completely skeptical, he set out on a search for truth.

The Muslim year 500 (which began on 2 September 1106 C.E.) marked the beginning of a new century. Muhammad was reported to have said that God would send a "renewer" (*mujaddid*) of his religion at the beginning of each century, and various friends assured al-Ghazali that he was the "renewer" for the sixth century. This induced him to take up an invitation from the vizier of the provincial governor in Nishapur to become the main professor in the Nizamiyah college there. He continued in this position for three or possibly four years and then returned to Tus, probably because of ill health; he died there in 1111. His brother Ahmad, himself a distinguished scholar, describes how on his last day, after ablutions, Abu Hamid performed the dawn prayer and then, lying down on his bed facing Mecca, kissed his shroud, pressed it to his eyes with the words, "Obediently I enter into the presence of the King," and was dead before sunrise.

At the present time it is still difficult to reach a balanced judgment on the achievement of al-Ghazali. After the first translation of his autobiography into a European language (French) was published in 1842, many European scholars found al-Ghazali such an attractive figure that they paid much more attention to him than to any other Muslim thinker, and this fashion has been followed by Muslim scholars as well. His importance has thus tended to be exaggerated because of our relative ignorance of other writers.

Part of al-Ghazali's aim in studying the various philosophical disciplines was to discover how far they were compatible with Islamic doctrine. He gave separate consideration to mathematics, logic, physics, metaphysics or theology, politics, and ethics. Metaphysics he criticized very severely, but most of the others he regarded as neutral in themselves, though liable to give less scholarly persons an unduly favorable opinion of the competence of the philosophers in every field of thought. He himself was very impressed by Aristotelian logic, especially the syllogism. He not only made use of logic in his own defense of doctrine but also wrote several books about it, in which he managed to commend it to his fellow-theologians as well as to expound its principles. From his time on, many theological

> "The proof of the possibility of there being prophecy and the proof that there has been prophecy is that there is knowledge in the world the attainment of which by reason is inconceivable."
> Abu Hamid Al-Ghazali, *Deliverance from Error*, c. 1100

treatises devote much space to philosophical preliminaries, and works on logic are written by theologians. The great positive achievement of al-Ghazali here was to provide Islamic theology with a philosophical foundation.

Sufism had been flourishing in the Islamic world for over two centuries. Many of the earliest Sufis had been chiefly interested in asceticism, but others had cultivated ecstatic experiences, and a few had become so "intoxicated" that they seemed to outsiders to claim unity with God. Such persons often also held that their mystical attainments freed them from duties such as ritual prayer. In al-Ghazali's time, too, yet other Sufis were becoming interested in **gnostic** knowledge and developing theosophical doctrines. For these reasons many religious scholars were suspicious of all Sufism, despite the fact that some of their number practiced it in a moderate fashion without becoming either heretical in doctrine or practice. Al-Ghazali adopted the position of this latter group and, after his retirement from the professorship in Baghdad, spent much of his time in ascetical and mystical practices. His great work the *Ihya'* provides both a theoretical justification of his position and a highly detailed elucidation of it, which emphasized the deeper meaning of the external acts. In this way both by his writing and by his own life al-Ghazali showed how a profound inner life can be combined with full observance of the *shari'ah* and sound theological doctrine. The consequence of the life and work of al-Ghazali was that religious scholars in the main stream of Sunnism had to look more favorably on the Sufi movement, and this made it possible for ordinary Muslims to adopt moderate Sufi practices. ◆

gnostic: one who believes that matter is evil and that salvation comes through esoteric knowledge of a spiritual truth

Gomes, Peter

1942– ● BAPTIST

Aclergyman, educator, and author, Peter John Gomes (rhymes with "roams") was born in Boston, Massachusetts, on May 22, 1942, the son of Peter L. Gomes and Orissa Josephine White. An African American, he grew up in Plymouth, Massachusetts, in a mostly white neighborhood. His maternal grandfather was a minister and his father was a deacon and an usher. As a youth, Peter was uninterested in sports and felt most comfortable while attending Sunday school and church.

At Bates College in Lewiston, Maine, which Gomes entered in 1961, his major interest was in history, not religion, and he considered doing graduate studies in history. However, during his senior year at Bates, where he obtained a bachelor of arts degree in 1965, a professor who had attended Harvard Divinity School convinced him to attend school there. At Harvard Divinity School, Gomes for the first time found people who were both intellectual and spiritual, and this reawakened his passion for religion.

Gomes obtained a bachelor of sacred theology degree from the Divinity School in 1968, and was ordained a Baptist minister that same year. That year he became an instructor of history and director of freshman studies at Tuskegee College in Tuskegee, Alabama. In 1970 Gomes accepted the post of assistant minister at The Memorial Church of Harvard University. He expected to return to Tuskegee but in 1974 became the minister of The Memorial Church and Plummer Professor of Christian Morals at Harvard.

Because of the decline in Bible literacy, Gomes has devoted much of his attention to making Scripture comprehensible to all. He argues that the Bible should not be seen as a single work with a consistent, clear doctrine. Although the Bible deals with universal spiritual themes, Gomes believes, it is 66 books written by different people at various times. Therefore, he has said, readers have to not only ask "What does it say?" but "What does it mean—what did it mean then and what does it mean now?" Given this perspective, Gomes naturally opposes biblical literalism, the belief that every word of the Bible is literally true and has only one meaning. Literalism, also known as fundamentalism, is the perspective of some Baptist denominations, and Gomes has said "I appreciate their rigor, but I don't

"A lot of people seem to believe that they must read the Bible differently from Shakespeare because it's holy. Ironically our most primitive ancestors understood the power of metaphor, whereas our contemporary sophisticates are terrified of it."
Peter Gomes, in *People Weekly*, 1997

agree with the kind of intellectual straightjacket they put around the Bible." In his *The Good Book: Reading the Bible with Mind and Heart* (1996), he notes the ways literalists have misread the Bible to justify the enslavement of blacks, anti-Semitism, prejudice against women and homosexuals, and opposition to evolution.

Gomes says that Jesus stated the most important message of the Bible: "You should love the Lord, your God, with all your heart, your soul and your mind; and your neighbor as yourself." In *Sermons: Biblical Wisdom for Daily Living* (1998), he applies the Bible to everyday topics including opportunity, depression, love, and death.

Gomes has a courtly, aristocratic bearing and a Massachusetts accent that sometimes sounds nearly English. However, he is also passionate—sometimes confrontational—as well as engaging, warm, and witty. Lord Runcie, a former archbishop of Canterbury, has described him as "one of the great preachers of our generation," and *Time* magazine has placed him among the seven leading American preachers.

A moderate Republican, Gomes describes himself as culturally conservative: "I value tradition. I believe in God, the enduring qualities of life. I believe in manners, style—I believe that you should make decisions carefully, and be skeptical of wild ideologies."

When religious conservatives on the Harvard campus denounced homosexuality as a practice opposed by the Bible, Gomes created a sensation by declaring that he was gay. With his urging, the Board of Ministry of The Memorial Church announced in 1997 that the church would allow gay and lesbian couples to conduct commitment ceremonies in the church. But Gomes has asserted that he does not want to be identified primarily as a homosexual: "I am more than my race. I am more than my sexuality. I am more than my professorship. The only thing I am known by is a Christian."

Gomes has a wide range of teaching and research interests. They include the history of the ancient Christian church, Elizabethan Puritanism, church music, and the history of the African-American experience. ◆

Graham, Billy

1918– ● EVANGELICAL CHRISTIAN

Billy Graham rose from an American tradition of evangelical preaching to become one of the world's most famous evangelists. Evangelists are traveling Protestant preachers who convert large numbers of people to Christianity. After World War II, Evangelicalism grew out of an American movement called Fundamentalism, which accepted the Bible as the literal word of God. Graham became a leading figure in Evangelicalism, and he held a unique historical position as counselor and companion to every U.S. president beginning with Dwight D. Eisenhower.

Graham was born November 7, 1918, near Charlotte, North Carolina. His name was William Franklin Graham, Jr., shortened to Billy Frank or Billy by family and friends. William Franklin ("Frank") Graham and his wife Morrow raised Billy, their eldest, and his brother and two sisters on their dairy farm near Charlotte. Billy helped his father milk cows and deliver milk to 300 homes. He sometimes worked the fields until sunset, often becoming too tired to concentrate at school. The farm prospered, and the Grahams kept their farm through the Depression of 1929.

The Grahams were faithful Presbyterians who committed their Sundays to church, Bible study, and prayer. Although Billy fidgeted during services at their small church, he discovered a more exciting form of worship when his parents took him to hear the famous evangelist, Billy Sunday. The sights and sounds captivated five-year-old Graham as the flamboyant Sunday waved his arms, shouted, and jumped around.

Graham enjoyed reading books on history, but one teacher told Mrs. Graham that, although Billy was a bright child, he spent too little time on schoolwork. During high school, Billy found trouble in pranks and fast cars. But in 1934, the 16-year-old Graham changed his life. That year, the evangelist Reverend Mordecai Ham held nightly services for

> "God reveals Himself in hundreds of ways in the Bible, and if we read the Bible as carefully and as regularly as we read the daily papers, we would be as familiar with and as well informed about God as we are about our favorite player's batting average during baseball season!"
>
> Billy Graham,
> *Peace With God*,
> 1984

1918 Graham is born in North Carolina.

1934 Graham is captivated during a service conducted by Mordecai Ham.

1940 Graham graduates from the Florida Bible Institute.

1939 Graham is ordained a Southern Baptist minister.

1943 Graham marries Ruth Bell; becomes pastor of a church in Western Springs.

1949 Graham conducts a landmark evangelical crusade in Los Angeles.

1950 Graham begins airing the *Hour of Decision* on the radio.

1953 During a crusade in Tennessee, Graham pulls down a curtain dividing black and white members of the audience.

1982 Graham preaches in the Soviet Union.

1994 Graham officiates at Richard Nixon's funeral.

11 weeks in Charlotte. Billy began attending and soon found himself captivated. Ham warned audiences of the threat of hell and, pointing to the crowd, declared them sinners. Billy cringed and hid behind a woman's hat, feeling that the accusation fit him. One night, Ham's calling to come forth and be saved by God overwhelmed Graham, and he walked to the altar with hundreds of others. Graham felt a new peace enter his life.

In 1936, after graduating high school, Graham entered the religious Bob Jones College in Tennessee but soon changed to the Florida Bible Institute near Tampa, Florida, where he graduated in 1940. While at the institute, Graham developed a modest ability to prepare and give sermons. In late 1938, Graham chose to be baptized into the Baptist religion, and he was ordained a Southern Baptist minister in early 1939.

Graham then entered Wheaton College, a Christian college of liberal arts and sciences in Wheaton, Illinois, near Chicago. School rules prohibited use of tobacco or alcohol, card playing, or dancing. Graham soon met Ruth Bell, a fellow student who had spent much of her life in China with missionary parents. The year 1943 held major milestones for Graham as he and Ruth graduated from Wheaton, the couple married, and Graham became pastor of a Baptist church in Western Springs, another Chicago suburb.

Reverend Torrey Johnson heard Graham speak and invited him to take over a radio program called "Songs in the Night," airing Sunday nights from Chicago. After his success with the show, Graham accepted Johnson's invitation to preach to a large group of servicemen in Chicago. The promoters called the rally "Youth for Christ," which became the name of a large organization. Graham became vice president of Youth for Christ and preached at their rallies around the United States and in England.

Graham's 1949 evangelical crusade in Los Angeles became a turning point. He preached in a large tent, using a fiery, energetic style. Hundreds of people came forward to accept Jesus. Originally planned for three weeks, the rally lasted eight, with crowds of more than 9,000 spilling out of the tent. The format Graham followed through the years consisted of about two hours of preaching, after which he called to the open floor anyone who wanted to know Jesus as their personal savior. Evangelicals call this an altar call.

Graham began airing a radio program called "The Hour of Decision" in 1950. Within five years, more than 800 radio stations carried the show, and millions of listeners tuned in each week to hear Graham preach. Soon after the show began, Graham set up the Billy Graham Evangelistic Association (BGEA) to oversee donations that began pouring in.

Graham faced a moral dilemma preaching in Southern cities. Many arenas prohibited blacks from sitting with whites, which Graham felt contradicted Christian values. In March 1953, at a crusade in Chattanooga, Tennessee, Graham pulled down ropes that divided the black and white sections of the audience. He later hired a black staff member, and in 1964 Graham held a large interracial service in Birmingham, Alabama, the site of a racist church bombing in which four had died. For years, Graham refused invitations to preach in South Africa until finally, in 1973, the government agreed to Graham's conditions, and he held large gatherings that included blacks and whites together.

Graham carried his message of salvation through Jesus to various troubled sites around the world. He often preached against Communism and its anti-religious beliefs. However, in 1982, Russian Orthodox Church leaders invited Graham to the Soviet Union. Some Americans criticized Graham for not denouncing Soviet political oppression of religion. But Graham felt it was more important to speak to practicing Soviet Christians. He did, however, attempt to pressure Soviet officials to release people who had been jailed for preaching the Gospel.

Although Graham declined requests to endorse political candidates, observers found political views implied in his sermons and by his attendance at many political events. While he sought to minister to all factions, his conservative leaning could be discerned. Graham's high political connections began with the friendship of President Dwight D. Eisenhower, who Graham privately supported in his run for office. During Eisenhower's administration, Graham helped start the annual Presidential Prayer Breakfast (now the National Prayer Breakfast). Recognizing Graham's large following among American evangelical Christians, every subsequent president, from John F. Kennedy to Bill Clinton, sought Graham's advice or personal counsel. Graham became a frequent guest at the White House as well as the private homes of presidents. He played golf with many presidents and senators, and they often called upon him to offer prayers at important occasions.

Graham formed a longtime friendship with Richard M. Nixon, who often sought Graham's spiritual guidance. Graham

"The Christian ideal certainly does not demand that a person renounce all interest in the affairs of this life; but rather that we seek God's guidance in performing our daily work to the best of our ability, and that we keep both our work and our ambitions in subordination to the Lord at all times."

Billy Graham,
Peace With God,
1984

Graham's evangelistic crusades had reached an estimated 210 million people in 185 countries in North America, Europe, the Middle East, the Far East, and Africa by the late 1990s.

believed Nixon to be a sincere Christian and defended Nixon publicly. When the extent of Nixon's illegal activities became public, Graham says, he was "deeply distressed." Graham's connection to Nixon blemished his reputation, but Graham loyally officiated over Nixon's funeral in 1994.

Graham's evangelistic crusades had reached an estimated 210 million people in 185 countries in North America, Europe, the Middle East, the Far East, and Africa by the late 1990s. Graham appeared often on television and made several religious films. He wrote many books, including *Peace with God* (1953), *The Secret of Happiness* (1955), *My Answer* (1960), *World Aflame* (1965), *The Challenge* (1969), and his autobiography, *Just As I Am* (1997).

Billy and Ruth Graham lived in the Blue Ridge Mountains in a log home overlooking Montreat, North Carolina. Ruth devoted herself to raising their five children while Billy traveled, though she sometimes accompanied him. In his many years of ministry, Graham stood out as a prominent evangelist who had not been touched by scandal. Early in his career, Graham and his advisers created a set of guidelines to avoid such problems, including never publicly criticizing other ministers, maintaining strict financial accountability, and making financial records public. In addition, Graham refused to meet alone with a woman other than his wife.

By age 80, suffering from Parkinson's disease, Graham only preached at a few rallies each year. By the late 1990s, the BGEA operated on a budget of about $109 million a year, had 565 employees, and produced the "Hour of Decision" for an audience of 600 radio stations. William Franklin Graham III, Graham's son, was expected to take over the BGEA when his father retired. ◆

Grimke, Francis James

1850–1937 ● PRESBYTERIAN

Francis James Grimke was a leading African-American Presbyterian minister and author. Francis Grimke was born on Caneacres, a rice plantation near Charleston, S.C. He was the son of Henry Grimke, a wealthy white lawyer, and his African-American slave Nancy Weston, who also bore him two other sons, Archibald (1849) and John (1853). Henry

Grimke died in September 1852, and the mother and children lived for several years in a de facto free status. This ended in 1860 when E. Montague Grimke, the boys' half-brother, to whom ownership had passed, sought to exercise his "property rights." Francis Grimke ran away from home and joined the Confederate Army as an officer's valet. Montague Grimke eventually sold him to another officer, whom Francis Grimke served until emancipation. In 1866, he began his educational journey at Lincoln University (Pennsylvania), where he came to the notice of his white abolitionist aunts. Angelina Grimke Weld and Sarah Moore Grimke, who acknowledged his kinship and encouraged his further study, providing moral and material support.

Francis Grimke began the study of law at Lincoln after graduating at the head of his undergraduate class in 1870. He continued to prepare for a legal career, attending Howard University in 1874, but felt called to the ministry and moved to the Princeton Theological Seminary in 1875. Upon graduation from the seminary in 1878, Grimke began his ministry at the 15th Street Presbyterian Church in Washington, D.C., and married Charlotte L. Forten of Philadelphia. In 1880, Theodora Cornelia, their only child, died in infancy. From 1885 to 1889, Grimke served the Laura St. Presbyterian Church in Jacksonville, Florida. He returned to Washington and remained as pastor at the 15th Street Church until 1928, when he became pastor emeritus.

Grimke's pulpit afforded him access to one of the most accomplished African-American congregations in America; the members expected and received sermons that addressed issues of faith and morals with ethical insight, literary grace, and prophetic zeal. He practiced what he preached, earning himself the sobriquet Black Puritan. Through printed sermons and articles, Grimke encouraged a national audience to agitate for civil rights "until justice is done." He campaigned against racism in American churches, and helped form the Afro-Presbyterian Council to encourage black moral uplift and self-help. He also participated in the creation of organizations such as the American Negro Academy, which nurtured African-American development.

While not normally an activist outside the church, Grimke was an active supporter of Booker T. Washington's self-help efforts. However, in the early years of the twentieth century, he joined the group of African-American "radicals" led by W. E. B. Du Bois. He sided with Du Bois against Washington at the

1850 ▶ Grimke is born on a plantation, to a wealthy white lawyer and a slave.

1852 ▶ Grimke's father dies; the family live briefly as free people.

1860 ▶ Grimke, no longer free, joins the Confederate Army as officer's valet.

1866 ▶ Grimke enrolls at Lincoln University, aided by anti-slavery white aunts.

1870 ▶ Grimke graduates college at head of class and begins studying law.

1875 ▶ Grimke begins studying at Princeton Theological Seminary.

1878 ▶ Grimke graduates, begins ministry in Washington, D.C., and marries.

1880 ▶ Grimke's only child, Theodora Cornelia, dies in infancy.

1923 ▶ Grimke arouses controversy challenging sincerity of President Wilson.

1937 ▶ Grimke dies.

Carnegie Hall Conference (1906), which led to the schism between Washington and the radicals, and later became a strong and longtime supporter of the NAACP.

In 1923, Grimke aroused a storm of controversy by a Howard University School of Religion convocation address, "What Is the Trouble with Christianity Today?" in which he denounced groups such as the YMCA and the "federation of white churches" for their racist practices and challenged the sincerity of the faith of former President Woodrow Wilson. Legislators, led by Rep. James Byrnes of South Carolina, protested the address, and tried to remove him from Howard's board of trustees by threatening Howard's federal budget appropriation. Grimke retired in 1925 and lived in Washington, D.C., until his death in 1937. ◆

Griswold, Frank

1937– ● EPISCOPAL

When Bishop Frank T. Griswold was installed as the 25th presiding bishop of the Episcopal Church on January 10, 1998, he took the helm of an institution buffeted by strong conflicting social currents. The Episcopal Church is the United States branch of the Anglican Communion, the descendent of the Church of England.

Frank T. Griswold III was born September 18, 1937, in Bryn Mawr, near Philadelphia, Pennsylvania. He attended St. Paul's School in Concord, New Hampshire. In 1959, he received a degree in English literature from Harvard University. Griswold earned Bachelor of Arts (1962) and Masters of Arts (1966) degrees in theology from Oxford in England. He also studied at the General Theological Seminary in New York City from 1959 to 1960.

Griswold became an Episcopalian deacon in 1962 and was ordained as a priest in the Diocese of Pennsylvania in 1963, becoming the Right Reverend Frank T. Griswold. In 1965, Griswold married Phoebe Woetzel, and the couple had two daughters, Hannah and Eliza.

Griswold served churches in Bryn Mawr, Yardley, and Philadelphia before leaving Pennsylvania to serve as bishop coadjutor (assistant bishop) of the Diocese of Chicago in 1985.

(The Episcopal Church is divided into over 100 dioceses administered by bishops.) In 1987, Griswold succeeded as bishop of Chicago, where he served ten years. During that time, he worked towards greater ecumenism unity among Chicago religious groups. Griswold participated in joint services with the Catholic Archdiocese of Chicago and hosted meetings of the Council of Religious Leaders of Chicago. He also committed his diocese to the Chicago Metropolitan Sponsors, Inc., a major interfaith community organizing project formed in 1995. He was known as a skillful bridge-builder among people and for his moderate stance on issues.

In addition to being remarkably well-read, Griswold became known for his quick wit and sense of humor, and discipline. He began his days at 5 A.M. with prayer and yoga and made two spiritual retreats each year, one at a monastery.

On July 21, 1997, 214 Episcopalian bishops gathered in the historic Christ Church in Philadelphia—a place where George Washington, Benjamin Franklin, and Betsy Ross once worshiped and where the American Episcopal Church was born in 1798. The bishops elected Griswold to lead their church for the next nine years. On January 10, 1998, the 60-year-old Griswold was installed in a majestic ceremony in the Washington National Cathedral. Often called the "nation's church," the cathedral is the official and ceremonial seat of the Episcopal presiding bishop, though church headquarters are located at the Episcopal Church Center in New York City.

At his installation, Griswold said, "The Church is not an object or an institution to be fixed or a building to be repaired. Instead, the church is a relationship to be lived. As such, the church is always, in every age, being rebuilt and reformed out of the struggles and witness of its members." Indeed, Griswold took over a church undergoing major struggles. Members were split along conservative and liberal lines over issues of women in the priesthood, the ordination of gay clergy, and same-sex unions. Griswold took on the challenge willingly, telling reporters, "By virtue of the office of presiding bishop, I'm going to become a center of controversy, like it or not." But he called for members to keep their minds open and to keep communicating. Of his own position, he said, "My door, my heart, must be open to everyone."

In 1999, Griswold and the 2.5 million Episcopal church members began preparing for their next General Convention, scheduled for July 2000 in Denver. At the convention, held

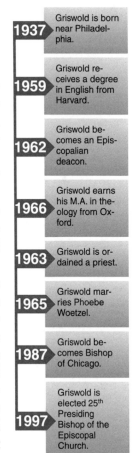

1937 Griswold is born near Philadelphia.

1959 Griswold receives a degree in English from Harvard.

1962 Griswold becomes an Episcopalian deacon.

1966 Griswold earns his M.A. in theology from Oxford.

1963 Griswold is ordained a priest.

1965 Griswold marries Phoebe Woetzel.

1987 Griswold becomes Bishop of Chicago.

1997 Griswold is elected 25th Presiding Bishop of the Episcopal Church.

Washington National Cathedral

Every United States president has been to the Washington National Cathedral since President Theodore Roosevelt presided over the laying of its cornerstone on September 29, 1907. However, the final stone was not set on the cathedral until President George Bush presided over the dedication on September 29, 1990. The Cathedral Church of Saint Peter and Saint Paul, as it is formally named, is administered by the Episcopal church and is the chief mission church of the Episcopal Diocese of Washington, D.C. It is the seat of the Episcopal bishop of Washington and the presiding bishop of the Episcopal Church USA. However, the cathedral is often the site of interfaith services, and everyone is welcome to visit the church.

The cathedral is laid out in the form of a cross, 525 feet long and 275 feet wide at the widest. It was built stone-on-stone with no structural steel, like a medieval church. Its English Gothic style features pointed arches and vaulted ceilings. Stone carvings and more than 200 stained-glass windows beautify the structure. Stones from historic buildings and shrines in all parts of the world were used in it's construction. The central tower is 676 feet above sea level, the highest point in the District of Columbia. Philip Hubert Frohman is considered to be the principal architect of the cathedral. Woodrow Wilson is among several well-known people buried there.

every three years, delegates create church policy. The 2000 convention would likely be the site of further conflict over issues that had split the church in previous conventions. Although the church had ordained women since 1976, four dioceses still refused to allow women priests. Non-celibate gays were still banned from the ministry. However, since the ban was not church law, but rather based on a General Convention resolution, some clergy were performing such ordinations. The battle over whether priests could officiate at same-sex unions would also be on the agenda.

Griswold also inherited the issue of full communion between the Episcopal Church and the Evangelical Lutheran Church in America, an idea that had been discussed for 30 years. An agreement would allow the two groups to share clergy, sacraments, and missions. Griswold supported this ecumenical move, still being negotiated in late 1999. In August 1999, a majority of Evangelical Lutheran delegates at their national convention in Denver voted to approve a full communion pact with the Episcopal Church, pushing the process a great step forward.

Anglicans, mainly Episcopalians, and Roman Catholics had also considered such a bond, but were stalled on such issues as the acceptance of women priests. Some Episcopalians see little difference between their religion and that of Roman Catholics, while some see themselves as closer to other Protestants. Griswold received both criticism and praise for reportedly taking communion at a Catholic church near his office at Episcopal headquarters in New York. ◆

Gutierrez, Gustavo

1928– ● CATHOLIC

Gustavo Gutierrez is a Peruvian Catholic priest and founder of Liberation Theology, which holds that God is on the side of the oppressed and requires that the church focus its efforts on liberating people from poverty and exploitation. Gutierrez's attempt to interpret the meaning of Christianity within the context of the struggle for justice unleashed a revolution in Latin American theological inquiry.

After training for the priesthood in Europe in the 1950s, Gutierrez became part of a South and Central American network of Catholic church reformers seeking to apply the teachings of the Second Vatican Council (1962–1965) to Latin American conditions. Influenced by radicalized students, the Peruvian Marxist Jose Carlos Mariategui, the author Jose Maria Arguedas, and dependency theory, Gutierrez came to champion the liberation of the Latin American poor. In 1968 he coauthored the central texts of the famous Medellin Latin American bishops' conference that denounced social and economic inequality. In his 1971 foundational text *Notes on a Theology of Liberation,* he proposed the new theological method of theology as reflection on the commitment of Christians to construct a just society.

> "The theology of liberation is a theology of salvation in the concrete, historical and political conditions of our day."
> Gustavo Gutierrez,
> *The Power of the Poor in History,*
> 1983

The liberation theology movement that his ideas spawned committed some members of the Catholic church to defend the rights of the marginalized. Because of his use of certain aspects of Marxist theory, Gutierrez's theology has attracted Vatican and conservative criticism. Nevertheless, he has continued to refine his ideas through conferences, international theological networks, and contact with the poor. In later works Gutierrez has developed a spirituality of suffering. ◆

Handsome Lake

1735–1815 ● NATIVE AMERICAN

Handsome Lake was a Seneca shaman, prophet, and **sachem** (leader) of the Six Nations of the Iroquois. He was born on the Genesee River opposite modern-day Avon, Livingston County, New York. Handsome Lake's life mirrors the history of the Iroquois people. Born at the zenith of Iroquois power and influence, he participated in major battles against Indian and American opponents and witnessed his people's loss of land and pride following the Revolutionary War. He later suffered a debilitating illness, exacerbated by bouts of drunkenness, but was revivified by a series of dream-vision experiences and led the way to a national revitalization of Indian values.

Early in 1799 Handsome Lake was confined to bed with a serious illness and seemed near death. During a series of dream-vision experiences in June and August 1799 he received many messages from the Creator through four intermediaries whom the prophet referred to as the Four Messengers or the Four Angels. They instructed him about his mission, guided him on a sky journey to the land of the damned and the blessed, and promised him shamanic powers. Handsome Lake recovered, and his sense of physical and spiritual rebirth intensified as he preached and worked for reform.

The earliest messages the prophet received condemned alcohol, witchcraft, and charms. The Creator was also displeased with wife beating and desertion by husbands, as well as by adul-

sachem: Native American chief or leader; chief of the Algonquin confederation of tribes of the North Atlantic coast

165

Handsome Lake

tery, interference in marriages by mothers-in-law, and the neglect and abuse of children and the elderly. Such activities reflected a serious breakdown in the traditional Iroquois way of life. Handsome Lake now called for a breakup of the traditional longhouse dwelling and instituted the building of single-family houses following the Quaker model. More radically, he preached that men must give up their rapidly declining occupations of hunting and waging war and instead take up farming, the traditional domain of women. At the same time, he warned against the private ownership of property as destructive of traditional Iroquois values, and he encouraged cooperative farming and other communal activities. He also condemned the cruelty to farm animals evident among many whites. Fearful of the corrosive effects of white education on Iroquois traditions, he said that only a few Iroquois children should be educated, and those for the express purpose of enabling the Iroquois to deal with the whites in legal and political matters.

His reforms of ritual life emphasized the communal ceremonies of thanksgiving centered on the agricultural cycle. Thus he tended to downplay and even denounce the role of the medicine societies. Eventually they regained their prominence, albeit within the context of an Iroquois life reformed by Handsome Lake and his half brother, Cornplanter.

As a religious leader, Handsome Lake differed from the Native American prophets who claimed that renewal would occur only when the people returned to the sacrifices and rituals they had neglected. The divine would then send forth its power and restore them. They also proclaimed that the whites would be destroyed if the people rejected all white influences and returned to the old ways. In contrast, Handsome Lake spoke in the name of a transcendent moral being who was seriously displeased with the sins of his people and would either reward them or punish them after death depending on whether they reformed themselves. The Creator did not promise that the whites would be destroyed or driven away but rather said that personal and social reforms would enable the Iroquois to be strong enough to maintain their own independence and to survive in a world increasingly controlled by whites. Rejecting both the assimilationism of the Mohawk leader Joseph Grant and the nativism of the Seneca leader Red Jacket, Handsome Lake presented the Iroquois with the will of the Creator: they must either accept the *gaiwiio* ("good word"), that is, the revelations and injunctions received by Handsome Lake, by repenting their deeds and embracing personal and social reform, or be lost in both a personal and a historical sense.

Unlike the biblical prophets, Handsome Lake's concern with ethical behavior was not accompanied by a desacralization of nature. Although he rejected any prescription for the ills of his people, Handsome Lake affirmed as integral to the Iroquois tradition the necessity of maintaining correct relationships with the spirit forces through ceremonial life. Only by enacting

> Handsome Lake spoke in the name of a transcendent moral being who was seriously displeased with the sins of his people and would either reward them or punish them after death.

the moral and socioeconomic reforms enjoined by the *gaiwiio* could the Indian tradition be fully effective.

Handsome Lake also maintained that the holy was both a transcendent moral being and an immanent presence and power. The present-day Longhouse religion, or Handsome Lake religion, while basing itself on the prophet's teachings, incorporates them into a religious structure that includes shamanic institutions and practices, agricultural and gathering ceremonies, and organizational meetings such as the Six Nations Conference. ◆

Harris, Barbara

1930– ● EPISCOPAL

> "There is room at
> the table for
> everybody."
>
> Barbara Harris,
> 1999

Barbara Clementine Harris was the first female bishop of the Protestant Episcopal Church. She was born in Philadelphia, where her father, Walter Harris, was a steelworker and her mother, Beatrice, was a church organist. A third generation Episcopalian, Harris was very active in the St. Barnabas Episcopal Church. While in high school, she played piano for the church school and later started a young adults group.

After graduating from high school, Harris went to work for Joseph V. Baker Associates, a black-owned public relations firm. She also attended and graduated from the Charles Morris Price School of Advertising and Journalism in Philadelphia. In 1968 she went to work for Sun Oil Company and became community relations manager in 1973.

During the 1960s, Harris participated in several civil rights events. She was part of the 1965 Freedom March from Selma, Ala., to Montgomery, Ala., with the Rev. Dr. Martin Luther King, Jr., and was also a member of a church-sponsored team of people who went to Mississippi to register black voters. Harris began attending North Philadelphia Church of the Advocate in 1968. That same year, the Union of Black Clergy was established by a group of black Episcopalian ministers. Harris and several other women lobbied for membership. Eventually, they were admitted and the word laity was added to the organization's name. Later it became the Union of Black Episcopalians.

Once the Episcopal Church began to ordain women in 1976, Harris began to study for the ministry. From 1977 to

OPPOSITE:
Barbara Harris

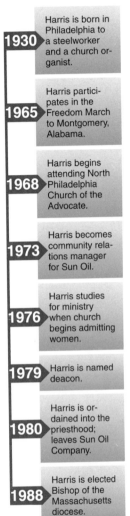

1930 Harris is born in Philadelphia to a steelworker and a church organist.

1965 Harris participates in the Freedom March to Montgomery, Alabama.

1968 Harris begins attending North Philadelphia Church of the Advocate.

1973 Harris becomes community relations manager for Sun Oil.

1976 Harris studies for ministry when church begins admitting women.

1979 Harris is named deacon.

1980 Harris is ordained into the priesthood; leaves Sun Oil Company.

1988 Harris is elected Bishop of the Massachusetts diocese.

1979 she took several courses at Villanova University in Philadelphia, and spent three months in informal residency at the Episcopal Divinity School in Cambridge, Mass. She was named deacon in 1979, served as a deacon-in-training in 1979–1980, and was ordained to the priesthood in 1980. She left Sun Oil Co. to pursue her new career full-time.

The first four years of Harris's ministry were spent at St. Augustine-of-Hippo in Norristown, Pa. She also worked as a chaplain in the Philadelphia County Prison System, an area in which she had already spent many years as a volunteer. In 1984 she became the executive director of the Episcopal Church Publishing Co. Her writings were critical of church policies, which she believed to be in contrast to social, political, and economic fairness.

In 1988 the Episcopal Church approved the consecration of women as bishops. Harris was elected to become bishop to the Massachusetts diocese in the fall of 1988. Her election was ratified in January 1989 and she was ordained in a ceremony in Boston on February 11, 1989 with over 7,000 in attendance.

As the first female Episcopal bishop, Harris was surrounded by controversy centered on three issues: her gender, her lack of traditional seminary education and training, and her liberal viewpoints. Policies toward women, black Americans, the poor, and other minorities were always at the forefront of Harris's challenges to the church and its doctrines. Harris overcame the objections and focused her attention on her duties as a bishop. She has served the diocese of Massachusetts, where she has been extremely active in local communities and prison work. Greatly concerned with the prison ministry, she represents the Episcopal Church on the board of the Prisoners Visitation and Support Committee. ◆

Harris, William Wade

c. 1865–1928 ● AFRICAN CHRISTIAN

William Wade Harris was the leader of a mass movement to Christianity in Africa that inspired creation of an African Christian church. The prophet Harris created the largest mass movement to Christianity in the history of the African continent and revolutionized the religious life of the southern Ivory Coast. He paved the way for the growth of the Catholic church and the establishment of the Protestant church and for the creation of several indigenous religious institutions. Most significant among these is the Harrist Church of the Ivory Coast, which institutionalized his teachings. His impact was unique among the movements to Christianity led by African prophets in that it reflected totally indigenous initiative in a population not previously christianized by missionaries.

A Grebo from southeastern Liberia, Harris was familiar with Western customs and literate in both English and Grebo as a result of mission schooling. He became an Episcopalian lay preacher, taught in a mission school, directed a boarding school, and worked as a government interpreter.

When antagonism between the Grebo and the Liberian government broke out, Harris led several acts of rebellion against the government. In 1909 he was imprisoned for treason for leading an alleged coup d'etat attempt. During his imprisonment he had a vision of the angel Gabriel that convinced him he was God's last prophet, charged with the divine mission of bringing Christianity to all those people not yet converted. In 1913, after his release from prison, Harris went to the Ivory Coast, where his message was well received. The Ivorians, who found their traditional spiritual guardians ineffective in warding off the colonial onslaught, welcomed Harris's message of a stronger spiritual force.

Harris told them to destroy the altars, masks, and other material representations associated with their indigenous religion and to worship the Christian god as he taught them. In little more than one year, he had baptized what colonial officials estimated at from 100,000 to 120,000 people; Catholic missionaries, who had been summoned by the colonial government to inculcate loyalty to France among its new subjects, had succeeded in baptizing only 400 people in the previous two decades.

To complete the christianization of those he baptized, Harris sent them to the Catholic missions and to his Protestant disciples from Sierra Leone and the Gold Coast (now Ghana) who were working in the Ivory Coast. In areas where there were neither missions nor disciples, Harris delegated village leaders to teach their fellow villagers what they had learned from him.

The Catholic missions were inundated with Harris's converts, and his African Protestant disciples continued to convert

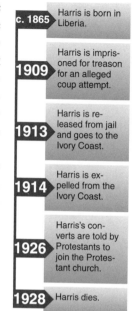

c. 1865 ▶ Harris is born in Liberia.

1909 ▶ Harris is imprisoned for treason for an alleged coup attempt.

1913 ▶ Harris is released from jail and goes to the Ivory Coast.

1914 ▶ Harris is expelled from the Ivory Coast.

1926 ▶ Harris's converts are told by Protestants to join the Protestant church.

1928 ▶ Harris dies.

and teach multitudes in the prophet's name. When a Protestant missionary from Europe arrived in the Ivory Coast in 1924, expecting to find no Ivorian Protestants because there had been no European Protestant missionaries there, he encountered tens of thousands of Ivorians worshiping autonomously, calling themselves Harrist Protestants and exhorting him to send the "teachers with Bibles" Harris had said would come to teach them the word of God.

Although some of the Ivorians who had been worshiping autonomously were initially drawn to the Protestant missionaries, they became disaffected when the Protestants attacked fundamental social institutions such as polygamy and sought to undermine the power of Harris's disciples. In 1926 a Protestant delegation returned from a visit to Harris in Liberia with a message telling his converts to join the Protestant church, but in 1928 an Ivorian delegation went to tell the prophet of their grievances against the missionaries. This group returned from Liberia with a "last will and testament" from Harris that supported their desire to worship independently. John Ahui, the young member of the delegation whom Harris chose to continue his mission, perpetuated the prophet's teachings and founded the Harrist Church of the Ivory Coast, of which he remains the patriarch.

Harris's message to the Ivorians was both spiritual and secular. He urged them to stop worshiping the nature spirits that had failed to protect them from conquest by the French and instead to worship the omnipotent creator god who would bring them prosperity, a return to their state of sovereignty, and access to the knowledge and technology of their conquerors. He offered them his own example as an African who, as a result of his schooling and resultant professional positions, could function in the world of the Europeans and Americans as well as in an African milieu. Thus the unprecedented movement of religious conversion that missionaries characterized as a "tidal wave" or "avalanche" to Christianity also had a secular influence; Harris's movement inspired Ivorians to learn the pragmatic tactics necessary to regain their sovereignty and to create new institutions within which to do so.

Because he inspired Ivorians to such manifestations of collective indigenous initiative, which the colonial administration perceived as a direct threat to its control over its subjects, Harris was expelled from the Ivory Coast in 1914. Those who persevered in worshiping as Harris had taught them were

> Harris's movement inspired Ivorians to learn the pragmatic tactics necessary to regain their sovereignty and to create new institutions within which to do so.

persecuted by the colonial officials, often with the assistance of the Catholic missionaries.

The Harris church appealed to Ivorians because it represented a form of Christianity based on indigenous organizational, conceptual, and ritual structures. Harris had such appeal to the Ivorians not only because he considered the conceptual structures and preoccupations of the traditional religion but also because he offered desirable solutions to the immediate problems engendered by the colonial situation. Additionally, Harris's style of presentation corresponded to the indigenous mold pioneered by priests of the traditional nature spirits.

That the prophet Harris was a native Liberian is significant because of Liberia's special meaning in Africa. Created by Afro-Americans seeking freedom from the oppression of American racism, Liberia was a symbol of the possibility of the redemption of Africa from European exploitation by and for Africans and their descendants abroad.

Influential Afro-American leaders in Liberia, such as Edward Wilmot Blyden, believed that Afro-Americans could share with the Africans the benefits of Western knowledge and experience, to be synthesized with the Africans' own wisdom and techniques for the creation of a new sovereignty. It is therefore particularly appropriate that William Wade Harris, a symbol of African potential for the Ivorians, should have brought his message from Liberia, a symbol of African potential and freedom from oppression. ◆

> Harris's style of presentation corresponded to the indigenous mold pioneered by priests of the traditional nature spirits.

Hasan Al-Basri

642–728 ● Muslim

Hasan Al-Basri was a famous Muslim ascetic of the generation following the prophet Muhammad. The son of a freed slave, he was born in Medina in Saudi Arabia. Hasan later moved to Basra, where he settled permanently after a brief career as holy warrior in what is now Afghanistan and as secretary to the governor of Khorasan in present-day Iran.

To a simple religious spirit such as Hasan, the social and economic changes accompanying the schisms and *coups d'etat* within Islam amounted to an excess of worldliness. Thus he reacted much more sharply to this disease in the hearts and behavior of the people than he did to the tyranny of the government, then personified in al-Hajjaj, the governor of Iraq. Though openly critical of the leaders of the government, Hasan refused to "bid them good and forbid them evil" (because, he said, their swords were faster than our tongues) or to participate in uprisings against them. Likewise, he advised others not to oppose by the sword a punishment or test from God, such as the tyrant al-Hajjaj, but to face it with patience and repentance: God, said Hasan, brings change and relief through these means rather than through hasty resort to violence.

hadith: narrative record of the sayings and customs of Muhammad and the collective body of Muslim traditions relating to him and his associates

Although he was an acknowledged expert in the Koran, Islamic law, and **hadith** (traditions of the Prophet), and he was also said to have lectured and written books on these subjects, Hasan's fame rests on his pietistic and dogmatic concerns. Here his interest lay not in theological doctrine but in the quality of faith and action, in the inner, genuinely sincere, pious life of the heart translated into an outer, morally upright, ascetic mode of living. Equipped with extensive knowledge and a living memory of the practice of the Prophet's companions, an attractive personality, an eloquent tongue, and most of all, a fearful heart and an upright character, Hasan engaged in preaching against worldliness and its resulting hypocrisy. His sermons and letters are grim reminders of the transience of worldly life, the permanent value of the life in the hereafter, and the inevitability of death and divine retribution, as well as moving exhortations to fear God and foster sincere faith and upright conduct. For Hasan, people with skin-deep faith and readiness to sin, were morally aberrant believers in acute danger of hellfire and hence urgently in need of help.

qadar: Arabic word meaning free will

Hasan's doctrine of **qadar** (free will) was also morally inspired, directed as it was against the sinners' deterministic rationalizations. Challenged by Caliph Abd al-Malik to defend and define his position, he indicated that humans have power (*qudrah*) to choose freely; that good and guidance come from God, who has foreknowledge of both good and evil (the latter coming from humans or the devil); that God's predestination is not coercive nor his foreknowledge prohibitive for human free choice. The reports that Hasan recanted his belief in free will were probably later attempts by the orthodox Sunnis to clear his reputation of what had come to be regarded as heresy, although the possibility remains that he did partially modify his position.

The fact that both the Sufis and the Multazilah regarded Hasan as one of their forerunners is a mark of his importance and influence as an ascetic and a theologian. It is even more remarkable that the Sunnis take pains to count him among their own predecessors despite his novel attitudes in matters of piety and dogma. And it is a measure of his immediate impact that on the day Hasan died, evening prayers could not be held in the mosques because the whole city of Basra was busy attending his funeral. ◆

Heschel, Abraham Joshua

1907–1972 ● JEWISH

Abraham Joshua Heschel was born in Warsaw, Poland, the youngest of five children born to Moshe Mordecai Heschel and Rivke Reizel Perlow. Heschel's male ancestors had been Hasidic rabbis for seven generations. Related to Hasidic nobility throughout Europe, and displaying precocious piety and intelligence, Heschel could have easily continued the Hasidic rabbinic line. Instead, he turned from Hasidism to pursue a secular education. While studying at Berlin's Humboldt University from 1929 to 1933, he was one of the few young scholars completely comfortable in both the orthodox Jewish and secular worlds.

Awarded a Ph.D. in philosophy and Semitics in February 1933, Heschel began teaching Talmud at the Hochschule, where in 1937 he impressed Martin Buber, who persuaded Heschel to succeed him as director of the Lehrhaus Freie J'dische (Free Jewish House of Learning), a school in Frankfurt. Deported to Poland by the Nazis in 1938, Heschel taught briefly at the Institute for Jewish Studies before emigrating to London, where he established the Institute for Jewish Learning.

Hebrew Union College, in Cincinnati, Ohio, brought Heschel to the United States in 1940; he served on the college's faculty as an associate professor of philosophy and rabbinics until 1945. The Cincinnati years were personally difficult for Heschel: his English was poor; he had no family; the college administration, faculty, and student body practiced Reformed Judaism, appreciating neither his orthodox diet nor his Hasidic piety; he agonized over the plight of European Jewry; and he

> "The meaning of man's life lies in his perfecting the universe. He has to distinguish, father and redeem the sparks of holiness scattered throughout the darkness of the world. This service is the motive of all precepts and good deeds."
>
> Abraham Joshua Heschel, *The Earth Is the Lord's,* 1950

1907 Heschel is born to a sixth-generation Hasidic rabbi and his wife.

1933 Heschel receives a Ph.D. in philosophy and Semitics.

1937 Heschel is persuaded by Martin Buber to become director of school.

1938 Heschel is deported to Poland by the Nazis, then emigrates to London.

1945 Heschel becomes a naturalized American citizen.

1946 Heschel marries Sylvia Straus; becomes the seminary's first ever Jewish ethics and mysticism professor.

1965 Heschel's efforts play key role in the Vatican II decision absolving Jews; Heschel marches with Martin Luther King in Alabama.

1972 Heschel dies unexpectedly in his sleep.

grieved for his mother and sister, who died at the hands of the Nazis. The most significant developments of these years were becoming a naturalized citizen in 1945, and meeting concert pianist and philosopher Sylvia Straus, whom he married in 1946. They had one child.

When New York's Jewish Theological Seminary invited Heschel to join its faculty in 1946, he gladly accepted, becoming its first professor of Jewish ethics and mysticism. It was only after marrying that Heschel began to write his theological works. Fluent in Polish, Yiddish, and Hebrew since his childhood, Heschel eventually mastered English. Indeed, by 1950 he had developed a lucid and elegant English prose in which he wrote prolifically for the next 20 years, establishing a worldwide reputation as one of the foremost Jewish theologians of the century. His theology reflected the inner tension he had felt since his youth, described in the posthumously published *A Passion for Truth* (1973).

Heschel's theological synthesis recognized Israel's God as one whose "divine pathos" makes him willing to involve himself in the history of man. Mankind's appropriate response to God is to bear witness to him in ethics and action. Such witness-bearing inspired Heschel to take militant, public stands against injustice and falsehood. One result of this "passion for truth" was his successful crusade to persuade Pope Paul VI to use Vatican II to absolve Jewry of the charge of deicide in the Crucifixion of Jesus. Personal contacts with Augustin Cardinal Bea in November 1961 resulted in Heschel's 13-page memorandum to Bea, "On Improving Catholic-Jewish Relations." This 1962 document, as well as Heschel's personal contact with Pope Paul VI in 1964, provided the thesis and language for Vatican II's "Declaration on the Relation of the Church to Non-Christian Religions." By personally lobbying the cardinal and the pope, Heschel played a central if hidden role in bringing about the 1965 Vatican II decision.

The publication of *The Prophets* in 1962 coincided with Heschel's emergence as a prophetic voice of conscience. At the National Conference on Religion and Race in 1963 he electrified a racially mixed audience, throwing the weight of the Jewish community behind the struggle of blacks for equal justice under law. In 1965, he risked injury from police dogs and fire hoses to march with Martin Luther King, Jr., from Selma to Montgomery, Alabama, later remarking, "When I marched in Selma, my feet were praying." In the same year, before the rise of broad popular opposition to the Vietnam War, Heschel joined Protestant theologian Reinhold Niebuhr and Roman Catholic priest Daniel Berrigan to form "Clergy and Laity Concerned About Vietnam." He regarded such involvement not as political entanglement, but as moral militancy. At one antiwar rally he declaimed, "This is not a political demonstration. It is a moral convocation, a display of concern for human rights." He cast a righteously indignant eye on the Soviet Union as well, and was one of the first to urge world Jewry to come to the aid of Soviet Jews.

Heschel, who had suffered a heart attack in 1969, died unexpectedly in his sleep in his home in New York City on Sabbath evening, December 23, 1972, timing which an ancient Jewish metaphor calls "God's kiss on the soul." Heschel's thoughts and actions influenced theology, ethics, and politics far beyond the boundaries of his orthodox Jewish faith. He had touched the world, changing the way Jews, Protestants, and Catholics think and behave. ◆

Hillel

c. 50 B.C.E.– c. 1st Century c.e. ● Jewish

Hillel was a Jewish sage and teacher. Although several modern scholars claim that Hillel, known as "the Elder," had roots in Alexandria, Egypt, there is no reason to doubt the Talmudic tradition that he was a native of Babylonia in present-day Iraq. Talmud reports that Hillel was designated *nasi* (patriarch, i.e., head of the court) in recognition for having been able to resolve a difficult question of Jewish law on the basis of a tradition he heard from earlier teachers named Shema'yah and Aytalyon. The later Jewish patriarchs were regarded as descendants of Hillel, who in turn was said to have been a scion of the house of David.

Talmudic tradition portrays Hillel as a great spiritual leader who embodied the qualities of humility, patience, peace, love of Torah, and social concern. Many of the well-known sayings attributed to Hillel emphasize these ideals. For example: "Be of the disciples of Aaron, loving peace and pursuing peace, loving people and bringing them near to the Torah." "A name made great is a name destroyed." "If I am not for myself who is for

The Talmud

The Talmud (Hebrew for "learning") is principally a detailed examination and interpretation of the Mishnah, the codification of Jewish oral law that was completed around 200 C.E. But it also contains discussions of every subject of interest to ancient rabbis. Until the eighteenth century, all Jews regarded the Talmud as a divine, mandatory guide to all aspects of Jewish life, public and private. Today, Orthodox Jews generally maintain this belief. There are actually two Talmuds, the Palestinian and Babylonian, produced by different groups of Jewish scholars. The Palestinian Talmud was completed around 400 C.E., and the Babylonian Talmud about a century later. It is the latter Talmud, the more thorough and clear of the two, that became the guide to Jewish life.

Implied in the supreme position of the Talmud is the belief that Talmudic learning is the basis for choosing Jewish community leaders. That is because only leaders steeped in the Talmud would be able to lead Jews in the direction prescribed by God. This view helped rabbis to establish themselves as the leading authorities in traditional Jewish communities. Just as the Talmud is a commentary on the Mishnah, so there are many commentaries on the Talmud. Among the best known is the one produced by Rashi, a European Jewish scholar, in the eleventh century.

me? And when I am for myself, what am I? And if not now when?" "Do not separate yourself from the community." "Do not judge your fellow until you are in his position."

A popular tradition illustrates Hillel's forbearance and contrasts it with the impatience of a colleague named Shammai, who often appears as his foil. Shammai is said to have rebuffed a heathen who demanded of him. "Make me a proselyte on condition that you teach me the entire Torah while I stand on one foot." When approached by the same heathen Hillel responded, "What is hateful to you do not do to your fellow man. That is whole Torah, the rest is commentary. Go and learn it." This negative formulation of what eventually circulated as the Golden Rule, like many of Hillel's saying, has parallels in ancient literature, so the intention is not simply to relate the uniqueness or essence of Judaism. Here Hillel appears as the teacher par excellence; in one utterance he conveys that the central ideals of Judaism are easily delineated, but the path to their fulfillment can be discerned only through further study and commitment.

taqqanot: Hebrew word meaning enactments

Several social **taqqanot** ("enactments") are associated with Hillel. The most important of these is the prozbul, a legal instrument that enabled creditors to claim their debts after the sabbatical year though biblical law prohibited it. The biblical law was intended to protect the poor in an agricultural society. In later times, when the economy depended upon the free flow of credit, people would refrain from lending as the sabbatical year drew near because they feared the money owned them would not be collectible By means of the prozbul, creditors transferred their bonds to the court, thereby retaining the right to collect after the sabbatical year.

Hillel's significance has been assessed in various ways, all of which acknowledge that he was a pivotal figure in Judaism during the late first century B.C.E. and the early first century C.E. Some scholars suggest that Hillel created the basis for the development of Jewish law, narrowing the differences between the Pharisees and Sadducees by showing how the oral law is inherent in the written. Other scholars credit Hillel with the transformation of the Pharisees from a political party to a society of "pious sectarians" committed to table-fellowship," that is, to the meticulous observance of tithing laws and the eating of everyday meals in a state of ritual purity. ◆

Hooker, Thomas

1586–1647 ● PURITAN

Thomas Hooker was an English and American Puritan minister. Born in Leicestershire, England Hooker took his B.A. and M.A. at Cambridge, where he was variously Dixie fellow, catechist, and lecturer in Emmanuel College. As a minister he became active in the unofficial meetings of Puritan ministers then taking place. When William Laud moved to restrict nonconforming ministers in the late 1620s. Hooker fled, first to the Netherlands, then to New England in 1633. He and Samuel Stone organized the first church in Newtown (now Cambridge), Massachusetts.

Partly because of religious and political disputes in the Bay Colony, partly because of his parishioners' dissatisfaction with their land allotments, Hooker led in 1636 a removal to Connecticut, where he and his group founded Hartford. When the General Court of Connecticut first met in May 1638 to draw up its Fundamental Orders, Hooker's sermon on the occasion described the proper relationship between the people and their magistrates. Although an important political statement of early

New England, the sermon is no longer commonly accepted, as it once was, as evidence of Hooker's democratic attitudes. Hooker maintained his influence in Boston, returning in 1637 to serve as a moderator of the synod called to deal with the Puritan heretic Anne Hutchinson, then later in 1645 to participate in the meeting called to consider responses to a Council of clergyman called the Westminster Assembly. The first of these meetings marked the triumph of Hooker's theology as a nearly official view of the process of salvation for the New England churches. At the later meeting Hooker presented his *Survey of the Summe of Church Discipline* (London, 1648), which became one of the definitive statements of the congregational church order in New England. He died at Hartford on 7 July 1647.

More than 30 volumes appeared over Hooker's name or were legitimately credited to him; the most important, in addition to the *Survey*, are collections of sermons that examine the spiritual stages the soul passes through on the way to conversion. Under the influence of Richard Sibbes and other English preparationist theologians who held that the individual soul could not earn grace but could prepare itself for its reception, Hooker preached extensively on the subject and made his final survey of the soul's progress during his pastorate at Hartford. These sermons were published posthumously in the two volumes entitled *The Application of Redemption* (London, 1656–1659). Hooker was well known in his own time for his direction of troubled spirits in the process of discovering saving grace in themselves, and this concern is evident in his various sermonic works on the theology and psychology of conversion. He was also interested in the role meditation could play in the spiritual life of a soul under the workings of grace, and he has been recognized in this century as one of the significant Puritan exponents of the meditative process. ◆

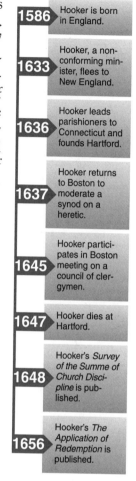

1586	Hooker is born in England.
1633	Hooker, a nonconforming minister, flees to New England.
1636	Hooker leads parishioners to Connecticut and founds Hartford.
1637	Hooker returns to Boston to moderate a synod on a heretic.
1645	Hooker participates in Boston meeting on a council of clergymen.
1647	Hooker dies at Hartford.
1648	Hooker's *Survey of the Summe of Church Discipline* is published.
1656	Hooker's *The Application of Redemption* is published.

Horn, Rosa Artimus

1880–1976 ● PENTECOSTAL

Rosa Artimus Horn, affectionately called "Mother," was an African-American minister best known for her radio program, the *You, Pray for Me Church of the Air*, which reached listeners as far as 1,000 miles away from her Harlem-

OPPOSITE:
Thomas Hooker
(standing, with staff)

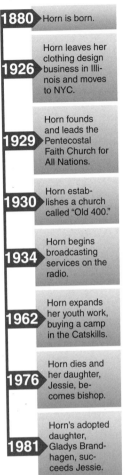

1880 ▸ Horn is born.

1926 ▸ Horn leaves her clothing design business in Illinois and moves to NYC.

1929 ▸ Horn founds and leads the Pentecostal Faith Church for All Nations.

1930 ▸ Horn establishes a church called "Old 400."

1934 ▸ Horn begins broadcasting services on the radio.

1962 ▸ Horn expands her youth work, buying a camp in the Catskills.

1976 ▸ Horn dies and her daughter, Jessie, becomes bishop.

1981 ▸ Horn's adopted daughter, Gladys Brandhagen, succeeds Jessie.

based congregation. Mother Horn began her ministry in Evanston, Illinois, where she was also a clothing designer. She moved to New York City in 1926, believing that God had sent her there to "establish true holiness." She began her work in Brooklyn, holding revivals and faith-healing meetings, with many reports of conversions and miracles.

Her following was interracial and intercultural, attracting members of the Italian and Jewish communities as well as African Americans and people from the Caribbean. In 1929 she became the founder and first bishop of the Pentecostal Faith Church for All Nations, also known as the Mount Calvary Pentecostal Faith Church. The following year, after a summer-long preaching and healing crusade in Harlem, she established a church at 392–400 Lenox Avenue, fondly referred to by long-standing members as "Old 400."

In 1934, Horn began her radio broadcasting. The *You, Pray for Me Church of the Air* reached audiences as far away as Tennessee, Massachusetts, and the Caribbean. In the New York metropolitan area, many joined Mother Horn's church after having heard the broadcasts of her services from "Old 400." She did not confine her outreach to the masses of poor during the depression to radio messages. With personal funds, she leased a house at the corner of 132nd Street and Madison Avenue and had it renovated as a shelter and soup kitchen for the hungry and homeless. Called the Gleaners' Aid Home, Mother Horn's facility provided breakfast and dinner for thousands, and housed many women and children. She also took great interest in the adolescent and young-adult populations, offering them alternatives to street life through religion and hard work.

During World War II, Mother Horn's church, consistent with the majority of African-American Pentecostal groups of the time, encouraged young men to register as conscientious objectors. She went to local draft boards to ensure that her young ministers were not drafted. Burdened by their plight, she decided to create work for them that would be approved by the federal government as an alternative to military service. She secured farmland near her birthplace of Sumter, S.C., and there personally trained young men in farming. The produce was sold to local supermarkets and hospitals.

During the 1950s and 1960s, Mount Calvary sponsored a mission home for the poor in Los Angeles. Mother Horn's ministry also included foreign missions in the Dominican Republic and the Bahamas.

She expanded her youth work in 1962 when the church purchased a camp in the Catskills. Named the Bethel Sunshine Camp, the 40-acre facility provided summer recreation and religious instruction for youth from poor communities. She was assisted in the development of these ministries by her natural daughter, Jessie Artimus Horn, who succeeded Mother Horn as presiding bishop upon her death in 1976, and by an adopted daughter, Gladys Brandhagen, who succeeded her adopted sister in 1981. Bishop Brandhagen, a woman of Norwegian ancestry, had become part of Mother Horn's movement in Evanston, after her father's conversion under Mother Horn's ministry. The Pentecostal Faith Church reports some 22 churches with an estimated membership of 1,200. ◆

Hubbard, L. Ron

1911–1986 ● SCIENTOLOGY

Lafayette Ronald Hubbard, who founded the Church of Scientology, was born in 1911 in Tilden, Nebraska, the son of Harry Ross Hubbard, a commander in the U.S. Navy, and Ledora May Waterbury de Wolfe. Raised on his grandfather's ranch in Helena, Montana, Hubbard claimed he was an adventurer and traveler during this time, probably referring to trips he made to visit his father, who was stationed in Guam. At the age of 12, Hubbard rejoined his family when his father was transferred to Washington, D.C. Hubbard enrolled at George Washington University in 1930 but left after two years because of poor academic performance. Claims that he studied mathematics at Princeton in 1945 are not confirmed by that university.

In the 1930s Hubbard began writing adventure stories. His first novel was *Buckskin Brigades* (1937), but he first gained notoriety for writing pulp science fiction stories and novels. A prolific writer for the rest of his life, Hubbard claimed he sold more than 23 million copies of his books. He married Margaret Louise Grubb sometime before 1940.

At the beginning of World War II, Hubbard was assigned to U.S. naval intelligence in Australia as a lieutenant. He commanded two ships, but he was removed from the first for ex-

> In the 1930s Hubbard began writing adventure stories.

ceeding orders and from the second for firing guns in Mexican waters and creating an international incident. Although he later claimed he was crippled and blinded during the war, no naval records substantiate that he was wounded. He spent the last few months of the war in the Oak Knoll Military Hospital in California, where he was treated for an ulcer. After leaving the service, he complained to the Veterans Administration (VA) about his "suicidal inclinations." The VA decided he suffered from numerous physical ailments and awarded him a 40 percent disability pension. Hubbard married Sarah ("Betty") Northrup in August 1946, more than a year before he and his first wife divorced in December 1947. He and Sarah had a daughter, Alexis, in 1950.

Around this time, Hubbard wrote *Dianetics: The Modern Science of Mental Health* (1950), which made him a best-selling author and set the course for the rest of his life. This book outlined a form of counseling that purported to cure emotional and psychological illnesses. Through a process known as "auditing," a counselor used questions and an electronic device called an "E-meter" to help the subject increase his or her analytical mind. This therapy uncovered painful experiences, "engrams," from past lives and helped patients heal themselves. Hubbard said this process was the result of 30 years of research. The book was tremendously popular despite criticism from psychiatrists and others. Some have suggested that Hubbard developed Dianetics in the hope that it would cure his own ongoing ailments.

In April 1950 Hubbard founded the Dianetics Research Foundation in Elizabeth, New Jersey, with branches in five major U.S. cities, and began giving lectures around the country. In 1951 Sarah Hubbard filed for divorce on the grounds that Ron Hubbard was suffering from paranoid schizophrenia. Ron Hubbard took their daughter with him to Cuba, where he received treatment in a military hospital. Meanwhile, the popularity of Dianetics had begun to wane. He wrote *The Science of Survival: Prediction of Human Behaviour* (1951), which explained the religious background of Dianetics, called Scientology. According to Hubbard, humans are eternal beings, called thetans, trapped in human bodies. Presumably, Scientology could help individuals recover memories from past lives and heal from painful experiences contained in those lives. After leaving Cuba in 1962, he began forming Scientology organizations, starting in Camden, New Jersey.

Hubbard married Mary Sue Whipp in March 1952. He opened the First Church of Scientology in Los Angeles in early 1954, and by 1959 the church had become successful, chiefly through the massive dissemination of the founder's books. Hubbard bought the Hill Manor castle and 55 acres in Sussex, England, to use for the worldwide headquarters of Scientology, which now had centers in England, France, South Africa, and New Zealand. The first of his two children by Margaret Grubb, Ron Hubbard, Jr., who had worked with his father from the beginning of the church, left the fold abruptly in 1959 and later changed his name to Ron de Wolfe.

In 1960 Hubbard declared that Scientology was a "new religion" that was not based on worship of a god. He began having problems with law-enforcement officials in several countries concerning fraud and other crimes. After an Internal Revenue Service ruling in 1967 stripped the mother church of its tax-exempt status in the United States, Hubbard moved the Scientology headquarters to a yacht called the *Apollo*, based in England. He lived on the yacht during much of the 1960s and 1970s. Church officials claimed that government agencies were harassing them because they did not practice a "traditional" religion. None of this apparently affected the success of the church, which in the 1970s boasted 6 million members worldwide. As his legal problems increased and the *Apollo* was denied permission to dock in many ports, Hubbard established new headquarters in Florida and in southern California.

Although Scientology continued to grow tremendously in the 1970s, the decade presented difficult times for Hubbard. In 1971 the French government found him guilty of fraud in absentia. A U.S. federal court ruled in the same year that Hubbard's medical claims were bogus, and an IRS investigation ruled that Hubbard was skimming millions from the church. In 1978 the Federal Bureau of Investigation raided Scientology offices, taking thousands of documents that purportedly showed an extensive intelligence organization engaged in burglaries

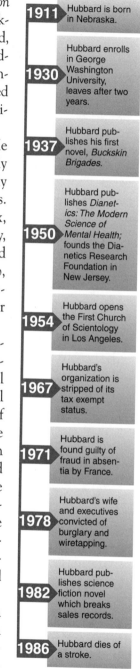

1911 Hubbard is born in Nebraska.

1930 Hubbard enrolls in George Washington University, leaves after two years.

1937 Hubbard publishes his first novel, *Buckskin Brigades*.

1950 Hubbard publishes *Dianetics: The Modern Science of Mental Health*; founds the Dianetics Research Foundation in New Jersey.

1954 Hubbard opens the First Church of Scientology in Los Angeles.

1967 Hubbard's organization is stripped of its tax exempt status.

1971 Hubbard is found guilty of fraud in absentia by France.

1978 Hubbard's wife and executives convicted of burglary and wiretapping.

1982 Hubbard publishes science fiction novel which breaks sales records.

1986 Hubbard dies of a stroke.

> "A high-tone individual thinks wholly into the future. He is extroverted toward his environment. He clearly observes the environment with full perception unclouded by undistinguished fears about the environment. He thinks very little about himself but operates automatically in his own interests. He enjoys existence."
>
> L. Ron Hubbard, *Advanced Procedure and Axioms*, 1951

and wiretapping of hundreds of government offices. Mary Sue Hubbard and other Scientology officials were convicted of these crimes. Hubbard himself could not be held liable because he had officially resigned from church management in 1966. Nevertheless, many observers felt that he had been closely involved in church affairs.

In the early 1980s the IRS challenged the tax-exempt status of the entire Scientology organization. Meanwhile, Great Britain banned Hubbard from entering the country, and Australia revoked the church's status as a religion. After further raids by the FBI, Hubbard withdrew to a ranch near San Luis Obispo, California, where he remained in seclusion for the rest of his life. He wrote and published his first science fiction novel in 30 years, *Battlefield Earth: A Saga of the Year 3000* (1982), as a commemoration of his writing career. The book rapidly made the *New York Times* best-seller list and broke all existing sales records for science fiction.

Hubbard spent the last few years of his life researching, writing, and publishing. He officially died in Creston, California, of a stroke on 24 January 1986, although some, including Hubbard's oldest son, believed he died years earlier. No autopsy was performed, and he was cremated without ceremony. His ashes were scattered in the Pacific Ocean by Church of Scientology officials. Hubbard had two children with Margaret Grubb and four with Mary Sue Whipp. Some sources mention seven children in all.

Hubbard attracted millions of followers with his ideas, touched them with his books of fiction and nonfiction, and changed lives through the founding of Dianetics and Scientology. He garnered love, hatred, loyal followers, and vehement detractors, and he lived a life of mystery, contradiction, and controversy to his end. ◆

Saint Jerome

c.347–c.420 ● CHRISTIAN

Saint Jerome was an early Christian saint, translator, and teacher. Also known as Eusebius Hieronymus, Jerome is revered as the most learned of the Latin church fathers; he and his two contemporaries, Saint Ambrose and Saint Augustine, are, along with Pope Gregory the Great, traditionally known as the four doctors of the Western church. His enduring monument is his translation of the Bible into a Latin comprehensible to the common people of his age, known as the Vulgate version, which became the authoritative translation in the Roman Catholic church. Also of great significance is the impulse to monasticism that he engendered in the church. Many of his letters have been preserved so that, in addition to his literary legacy, there remains a volume of detailed personal information.

Born to affluent parents in Stridon, near Ljubljana in Slovenia, Jerome was a precocious student in his youth; at 12 he was sent to Rome to study grammar, rhetoric, and philosophy. He leavened his scholastic duties with liberal doses of the pleasures of the flesh; his sins were to return to haunt him in his years of asceticism. In Rome he was baptized by Pope Liberus. After his studies, he spent the next 20 years in travel; this was the period when he first became attracted to the monastic way of life. He also developed links with an Italian ascetic elite grouped round Bishop Valerius and hence formed a friendship with Rufinus; both men greatly admired the writings

> Jerome's enduring monument is his translation of the Bible into a Latin comprehensible to the common people of his age.

of the Alexandrine scholar, Origin, who had done much work in establishing the text of the Old Testament.

A naturally passionate man of robust appetites as well as a lover of the classical authors, Jerome was to find the ascetic life a great trial. He relates in one of his letters how hard it was to cut himself off from his friends "and—harder still—from the dainty food to which I had become accustomed." The Greek and Roman authors he loved were pagan and considered inappropriate reading for the faithful; nonetheless, he admits that "miserable man that I was, I would fast only that I might afterwards read Cicero," after whom the style of the prophets seemed "rude and repellent."

The revelation, beloved of early church literature, that led to his renunciation of pagan writers occurred in Antioch in 374: he beheld the Last Judgment, where Jesus asked him who he was; upon his answering that he was a Christian, the reply descended that "thou liest, thou art a follower of Cicero and not of Christ." Thereafter he seems to have avoided the temptations of paganism, although references to Virgil, Horace, and Ovid would reappear in his letters on occasion. During his lonely years as a hermit in Chalcis from 375 to 377 Jerome learned Hebrew from a Jewish convert, but he left when the place became suspected of harboring heretical views. He agreed to be ordained a priest in 378, on condition that his monastic aspirations not be prejudiced and that he be allowed to continue his studies.

As secretary to Pope Damasus between 382 and 385, Jerome was able to progress in his translation of many key early Christian texts. He also held classes for pious gentlewomen, to whom he was fond of extolling the virtues of virginity. The erotic mysticism with which he praised the joys of convent life is apparent in his letters to Eustochium, daughter of his most devoted disciple, the widow Paula, preparing her for her chosen vocation as a nun: in them, he used the now-familiar description of nuns as the Brides of Christ and cited the Song of Solomon as the biblical text celebrating this marriage.

His success in persuading some of these aristocratic ladies to adopt the ascetic life made him unpopular among many of his peers, and also with the pope who succeeded his patron Damasus. Jerome's tirades against the lax lifestyles of monks and clergy further increased resentment against him and in 386 he left Rome for the Holy Land, vehemently decrying the papal city as "Babylon"; he remained in Bethlehem until his death, grieving at the barbarian invasion of the Roman Empire and ruing the hypocrisy that plagued the priesthood: "Our walls shine with gold…yet Christ dies before our doors naked in the person of His poor," he lamented.

It was in the monastery financed by Paula (who had accompanied him to Bethlehem) that, between 391 and 406, Jerome undertook and completed his translation of the Bible on the basis of the original text. While always anxious to remain strictly orthodox, Jerome did not allow this determination to cloud his conclusions as to the authenticity of his sources. Thus, although Christians had traditionally maintained that the Jews had falsified the Hebrew text where it seemed to predict the Messiah, Jerome dismissed this view outright as incompatible with the findings of scholarship. He even took the help of rabbis to clarify textual difficulties for him. His acceptance of the text endorsed as correct by Jews ("Let him who would challenge aught in this translation ask the Jews," he proposed) led to his translation initially receiving a hostile reception; Saint Augustine's championing helped it win approval.

Strong-willed and temperamental. Jerome was sometimes involved in petulant dispute: he argued with Saint Augustine over the behavior of Saint Peter; he was moved to break with his friend Rufinus when he found it prudent to disavow his own youthful espousal of Origin, whose doctrines had fallen out of favor; he was so vehement in his opposition to the Pelagian heresy of questioning the doctrine of original sin that his monastery was attacked by a mob; he penned savage attacks on the married state in response to Jovian.

In his homilies to his monks, however, his depth of learning as a scholar is evident; it was as a scholar rather than as a thinker that he accomplished his greatest achievements, not least in transmitting Greek thought to the West. ◆

> "It is hard for the human soul to avoid loving something, and our mind must of necessity give way to affection of one kind or another. The love of the flesh is overcome by the love of the spirit. Desire is quenched by desire. What is taken from the one increases the other."
>
> Jerome, letter to Eustochium, late 4th century

Jesus Christ

C. 4 BCE–30 C.E. ● CHRISTIAN

> "And Jesus cried with a loud voice, and gave up the ghost. And the veil of the temple was rent in twain from the top to the bottom. And when the centurion, which stood over against him, saw that he so cried out, and gave up the ghost, he said, Truly this man was the Son of God."
>
> Bible,
> Mark 15:37–39

Jesus Christ also known as Jesus of Nazareth was the founder of Christianity. Regarded by Christians as the universal messiah or savior, Jesus (the Greek form of the Hebrew name, Yehoshua) was a Jew who lived in Judea during the Roman occupation. He taught a message of forgiveness of sins, love of neighbor, and the reign of the Kingdom of God.

The Gospels of the New Testament, all written by the first part of the second century C.E., are the main source of information about Jesus. Gathered from various traditions after his death, they trace the genealogy of his parents, Joseph and Mary, back to King David, from whose descendants the Messiah (or "Christ" in Greek) was traditionally expected to originate. The couple lived in Nazareth, in the Galilee region of northern Israel, but because of a census they traveled to Bethlehem where Jesus was born in a stable. Joseph was a carpenter and Jesus seems to have practiced this trade as well. Not much is known of his early life; the Gospels tell of his encounter with John the Baptist when he was already an adult. In about 26 B.C.E. John, following the words of the prophet Isaiah, "to make a way for the Lord in the wilderness," had left the towns of Judea to dwell in the desert, baptizing adherents to his prophetic message in the waters of the Jordan River. John preached that the present age was corrupt and that a heavenly judgment was imminent that would cleanse the world through fire. Those who wished to live in the new age that he prophesied were enjoined to repent of sin and do good deeds as well as be baptized by immersion. This was a period of intensive messianic anticipation among the Jews, precipitated by the curtailment of their independence by the Roman rulers of their country.

Jesus's own sense of destiny was catalyzed by John's teaching, but before he began to preach he underwent a period of trial, tempted with spiritual and material power. After surviving these tests he began to travel throughout Galilee, preaching his message in the towns and villages there, gathering around him numerous disciples and an inner group, the Twelve Apostles: Peter, James, John, Andrew, Philip, Bartholomew, Matthew, Thomas, James the son of Alphaeus, Thaddaeus, Simon the Cananite, and Judas Iscariot (later replaced by

OPPOSITE:
Jesus Christ

The Bible

The Bible, the most widely published and read book in human history, includes the sacred texts of Judaism (referred to by Christians as the "Old Testament") and Christianity (the Hebrew scriptures with the "New" Testament). The Hebrew scriptures include 39 books, recorded in Hebrew and Aramaic over the course of several centuries. The New Testament contains 27 books, written in Greek over a relatively brief period of time following the death of Jesus.

One traditional arrangement of the Hebrew scriptures divides them into the Torah, histories, prophetic writings, and wisdom literature. The Torah, traditionally ascribed to Moses, includes the first five books of the Bible, and covers God's creation of the world and first humans, and the earliest development of the Hebrew nations. The histories chronicle the reigns of leaders and the struggles of the Hebrew peoples to overcome political oppression and exile. The prophesies include both God's warnings and promises to the Jews. The wisdom writings include the poetry of the Song of Songs, the wise reflections of Ecclesiastes, and the pithy moral advice of Proverbs.

The Hebrew scriptures are united by their account of the rise and struggles of the Hebrew nation. The Christian scriptures are united by their focus on the life and teachings of Jesus of Nazareth and the new religion he inspired. The four Gospels give details of his life, ministry, death, and reported resurrection. Later works tell of how Jesus' followers attempted to adopt his teachings in their own communities, and the struggles they faced. Revelation, the last book of the New Testament, offers a violent account of the end of time, when Jesus Christ will return to triumph over Satan and redeem those who have been faithful to him.

The Bible has been a formative text for Western civilization, giving shape to the way Jews and Christians understand God, human ethics, and the meaning and goal of human life. In its English translation in the King James Version, the Bible has had an influence on the formation of the language rivaled only by Shakespeare.

Matthias). The Apostles accompanied Jesus on his mission, with Peter given authority above the rest and being privy to miracles and teachings the other Apostles did not witness.

Jesus' first miracle was changing water into wine at a marriage feast in Cana in Galilee. Thereafter, he cast out demons, healed the blind and leprous, and raised the dead. He also walked on the waters of the Sea of Galilee, and fed the multitudes in the wilderness. In his Sermon on the Mount, Jesus preached the love of God and man and taught that salvation rested on fulfilling the inner meaning of the law and not its outward performance. A healer in the tradition of Elijah and Elisha, his works attracted crowds of people who had heard of his deeds. Without claiming to be the Messiah, Jesus spoke of the coming of the Kingdom of Heaven, teaching in parables that contained spiritual insights veiled in everyday stories. He proclaimed that God was forgiving, as in the parable of the prodigal son, but could also be wrathful, as in the parable of the unmerciful servant. Both these attributes became more accentuated in Jesus' teaching than they had been in Jewish tradition. He offered a threat of damnation if God's will was not obeyed, a promise of salvation if it was. The kingdom of God was not a temporal reality that would mean salvation from the Roman enemy, but a new reality of which Jesus was the sign.

While he sometimes set aside the Jewish law in order to accomplish a pressing task, he insisted that his message was to his fellow Jews and that they should adhere strictly to the Law. He spent a year in the north of Israel, healing the sick and curing people of demons before heading south for Jerusalem, which he had prophesied would be the place where he would die.

Jesus arrived in Jerusalem in the spring, the season of the Passover festival. By this time, the radical nature of his teachings had produced many enemies antagonized by his attacks on the religious establishment, which he accused of injustice and hypocrisy. At his last meal, known as the Last Supper, he blessed and gave out bread and wine to his Apostles, instituting the sacrament of Communion. Jesus's preaching of the forthcoming destruction of the Temple angered the Sadducees, the priestly caste. While he was in the garden of Gethsemane on the Mount of Olives, he was arrested by the Temple guard—who had been led there by one of the Apostles, Judas Iscariot—and brought to the high priest. The Sanhedrin, the Jewish court, was convened and Jesus, suspected of being a false messiah, was condemned as a blasphemer and was handed over to Pontius Pilate, the Roman procurator of Judea, on the grounds that he claimed to be king of the Jews. Pilate, initially finding no fault with Jesus, relented to pressures from the Sanhedrin and ordered Jesus to be crucified, the usual form of execution. On a hill called Golgotha outside the city walls, Jesus was crucified and, after a three-hour ordeal, died and was entombed. Three days later his tomb was discovered to be empty. His disciples recorded Jesus's appearances before them during the next weeks, until on the fortieth day after the Resurrection they declared that he had ascended to Heaven. Following this his disciples began their own mission of proclaiming his life and establishing communities in Jerusalem and throughout the Mediterranean region. ◆

The Sanhedrin, the Jewish court, was convened and Jesus, suspected of being a false messiah, was condemned as a blasphemer and was handed over to Pontius Pilate.

John XXIII

1881–1963 ● Catholic

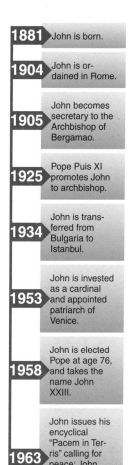

1881 John is born.

1904 John is ordained in Rome.

1905 John becomes secretary to the Archbishop of Bergamao.

1925 Pope Puis XI promotes John to archbishop.

1934 John is transferred from Bulgaria to Istanbul.

1953 John is invested as a cardinal and appointed patriarch of Venice.

1958 John is elected Pope at age 76, and takes the name John XXIII.

1963 John issues his encyclical "Pacem in Terris" calling for peace; John dies before the council's second session.

John XXIII was a Catholic Pope who initiated far-reaching reforms in the Roman Catholic church during his short pontificate. Pope John was born Angelo Roncalli in Bergamo, Italy, to poor tenant farmers.

He was ordained in Rome at the age of 22. In 1905 he became secretary to the archbishop of Bergamo, with whom he had a close relationship. He served as spiritual director at the Bergamo seminary until the new pope, Benedict XV, called him to Rome to take charge of missionary activities and elevated him to the rank of monsignor.

In 1925 Pope Pius XI removed Roncalli from the Vatican by promoting him to archbishop and sending him to Bulgaria as an apostolic vicar, where only 1 percent of the population was Catholic. Lonely and hurt by the Vatican's treatment, Roncalli visited Bulgaria's impoverished and scattered Catholic communities, ordered communal prayers to be said in the vernacular (the Vatican refused or ignored his requests for other changes), and developed his diplomatic skills. His diplomacy was based on the motto "see everything, ignore a good deal, improve things where possible;" he optimistically believed that time, opportunity, and patience improved almost any situation. He accomplished his goals by generating good will through friendly gestures and using his warmth and good humor to defuse antagonism caused by individual or ideological differences.

When Roncalli was transferred to Istanbul in 1934, these skills helped him overcome the hostility of different Christian denominations, the anti-Italian Orthodox Greeks, and the secular anti-Western Turks. During World War II, he maintained relations both with Nazi occupiers and the local community in Greece and negotiated grain shipments to alleviate the 1941 famine. Roncalli's friendliness with Germany's ambassador in Istanbul ensured German noninterference with attempts to save Jews (in which he was involved), while his peace keeping activities within Istanbul's divided French community influenced his appointment as papal nuncio to France in 1944.

The new French government had dismissed Roncalli's predecessor from France and demanded that 33 bishops be removed from office for their acquiescence in the Vichy regime.

However, Roncalli's tenure as papal nuncio was so effective that the French president insisted on attending his investiture as a cardinal in 1953, when he was appointed patriarch of Venice.

In 1958, aged 76, Roncalli was elected pope, taking the name John XXIII. He was a compromise candidate because it was believed that as an elderly man he would not be too active in introducing innovation. He however, called for *aggiormento:* the updating and renewal of the church in the modern world.

In 1959 Pope John proposed three undertakings: a diocesan synod for Rome, the revision of the code of the canon law, and the calling of an ecumenical council—the first in nearly a century. He attributed his inspiration for convoking the Second Vatican Council The council issued decrees on religious freedom and conscience, the liturgy, the church as the people of God, and on was and peace, unequivocally condemning the arms race. He invited non-Catholic observers and established a Secretariat for Promoting Christian Unity. In 1963 he issued his encyclical *Pacem in Terris,* calling for peace among nations based on justice, charity, and the right organization of society, and calling for an end to the arms race, a ban on nuclear weapons, and eventual disarmament.

Pope John was warm and friendly, a kind of father figure; he was accessible and often walked through Rome talking to the people. He became a voice for unity and peace, appealing to "all men of good will" to learn to live together. Pope John died before the council's second session but in his short reign he had revitalized the church, raising its moral prestige to unprecedented heights and becoming the most popular pope of modern times. ◆

> "All the evils which poison men and nations and trouble so many hearts have a single cause and a single source: ignorance of the truth—and at times even more than ignorance, a contempt for truth and a reckless rejection of it."
>
> John XXIII, encyclical, 1959

John Paul II

1920– ● ROMAN CATHOLIC

When the Sacred College of Cardinals of the Roman Catholic Church gathered at the Vatican in 1978 for the solemn election of a new pope, nobody could have guessed the outcome. After two days of discussion, on October 16 at 6:10 P.M., white smoke from the Vatican smokestack signaled to the world that the cardinals had made their

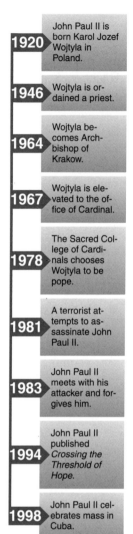

decision. They had chosen Cardinal Karol Wojtyla of Poland. John Paul II, as he became known, became the first non-Italian pope of the Roman Catholic Church in over 450 years. But if the Italians gathered outside the Vatican were alarmed, that concern faded as the new pope emerged on the balcony and addressed them in fluent Italian. John Paul soon endeared himself to the rest of his flock through his language skills and for the care he expressed for all the people of the world.

Pope John Paul II was born Karol Jozef Wojtyla on May 18, 1920, in the small town of Wadowice, Poland, near Krakow. He had one brother, Edmund, 15 years his senior, who left home to study medicine. When Karol was only nine years old, he lost his mother, Emilia, who died giving birth to a girl, who also died. The saddened boy grew closer to his father, also named Karol Wojtyla, a Polish administrative army lieutenant. His father's strong discipline, after the guidance of his former schoolteacher mother, shaped Karol into a hard-working student. But Lolek, as his family called him, also had time to play soccer in the streets and to ski in the winter. He loved to hike and swim in the forests and rivers near his home, pastimes he continued in his years ahead.

After young Wojtyla entered high school, another tragedy struck. His brother died in 1932 after contracting scarlet fever from patients. Lieutenant Wojtyla had retired, so he now devoted all his attention to his remaining son. They moved to Krakow in 1938 so young Karol could attend Jagellonian University, one of Europe's oldest learning institutions. There he began studying theater, which he had come to love in high school.

On September 1, 1939, the young student's life changed drastically when Germany invaded Poland, beginning World War II. Wojtyla learned quickly that student life could be dangerous, as Germans rounded up teachers and other intellectuals. However, he helped form a small theater group that performed political plays and met with a Catholic prayer group. To avoid suspicion, Wojtyla began working at a quarry in 1940 and later in a chemical factory.

While German occupation ravaged his country, another blow hit Wojtyla in 1941 when he found his father dead of a

Saint Peter's Basilica

Saint Peter's Basilica is the world's largest Christian church. It is the crown jewel of Vatican City, home of the pope and world center of Roman Catholicism. The original St. Peter's, begun by Constantine the Great about 325, was built above a tomb believed to hold the body of Peter, apostle of Jesus. Designers modeled the church after the *basilica,* a rectangular meeting hall used by Romans. In 1506, Pope Julius II began rebuilding the church completely, leaving only Peter's tomb and bits of the earlier structure. The first design for the current St. Peter's was developed by Donato Bramante, and construction continued through the mid-1600s.

St. Peter's is shaped like a cross, with a length of 700 feet and a width of about 450 feet at its widest. At the center aisle, the ceiling reaches 150 feet. The magnificent dome, designed by Michelangelo, rises more than 400 feet from the floor. The church interior is richly decorated with marble, gold leaf, and mosaics. Sculptor Bernini built an elaborate bronze canopy over the main altar and also designed several magnificent papal tombs. In one of several chapels lining the sides, stands Michelangelo's sculpture the *Pieta.* The Square of St. Peter is a large space in front of the church embraced by two semicircles of columns, topped by sculptures of saints.

sudden heart attack. For 12 hours, the anguished son prayed over his father's body. Alone in the world, Wojtyla began changing his life. "After my father's death, I gradually became aware of my true path," he later said. As he sought spiritual strength, he found himself drawn to the priesthood. The following year, he said, "I knew that I was called." Wojtyla continued his studies in a secret theology department run by surviving professors of the Jagellonian University. When Communists ousted the Germans from Poland, Wojtyla emerged from hiding. On November 1, 1946, the archbishop of Krakow ordained the 26-year-old a priest. The archbishop then sent Wojtyla to Rome to study for two years.

Wojtyla returned to a Communist Poland that offered its Catholic majority limited freedom. Nevertheless, Father Wojtyla served two parishes while continuing his studies, and his two doctorate degrees in theology earned him a teaching position in 1953. He taught philosophy at universities in Krakow and Lublin.

Wojtyla's intellectual and social skills led him to rise in the church. In 1958, the pope chose him to become an auxiliary bishop of Krakow, and in 1964 he became archbishop of Krakow. In 1967, he was elevated to cardinal, one of the select clergymen who rank immediately below the pope in the Catholic hierarchy. As a cardinal in Poland, Wojtyla struggled against Communist opposition. Partly through his influence, government leaders learned to compromise with the nation's Catholics. Wojtyla also worked to modernize the Polish church in keeping with the efforts of Pope John XXIII and Vatican Council II (1958–1963).

In a remarkable turn of events, Cardinal Wojtyla came to Rome twice in 1978 to select a pope. First, Pope Paul VI died in August, and the College of Cardinals chose for his replacement an Italian cardinal who became Pope John Paul I on August 26. To everyone's shock, the new pope died of a massive stroke weeks later on September 28. Cardinal Wojtyla returned to Rome to vote again. With few eligible Italians left, the cardinals considered non-Italian candidates. Cardinal Wojtyla had impressed many of them with his multi-lingual abilities and his travels to their regions. After their vote, the cardinals asked Cardinal Wojtyla to be their new leader. A humbled Wojtyla replied, "I accept." In honor of his immediate predecessor, Wojtyla took the name John Paul II.

As a cardinal in Poland, Wojtyla struggled against Communist opposition.

The Roman Catholic Church regards the pope as its visible, worldly head, with Jesus Christ as its supreme head. The pope is believed to be heir to the position that Jesus established with his apostle Peter. Throughout Poland, Catholics celebrated in the streets at the news of their beloved cardinal's new role.

John Paul earned the nickname "the pilgrim pope" by traveling more than any previous pope. In 1979, the new pope toured the United States, Latin America, and Poland. John Paul also attracted large crowds to his weekly audiences in the square outside St. Peter's Basilica. In May 1981, a Turkish terrorist in the audience shot and seriously wounded the pope. On Christmas Day in 1983, John Paul met with his attacker in prison and forgave him.

John Paul often urged governments to improve the conditions of their nations' poor and called upon rich nations to create a fair world economic order. The pope strongly defended human rights and spoke of all human beings as part of God's family. During the 1980s, he supported the Solidarity movement in Poland and has been credited with influencing the collapse of Communism in Eastern Europe and the Soviet Union from 1989 to 1991. In January 1998, more than a half million Cubans gathered at Revolution Square in Havana for a Catholic Mass celebrated by Pope John Paul II. Cuba's Communist leader, Fidel Castro, had welcomed the pope to Cuba. The pope called upon Cuban leadership to end religious restrictions and also called upon the United States to end its embargo against Cuba.

John Paul II firmly upheld traditional Roman Catholic teachings, including opposition to divorce, artificial birth control, abortion, and homosexuality. He also opposed such ideas as marriage for priests or admitting women to the priesthood. Through the years, the pope disciplined several Catholic clergy for liberal liturgical practices. Nonetheless, John Paul made many progressive political moves in his role as head of the Vatican. He helped the Italian parliament approve an agreement in 1985 recognizing the separation of church and state in Italy. In 1984, the Vatican and the United States established diplomatic relations and the exchange of ambassadors. In 1994, the Vatican established full diplomatic relations with Israel. John Paul also met with many leaders of various world faiths to encourage harmony between religions.

In June 1999, John Paul made his 87th pastoral trip to a foreign country, spending two weeks visiting 21 cities throughout

John Paul often urged governments to improve the conditions of their nations' poor and called upon rich nations to create a fair world economic order.

Poland. Millions of Poles turned out to greet their native son. The Pope announced in July 1999 that he intended to make a pilgrimage to the Holy Land in the year 2000 to celebrate the millenium. He planned to visit Iraq, Egypt, Syria, Greece, and cities ruled by Israel and the Palestinian Authority.

Among John Paul's published works are *Crossing the Threshold of Hope* (1994), containing his written responses to interview questions, and *Gift and Mystery* (1996), a personal memoir. ◆

Jonas, Regina

1902–1944 ● JEWISH

1902 Jonas is born into a poor Berlin household.

1930 Jonas passes her final oral exams for the rabbinate, but is granted a teaching certificate rather than ordination.

1935 Jonas is ordained a rabbi.

1942 Jonas is deported by the Nazis to Theresienstadt concentration camp.

1944 Jonas is deported to the Auschwitz death camps and murdered.

Regina Jonas was the first woman to be ordained as a rabbi. Born in Berlin, she was raised in a poor, religious home. She completed rabbinical studies in Berlin with a thesis entitled "Can women perform the rabbinical appointment?" Jonas concluded that, "except for prejudice and novelty ...hardly anything" stood against it. In July 1930 she passed her final oral examinations administered by some of the leading rabbis and scholars of liberal Judaism in Germany, including Leo Baeck, Julius Guttmann, Ismar Elbogen, and Eduard Baneth. The latter had marked her thesis as "Good" and probably intended to agree to her ordination. After his sudden death in the summer of 1930, however, Jonas was not ordained but given a certificate as an "academically approved teacher of religion." Finally, on 27 December 1935 Jonas was ordained privately by the liberal rabbi of Offenbach, Max Dienemann.

Following her ordination, the Jewish community of Berlin employed Jonas, but only as a religion teacher. She was also allowed to take over the "rabbinical-pastoral care" at the Jewish old-age home, hospital, and public institutions. Jonas was considered a gifted preacher and pastor. She often lectured about religious, biblical, and historical topics and about the status of women in Judaism.

In her writings Jonas insisted on the traditional Jewish separation of men and women in synagogues and stressed the Jewish principle of chastity. She also believed that the responsibilities of motherhood meant that only unmarried women should be rabbis.

Jonas was deported by the Nazis to the Theresienstadt concentration camp on 6 November 1942 where she continued her pastoral work as a rabbi among the inmates. On 12 October 1944, she was deported to the Auschwitz death camps and murdered. ◆

Jones, Absalom

1716–1818 ● Episcopal

Absalom Jones was an African American Episcopal minister and community leader. Among the enslaved African Americans who gained their freedom in the era of the American Revolution, Absalom Jones made some of the most important contributions to black community building at a time when the first urban free black communities of the United States were taking form. Enslaved from his birth in Sussex County, Delaware, Jones served on the estate of the merchant-planter Benjamin Wynkoop. Taken from the fields into his master's house as a young boy, he gained an opportunity for learning. When his master moved to Philadelphia in 1762, Jones, at age 16, worked in his master's store but continued his education in a night school for blacks. In 1770 he married, and through unstinting labor he was able to buy his wife's freedom in about 1778 and his own in 1784.

After gaining his freedom, Jones rapidly became one of the main leaders of the growing free black community in Philadelphia—the largest urban gathering of emancipated slaves in the post-Revolutionary period. Worshiping at Saint George's Methodist Episcopal Church, Jones soon began to discuss a separate black religious society with other black Methodists such as Richard Allen and William White. From these tentative steps toward community-based institutions came the Free African Society of Philadelphia, probably the first independent black organization in the United States. Although mutual aid was its purported goal, the Free African Society was quasi-religious in character; beyond that, it was an organization where people emerging from the house of bondage could gather strength, develop their own leaders, and explore independent strategies for hammering out a postslavery existence that went beyond formal legal release from thralldom.

Among the enslaved African Americans who gained their freedom in the era of the American Revolution, Absalom Jones made some of the most important contributions to black community building. . . .

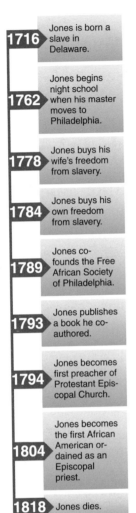

1716 Jones is born a slave in Delaware.

1762 Jones begins night school when his master moves to Philadelphia.

1778 Jones buys his wife's freedom from slavery.

1784 Jones buys his own freedom from slavery.

1789 Jones co-founds the Free African Society of Philadelphia.

1793 Jones publishes a book he co-authored.

1794 Jones becomes first preacher of Protestant Episcopal Church.

1804 Jones becomes the first African American ordained as an Episcopal priest.

1818 Jones dies.

Once established, the Free African Society became a vehicle for Jones to establish the African Church of Philadelphia, the first independent black church in North America. Planned in conjunction with Richard Allen and launched with the assistance of Benjamin Rush and several Philadelphia Quakers, the African Church of Philadelphia was designed as a racially separate, nondenominational, and socially oriented church. But in order to gain state recognition of its corporate status, it affiliated with the Protestant Episcopal Church of North America and later took the name Saint Thomas's African Episcopal Church. Jones became its minister when it opened in 1794, and served in that capacity until his death in 1818. For decades, Saint Thomas's was emblematic of the striving for dignity, self-improvement, and autonomy of a generation of African Americans released or self-released from bondage, mostly in the North. In his first sermon at the African Church of Philadelphia, Jones put out the call to his fellow African Americans to "arise out of the dust and shake ourselves, and throw off that servile fear, that the habit of oppression and bondage trained us up in." Jones's church, like many others that emerged in the early nineteenth century, became a center of social and political as well as religious activities, and a fortress from which to struggle against white racial hostility.

From his position as the spiritual leader at Saint Thomas's, Jones became a leading educator and reformer in the black community. Although even-tempered and known for his ability to quiet controversy and reconcile differences, he did not shrink from the work of promoting the rights of African Americans. He coauthored, with Richard Allen, *A Narrative of the Proceedings of the Black People, During the Late Awful Calamity in Philadelphia, in the year 1793*, a resounding defense of black contributions in the yellow fever epidemic of 1793—Jones himself assisted Benjamin Rush in ministering to the sick and dying in the ghastly three-month epidemic—and a powerful attack on slavery and white racial hostility. In 1797, he helped organize the first petition of African Americans against slavery, the slave trade, and the federal Fugitive Slave Law of 1793. Three years later, he organized another petition to President Jefferson and the Congress deploring slavery and the slave trade. From his pulpit he orated against slavery, and he was responsible in 1808 for informally establishing January 1 (the date on which the slave trade ended) as a day of thanksgiving and celebration, in effect an alternative holiday to the Fourth of July for black Americans.

Typical of black clergymen of the nineteenth century, Jones functioned far beyond his pulpit. Teaching in schools established by the Pennsylvania Abolition Society and by his church, he helped train a generation of black youth in Philadelphia. As Grand Master of Philadelphia's Black Masons, one of the founders of the Society for the Suppression of Vice and Immorality (1809), and a founder of the literary Augustine Society (1817), he struggled to advance the self-respect and enhance the skills of the North's largest free African-American community. By the end of Jones's career, Saint Thomas's was beginning to acquire a reputation as the church of the emerging black middle class in Philadelphia. But he would long be remembered for his ministry among the generation emerging from slavery. ◆

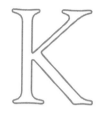

Kang Yu-Wei

1858–1927 ● CONFUCIAN

Kang Yu-Wei was a political reformer and Confucian thinker of modern China. He first attained national prominence as leader of the political reform movement that ended in the defeat of the Hundred Days Reform of 1898. Although primarily political, the movement also had a spiritual and moral dimension. Kang called not only for the "protection of the nation" but also for the "preservation of the faith," by which he meant the spiritual revitalization of Confucianism and the promotion of its teachings as the state religion. This position was partly a response to the cultural and political crises that China was undergoing at the time. By revitalizing Confucianism, Kang hoped to strengthen China's self-esteem and national solidarity. But his call for the "preservation of the faith" must not be seen solely in this practical light; it was also the culmination of a moral and spiritual quest that had started in his early youth.

1858 Kang is born into a family scholars and officials in China.

1898 Kang first attains prominence helping defeat Hundred Days Reform; flees China.

1913 Kang returns to China after long exile.

1917 Kang joins a warlord in a failed attempt to restore Manchu rule.

1927 Kang dies.

Kang Yu-wei was born to a family of scholars and officials in Nan-hai County, Kwangtung Province. His father died while Kang was still a child, and thereafter his grandfather, a devoted Neo-Confucian scholar, personally took charge of the boy's education. Shortly before the age of 20, Kang entered a period of spiritual restlessness, triggered by the sudden death of his grandfather and by the beginning of his subsequent apprenticeship under an inspiring Confucian teacher. He rebelled against his conventional Confucian education and temporarily withdrew from society altogether. Plunging into a frantic intellectual search, he fell under the influence of various non-Confucian persuasions, especially Buddhism, Taoism, and "Western learning."

Kang's intellectual quest finally culminated in the formation of a moral and historical worldview that he expressed in a series of writings published in the decade from the early 1890s to the early 1900s. Based on a bold and comprehensive reinterpretation of Confucianism that centered on the pivotal Confucian ideal of *jen* (human-heartedness), this view also reflected, in its redefinition of *jen*, Kang's interest in non-Confucian thought. *Jen* provided Kang with a worldview that saw the essential and ultimate state of the cosmos as a selfless all-encompassing whole. Kang also retained the Confucian belief central to *jen* that the intrinsic goal of human existence is the moral perfection of individual and society. But his definition of moral perfection bears the profound influence of non-Confucian thought, for his vision of the ideal society, the "great unity" (*ta-t'ung*), was that of a universal moral community where egalitarianism, libertarianism, and hedonism would prevail. Since his conception of hedonism resulted from the impact of the materialistic doctrines of Western industrial society, his ideal society offered the radical combination of moral perfection, technological development, and material abundance.

The radical tendencies in Kang's conception of *jen* were tempered by his historical interpretation of that ideal. In his view, the full realization of the ideal can be attained only through the gradual course of human history. Borrowing a scheme from an ancient commentary on the Confucian classic *Ch'un-ch'iu*, Kang took the view that human history evolves through three stages, from "the age of chaos," which lay in the past, through an intermediate age of "emerging peace," to the final stage of "universal peace," or "great unity," to be realized in the future. Kang insisted that it was for this latter age alone that his radical reevaluation of *jen* was appropriate. He believed that, meanwhile, in the era preceding the "age of great unity," many of the conventional values of Confucianism remained relevant. These were the tenets of the worldview that lay at the core of his efforts to have Confucianism accepted as a state religion.

Kang's reform movement culminated in 1898, when, under his guidance, the emperor of China attempted to put into practice a wide-ranging program of political reform. The intervention of the dowager empress Tz'u-hsi, who moved to imprison the emperor and nullify the imperial edicts little more than three months after they were issued, brought Kang's reforms to an end. Together with his student Liang Ch'i-ch'ao, Kang fled China and began an exile that lasted until 1913. During this period he continued his reformist efforts abroad and traveled extensively, deepening his understanding of the social and political forces that were shaping the modern world.

Upon his return to China, Kang resumed his efforts to implement the promotion of Confucianism as a state religion. Convinced that the revolution of 1911, in which the traditional monarchy had been replaced by a republican form of government, had only served to impede the historical evolution of the ideal society, he joined the warlord Chang Hsun in an ill-fated attempt to restore Manchu rule in 1917. In the writings of his later years, Kang remained faithful to the interpretation of Confucianism that he had formulated in the 1890s, but, because the intellectual climate of China had changed, his views never regained their former influence. ◆

> Kang's reform movement culminated in 1898, when, under his guidance, the emperor of China attempted to put into practice a wide-ranging program of political reform.

Kaplan, Mordecai

1881 – 1983 ● Jewish

Mordecai Kaplan was an American rabbi, author, and religious leader; creator of the theory of Reconstructionist Judaism; and founder of the Reconstructionist movement. The son of Rabbi Israel Kaplan, a Talmudic scholar, Mordecai Menachem Kaplan was born in Svencionys, Lithuania, on 11 June 1881. The family left eastern Europe in 1888 and reached the United States in July 1889. Kaplan was instructed in traditional Jewish subjects by private tutors while

attending public schools in New York City. He received degrees from the City College of New York and Columbia University, and rabbinic ordination from the Jewish Theological Seminary of America. In 1909, following a tenure as minister and rabbi of Kehillath Jeshurun, an Orthodox congregation, Kaplan returned to the Jewish Theological Seminary, where he served for more than 50 years: as principal (later dean) of the recently established Teachers Institute until 1945, and as professor of homiletics and philosophies of religion until his formal retirement in 1963.

Beyond his roles as a leader within the Conservative rabbinate and the Zionist movement and as an important contributor within the field of Jewish education, Kaplan's major achievement remains his formulation of Reconstructionism, which he presented to the public through a series of lectures and publications, chief among which was *Judaism as a Civilization* (1934). Kaplan developed his theories in response to his own loss of faith in the traditional concept of revelation as a result of his studies with the iconoclastic Bible scholar Arnold Ehrlich. Attempting to rebuild a personal cosmology, Kaplan drew from Western philosophers and social scientists as well as Jewish sources, using the findings of French Sociologist Emile Durkheim, the pragmatic philosophy of John Dewey and William James, and the theological insights of British author Matthew Arnold in combination with the spiritual Zionism of Asher Ginsberg. This synthesis of materials made Kaplan unique among twentieth-century Jewish thinkers for seeking to combine modern science with an affirmation of Judaism.

At the heart of Kaplan's thought is his definition of Judaism as an "evolving religious civilization." Opposing those who sought the maintenance of Jewish life solely through preservation of the religion, he argued that a Jewish civilization that included within it a land, language and literature, mores, laws and folkways, arts, and a social structure transcended reli-

> "We want our religious traditions to be interpreted in terms of understandable experience and to be made relevant to our present-day needs."
>
> Mordecai Kaplan,
> *The Thirteen Wants*, 1926

gion. Kaplan also presented a radical change in the God-idea. Preferring to use the term *divinity*, he rejected notions of a personal God active in human history, favoring instead a functional understanding of God as the creative source within the universe, the Power that engenders a salvation to which the Jewish people have long been particularly responsive. These conceptual shifts infuriated Orthodox Jewry, creating a division exacerbated further by Kaplan's efforts to transfer the center of concern and authority from divinely revealed text to the Jewish people itself, as well as by his justification of the transcendence of Jewish law and custom when those sources no longer met the needs of the Jewish people. Kaplan differed from his Conservative colleagues in his use of extra traditional resources; his approach remained distinct from that of Reform Judaism through his efforts to retain traditional forms while providing new content.

Kaplan also sought to modernize Jewish organizational structure. Realizing the superior strength of the Diaspora cultures, he argued that emancipated Jews lived within two civilizations and that, on most occasions, the general (gentile) culture exerted the primary hold upon the individual. In an effort to counterbalance the impetus toward total assimilation, Kaplan called for maximal development of opportunities for the individual to function within a Jewish environment. The locus of those activities was to be the synagogue, which Kaplan sought to transform from a simple prayer room to a modern institution, the focus for worship, study, and recreation. Attracting supporters for these theories, Kaplan supervised the creation of the first such community and synagogue center, The Jewish Center on Manhattan's West Side, in 1918. The commitment of the lay leadership to Orthodox Jewish practice, as well as Kaplan's own temper, soon led to difficulties, however, resulting in his resignation from the Center in 1922. Kaplan next established the Society for the Advancement of Judaism, which served thereafter as the living laboratory for his experiments with Jewish worship, such as the inclusion of women within the *minyan* (prayer quorum) and the creation of *bat mitsvah* as a young woman's rite of passage equivalent to the **bar mitsvah.**

When editing the *Sabbath Prayer Book* (1942), Kaplan retained the traditional service structure, but replaced statements regarding resurrection of the dead with declarations that God remembered the living. In a similar manner, prayers for restora-

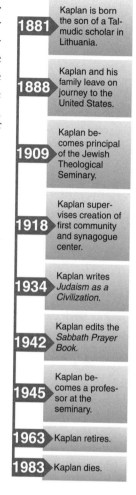

1881 Kaplan is born the son of a Talmudic scholar in Lithuania.

1888 Kaplan and his family leave on journey to the United States.

1909 Kaplan becomes principal of the Jewish Theological Seminary.

1918 Kaplan supervises creation of first community and synagogue center.

1934 Kaplan writes *Judaism as a Civilization.*

1942 Kaplan edits the *Sabbath Prayer Book.*

1945 Kaplan becomes a professor at the seminary.

1963 Kaplan retires.

1983 Kaplan dies.

bar mitsvah: rite of passage for young Jewish men, usually at about 13 years of age, when religious responsibilities are assumed

tion of the Temple and the coming of the Messiah were removed in favor of recollections of the faith of those who had worshiped within the Temple and prayers for a messianic age, to be achieved through human efforts. Perhaps most controversial, because it was most readily apparent, was Kaplan's replacement of the phrase "who has chosen us from all the nations" in the benediction prior to reading of the Torah with "who has brought us near in His service." Copies of the prayer book were burned at a rally of Orthodox Jews in New York City in 1945, and a ban was pronounced against Kaplan.

Kaplan's followers included Conservative rabbis Eugene Kohn, Ira Eisenstein, and Milton Steinberg, as well as laypeople throughout the country. Kaplan resisted their desire to establish Reconstructionism as a fourth movement within American Judaism, and Reconstructionism thus remained identified as the "left wing" of Conservative Judaism until the 1960s. Only upon his retirement from the seminary did Kaplan devote himself to the establishment of a distinct Reconstructionist movement; by then, many of his concepts and practices had diffused and become accepted within Reform and Conservative Judaism. As a result, although the influence of Kaplan's ideas has been broad, the Reconstructionist movement has remained small. ◆

> Kaplan resisted their desire to establish Reconstructionism as a fourth movement within American Judaism, and Reconstructionism thus remained identified as the "left wing" of Conservative Judaism until the 1960s.

Kelly, Leontine

1920– ● METHODIST

Leontine Turpeau Current Kelly was born in Washington, D.C., and attended public schools in Cincinnati, where her family moved in the late 1920s. In 1938, Turpeau entered West Virginia State College (later renamed West Virginia State University), but withdrew in 1941 to marry Goster Bryant Current.

The Currents divorced in the early 1950s, and Leontine Turpeau Current remarried in 1956. In 1958, she moved with her second husband, James David Kelly, a United Methodist minister, to Richmond. Leontine Kelly enrolled at Virginia Union University in Richmond and received her bachelor of arts degree in 1960. That same year, Kelly took a job teaching social studies and became a certified lay speaker in the Methodist Church. In 1966, Leontine Kelly quit her teaching job after her husband accepted the pastorship at Galilee United Methodist Church in Edwardsville, Va.

When James Kelly died in 1969, Galilee Church asked his wife to assume responsibility for running the church. Leontine Kelly accepted and began her theological studies shortly thereafter. In 1975, she left Galilee to accept a two-year position as director of the programs of social ministry at the Virginia Conference Council of Ministries. In 1976, Kelly received a master's of divinity from Union Theological Seminary in Richmond, and one year later, she was ordained an elder in the Methodist church.

In 1977, Kelly became pastor at Asbury United Methodist Church in Richmond. In 1983, she moved to Nashville, to accept an executive position on the board of discipleship of the national staff of the United Methodist Church. During this time, Kelly was active in the clergywomen's movement, struggling for greater opportunities for women in the ministry. In July 1984, Kelly was elected bishop of the Western Jurisdiction of the Methodist Church, becoming the second woman and the first African-American woman ever to hold this position.

Kelly moved to San Francisco to assume her duties, supervising close to 400 churches in the California and Nevada conferences. As bishop, Kelly focused on improving the positions of women and ethnic groups within the church and on increasing church involvement in the social and economic development of black communities. During her term, Kelly served on the executive committee of the Council of Bishops and as president of the six-member Western Jurisdictional College of Bishops. In 1988, Kelly retired as bishop and accepted a part-time teaching position at the Pacific School of Religion in Berkeley, Calif. Since her retirement, she has remained active in the religious community, devoting her attention to church involvement in the country's health care crisis. In 1988, she accepted a one-year term as president of the board of directors of the AIDS National Interfaith Network. In January 1992, Kelly was elected to serve as president of the Washington, D.C.-based Interreligious Health Care Access Campaign, an organization devoted to achieving universal access to health care benefits. ◆

"As a child I asked my father how black people could be Christian. How could they accept it when the very people that enslaved them taught them Christianity? My father said that in God there was the strength and the source for patience to wait for freedom. What I found is that everybody wasn't waiting. People were working."

Leontine T. C. Kelly, quoted in *U.S. News and World Report*, 1989

Kelman, Wolfe

1923–1990 ● Jewish

Wolfe Kelman was a Conservative Jewish leader who was instrumental in the modernization of the rabbinate and in extending ordination to women.

Kelman was born in Vienna, Austria, in 1923. He was the second of six children of Mirl Fish and Zvi Yehuda (Hersh Leib) Kelman, a rabbi descended from a long line of Hasidic rabbis. Wolfe's father immigrated to Canada in 1929, and Wolfe and his mother and siblings joined him there in 1930. Wolfe attended public school in Toronto. When, at age 13, his father died, his mother stepped into the role of communal leader, offering religious and personal guidance.

Kelman's studies at the University of Toronto were interrupted by service in the Royal Canadian Air Force from 1943 to 1945. He received his B.A. degree in 1946. Kelman moved to the United States that year and earned his rabbinical degree and M.A. degree in Hebrew literature from the Jewish Theological Seminary (JTS) in New York City, both in 1950. He did postgraduate studies at Columbia University.

> At JTS, Kelman became a disciple of Rabbi Abraham Joshua Heschel, whose dedication to Judaism, civil rights, and interfaith dialogue helped shape Kelman's professional life. . . .

At JTS, Kelman became a disciple of Rabbi Abraham Joshua Heschel, whose dedication to Judaism, civil rights, and interfaith dialogue helped shape Kelman's professional life: "Heschel taught us that no religion has a monopoly on holiness," Kelman later wrote. He followed the advice of Heschel and JTS chancellor Louis Finkelstein, who urged Kelman not to become a congregational rabbi but rather a "civil servant" in the Conservative movement or, as he jokingly called himself, "an *un*civil servant." In 1951 Kelman became chief executive of the Rabbinical Assembly (RA), the professional association of Conservative rabbis. He then served as executive secretary, executive director, and finally, from 1951 to his retirement in August 1989, executive vice president. For many years Kelman oversaw RA publications such as the annual *Proceedings of the Rabbinical Assembly* and the *Weekday Prayer Book* (1961). On 2 March 1952 he married Jacqueline Miriam Levy, the daughter of the noted Reform rabbi Felix Levy. Their son, Levi Yehuda, was born in 1953. Their daughters were born soon after: Naamah Kathrine in 1955 and Abigail Tobie in 1956. The family lived in Riverdale in the Bronx and then moved to

Manhattan, living in various apartments, finally settling on the Upper West Side.

As executive vice president of the Rabbinical Assembly, Kelman presided over what he labeled "the professionalization of the rabbinate" during a period of extraordinary growth for the Conservative movement. He fought to obtain competitive salaries and benefits for rabbis, yet he personally took little credit for the reforms: "The status of rabbis improved because of the hundreds of good rabbis out there," he commented. As director of the Joint Placement Committee of the RA, United Synagogue, and JTS from 1951 to 1966, he helped more than 1,500 rabbis and rabbinical students find pulpits. Kelman mentored hundreds of rabbis, dispensing spiritual and practical advice, even occasionally counseling a rabbinical student that his talents might be better suited running a pizza parlor. During his tenure at the RA, membership grew from approximately 300 rabbis in 1951 to some 1,200 in 1989.

Kelman served on the executive council of the United Synagogue of America during the 1950s and early 1960s and on various committees of JTS. He spent 1957 and 1958 as visiting rabbi of the West London Synagogue. In 1962 Kelman became an American citizen. During the 1960s he helped revive the RA's 1930s social justice program, which led to Conservative rabbis championing civil rights on picket lines and marches, as well as from the pulpit. Joining Heschel in 1965 in Selma, Alabama, he marched with the Reverend Martin Luther King, Jr. Beginning in 1974 he served on the board of directors of the Hebrew Immigrant Aid Society. In 1986 he chaired the American section of the World Jewish Congress. He had served since 1968 on the governing council and from 1975 as chair of the cultural commission.

Kelman participated in many interfaith organizations. Serving on the International Jewish Committee on Inter-religious Consultations, he represented the Jewish community with the Vatican, the World Council of Churches, and major Christian organizations in the United States, and he helped prepare Heschel for his meeting with Pope Paul VI. Kelman was a key participant in the talks that led to a Jewish delegation meeting for the first time with Pope John Paul II in Rome and Miami in 1987.

Meanwhile, Kelman taught homiletics from 1967 to 1973 at the Jewish Theological Seminary and history from 1973 to 1988. He was chair of the academic board of the Melton Re-

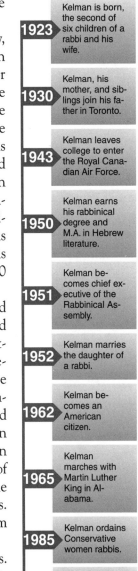

1923 Kelman is born, the second of six children of a rabbi and his wife.

1930 Kelman, his mother, and siblings join his father in Toronto.

1943 Kelman leaves college to enter the Royal Canadian Air Force.

1950 Kelman earns his rabbinical degree and M.A. in Hebrew literature.

1951 Kelman becomes chief executive of the Rabbinical Assembly.

1952 Kelman marries the daughter of a rabbi.

1962 Kelman becomes an American citizen.

1965 Kelman marches with Martin Luther King in Alabama.

1985 Kelman ordains Conservative women rabbis.

1990 Kelman dies of malignant melanoma.

search Center from 1969 to 1971. In 1976 he was invited to the Oxford Centre for Postgraduate Hebrew Studies in England as a visiting lecturer and he spent 1984 and 1985 in Israel as visiting professor of contemporary Jewish history at Hebrew University in Jerusalem.

Keenly interested in Jewish cultural, educational, historical, and sociological life, Kelman championed the writings of Elie Wiesel, Chaim Grade, and Heschel. He wrote major articles and reviews for the *American Jewish Year Book, Conservative Judaism* (a journal he helped found), and other publications. In 1978, to commemorate Kelman's 25 years of service to the Rabbinical Assembly, the RA published a Festschrift, *Perspectives on Jews and Judaism: Essays in Honor of Wolfe Kelman*, edited by Arthur Chiel. In 1986 Kelman agreed to serve on the first editorial board of the progressive journal *Tikkun*.

> Kelman was most proud of his instrumental role in increasing women's participation in communal religious life, culminating in the ordination of Conservative women rabbis in 1985.

Kelman was most proud of his instrumental role in increasing women's participation in communal religious life, culminating in the ordination of Conservative women rabbis in 1985. "It was [my mother's] example," he explained, "that made me believe women could function as rabbis." On 24 July 1992, two years after Kelman's death, his daughter Naamah became the first woman rabbi ordained in Israel.

Maintaining an open house, Kelman was always available to his various constituencies in person or by telephone. His students joked that the afterlife had better have telephones for Kelman's use.

Diagnosed with malignant melanoma in 1989, Kelman retired from the RA that August but remained active in communal life. In 1990 he was appointed director of the Finkelstein Institute of Religious and Social Studies of the Jewish Theological Seminary and honored by New York City mayor Edward Koch at a special reception for service as a member of the informal Mayor's Advisory Board of Religious Leaders and for helping revive Jewish life on Manhattan's Upper West Side. Kelman died of cancer in 1990. He was buried in Lodi, New Jersey.

Although Wolfe Kelman worked behind the scenes, he was a major and vital force in American Conservative Judaism, helping to modernize, professionalize, and expand the rabbinate. Through an extraordinary network of contacts throughout the world, Kelman was involved in civil rights, interfaith work, and political and business affairs. ◆

Kimbangu, Simon

1889–1951 ● KIMBANGUIST

Simon Kimbangu was an African religious prophet and founder of the Church of Jesus Christ on Earth through the Prophet Simon Kimbangu. Kimbangu was born on 24 September 1889 in the village of N'Kamba, located in the Ngombe district of lower Zaire (the former Belgian Congo). In Kikongo, the word *kimbangu* means "one who reveals the hidden truth." Many legends surround Kimbangu's youth and early religious activities. Some accounts claim that both his mother and father were traditional Kongo healers and that his visionary activities were related to theirs. Only since the mid-1970s has much of the original missionary and government documentation on Kimbangu's early activities become available to scholars.

Kimbangu attended a Baptist Missionary Society school at Wathen, near his home village. He became a Christian as a young man and was baptized on 4 July 1915 along with his wife, Marie-Mwilu, in the Baptist mission at Ngombe-Luete. He was trained as a religious instructor by the Baptist Missionary Society but failed his examination to become a pastor. During the typhoid epidemic of 1918 and 1919, in which many residents of his area died, Kimbangu is reputed to have received a calling to heal the sick. He is alleged to have heard a voice that said, "I am Christ. My servants are unfaithful. I have chosen you to bear witness before your brethren and convert them. Tend my flock." Frightened, Kimbangu was unable to respond and fled to the capital city of Kinshasa (then Leopoldville), where he worked briefly as a migrant laborer at an oil refinery.

Upon returning to his village, Kimbangu again received the calling to heal. On 6 April 1921 he performed his first public act of faith healing. He is reported to have laid hands on a critically ill woman and healed her. This act marked the beginning of Kimbangu's healing revival and six months of intensive religious activity. N'Kamba, the seat of Kimbangu's healing ministry, became known as the "New Jerusalem," and over 5,000 local converts are reported to have flocked to him.

As the healing movement spread in popularity, colonial officials and merchants began to perceive it as a revolutionary

> Kimbangu is alleged to have heard a voice that said, "I am Christ. My servants are unfaithful. I have chosen you to bear witness before your brethren and convert them. Tend my flock."

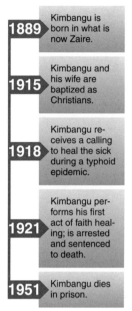

1889 Kimbangu is born in what is now Zaire.

1915 Kimbangu and his wife are baptized as Christians.

1918 Kimbangu receives a calling to heal the sick during a typhoid epidemic.

1921 Kimbangu performs his first act of faith healing; is arrested and sentenced to death.

1951 Kimbangu dies in prison.

threat. Missionaries were skeptical of Kimbangu's new teachings, and merchants complained that he incited followers to abandon their work and neglect the payment of taxes. With a small cadre of leaders to assist him, Kimbangu continued to preach and perform inspired acts of healing. On 6 June 1921, Leon Morel, a Belgian official, attempted to arrest Kimbangu and four of his most loyal assistants. Kimbangu eluded colonial officials until, prompted by a divine vision, he voluntarily surrendered on 12 September.

On 3 October 1921 Kimbangu was sentenced to death by 120 strokes of the lash for sedition and hostility toward the colonial authorities. His court-martial was characterized by arbitrary proceedings and legal irregularities. In November, the death sentence was commuted to life imprisonment by King Albert, who was reportedly influenced by the pleas of Belgian missionaries to exercise some leniency. Kimbangu was transported to Lubumbashi (then Elisabethville) in Shaba province, where he was imprisoned until his death on 12 October 1951 in the "hospital for Congolese." There is some debate concerning whether Kimbangu, whose teachings resembled those of fundamentalist Protestantism, converted to Catholicism on his deathbed. This possibility has been vehemently denied by his family and followers.

Kimbangu's arrest augmented the aura of mystery surrounding him as a prophetic figure and increased the popular appeal of his charismatic movement. Between 1924 and 1930, Belgian colonial authorities continued overt attempts to suppress the movement. Kimbangu's principal followers were imprisoned at Lowa, and others were confined over the years in 30 detention centers spread throughout the country. The Kimbanguist church estimates that there were 37,000 exiles, of whom 34,000 died in prison between 1921 and 1956. Recent scholarship, however, has established that this figure resulted from a typographical error in a newspaper article; the official exile and imprisonment figure was closer to 2,148. Although Kimbanguist detainees were isolated and kept under martial surveillance, the policy of detention eventually led to the spread of the Kimbanguist movement in various regions of what is now Zaire.

The movement gained strength, forming itself into a group that became known as the Church of Jesus Christ on Earth through the Prophet Simon Kimbangu. Followers were called *ngunza* ("prophets" or "preachers"). Kimbanguist offshoots, such as Salutism and Mpadism, and other manifestations of Kimbangu's influence appeared throughout present-day Zaire, Congo, and Zambia among populations with whom Kimbangu never had direct contact.

Between 1955 and 1957, Kimbangu's movement experienced a renewal and continued to spread throughout the Belgian Congo. After the prophet's death, his youngest son, Kuntima (Joseph) Diangienda, assumed leadership of the church in accordance with Kimbangu's wishes. He formalized its doctrine, sacraments, and egalitarian organizational structure. In 1969, the Kimbanguist church was admitted to the World Council of Churches, and in 1971, it was proclaimed as one of the four officially recognized ecclesiastical bodies in Zaire. By the end of the 1980s there were nearly four million Kimbanguists in Zaire.

Simon Kimbangu's direct and indirect influence on African prophetic movements has been far-reaching. The Kimbanguist church is one of the most extensively documented African religious groups. It is possible to view the history and transformation of the Kimbanguist church as a prototype for many contemporary African religious groups that have made the transition from grass-roots movements to established churches. ◆

King, Martin Luther, Jr.

1929–1968 ● Baptist

Martin Luther King, Jr., was an American Baptist minister, leader of the U.S. civil rights movement, and winner of the Nobel Prize for peace. Born the son and grandson of Southern Baptist preachers, King was originally christened Michael Luther, but his father changed both their names in honor of the sixteenth-century religious reformer, Martin Luther. When 15 he went to Morehouse College, Atlanta, under the auspices of the special program for gifted students. Despite an early interest in medicine and law, he decided to follow in his father's footsteps and enter the ministry. In 1951 he was awarded his Bachelor of Divinity degree from Crozer Theological Seminary, where he was first exposed to the ideas of Mahatma Gandhi and modern Protestant the-

> When 15 King went to Morehouse College, Atlanta, under the auspices of the special program for gifted students.

ologians such as Paul Tillich, who brought existentialism, depth psychology, and neo-Scholastic ontology to bear on their religious thinking. King himself was always to see God as an active personal entity and salvation as resulting through faith in God's guidance.

In 1955 King received his doctorate from Boston University. Two years earlier, he had met and married Coretta Smith; the young couple moved to Montgomery, Alabama, where

King took up his pastoral duties. When, in December 1955, Rosa Parks was arrested for refusing to surrender her seat on a bus to a white passenger, King was chosen to head the Montgomery Improvement Association to oppose the segregated transport system. Although he was from a comfortable middle-class black family and had therefore been cushioned from the worst excesses of racial discrimination and prejudice that were the common experience of many black people, King identified passionately with the cause of black liberation.

King immediately avowed his commitment to the principle of nonviolence in thought as well as deed: "We will not resort to violence. We will not degrade ourselves with hatred. Love will be returned for hate." He and his supporters faced violent opposition, his family was threatened and his home dynamited, but a year later the protesters achieved the desegregation of both inter and intrastate transportation and King was launched to national prominence. He immediately organized the Southern Christian Leadership Conference to unify those forces working for black civil rights; this gave him a national platform for the dissemination of his views. A magnificent and emotive speaker, he fused the rhetoric of a Southern preacher with the cogency of a philosopher, expressing his nonviolent philosophy of social justice in lectures throughout the country.

While continuing to organize, agitate, and educate for change, King also traveled widely, winning worldwide support for both his cause and his methods. In India, which he visited in 1959, he was warmly welcomed by Jawaharlal Nehru and became even more convinced of the potency of nonviolent resistance methods as a weapon for the oppressed through his meeting with Gandhian workers. He returned to his home town of Atlanta convinced that "the psychological moment has come when a concentrated drive against injustice can bring great, tangible gains."

In October 1959, King was arrested while leading a demonstration protesting the segregation of an Atlanta lunch counter. The charges were dropped, but a national outcry resulted when he was imprisoned for having violated the terms of his probation on a minor traffic offense some months previously. He was eventually released through the personal intervention of Democratic presidential candidate John F. Kennedy; the latter's slender victory in the presidential election a few days later has been attributed to the swing in the black vote which his support for King occasioned.

"Now is the time to make real the promises of democracy; now is the time to rise from the dark and desolate valley of segregation to the sunlit path of racial justice; now is the time to lift our nation from the quicksands of racial injustice to the solid rock of brotherhood; now is the time to make justice a reality for all God's children."

Martin Luther King, 1963

1929 King is born the son and grandson of Baptist preachers.

1951 King receives his Bachelor of Divinity degree.

1953 King meets and marries Coretta Smith.

1955 King receives his doctorate.

1959 King is arrested while leading an anti-segregation protest.

1963 King and other demonstrators are jailed by Alabama police; King gives a moving oration in Washington, D.C.

1964 King is awarded the Nobel Peace Prize.

1967 King speaks out against the Vietnam War.

1968 King is assassinated in Memphis.

1986 King's birthday is proclaimed a national holiday.

King, still only 31 years old, was now undisputed leader of the civil rights movement, which succeeded in attracting the support of many black and liberal white supporters and of successive Democratic administrations under Kennedy and Lyndon B. Johnson. Reactionary white retaliation against the movement could be brutal, however. In spring 1963, police in Birmingham, Alabama, turned dogs and fire hoses on peaceful demonstrators led by King: he and hundreds of his supporters, including schoolchildren, were jailed. At the same time, a local black church was bombed and four girls attending Sunday school there were killed. King's open letter from the Birmingham jail constituted an eloquent rejoinder to those more conservative elements within the black establishment who questioned his confrontational tactics.

The acme of the civil rights campaign was the August 1963 march on Washington, the largest peacetime demonstration ever seen in the United States, in which a peaceful multiracial crowd of over 200,000 people marched to the Lincoln Memorial in support of the equal rights platform. There, they heard King give a moving oration, part vision, part statement of intent: many were moved to tears by the power of his words. The Civil Rights Act passed the following year authorized the federal government to enforce desegregation of public housing, and outlawed discrimination in publicly owned facilities and employment. In 1964 King was awarded the Nobel Peace Prize for his work.

Despite the achievements of the civil rights movement under his leadership, the lack of greater substantive progress led to increasing frustration with King's nonviolent methods among younger radicals. Thus, an incident at Selma, Alabama, in 1965, when demonstrators demanding a federal voting rights law turned back to avoid confronting a police cordon, led to accusations that King had struck a deal with the state authorities. Increasingly, it became apparent that the strategy that had broken segregation laws was not adequate in dealing with some of the more complex racial problems, such as the disadvantaged socio-economic position most blacks occupied within American inner cities.

King's response was to seek to broaden the scope of his nonviolent vision to address other concerns that had a bearing on the black cause. Thus, a year before his death he came out against the war in Vietnam, despite strong opposition from many within the civil rights camp. His plans for a Poor People's March on Washington were interrupted by a trip to Memphis, Tennessee, in support of a strike by city sanitation workers. There, he was shot and killed while standing on the balcony of his motel room. Countrywide rioting followed the news of his murder, and a massive hunt was launched for his killer. James Earl Ray was eventually apprehended in London and pleaded guilty to the crime.

Since 1986, the third Monday in January has been a United States federal holiday marking the anniversary of King's birth. ◆

Kinjikitile

?–1905 ● Traditional African

Kinjikitile was a religious leader in southeastern Tanganyika (now Tanzania) who provided inspiration for the anticolonial struggles known as the Maji Maji Wars. In 1904, Kinjikitile became famous as a medium in a place called Ngarambe in Matumbi country, where the oppressions of the German colonial system were severe. He was possessed by Hongo, a deity subordinate to the supreme being, Bokero, whose primary ritual center was at Kibesa on the Rufiji River. At Ngarambe, Kinjikitile blended the spiritual authority of Bokero and Hongo with more local elements of ancestor veneration at a shrine center where he received offerings from pilgrims seeking intercession with the spiritual world and relief from the adversities they faced, both natural and political. In the latter part of 1904 and early 1905, Kinjikitile advised the pilgrims to prepare themselves to resist the Germans and dispensed a medicine that he promised would turn the enemy's bullets into water when combat commenced. The rebellion broke out in late July 1905 without the order coming from Kinjikitile, but the ideological preparation provided by his message and the system of emissaries that spread the word and the medicine have been viewed as critical in the Maji Maji Wars.

The Maji Maji Wars continued from July 1905 to August 1907, extending over more than 100,000 square miles and causing terrible loss of life, estimated officially at 75,000 by the Germans and at over 250,000 by modern scholars. Out of this

> In 1904, Kinjikitile became famous as a medium in a place called Ngarambe in Matumbi country, where the oppressions of the German colonial system were severe.

struggle, Kinjikitile emerged as a figure of epic proportions; he is said to be a religious innovator who devised a spiritual appeal that transcended particularism and allowed the people to unite against German rule.

By 1904, resentment of colonial rule and the desire to overthrow it had become widespread in southeastern Tanganyika. The times were especially troubled in Matumbi country, which experienced a succession of adversities that went beyond the capacity of political agents to handle. In 1903 there was a severe drought, and from 1903 to 1905 the Germans increasingly insisted that the people of Matumbi engage in communal cotton growing, promising payment for the crop once it had been marketed and the administration's overhead covered. Much to the anger of the people, the payments did not materialize.

Of Kinjikitile the person very little is known. The most certain event in his biography was his death by hanging on 4 August 1905 when, together with an assistant, he became the first opposition leader to be summarily executed by the German military forces. He had lived in Ngarambe for some four years prior to this time and had emerged as an influential person; the recipient of many gifts, he had become an object of jealousy on the part of local political leaders.

Kinjikitile was a synthesizer of many religious elements. There had long been a territorial shrine to Bokero on the Rufiji to which the people had recourse in times of drought. The drought of 1903 had activated this shrine and extended its range of influence as pilgrims came from greater and greater distances. Kinjikitile's teachings drew upon this long-standing religious institution, joining the territorial authority of Bokero with local beliefs in divine possession. At Ngarambe, he also built a huge *kijumbanungu* ("house of God") for the ancestors; drawing on a resurrectionist theme, he announced that the ancestors were all at Ngarambe, ready to help their descendants defeat the Germans and restore the earthly realm. Furthermore, Kinjikitile's teachings contained elements of witch cleansing, whereby the evil within society was to be eliminated and the community morally purified. By drawing upon these traditional beliefs and using them to create an innovative ideology, Kinjikitile provided a regional and multi-ethnic basis for the spread of his message of resistance.

Maji Maji warriors knew that their weapons were inferior to those of the colonial forces, but the German presence was

> Kinjikitile's teachings contained elements of witch cleansing, whereby the evil within society was to be eliminated and the community morally purified.

not so strong as to overawe them. They hoped for a political restoration, not of indigenous rulers, but of the Sultan of Zanzibar, whose regime became idealized because of the relatively benign form of commercial hegemony with which it was associated. Hence there was room for the Germans to investigate the possibility that Islamic propaganda or belief had played a role in the mobilization of resistance. Their conclusions were negative. Indeed, although Kinjikitile wore the traditional garb of Muslims, a long white robe called the *kanzu*, his message and idiom were decidedly drawn from traditional sources. ◆

Kiwanuka, Joseph

c. 1896–1966 ● Catholic

Joseph Kiwanuka was a pathbreaking black Catholic bishop in Uganda. Kiwanuka was educated at Katigondo Seminary and ordained a priest in 1929. After studying in Rome and becoming the first African doctor of canon law, he joined the White Fathers missionary society and made his novitiate in North Africa. In 1939 he was chosen as first vicar apostolic of Masaka, Uganda, and consecrated bishop by Pope Pius XII in Rome. Twenty years later Kiwanuka became archbishop of Kampala, and he attended the Second Vatican Council (1962–1965). He died at Rubaga.

Kiwanuka's importance lies in his having been the first black diocesan bishop in any mainline church since the Nigerian Samuel Crowther died in 1891. For more than 12 years, he remained the sole African bishop in the Catholic Church (outside Ethiopia and Madagascar). The diocese of Masaka, wholly staffed by local priests, was seen as an experiment. Kiwanuka's achievement was outstanding. His clergy multiplied and he sent several overseas for further training, but his development of elected lay parish councils and parents' associations for church schools was no less significant and quite out of line with contemporary missionary practice. His political influence was considerable. In a colonial age and under considerable missionary suspicion, Kiwanuka pioneered the way for the hundreds of African bishops of the next generation. ◆

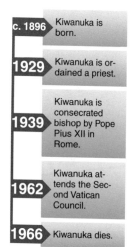

c. 1896 — Kiwanuka is born.

1929 — Kiwanuka is ordained a priest.

1939 — Kiwanuka is consecrated bishop by Pope Pius XII in Rome.

1962 — Kiwanuka attends the Second Vatican Council.

1966 — Kiwanuka dies.

Knox, John

c. 1514–1572 ● PROTESTANT

John Knox was a Protestant reformer of Scotland. Born in Haddington, Knox likely studied at Saint Andrews under the theologian John Major. He was ordained to the priesthood at the age of 25 and served as a tutor to the children of gentlemen in East Lothian.

Knox was a rugged political fighter, but he was also a person of profound religious sensitivity. The source of this sensitivity was the Bible, which he apparently studied with devotion early in life. When dying, he asked his wife to "go read where I cast my first anchor" in the seventeenth chapter of *John*.

Knox, converted to Protestantism by the preaching of Thomas Gwilliam in Lothian, was confirmed in the Protestant movement by his association with Protestant reformer George Wishart. After the burning of Wishart, Protestants took the castle at Saint Andrews and the life of Cardinal Beaton, Scotland's Catholic leader. Knox, under threat of persecution, 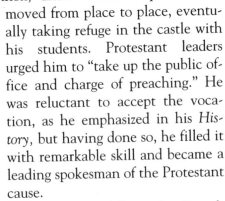 moved from place to place, eventually taking refuge in the castle with his students. Protestant leaders urged him to "take up the public office and charge of preaching." He was reluctant to accept the vocation, as he emphasized in his *History*, but having done so, he filled it with remarkable skill and became a leading spokesman of the Protestant cause.

The castle fell to the French fleet in 1547, and Knox became a galley slave until his release was arranged by the English. For five years (1549–1554) he was active in the Puritan wing of the English Reformation movement. With the accession of the Catholic Mary Tudor as queen in 1553, Knox left England and was named the minister of the church of the English exiles in Frankfurt. The exiles soon divided over the use of *The Book of Common Prayer,* whether to revise it or to substitute a new liturgy. As a result of the controversy, Knox left Frankfurt for Geneva, where he became pastor of the English congregation. Knox's stay there was significant for the consolidation of his own theology, as he was impressed by Protestant leader John Calvin's achievement in establishing the Reformed church in Geneva.

Knox visited Scotland briefly in the autumn of 1555 to encourage the Protestant leadership. When the religious and political struggle came to a crisis in 1559, Knox left Geneva to assume a leading role in the Protestant cause. His powerful preaching, political wisdom, and determination contributed significantly to the Scottish Parliament's action in 1560 abolishing the papal jurisdiction and approving a confession of faith as a basis for belief in Scotland.

In addition to his public leadership, Knox had a role in three major documents of the Scottish Reformation of 1560. The Confession of Faith was written in four days by John Knox and five others. It conveys the intensity of the moment and the personal quality of the confession of believers who were putting their lives at risk for their faith. It has been described as "the warm utterance of a people's heart." It states the Protestant faith in plain language and is more pictorial and historical than abstract in style.

The *First Book of Discipline* was written by Knox in collaboration with four others. It is notable not only for its reform of the church but also for its vision of universal compulsory education up to the university level and for its provisions for relief of the poor. The book was never adopted by Parliament because its members did not want the wealth of the church expended on Knox's "devout imaginings."

Knox's third contribution to the official documents of the church was *The Book of Common Order,* which Knox and his collaborators had written in Frankfurt and used in Geneva. It now became the worship book of the Church of Scotland.

Knox disavowed speculative theology, but his writings, filling six volumes, were as powerful as his preaching. "The First Blast of the Trumpet against the Monstrous Regiment of Women" (1558), although dealing with the situation in Scotland, caused him difficulty with Elizabeth I of England when he needed her support. Knox's *History of the Reformation of Religion within the Realm of Scotland* is a history of the man and the

c. 1514 — Knox is born in Scotland.

1547 — Knox becomes slave when French overtake a castle he teaches in.

1549 — Knox, released by the English, becomes active in Puritan wing.

1553 — Knox leaves England and is named minister of exiles in Frankfurt.

1560 — Knox's preaching leads to Scotland's abolishing papal jurisdiction.

1572 — Knox dies.

> "The poor we see altogether neglected by the bishops, proud prelates, and filthy clergy, who upon their own bellies, license, and vanity consume whatsoever was commanded to be bestowed upon the poor. They preach not truly and sincerely, but their lands, rents, and pompous prelacies are all they care for, and sit reckoning of."
>
> John Knox, 1556

cause and a justification of both. Other notable writings include "Letter of Wholesome Counsel" and "Treatise on Predestination."

Knox was a remarkable human being. Scholars have debated whether or not he was a man of courage, perhaps because of his own misgivings. He took precautions, but he did "march toward the sound of guns." Scholars have accused him of demagoguery, but a supporter declared that he was able in one hour to do more for his contemporaries than 500 trumpets continually blustering in their ears. He believed that he had been called by God, that through his life God's purposes were being fulfilled, and that the Reformation was God's cause and must triumph.

Catholicism would probably have been overthrown in Scotland without Knox, but it is due to Knox that the Church of Scotland was Calvinist rather than Anglican, and that after his death it became presbyterian rather than episcopal. Knox also contributed significantly to the struggle for human freedom. His emphasis on the responsibility not only of lower magistrates but of individuals to resist evil rulers, and the dramatic way he expressed this idea in his own life, especially in his encounters with Queen Mary, and in his sermons and writings cannot be overestimated. His Presbyterian and Puritan followers made these ideas part of the tradition of public and political life in the English-speaking world. ◆

Krishnamurti, Jiddu

1895–1980 ● THEOSOPHIST

Jiddu Krishnamurti was a leading Indian spiritual leader. Jiddu Krishnamurti attained fame through his presentation of a unique version of Indian philosophy and mysticism in a charismatic, even mesmerizing, style of lecturing that attracted large audiences around the world.

Although Krishnamurti taught a philosophy that seemed to border on atheism, it is made clear in his authorized biography that throughout his life he was subject to a profound spiritual purgation. This purgation came to be called "the Process" and suggested to those who witnessed it that his "higher self" departed from his body and entered into what appeared to be a transcendent state of consciousness. This state was accompanied at times by severe pain in his head and back.

Krishnamurti's experience has been likened to the awakening of the *kundalini* power, practiced in some forms of Indian spirituality. The suffering accompanying this experience occurred only under certain circumstances and did not impede his teaching work; in fact, it contributed to the exalted state in which Krishnamurti knew the oneness with all life and the unconditioned freedom that he tried, through his continual lecturing and the books, tape recordings, and videotapes published by his organization, to convey to thousands of persons under his influence.

Krishnamurti was born in Madanapalle, a small town in what is now the state of Andhra Pradesh, north of Madras. He was a member of the Brahman caste of religious leaders & scholars. His father, Narianiah, was a rent collector and, later, a district magistrate under the British government. His mother, Sanjeevama, died when Krishnamurti was ten years old. His father cared for him and his brothers until he retired from government service and was granted permission to move to the estate of the Theosophical Society, located just outside Madras. This move occurred in January 1909, when Annie Besant was the international president of the Theosophical Society. Her close collaborator was Charles W. Leadbeater, whose clairvoyant powers, he claimed, enabled him to recognize Krishnamurti's potential for spiritual greatness when he observed the boy's aura as he was playing on the beach at the seaside edge of the Theosophical Society estate.

The teaching of theosophy, as promulgated by H. P. Blavatsky and H. S. Olcott, the founders of the Theosophical Society, held that the spiritual destiny of humanity was in the hands of "Masters," highly evolved human beings who had

1895 Krishnamurti is born into the Brahman caste in a small town in India.

1911 Krishnamurti travels to England for the first time.

1912 Krishnamurti's father files a sexual harassment suit to protect his son.

1914 Krishnamurti's father loses the lawsuit.

1920 Krishnamurti's gifts as public speaker become evident.

1925 Krishnamurti's brother and constant companion dies of pneumonia.

1933 Krishnamurti breaks from the Theosophical Society upon the death of its leader.

1985 Krishnamurti writes *The Ending of Time* with physicist David Bohm.

1986 Krishnamurti dies.

transcended material existence and lived on a higher plane. Leadbeater and Besant taught that the Lord Maitreya, the World Teacher, would become incarnate in this age in a manner similar to the way that Krishna (the Hindu deity) and Jesus had appeared in the world in earlier eras. Krishnamurti was a likely candidate to become the vehicle for such a manifestation but it remained for him to be trained and tested before he could actually take on such a role.

Krishnamurti and his brother Nitya were "put on probation" (i.e., rigorously tested and prepared for spiritual leadership) by a Master named Kuthumi on 1 August 1909, when Krishnamurti was 14 years old. From that time onward Krishnamurti was nurtured and financially supported by a circle of upper-class English and American men and women and was under the scrutiny of the larger group of Theosophists who saw him at public gatherings. An organization called the Order of the Star in the East was founded by George Arundale, a prominent Theosophist of the period, to promote Krishnamurti's projected vocation.

Krishnamurti and Nitya left India in 1911 for their first visit to England. After their return to India, Krishnamurti's father allowed Krishnamurti and Nitya to be taken back to England for education by Besant and signed a document to that effect in 1912. By the end of 1912 Narianiah had filed suit against Besant to regain custody and charged that Leadbeater and Krishnamurti were involved in a sexual relationship. In 1914, after a judgment against her in the Indian courts, Besant won an appeal to the Privy Council in London. Both she and Leadbeater were exonerated from the charges brought by Narianiah. Krishnamurti and Nitya remained in England during this period and were prepared by a tutor for university studies. However, Krishnamurti was not able to pass the entrance examinations for Oxford and never obtained a university degree, although he studied for many years privately and learned English, French, and some Sanskrit.

From about 1920 until the dissolution of the Order of the Star (formerly the Order of the Star in the East) in 1929, Krishnamurti's extraordinary gifts as a public lecturer and his independent viewpoint on the spiritual quest became evident. He spoke more and more frequently at gatherings of the Theosophical Society in India, the Netherlands, and North America. At some of these meetings he referred to himself in a way that implied he was speaking as the World Teacher. (Krishnamurti's brother and constant companion, Nitya, died of tuberculosis in Ojai, California, on 13 November 1925; Krishnamurti's struggle with the ensuing sorrow was formative of his judgment about the "bondages of the mind.") However, the articulation of his own special teachings alienated him from the inner circle of the leadership of the Theosophical Society, including Besant, Leadbeater, Arundale, and C. Jinarajadasa, each of whom claimed to have received communications from the Masters consisting of instructions for the Theosophical Society that were contrary to Krishnamurti's increasingly independent course. Besant's death in 1933 ended Krishnamurti's ties to the Theosophical Society, and for this break he was repudiated for some time by its leading officials. However, Jinarajadasa's successors to the presidency of the Theosophical Society, Nilakanta Sri Ram and Radha Burnier, sought cordial relations with Krishnamurti, who visited the Theosophical Society compound in the years before his death.

Krishnamurti's work as an independent teacher eventually combined two approaches. First, he traveled around the world on a schedule of lectures. In India he spoke often in Madras and Bombay, and occasionally in Delhi and Banaras. He lectured at Saanen in Switzerland, Brockwood Park in England, and New York City and Ojai (where he maintained his residence) in the United States. Second, he founded several schools in the United States, Canada, Europe, and India, where students through high-school age were instructed in ways to reduce aggression and to aid in acquiring Krishnamurti's universal insight. A noteworthy feature of Krishnamurti's later life was the interest he attracted from scientists. He participated in various dialogues with groups or individuals from the scientific community on the possible connection between his teachings and various contemporary theories of, for example, physics. One of the last books he published, *The Ending of Time* (1985), was co-written with David Bohm, a professor of theoretical physics at Birkbeck College, University of London. ◆

"Truth is a pathless land, and you cannot approach it by any path whatsoever, by any religion, by any sect."

Krishnamurti, 1929

Kroloff, Charles

1935– ● JEWISH

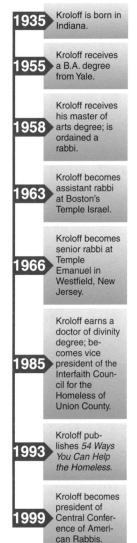

A Reform rabbi and social activist, Charles Kroloff is the son of Max N. Kroloff and Mary Goldstein. Born on June 1, 1935 in East Chicago, Indiana, he grew up in Chicago and Atlanta. In 1955 he was awarded a bachelor of arts degree magna cum laude from Yale University in New Haven, Connecticut. Three years later he obtained a master of arts degree from Hebrew Union College-Jewish Institute of Religion, the major educational institution of Reform Judaism, where he was also ordained as a rabbi. In 1985 he earned a doctor of divinity degree there.

Kroloff was assistant rabbi of Temple Israel in Boston from 1963 to 1966. He then served as rabbi of the Community Reform Temple in Westbury, New York. In 1966 he was appointed senior rabbi of Temple Emanu-el in Westfield, New Jersey, a post he still held at the turn of the twenty-first century.

As a part of the Reform movement in Judaism, Kroloff supports its central principles. One is a commitment to the autonomy of the individual, or the right of Reform Jews to decide whether to accept a particular belief or practice. Another is the belief that traditional Jewish ritual must evolve with a changing world. Also central to Reform Judaism is a dedication to "tikkun olam," Hebrew for "the improvement of the world," which has aligned Reform Jews with many liberal causes.

Kroloff has made clear his dedication to "tikkun olam" through his role as an advocate for the homeless. His temple's school is a homeless shelter at night, and Kroloff has devoted many nights to talking to and sleeping alongside homeless people who take refuge there. From 1985 to 1987 Kroloff served as vice president of the Interfaith Council for the Homeless of Union County, New Jersey. He has also written two books on homelessness: *When Elijah Knocks: A Religious Response to Homelessness* (1992), and *54 Ways You Can Help the Homeless* (1993). In both he offers practical advice on the small and large ways in which the average person help homeless people.

From 1978 to 1982 Kroloff was vice chairman of the Commission on Social Action of Reform Judaism. A staunch supporter of Israel, he was national president of the Association of

Reform Zionists of America from 1984 to 1989. He served on the Committee on Human Sexuality of the Central Conference of American Rabbis (CCAR), an association of Reform rabbis, from 1993 to 1998.

In the late 1990s, the CCAR debated whether to adopt a new platform moving Reform Judaism toward historical Jewish practices. The outcome was a new set of principles for Reform Judaism, overwhelmingly adopted by the CCAR in May 1999. It urged Reform Jews to give greater attention to traditional ritual (although references to specific practices, such as keeping a kosher home and wearing a skullcap and prayer shawl, were omitted in the final draft). It also urged them to become more familiar with Hebrew, the original tongue of the Jewish people. Kroloff supported the new platform, stressing, however, that while "the principles do call for more tradition," they do so "in a very modest way that emphasizes personal autonomy. No one says you must do X, Y, or Z in order to be a good Jew."

At the May 1999 gathering of the CCAR, Kroloff was elected to a two-year term as the Central Conference's president. He stated that one of his priorities was dealing with the shortage of Reform rabbis and other religious professionals. But, he said, "My main crusade for the next two years will be to put more emphasis on taking care of ourselves [the rabbis] so that we can take better care of others and also have a life." In his own personal life, Kroloff sails, works out, and plays golf. "If I were not a rabbi," he has confessed, "what I really wanted to do was to be first baseman for the Mets." ◆

"Amazingly, we can make quite a difference in the lives of the homeless when we respond to them, rather than ignore or dismiss them. Try a kind word. Remember, their self confidence is nearly nonexistent. Whatever we can say or do that gives them even an iota of self-worth will have some benefit."

Chuck Kroloff, 54 *Ways You Can Help the Homeless*, 1993

Lao–Tzu

700s B.C.E. ● TAOISM

Lao-Tzu was a Chinese sage who would probably have been satisfied with the confusion and mystery that have surrounded attempts to uncover hard evidence about him. It was said of him that "he strove towards self-concealment and remaining without name." He has been variously identified as a court scholar who was an historical contemporary of Confucius; as the great astrologer Tan; as a chimerial personification of what was in fact a group of sages and scholars working independently and at different times during the fifth to third centuries B.C.E.; as the immortal personification of the Tao; as the Buddha incarnate. The significance of this mysterious personality rests on his composition of the *Tao te Ching* (translatable as "The Way and its Power" or "Life and its Meaning"), a treatise that has had a fundamental and lasting effect on Chinese

> "Heaven is long-enduring and earth continues long. The reason why heaven and earth are able to endure and continue thus long is because they do not live of, or for, themselves. This is how they are able to continue and endure."
>
> *Tao te Ching*, c. 6th century B.C.E.

thought for over 2,000 years. The work is a poetic celebration of the Way (Tao) of the primordial forces of nature, and describes how the man of virtue identifies himself with these forces through his conduct. It is the fundamental Taoist text.

Alternative suggestions notwithstanding, Lao-tzu (this epithet is best translated as "the Old One") is most credibly identifiable as an archivist at the imperial court of the Zhou dynasty in Luo-Yang, in what is now the province of Henan in central China. The family name of the scholar in charge of the sacred books of the royal court was Li, his proper name Erh, and his appellation Tan. What little is known about him is inextricably entangled with myth and legend.

Lao-tzu is said to have met Confucius when the latter visited the royal court. Much has been talked and conjectured about the meeting of these two giants of Chinese letters: the schools they founded, Taoism and Confucianism respectively, represent the two most significant strands of Chinese philosophy. All reports agree that Lao-tzu spoke in rather a deprecatory manner about Confucius's honored idols, the heroes of ancient times, and tried to convince Confucius of the futility of his cultural pursuits. Confucius, on the other hand, expressed his respect for the sage's wisdom, comparing him to a dragon who rises up to the clouds (unlike their counterparts in European mythologies, Chinese dragons represent powerful and beneficent forces).

Chinese society was experiencing uncertainty, civil strife, and change in Lao-tzu's day. The period is known as the time of the Warring States, and lasted for some 200 years. Lao-tzu is said to have left the court when political conditions had deteriorated beyond hope of repair. Traveling westward, he arrived at the Hsien-ku pass (riding, some say, on the back of a black ox) where he was confronted by its legendary guardian, Yin Hsi. Yin Hsi begged the sage to leave him some written record; without further ado, Lao-tzu composed the *Tao te Ching* on the spot, handed it over, and disappeared into the west.

Lao-tzu's weariness with the world of current affair is suggested by the fact that there is not one historical reference in the *Tao te Ching*. However, the text is not simply a mystical treatise unrelated to worldly considerations; it does implicitly address issues of government and society. Faced with the hypocrisy and moral turpitude that characterized the latter days of the Zhou dynasty, he felt that all forceful attempts to put things right were inevitably corrupted by the prevailing malaise. Hence the *Tao te Ching* indicates that conventional moral, political, and social standards need to be discarded because they are based on value judgments and lead people to undertake activities that alienate them from nature. Rather, the individual should seek to pursue the way of the Tao, a path beyond praise or blame that conforms to cosmic principles.

The Tao is perhaps best understood as the universal force that animates the cosmos, an ineffable reality experienced in ecstacy, empty of inherent qualities but manifest in everything. It is the unchanging unity that underlies the transient plurality of appearances. If this force is allowed to flow smoothly and uninterruptedly, harmony will be achieved through the balancing of opposing forces. Lao-tzu's superior man empties himself of desires, preconceptions, and goals so that the Tao can work through him unobstructedly. By so doing he reaches a state where his actions are so completely in accord with the proper and natural harmony of things that no trace is left of the author of the action. Lao-tzu denominates such action as *wu wei,* or nondoing, and equates it with the behavior of the ideal leader, who effectively becomes the personification of the Tao itself.

While the influence of Taoism and the *Tao te Ching* grew, so too did the legend of Lao-tzu. It was widely believed that the Old One had discovered the secret of immortality through his world-shunning practices, and he came to be revered as a cosmic force himself, a physical manifestation of the Tao. By the time of the later Tan dynasty (23–220 C.E.), he was even worshiped by the emperor himself. Other tales of the period credited Lao-tzu with a miraculous childhood akin to that traditionally ascribed to the Buddha—his mother was supposed to have borne him in her womb for 72 years, for instance. Any historical evidence about the individual was thus buried beneath the welter of supposition and legend.

Western interest in Taoism and the *Tao te Ching* is of more recent origin. However, Leo Tolstoy acknowledged his indebtedness to the sage for the doctrine of nonaction, closely related to *wu-wei,* while Carl Jung was also fascinated by Taoist teachings. Lao-tzu's work has been through innumerable translations in the west in the course of the last 180 years, while the upsurge of interest in Eastern philosophy and religion has rendered the Old One's teachings accessible to a wider audience than ever before. ◆

> "Gravity is the root of lightness; stillness, the ruler of movement."
> *Tao te Ching,* c. 6th century B.C.E.

Las Casas, Bartolome de

c. 1474–c. 1566 ● CATHOLIC

Bartolome de Las Casas was a Spanish bishop, defender of human rights, and author who remains one of the most controversial figures in Latin America's conquest period. His expose of Spanish mistreatment of Amerindians produced public outrage that was directed at both the conquistadores who were committing the atrocities and at the writer who had made them public. Las Casas's vast output of political, historical, and theological writing forms one of the basic sources for contemporary understanding of the conquest period and of some of the most important individuals involved in the initial colonization of the Spanish Indies.

Las Casas was the son of a Seville merchant, Pedro de Las Casas. In 1493 the young Bartolome saw Christopher Columbus's triumphant return to Spain and the small group of Taino Indians Columbus brought with him. Las Casas remained at home in school while his father and other members of his family accompanied Columbus as colonists on the second voyage to the Indies. Five years later Pedro de Las Casas returned to Spain for a short period, bringing with him a Taino boy named Juanico. While his father was at home, Bartolome declared his desire to become a priest and went to Salamanca to learn canon law. He also began to learn about the Indies from Juanico, with whom Las Casas struck up a lifelong friendship. In 1502 Las Casas quit school and sailed to the West Indies. His first years in Hispaniola were spent helping his father and aiding in the provisioning of Spanish military expeditions. At the same time, young Las Casas began learning sev-

eral native languages and befriending local Indians; he had already begun deploring the violence he witnessed. He returned to Europe, first to Spain and then to Rome where, in 1507, he was ordained a priest.

In 1510 Las Casas returned to Hispaniola. These years were to be crucial both for Las Casas and for the nature of Spanish-Indian relations. His return coincided with the arrival of the Dominicans. In 1511 the Dominican priest Antonio de Montesino represented his order in a highly public condemnation of the Encomienda system that outraged the island's entire Spanish community. The message was not lost on Las Casas, who then held Indians as an *encomendero* (land grantee). Las Casas was ordained priest in 1512 or 1513, and in 1513 he joined Diego de Velazquez and Panfilo de Narvaez in the conquest of Cuba. Las Casas preached to and converted the natives in preparation for the Spanish conquistadores, and those efforts largely succeeded. In reward for his services, Las Casas received land together with a grant of Indians and by all appearances had established himself as a typical *encomendero*.

The decimation of Cuba's native population by Spanish *encomenderos* through overwork, starvation, and murder made Las Casas realize that the real solution for Indian mistreatment lay not with challenging the conduct of individual *encomenderos* but by calling into question the entire system and its relationship to Christian morality. In 1514 he astonished his parishioners by condemning the *encomienda* in its entirety, freeing his Indians, and then vigorously interceding with local authorities on the natives' behalf. Failing to convert even a single *encomendero* to his position, he went to Europe in 1515 to plead his case with the king of Spain. Las Casas spent the next six years arguing that the period for military conquest of the Indians had passed. The time had arrived, he claimed, for peaceful conversion of natives and the promotion of agricultural colonization. He did not stand alone in condemning Spanish cruelties against Indians. Other voices had begun to sound in the Americas, and a small but influential group of royal ministers and Spanish churchmen supported the goal of protecting Indians. After heated debate, Emperor Charles V (Charles I of Spain) sided with Las Casas in 1519, ruling that the Indies could be governed without the force of arms. The ruling, however, had little practical effect in the distant Western Hemisphere.

c. 1474 — Las Casas is born in Spain.

1493 — Las Casas sees Columbus return home.

1502 — Las Casas quits school and sails to the West Indies.

1513 — Las Casas joins Velasquez and Narvaez in the conquest of Cuba.

1523 — Las Casas becomes a Dominican monk.

1537 — Las Casas publishes *The Only Way*.

1544 — Las Casas sails to Indies for brief tenure as Bishop of Chiapas.

1545 — Las Casas issues a controversial confessor manual for priests.

1555 — Las Casas has his last great success acting on the Indians' behalf.

1566 — Las Casas dies.

During the next quarter century, Las Casas repeatedly suffered defeats in his efforts to defend the Americas' native populations. In 1520 he left Spain to establish a settlement in Venezuela, hoping to peacefully convert local Indians and create an economically self-sufficient community. But opposition from *encomenderos* and colonial officials helped to incite an Indian rebellion that wrecked the project. Despondent over its failure, he entered the Dominican order as a monk in 1523. The years that followed were ones of intellectual growth and personal frustration for Las Casas. He outlined his program for peaceful conversion, in opposition to military conquest, in *The Only Way* (1537). While in the monastery, he began his monumental *In Defense of the Indians* and the *History of the Indies* and continued a lifelong passion of collecting documents.

Although colonial Spaniards scorned any attempt to ameliorate the Indians' plight, moral encouragement arrived from Europe in the form of Pope Paul III's **bull** *Sublimis Deus* (1537), which proclaimed that American Indians were rational beings with souls, whose lives and property should be protected. During the same year Charles V supported an effort by Las Casas and the Dominicans to establish missions in Guatemala based on the precepts laid out in *The Only Way*. The high point of the crown's efforts came in 1542 with the so called New Laws, which forbade Indian slavery and sought to end the *encomienda* system within a generation by outlawing their transference through family inheritance. Las Casas, who was in Spain at the time, directly influenced the direction of the New Laws in part by reading the first version of *The Devastation of the Indies* to a horrified royal court.

In 1544 he sailed to the Indies for a brief and tempestuous tenure as the bishop of Chiapas. Although he had been offered the Cuzco bishopric, the richest in the Americas, Las Casas instead accepted one of the poorest. When he tried to implement the New Laws in his see, local clergy who had ties to *encomenderos* defied him. After Las Casas denied final absolution to any Spaniard who refused to free his Indians or pay restitution, he received threats against his life. Proclamation of the New Laws brought outright revolt in parts of Spanish America and fierce antagonism everywhere. Even the Viceroyalty of New Spain and its high court openly refused to enforce them. In 1545 colonial opposition persuaded Charles V to revoke key inheritance statutes in the New Laws. Las Casas went to an ec-

bull: a papal letter with the imprint of the bulla (a round seal)

clesiastical assembly in Mexico City and persuaded his fellow bishops to support a strongly worded resolution defending Indian rights. At the same time he publicly humiliated the viceroy, Antonio de Mendoza, for attempting to silence him. But he left his most defiant act for last.

Just after arriving, Las Casas issued a confessor manual for the priests in his diocese that essentially reinstituted the inheritance statutes of the New Laws. His *Confesionario* produced public outrage by reiterating that all Spaniards seeking last rites must free their Indians and make restitution, even if the Indians were part of a deeded estate. Las Casas justified his decision by arguing that all wealth acquired through *encomiendas* was ill-gotten, declaring, "There is no Spaniard in the Indies who has shown good faith in connection with the wars of Conquest." This last statement put at issue the very basis of Spain's presence in the Americas. Las Casas contended that the Spanish had acquired all their wealth by unjustly exploiting Indians; if all of their activities since Columbus's landing were unjust, so too, logically, was the crown's American presence. Not surprisingly, the Council of the Indies recalled Las Casas to Spain in 1547 and ordered all copies of the *Confesionario* confiscated.

Colonial and Spanish opposition to Las Casas coalesced around Juan Gines de Sepulveda, one of Spain's leading humanists. Sepulveda used Aristotle's doctrine of just war to defend Spanish conduct in the Americas. The vigor of Las Casas's counterattack led the Council of the Indies to call for a court of jurists and theologians to ascertain "how conquests may be conducted justly and with security of conscience." Charles V then ordered the two men to debate their positions before the court.

Much popular misconception has surrounded the 1550 "great debate" between Las Casas and Sepulveda in the Spanish city of Valladolid. The two men never debated face to face but stated their cases individually before the court. In the end, the majority of judges sided with Las Casas but, perhaps fearing controversy, refused to render a public decision. Legislation by the crown continued to move slowly toward the abolition of Indian slavery and some of the egregious features of the *encomienda* system.

Las Casas left Chiapas in 1547 and, in August 1550, resigned the Chiapas bishopric. He assumed residency in the Dominican San Gregorio monastery, where in 1552 he produced

> Las Casas contended that the Spanish had acquired all their wealth by unjustly exploiting Indians; if all of their activities since Columbus's landing were unjust, so too, logically, was the crown's American presence.

his most important work, *The Devastation of the Indies: A Brief Account*. *A Brief Account* was immediately translated into several languages and ignited a firestorm of controversy that continues today. Next came his two largest works. The first, *Apologetica historia sumaria*, argued for the rationality of American Indians by comparing them favorably to the Greeks and Romans. After research in Hernando Columbus's library; he rewrote his three-volume *History of the Indies*, which remains a standard source on Columbus and Spain's first decades in the Americas.

Las Casas continued to champion Indian rights in the final phase of his life. His last great success occurred in 1555, when Peruvian conquistadores offered 8 million **ducats** to Philip II in exchange for perpetual *encomiendas*. Las Casas adroitly had the decision postponed while he gained the power of attorney, enabling him to act officially on the Indians' behalf. With their backing, he made a counteroffer that surpassed the conquistadores' bribe and led to its summary withdrawal. Despite that triumph, Las Casas's final years were characterized by urgent pleas about the Indians' circumstances and the belief that God might destroy Spain for its sins against them. On the day he died, Las Casas voiced regret for not having done more. He was buried in the convent chapel of Our Lady of Atocha in Madrid.

ducat: gold coin used in European nations around the 14th century

Today Las Casas is largely remembered for *A Brief Account* and his role in the controversy surrounding the black legend of Spanish conquest. Whether or not Las Casas exaggerated Spanish atrocities, as his critics claim, does not alter the fact that *A Brief Account* remains one of the most important documents ever written on human rights. The issues Las Casas raised in 1552 remain pertinent today. Modern scholarship has supported Las Casas's staggering toll of native deaths but assigns the principal responsibility to Afro-European diseases rather than Spanish cruelty. Recent work has also refuted the claim that Las Casas promoted the African slave trade as a substitute for Indian slavery, pointing out that his *History of the Indies* explicitly condemns African slavery. Although Las Casas never claimed to be an impartial historian, his historical texts continue to provide information on the conquest period. Ultimately, however, it is Las Casas as a crusader and symbol of the struggle for human rights that keeps him in our historical memory. Perhaps no one else in history has been more insistent or clear in articulating Western culture's moral responsibility to the oppressed. ◆

Lee, Ann

1736–1784 ● SHAKER

Ann Lee was an English religious visionary and the founder of the American Shakers. Growing up in a poor, working-class family in Manchester, England. Ann Lee was attracted in 1758 to the Shakers, a Christian group that engaged in ecstatic dancing and other charismatic activities. Married in 1762, Lee had four children, all of whom died in infancy or early childhood. She interpreted these losses and the pain that she experienced in childbirth as a judgment on her concupiscence. In 1770 a vision convinced her that lust was the original sin in the Garden of Eden and the root of all human evil and misery. Only by giving up sexual intercourse entirely, following the heavenly pattern in which "they neither marry nor are given in marriage," could humankind be reconciled to God.

The Shakers and the celibate message that Ann Lee introduced among them experienced little success in England, where the group was sporadically persecuted but generally ignored. In 1774 Lee and eight of her followers emigrated to America and two years later settled at Niskeyuna (now Watervliet), New York, near Albany. Between 1781 and 1783, during the troubled aftermath of the American Revolution, Lee and the Shakers undertook a major proselytizing effort in New York and New England in the course of which they attracted support primarily from Free Will Baptists. Ensuing persecution, including brutal beatings and harassment, weakened Ann Lee and her brother William, contributing to their premature deaths in 1784.

Although Ann Lee's involvement with the Shakers in America lasted only a decade, her influence at that time was profound and has continued to be so during the groups's subsequent 200-year history. Intelligent, dynamic, and loving, she was revered by her followers. They came to believe that in "Mother Ann," as they affectionately called her, God's spirit had been incarnated in female form just as they believed that in Jesus, God's spirit had been incarnated in male form. Whether Lee herself ever claimed such quasi divinity—except in ecstatic utterances subject to symbolic interpretation—is questionable. Yet the conviction that Ann Lee was the second embodiment of Christ's spirit and the inaugurator of the millennium is central to the Shaker faith. ◆

> "Conviction of sin, godly sorrow, and repentance, are the first effects of the Spirit of God upon the conscience of a sinner. And when sin is fully removed, by confessing and forsaking it, the cause of heaviness, gloom and sorrow is gone; and joy and rejoicing, and thanksgiving and praise, are then spontaneous effects of a true spirit of devotion."
>
> *Shakers' Compendium*, 185

Lee, Chung Ok

1955– ● BUDDHIST

Rev. Dr. Chung Ok Lee is a spiritual teacher, peace activist, and scholar who served as a key representative of Won Buddhism to the United Nations. Won Buddhism is a form of Buddhism that began in Korea in the early 1900s.

Lee was born on August 20, 1955 in a small tribal village in Korea. Her father, Choon Wha Lee, and her mother, Kil Sung Kim, were farmers. Her father was Confucian and her mother was Buddhist. Lee grew up witnessing what she later termed as the oppression and suffering of women in her village. "My feminist journey began at a young age, when I worked alongside village women and listened as they told about the abuse their husbands and in-laws made them suffer." She also recalled the Korean custom of maintaining a family book recording the family's lineage. She was surprised as a fifth grader to discover that her name was not included because female family members were not listed.

Lee's father denied her education beyond ninth grade, because, he said, "modern education spoils women." But Lee, with help from some teachers, moved to a city to continue her education. There she became interested in religion. As a tenth grader, she visited a Won Buddhist temple, where she saw a woman giving a sermon. She began teaching public school when she was 22 years old. In spite of criticism from her family and her village, Lee entered the monastery at Won Buddhist Headquarters and began the community life that she continues until today.

Won Buddhism began when a Korean man named Pak Chung-bin (1891–1943) experienced a great spiritual awakening in 1916. The core of his vision was that human beings were going to be enslaved to the power of material civilization. Humankind needed to strengthen their spiritual power in order to restore and protect their dignity from materialism. Pak Chung-bin was regarded as the new Buddha by his followers.

In 1919, Pak Chung-bin, together with a few disciples, moved to a remote monastery where he spent five years developing the doctrine and system of his new religious order. In 1924, followers of Pak Chung-bin began living communally. Pak Chung-bin taught his disciples how to attain Buddhahood

1955 Lee is born in a small tribal village in Korea to a farmer couple.

1981 Lee receives full ordination and goes on to earn masters and doctorate.

1992 Lee becomes main UN representative of Won Buddhism International.

1993 Lee becomes international head of Parliament of World's Religions and abbot of Won Buddhism in America.

1994 Lee is founding co-chair of United Nations Values Caucus.

1995 Lee is head of UN Committee of Religious Non-Governmental groups.

1998 Lee becomes a professor at Mount Saint Mary College in New York.

and sent disciples out to create branch temples, where they taught their new religion to the general public.

In 1943, Pak Chung-bin died. Master Chongsan (Song Kyu, 1900–1962) succeeded him and named the order Won Buddhism in 1947. Under Chongsan's leadership, the Won Buddhist Order grew to a major religion in Korea, establishing over 400 temples throughout South Korea. It has established 30 branch temples in the United States and Europe.

Rev. Chung Ok Lee received full ordination in 1981 in Korea. She went on to earn her masters and doctorate degrees from New York University in New York City. Lee became active in global inter-religious dialogue in the 1980s. From 1989 to the late 1990s, she served on the Executive Council of the World Conference on Religion and Peace in the United States. She was an International President of the Parliament of World's Religions in Chicago in 1993. From 1994 to 1995, she was Founding Co-Chair of the Values Caucus at the United Nations. Lee served as President of the Committee of Religious Non-Governmental Organizations at the United Nations from 1995 to 1997. Lee served as Co-President of the Oslo Conference on Freedom of Religion or Belief in celebration of the 50th Anniversary of the Universal Declaration of Human Rights in August 1998.

Lee has written various publications and delivered keynote addresses on topics concerning women's issues, the environment and ecology, human rights, social development, religious pluralism, and global ethics at many international conferences. Rev. Chung Ok Lee became the Main Representative of Won Buddhism International to the United Nations in 1992. She became the abbot of Won Buddhism of American in 1993. In 1998, she became a professor at Mount Saint Mary College, Newburg, New York. ◆

> "In the coming new era, we cannot practice our own religious life without some understanding of other religions because we are part of a single world. Building a peaceful world through inter-religious dialogue in the world community is the new mission of religious people in these days."
>
> Chung Ok Lee, 1999

Lenshina, Alice

c. 1910–1978 ● Lumpa

Alice Lenshina was the founder of the African prophetic movement referred to as the Lumpa church. A barely literate peasant woman, Alice Lenshina Mulenga, from Kasomo village, Chinasali district, in the northern province of

Northern Rhodesia, started the movement among the Bemba, a matrilineal Bantu-speaking people of Northern Rhodesia (now Zambia). In 1953, Lenshina claimed to have had a spiritual experience in which she died, went to heaven, and met a Christian spirit, described variously as Jesus, God, or an angel, who told her to return to earth to carry out God's works. She told her story to the minister of the nearby Church of Scotland mission at Lubwa (founded by David Kaunda, the father of Kenneth Kaunda, the president of Zambia) and was baptized into the church, taking the name Alice. In 1954, she began holding her own services and baptizing her followers. Her meetings drew large crowds, and by 1955 her following was more or less distinctive from the Church of Scotland mission. One characteristic feature of Lenshina's movement was the singing of hymns, many of which were closer in form to traditional Bemba music than were the hymns of the Church of Scotland. Moreover, Lenshina's followers believed that she could provide protection against witchcraft, the existence of which the Church of Scotland denied.

By 1956 the Lenshina movement, with a membership of over 50,000, could be considered a church of its own. As the movement grew it drew members from different ethnic and religious backgrounds—urban workers and rural subsistence farmers—and from a range of social statuses, although its appeal was strongest among the poorer, less educated sections of Northern Rhodesian society. The movement spread along the line of the railroad into the towns of the Copper Belt, one of the main urban, industrial regions of central Africa. It also spread to the remote rural areas of the northern and eastern provinces, and poor peasants would walk hundreds of miles to contribute their labor and money to construct the monumental cathedral at Kasomo, Lenshina's religious headquarters. Lenshina's followers became known as *Lumpa* (a Bemba term meaning "excelling," "the most important").

In its early years, from the mid-1950s to the early 1960s, the Lumpa church, with its anti-European stance, was viewed as a political ally of the independence movement in Northern Rhodesia, and Lumpa meetings incorporated nationalist propaganda. Afterward, however, the church became increasingly nonpolitical and otherworldly in its outlook, and conflicts developed with the United National Independence Party, a political party founded under the leadership of Kenneth Kaunda and the main political contender to establish Zambian independence from colonial rule. In 1957 the Lumpa church, in its constitution, had stated that it was not opposed to the laws of the country; its solution to the problem of colonialism, African political nationalism, and rapid economic change was withdrawal. By 1963 church members refused to obey the laws of the colonial state or to join political parties. They believed that the end of the world was at hand, and they withdrew from the secular world and built their own separate communities in anticipation of the end. These communities were believed to be sacred domains, immune from the evils of the external world, which was thought to be under the control of Satan and his evil influence and agents.

By 1964, at a time when Northern Rhodesia's independence was imminent, both the colonial administration and the African independence movement attempted to control the Lumpa church. This led to fighting between church members and the recently elected Northern Rhodesia government, and between July and October 1964 over 700 people were killed. The Lumpa, armed with indigenous weapons such as spears, axes, and muzzle loaders, confronted soldiers with automatic weapons. As the Lumpa attacked they shouted, "Jericho!" in the belief that the walls of evil would tumble down and that they would triumph in battle. As they were shot they shouted, "Hallelujah!" in the belief that they would be transported directly to heaven, only to return to rule the world. The Lumpa were defeated, the church was banned, and Lenshina herself was imprisoned. Some of her followers fled to Zaire, where the Lumpa church continued to exist.

In its beliefs and practices, the Lumpa church combined both African and European elements. Movements of this type were and are characteristic of southern and central Africa. At the core of such movements is a prophet who is believed to have had a Christian experience. As is typical of such movements, Lenshina's prophecy was ethical in that it imposed a

c. 1910 Lenshina is born into a poor village in Northern Rhodesia.

1953 Lenshina has a near death experience that sets her on her path.

1954 Lenshina begins holding services and baptizing her followers.

1956 Lenshina's movement has a membership of more than 50,000.

1978 Lenshina dies.

strict, puritanical moral code upon her followers. She forbade adultery, polygamy, divorce, dancing, and drinking. Lenshina herself was the ultimate source of authority, and some Lumpa hymns even represented Lenshina as the savior. Baptism, the most important rite of the church, could only be performed by Lenshina herself, using water which she claimed to have received from God himself. Baptism was believed to wash away sins and ensure salvation.

> In Lumpa theology, God was viewed as the creator of all things. Satan was thought to have been created by God as a good spirit who turned against God.

In Lumpa theology, God was viewed as the creator of all things. Satan was thought to have been created by God as a good spirit who turned against God. Witchcraft, thought to stem from Satan, could be safeguarded against by church membership. Unlike the European mission churches, the Lumpa church did not deny the existence of witchcraft; instead it gave its members a means of combating it. Lenshina was believed to be the personification of good and to provide protection against evil. For the Lumpa, evil came to be the world outside their church, including the colonial administration, and the United National Independence Party represented evil.

The movement gradually acquired a structure, with Lenshina, her disciples, and spiritual and secular advisers at the center. Deacons supervised congregations, and within congregations preachers and judges ministered to the needs of local members and adjudicated their disputes. The church was itself a complete community, meeting its own spiritual, social, judicial, and economic requirements. In the historical context of the struggle for Zambian independence, a movement that demanded the complete allegiance of its members was bound to come into conflict with secular authorities. The Lenshina cult was not an atypical African religious expression; what brought it into prominence and led to its destruction was its unfortunate timing and conflict with the movement for Zambia's independence. ◆

Lord, John Wesley

1902–1989 ● Methodist

John Wesley Lord was a churchman who forthrightly expressed and acted upon his deep liberal convictions on controversial political and social issues in his effort to defend the Bill of Rights, to promote social and economic justice, to improve race relations, and to advance the cause of world peace.

He was born in Patterson, New Jersey, the second of the three sons of John James Lord, a letter carrier, and Catherine Carmichael, who wanted her son to be a minister. Lord was named after the founder of Methodism. After completing high school in suburban Montclair, New Jersey, Lord attended the New Jersey State Normal School at Montclair, from which he graduated in 1922. He was a public school teacher and principal in New Jersey from 1922 to 1924. He then entered Dickinson College in Carlisle, Pennsylvania, and received his A.B. degree in 1927. Deciding that the ministry was his true vocation, he then enrolled in Drew Theological Seminary in Madison, New Jersey, and obtained the bachelor of divinity degree in 1930. During his three years at Drew, he was assistant pastor of the Emory Methodist Church in Jersey City, New Jersey. After some graduate study in philosophy at New College, University of Edinburgh, Scotland, from 1930 to 1931, he married Margaret Farrington Ratcliffe on 29 April 1931. They had one daughter, Jean.

Lord's first pastorate was at the Union Community Church in Union, New Jersey, where he served from 1931 to 1934. He was then pastor of the First Methodist Church in Arlington, New Jersey, from 1935 to 1938, followed by the First Methodist Church in Westfield, New Jersey, from 1938 to 1948. One of the youngest Methodist bishops to be ordained in the United States, he was elected to the episcopacy of the Methodist church in June 1948 and served for 24 years. In 1948 he was assigned to the Boston area and made his home in Wellesley, Massachusetts. In 1960 he was reassigned to the Washington, D.C., area, where he remained until his retirement in 1972. From 1970 to 1971 he was president of the Council of Bishops of the United Methodist Church.

In Washington, Lord became a social activist. He upheld President John F. Kennedy's plea for the enactment of the School Assistance Bill of 1961, which provided federal aid to public schools. He explained that the public school system was the "bulwark of democracy," essentially different from the private parochial system, and that it would be unconstitutional to include the latter in the bill because of the First Amendment's strictures against the "establishment of religion." Committed to the principle of separation of church and state, Lord appeared

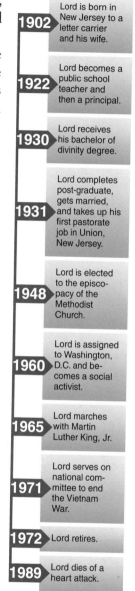

1902 Lord is born in New Jersey to a letter carrier and his wife.

1922 Lord becomes a public school teacher and then a principal.

1930 Lord receives his bachelor of divinity degree.

1931 Lord completes post-graduate, gets married, and takes up his first pastorate job in Union, New Jersey.

1948 Lord is elected to the episcopacy of the Methodist Church.

1960 Lord is assigned to Washington, D.C. and becomes a social activist.

1965 Lord marches with Martin Luther King, Jr.

1971 Lord serves on national committee to end the Vietnam War.

1972 Lord retires.

1989 Lord dies of a heart attack.

before the House Judiciary Committee in Washington on 27 May 1964 to oppose the proposed constitutional amendment, known as the Becker amendment, that would allow doctrinal exercises in public schools. He argued that the First Amendment, as it then stood, was adequate to protect "the free exercise of religion." Further, he emphasized that the 1962 Supreme Court decision in *Engle v. Vitale,* which forbade a state composed prayer and Bible reading in public schools, excluded neither teaching about religion nor studying the Bible for its "literary and historical qualities" in public schools. "The school may not pray, but it must teach," he admonished.

Dedicated to the struggle for racial equality, Lord participated in the 28 August 1963 civil rights demonstration in Washington, D.C., known as the "March on Washington for Jobs and Freedom." On 9 March 1965 he joined the abortive second attempt to stage a protest march from Selma to Montgomery, Alabama, in support of voting rights for African Americans. Motivated solely by his conscience, he demonstrated as an individual citizen and marched arm in arm with Dr. Martin Luther King, Jr. Championing racial integration in the Methodist church, Lord had, as bishop, by 1964 appointed in the Washington area black district superintendents to head predominantly white districts and churches and, beginning in 1966, black pastors to white parishes. In March 1972 he stated that "separate but equal" was the **shibboleth** used for many decades in some parts of the United States to defend the outrageous practice of busing black children to black schools. He favored instead busing them to better neighborhoods and better school systems, but only as a "temporary expedient." He warned that if busing were thought of simply as a means of integrating the "school," it would be a wasteful effort. The objective, in his view, was to make all neighborhoods "good" and to extend their services to all children.

shibboleth: common custom or methodology

A social reformer, Lord preached abstinence from alcoholic beverages and advocated penal reform and rehabilitation. As chairman of the Interreligious Committee on Race Relations from 1967 to 1969 and with the plight of America's cities in mind, he implored that "social service is not enough; we need social change" to address effectively problems stemming from poverty and racism.

A sharp critic of the Vietnam War, Lord faulted President Lyndon Johnson in December 1966 for escalating it, thus undercutting the president's call for negotiations and peaceful settlement. In May 1970 Lord accused President Richard Nixon of indifference to the moral issues of the war. He joined the Citizens Committee for the Amendment to End the War, formed in 1970, which aimed to restore to Congress its constitutional role in making war. In 1971 he served on the national committee Set the Date Now: An Interreligious Campaign to End the War and urged Congress to vote against the two-year extension of conscription that Nixon sought that year. Lord also argued that war resisters should be granted unconditional amnesty and repatriation in recognition of their right to dissent under constraint of conscience. His humanitarian efforts on the national level included accepting in 1966 an honorary chairmanship of the Committee of Responsibility to Save War-Burned and War-Injured Vietnamese Children.

Lord also disagreed with U.S. policy on China and joined the National Board for New China Policy, organized in 1970. He contended that Taiwan was historically, culturally, and linguistically Chinese and that the People's Republic of China (mainland China) was entitled to the Chinese seat on the United Nations Security Council. Concerned with the ravages caused by overpopulation, Lord explained that the Methodist (and Protestant) position was to make information and medical assistance regarding birth control available to families worldwide through public and private programs. Arguing for a more responsible attitude toward family planning, in 1972 he asked Nixon to recommend strongly to the American people his presidential commission's report *Population Growth and the American Future*, which called for a gradual stabilization of population, a national population policy, and U.S. assistance to developing countries in seeking solutions to the problem; Nixon rejected the report.

Lord sought a stronger United Nations. As a representative of the United States Interreligious Committee on Peace, he participated for 22 days in 1968 in a tour of seven countries to promote peace, calling on all nations to "surrender some of their sovereignty" to achieve a "world perspective." He pressed the U.S. Senate to reject Nixon's proposal in 1969 to deploy the antiballistic missile system.

After retiring in 1972, Lord lived in Wolfeboro, New Hampshire, and spent his winters in Lakeland, Florida. He preached often in New Hampshire and ministered around Lakeland. Lord used his mellifluous and stentorian voice both as a preacher and as a fighter for human rights. As he ex-

> Lord also argued that war resisters should be granted unconditional amnesty and repatriation in recognition of their right to dissent under constraint of conscience.

plained, "Methodists have a social passion." His reformist articles appeared in such Methodist periodicals as *Christian Advocate, Concern, Engage, Interpreter, Methodist Story, Together,* and *Wesley Quarterly.* As he once wrote, "In a long and arduous career, I was sustained by the thought that the work was not mine to finish, nor was I free to take no part in it." Lord died of a heart attack in Wolfeboro, New Hampshire, where he was buried. ◆

Saint Ignatius of Loyola

1491–1556 ● Catholic

Saint Ignatius of Loyola was a leader of the sixteenth-century Catholic reformation and founder of the Society of Jesus (the Jesuits). Born at a critical juncture in the history of the Roman Catholic church, when its spiritual life had deteriorated, plagued by impiety, simony, and laxity, Loyola, from a noble and wealthy background, helped to renew the life of the church, setting an example of poverty, devotion, and loyalty to the pope.

Baptized Inigo Lopez de Loyola in the Basque country of Spain, Loyola had an aristocratic upbringing. When he was 12, his parents arranged a position for him in the household of Juan Velazquez de Cuellar, King Ferdinand's treasurer. Velazquez educated Loyola to be his page in the royal court, grooming him impeccably and teaching him courtly manners as well as martial arts. Loyola read the chivalric tales that were popular at the time, seeing his own life on the way to high accomplishments.

By 1507 both his parents were dead. In 1517, when Velazquez died, Loyola left Cuellar for Navarre, also in northern Spain, pledging his loyalty and military services to the duke of Najera. In the revolt of the Comuneros, Loyola fought to put down the rebellion, but withdrew for reasons of conscience when the troops began the traditional plunder of the defeated town. In 1521 the French attacked the Navarre region at Pamplona, its capital. Loyola hid out, refusing to surrender with the rest of the town. He took refuge in the city's fortress, convinced that he would be killed by the French army which greatly outnumbered Navarre's forces. In the battle that ensued, he was hit by a cannonball, injured in both his legs. When the Spanish forces surrendered, the French treated Loyola's wounds; he was left limp and deformed from his injuries. He refused to accept his fate, suffering through excruciatingly painful surgery to correct his condition so that he could return to his chivalrous lifestyle. The period of his convalescence turned out to be the beginning of a spiritual revolution in his life. During this time his readings of the life of Christ and the saints led him to turn away from his martial pursuits toward a devout life of Christian spirituality.

In 1522 he left Navarre to go on pilgrimage to the Holy Land. In transit he stopped at Monserrat, a pilgrimage site in northeastern Spain. Here he divested himself of his wealth, taking the rough clothes of a beggar and discarding the weapons of his military career. He then continued to Manresa where he stayed for 11 months doing penance, dwelling in a cave, begging for food, breaking his bodily strength, and formulating what would become his great devotional work, *Exercitia Spiritualia*, Spiritual Exercises.

The *Exercises* was based on Loyola's own experiences of transformation, intended as a guide, leading the believer through a process of Christian self-examination, penitence, recommitment of faith and strengthening. Accordingly, the *Exercises* was divided into four weeks, each week concentrating on another stage of the process of restoring Christian commitment. Although formulated during these critical months at Manresa in 1522, the work did not reach its completed form until 1541.

From Manresa, Loyola went on to the Holy Land, leaving from the port of Barcelona to sail to Italy before finally arriving on foot in Jerusalem. Denied permission to stay there, Loyola returned to Barcelona in 1525 after making pilgrimages to various sites in the Holy Land. Back in Spain he studied Latin and philosophy, while also counseling those who sought his wisdom

1491 Loyola is born into an aristocratic family.

1507 Loyola becomes an orphan.

1517 Loyola pledges his loyalty to the duke of Najera.

1521 Loyola hides out, refusing to surrender to the French, and is maimed.

1522 Loyola leaves on a pilgrimage to the Holy Land.

1525 Loyola returns to Spain and is imprisoned for heresy.

1534 Loyola receives his masters degree in philosophy in Paris.

1539 Loyola's group becomes the Society of Jesus.

1540 Loyola's Society of Jesus is confirmed by Pope Paul III.

1541 Loyola publishes *Spiritual Exercises*, drafted in 1522.

1556 Loyola dies.

> "In those who go on from good to better, the good Angel touches such soul sweetly, lightly and gently, like a drop of water which enters into a sponge; and the evil touches it sharply and with noise and disquiet, as when the drop of water falls on the stone."
>
> Ignacius of Loyola, *Spiritual Exercises*, 1548

in spiritual matters. Gaining followers, many of whom were women, he was accused of heresy and imprisoned for a period of time.

When he gained his freedom, he went to Paris where he resumed his study of philosophy, receiving a master's degree in 1534. That same year, six men joined him in taking vows and studied his *Spiritual Exercises*, performing the prayers and meditations under his direction. Soon Loyola attracted more followers, increasing the group's number to ten before they departed for Jerusalem. On the way, in Venice, seven of the pilgrims were ordained as priests.

In 1539 the group became the Society of Jesus, and Loyola sent the principles of the Society to Pope Paul III, who confirmed it the next year. Loyola became general of the order, leading it until his death. His pleas to resign his duties during his last years when he suffered severe illness went unheeded by his followers, who looked to him for guidance. By the time of Loyola's death there were 1,000 members of the Society spearheading the church's Counter-Reformation against the Protestants while working within the Catholic church for its spiritual revival.

Loyola set a precedent of strong central authority for the Jesuits and this has continued throughout their history. They combated the trend in the sixteenth century away from religion—a move that had been accompanied by the study of classical texts—by teaching theology with rigorous scholarship and preaching the gospels. In addition the Society continued to emphasize education, good works, and helping the underprivileged. Already during Loyola's lifetime, the Jesuits were active in Asia, Africa, the New World, and throughout Europe. By 1626 their membership numbered over 15,000 and 100 years later this number had grown to 22,000.

The *Spiritual Exercises* became one of the church's most influential writings. In 1548 it received high praise from Pope Paul III and this was just the first of the book's accolades, reaffirmed again and again by the church through the centuries. Loyola's concept of spiritual retreat has sometimes been a subject of controversy, criticized because of the influence of the Jesuit leader over the practitioner in directing his prayer and spiritual life. Others focusing on the private nature of the meditations have criticized them for encouraging an inappropriate individuality in spiritual life. Loyola himself aroused differing appraisals. For some he was a militaristic leader of an authoritarian, secretive group. For others, he was a paternal figure whose strictness was a natural and necessary response to the Reformation as well as the need for reform within the church itself. Through Loyola's combination of pragmatism and spiritual rigor and sincerity, he became one of the major figures that rescued the Catholic church from one of its worst crises. ◆

Luther, Martin

1483–1546 ● Protestant

Martin Luther was a German theologian, ecclesiastical reformer, and the founder of Protestantism. Luther was born in Saxony, where his father worked in the copper mines and rose to a position of some authority and affluence. Somber piety and strict discipline characterized the family's home life. The elder Luther wished for his son to better himself and the family, and it was therefore decided that he should study for a career in law. To this end he entered university, where his manner earned him the nickname "the Philosopher" among his fellow students; he graduated with a master's degree in 1505.

To his father's chagrin, Luther was destined never to pursue a legal career. At an early age he had come into contact with the Brethren of the Common Life, one of the most pious and spiritual of late medieval religious movements, and was much influenced by them. His heightened religious sensibilities drew him inexorably toward the life of the spirit; then, on experiencing a ferocious thunderstorm near Stotterheim while on his way to university, he vowed to become a monk if he should survive. He was as good as his word, and entered the Augustinian monastery at Erfurt and was ordained in 1507.

> "If your faith and trust be right, then is your god also true; and, on the other hand, if your trust be false and wrong, then you have not the true God; for these two belong together faith and God. That now, I say, upon which you set your heart and put your trust is properly your god."
>
> Martin Luther, *The Great Catechism*, 1529

His diligence and talent marked him out as a fine scholar, and in 1508 he was sent by his order for further studies at Wittenburg. During a visit to Rome in 1510, on a mission to present the viewpoint of the German Augustinians in debate, he was shocked and disillusioned by the worldliness of the clergy there and the apparent absence of genuine spiritual values; this was to exacerbate his increasing alienation from the church of Rome.

The peculiarities of Luther's complex personality are a central component among the factors that precipitated his revolutionary theological formulation. Standing as he did at the gateway between the medieval and modern ages, he heralded the latter while manifesting the temperament of the former; the road to revolt was not an easy one for him, and his spiritual dilemmas can be seen to represent those of his age. Alternating between bouts of ecstasy and depression, and constantly and painfully oppressed by a sense of guilt at his own sinfulness, Luther increasingly came to feel that the established church could offer him little spiritual succor. The angry God of the Old Testament aroused in him no love, only fear. Moreover, he came to feel that human acts of repentance and good works were insufficient to expunge the burden of sin that each individual carried and accreted from cradle to grave. Salvation depended entirely on the grace of God rather than on human merit, he concluded; faith, therefore, became the cornerstone of his theology. He stressed the need for each man to minister to himself in the sovereign solitude of his conscience.

In 1512 Luther gained the title of doctor of theology; thereafter, regardless of the momentous religious controversies in which he became embroiled, his chief function remained lecturing in the chair of biblical theology at Wittenburg, while from 1514 he pursued an influential teaching ministry from the pulpit. He was vehemently anti-philosophical, characterizing himself as the northern barbarian storming the strongholds of the effete southern papists; in his autobiographical *Table Talk* he rued the time spent "on philosophy and all that devil's muck, when I could have been busy with poetry and legend and so many good things." Through his influence, Wittenburg forsook the study of Aristotle and the Scholastics for direct study of the Bible in a humanist framework: "Our theology, and that of Saint Augustine, reign," he declared triumphantly.

If a single date can be identified as signaling the advent of Protestantism, it is October 31, 1517, when Luther nailed his

95 theses to the door of All Saints' Church in Wittenburg, roundly attacking the practice of selling indulgences (the remission of sins under certain conditions). The theses were a declaration of the inward nature of Christianity, a criticism of the corruption rife in the established church, and an attack on papal policies. Luther outlined his "theology of the cross," which stressed the need of each Christian to share the temptation and suffering of Christ and argued that a person's communion with God requires no intermediary.

In the ensuing furor, Luther was supported by the chapter of his own Augustinian order, but nonetheless there were calls for his condemnation. In his debate with the theologian Johann van Eck in 1519, he was maneuvered into casting doubt on the findings of the General Council of Constance (1414–1418) and into supporting some of the doctrines of Jan Hus; within a year a papal bull had been issued against him and his works were publicly burned. However, Luther enjoyed strong popular support within Germany, and reacted combatively to church condemnation with two of his most influential tracts: his *Address to the Christian Nobility of the German Nation*, which protested the need for the secular powers in Germany to intervene to ensure reform within the church, and his *Prelude Concerning the Babylonian Captivity of the Church*, which argued for the reduction of the seven sacraments to just three—baptism, the Lord's Supper, and penance—on the ground that only these were sanctioned by Scripture. This latter stance was consistent with his belief in "sola Scriptura": that is to say, that Holy Scripture, not the word of the pope, is the supreme authority and guide for the true believer. His rejection of the established ecclesiastical order was now complete.

Following his public burning of the papal bull against him, Luther was formally excommunicated in January 1521. Nonetheless, such was the popular support for him within Germany that Emperor Charles V, despite his pro-Catholic and anti-reformist sentiments, agreed that Luther should be allowed to present his own case to the Diet of Worms. Apocryphally uttering "Here I stand; I can do no other," Luther evidenced his undisputed moral courage and rectitude by saying that he would not recant unless convinced of his error by Scripture or evident reason. The diet marked him as an outlaw whose works were proscribed; spirited away by influential supporters to Warburg Castle, he remained in hiding for a year; many presumed him kidnaped or dead.

1483 Luther is born son of a copper miner in Saxony.

1507 Luther becomes an Augustinian monk.

1510 Luther's visit to Rome exacerbates his alienation from the church.

1512 Luther gains the title of doctor of theology.

1517 Luther's 95 anti-papal theses mark the advent of Protestantism.

1520 Luther's works are publicly burned because of a papal bull against him.

1521 Luther is excommunicated, but Emperor lets him present case.

1524 Luther advocates persecution of the Jews when they will not convert.

1534 Luther completes his translation of the Bible into German.

1546 Luther dies.

An emotionally turbulent individual, Luther found his period of enforced retreat difficult; he plunged into deep depression and put on weight. He did not, however, remain wholly inactive, for this was the time in which he commenced his translation of the Bible into German, which was completed in 1534. The poet Heinrich Heine was to say that the creator of the German language was Luther: the foundation of a common German literary experience did not exist until Luther provided it. His biblical translations and political and theological pamphlets were written in a language of unprecedented lucidity and richness, with a vigor and flexibility of expression equally suited to the requirements of exposition and argumentation, of satire and humor. When the new printing presses made them available throughout the German states, they transformed the tongue which his adversary Charles V had described as fit only for speaking to horses. His noble hymns were a major contribution to the German language and to Protestantism, and encouraged the congregation to participate in religious services.

"Our manner of life is as evil as that of the papists," Luther admitted, "but when I can show that their doctrine is false, then I can easily prove that their manner of life is evil."

Returning to Wittenburg in March 1522, Luther joined in the administration and control of the expanding movement he had initiated. His aims were political as well as purely spiritual: "Our manner of life is as evil as that of the papists," he admitted, "but when I can show that their doctrine is false, then I can easily prove that their manner of life is evil." He accepted the concept of the division of church and state, and his assertion that a citizen must obey the laws of the latter paved the way for the increase in the power of kings that was seen in the succeeding century.

Luther's quarrelsome nature involved him in many arguments: he accused the radical reformers who flocked to his cause of being more interested in honor and glory than the salvation of souls. During the 1524 Peasants' War his brutal *Against the Murdering and Thieving Hordes of Peasants* drove many of those unfortunates into the Anabaptist fold, and once he realized the Jews would not convert, he advocated persecution of them. He also alienated many humanists by his vindictive personal assault on Disadrus Erasmus, whose views on free will conflicted with his own, and he disputed vigorously with the Swiss reformer Huldrich Zwingli over communion.

The Edict of Worms was suspended in 1526, and in 1530 Luther's assistant Philipp Melanchthon produced, in the *Augsburg Confession*, the great document of the reform movement. In 1525 Luther married a former nun and watching his baby

son, Martin, at his mother's breast, he commented, "Your enemies are the Pope, the Bishops, Duke George, Ferdinand and
the Devil. And there you suck and take no heed." Luther's preoccupations in his last years turned increasingly toward consol-
idating Protestant gains through education. ◆

Mahavira

c. 549–477 ● Jainist

Mahavira also known as Vardhamana was an Indian religious reformer and Jain prophet. Tales and legends of Mahavira abound, but there is little indisputably factual material to corroborate them. Sources relate that he was born near what is now the city of Patna, in the northern Indian province of Bihar. The stories concerning the young Mahavira are sufficiently similar to those woven around the youth of Gautama Buddha to suggest that they constitute elements of a conventional hagiography of the time rather than representing an accurate reflection of actual events. Thus, like Buddha, Mahavira is said to have been of noble birth, while the details and significance of his conception were foretold to his mother (as they were to Buddha's) in a series of dreams. He enjoyed a princely education; his compassion and love for his parents led to his delaying his renunciation of worldly affairs and concerns until their deaths, by which time he was 30 years old. Some legends relate that they starved themselves to death; in theory, this remains the most impeccable manner for a Jain of the requisite level of spiritual development to die, since once one has no further use for one's body as a vehicle for the quest for enlightenment, one abstains from the harmful practice of consuming other living things simply to sustain it.

Mahavira is commonly regarded as the founder and systematizer of Jainism as it is now practiced; within the Jain pantheon, he is revered as the 24th and last of the *Tirthankars*

> Tales and legends of Mahavira abound, but there is little indisputably factual material to corroborate them.

("finders of the path"), mythical prophet-reformers of Jainism. Living the life of a naked ascetic in the eastern region of the Ganges valley, he attained to *kevala-jnana* ("the highest knowledge") after 12 years; he vowed to refrain from violence, stealing, lying, unchastity, and owning possessions. After his full spiritual awakening, he proved himself an able administrator as well as an enlightened teacher, successfully revitalizing Jainism by organizing his followers into groupings of monks, nuns, and male and female laity. His reforms laid the foundations for a dynamic and successful Jain community that continues to thrive more than two millennia later.

Mahavira's Jainism holds that the universe is infinite and was not created by a deity, and believes in reincarnation according to the law of *karma*, or cause and effect; eventual spiritual salvation and liberation from the endless cycle of rebirths (*moksha*) is achieved through following the path of the *Tirthankars*. Mahavira stressed and practiced *ahimsa*, reverence for all life and the avoidance of injury to any living thing, as an indispensable component of the spiritual life. Due to this belief Jains are strict vegetarians and monks often cover their mouths with a piece of cloth to avoid accidentally swallowing even the tiniest insect. Mahatma Gandhi was greatly influenced by Jainism and adopted the doctrine of *ahimsa* as an integral part of his concept of *satyagraha* ("truth force").

Mahavira was one of the first Indian spiritual leaders to challenge the ritualistic orthodoxy of the Brahmin-dominated Hinduism of his day and to replace it with an ethical and metaphysical system stressing individual responsibility and equality. Today, there are some four million Jains in India; the high levels of education and commercial success they enjoy mean that they have an influence disproportionate to their numbers. ◆

Maimonides, Moses

1135–1204 ● JEWISH

Moses Maimonides, also known as Moses ben Maimon, was a Spanish philosopher, legal codifier, rabbi, and physician. He was born in Cordoba, Spain, to Rabbi Maimon, a rabbinical judge, scion of a long chain of rabbis. The family left Cordoba in 1148 to escape religious persecution. After wandering in Spain and North Africa, they settled in Fez in 1160. Maimonides had begun writing even before then; his first compositions, written in Arabic, included one on the terminology of logic and metaphysics and a work on the Jewish calendar.

During this period, many Jews faced with forced conversion adopted Islam but in name only, remaining secretly loyal Jews. This phenomenon prompted Maimonides to write a "Letter on Forced Conversion," in which he concluded that a Jew must not remain in any country where he is subject to forced conversion.

In about 1165 Maimonides left Fez with his father and brother, heading for the Holy Land, where

they stayed for five months. They went from there to Egypt, where they settled in Fostat, the old city of Cairo. Supported by his brother David, a dealer in precious stones, Maimonides was free to write and serve as religious and lay leader of the Jewish community, of which he became the head around 1177. His brother's death in 1169—he was lost at sea in the Indian Ocean, along with the entire family fortune, while on a business trip—made it necessary for him to find a livelihood, and he chose the medical profession. He attained prominence in this field with his appointment as one of the physicians to al-Fadil, a powerful vizier, while his medical writings became classics that were studied for centuries.

In the early 1170s Maimonides wrote an open letter to the Jews of Yemen, who had turned to him for guidance when faced with a false messiah as well as forced conversion to Islam. His response gave them courage to withstand the pressure toward conversion and reject the attraction of the would-be messiah. Maimonides's *Commentary on the Mishnah* (one of the basic rabbinical lawbooks) was finished in 1168. It included 13 principles expressing the fundamental beliefs of Judaism, which represent the first formulation of a Jewish creed. His *Book of the Commandments* defined and categorized the traditional 613

> "We honor not the commandments but the Commander, who saved us from groping in the dark and provided us with a lamp to make clear what is obscure."
>
> Moses Maimonides, 1180

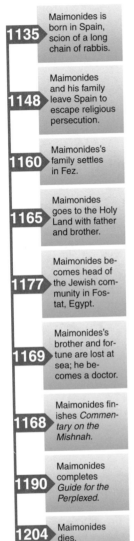

1135 Maimonides is born in Spain, scion of a long chain of rabbis.

1148 Maimonides and his family leave Spain to escape religious persecution.

1160 Maimonides's family settles in Fez.

1165 Maimonides goes to the Holy Land with father and brother.

1177 Maimonides becomes head of the Jewish community in Fostat, Egypt.

1169 Maimonides's brother and fortune are lost at sea; he becomes a doctor.

1168 Maimonides finishes *Commentary on the Mishnah*.

1190 Maimonides completes *Guide for the Perplexed*.

1204 Maimonides dies.

commandments identified in rabbinical law. This was a preparatory step toward the *Mishneh Torah* ("Repetition of the Law"), a 14-volume code of Jewish law compiled by him and written in clear Hebrew. His goal was to codify all literature on Jewish law in the Talmud and post-Talmudic works according to subject matter. Previously, the vast corpus of Jewish law had been diffuse and unsystematic. This was one of the first attempts at such a compilation, but it drew widespread criticism through its very success, the more so because Maimonides had cited neither his sources nor his authorities.

Maimonides completed his *Guide for the Perplexed*, aimed at showing that reason and revelation are compatible, in about 1190. It was written in Arabic using Hebrew letters, and a Hebrew translation was completed by Samuel ibn-Tibbon before Maimonides's death. This translation and a subsequent one were the source for the Latin translation through which Maimonides became known to Christian philosophers, and deeply influenced Scholastic philosophers such as Thomas Aquinas and Albertus Magus. Maimonides set medieval Jewish philosophy on an Aristotelian basis, seeking to reconcile Jewish revelation with Aristotle's rationalism. His target audience was those among the Jewish intellectual elite who were wavering in their faith, and he couched his text in such terms that only persons with an adequate intellectual background would be able to ascertain its true meaning. The result led to immense controversy in parts of the Jewish world, leading in some places to a ban on his works. Eventually, however, his views were universally accepted as authoritative.

Although Maimonides's literary output ceased after *The Guide*, he continued his energetic letter writing. The many letters that have survived exhibit a human warmth which complement the dispassionate, rational nature of his serious works.

Maimonides married rather late and had one son, Abraham, who also became a well-known Jewish scholar and succeeded him to leadership of the Egyptian Jewish community, a position which, as a mark of respect to Maimonides, remained hereditary among his descendants for two centuries. Maimonides's reputation was so great that when he died public mourning was declared by Jews wherever they lived. He was buried in Tiberias with a tombstone reading:

"From [biblical] Moses to Moses [Maimonides], there was no other like Moses." ◆

Maranke, John

1912–1963 ● Apostolic Church of John Maranke

John Maranke was the founder in 1932 of what is now an independent church with an international following, the Apostolic Church of John (or Johane) Maranke (Vapostori or Bapostolo). Maranke was born in the Bondwe area of the Maranke Tribal Trust land of Southern Rhodesia (now Zimbabwe) under the name of Muchabaya Ngomberume. He was a descendant of the royal Sithole lineage on his father's side. His mother was daughter of the Shona chief Maranke, whose clan name he adopted after a dramatic spiritual calling to found the church.

Little accurate information is available about Maranke's childhood. According to local missionaries, Maranke attended the American Methodist mission school under the name of Roston, after which he migrated to the town of Umtali in eastern Zimbabwe as a laborer. Close family and church members, however, dispute Maranke's affiliation with the Methodist mission.

In the official testament of the church, *Humbowo Hutswa we Vapostori* (The New Revelation of the Apostles), John recounts his first spiritual vision, which took place in 1917, when he was five. Over the years, he experienced a series of mysterious illnesses and dreams, culminating in a near-death experience in 1932. On 17 July 1932, John claimed to have seen a sudden flash of lightning and to have heard a booming voice dubbing him John the Baptist, instructing him to preach and seek converts from many nations. John began by proselytizing within his immediate family, converting his older brothers, Conorio (Cornelius) and Anrod, and his uncle, Peter Mupako. The first public sabbath ceremony was held on 20 July 1932 near the Murozi River (dubbed the Jordan) in the Maranke Reserve. Approximately 150 people joined the new group.

Maranke used visionary experiences as the inspiration for establishing the ritual practices and social hierarchy of the church. These practices drew heavily on Old Testament doctrines and showed evidence of influences from Methodist liturgy, Seventh-Day Adventism, and traditional Shona religion. By 1934, the social organization of the group was firmly in place. Maranke, who considered himself to be a *mutumwa*,

> Over the years, Maranke experienced a series of mysterious illnesses and dreams, culminating in a near-death experience in 1932.

1912 Maranke is born of part royal lineage in present-day Zimbabwe.

1917 Maranke has his first spiritual vision.

1932 Maranke has a vision instructing him to preach.

1934 Maranke's group's social organization is firmly in place.

1963 Maranke dies, and leadership passes to his sons, Abel and Makebo.

1988 Makebo dies.

1992 Abel dies, and leadership is transferred to Mambo Noah.

or holy messenger and reinterpreter of Christian doctrines, devised a Saturday sabbath ceremony (*kerek*) consisting of prophetic readings, preaching, and hymns in Shona, interspersed with songs in various local dialects. Other ritual practices included a Eucharist or Passover celebration (*paseka* or *pendi*), mountain prayer retreats (*masowe*), and healing rituals. Maranke maintained tight control over the group's leadership hierarchy by bestowing the spiritual gifts (*bipedi*) of preaching, baptism, healing, and prophecy, and a series of ranks (*mianza*) at the annual Passover ceremony. He further elaborated this leadership structure following minor internal conflicts in local congregations during the 1940s and 1950s.

Until his death in 1963, John and his immediate relatives controlled the *paseka* and the leadership hierarchy from Bocha, Zimbabwe. John's eldest sons, Abel and Makebo, initiated a traveling *paseka* to neighboring countries in 1957. After John's death, leadership was passed to Abel and Makebo. There was a brief schism resulting in the founding of a spin-off Apostolic group under Simon Mushati, John's maternal cousin.

After Makebo's death in the late 1980s, Abel assumed leadership until his death in 1992. The church expanded rapidly across several African nations, establishing large congregations in Zaire, Zambia, Malawi, Mozambique, and Botswana, and with some European converts within and outside of Africa. The 1992 succession was initially smooth, and leadership was transferred, by spiritual consensus, to Mambo Noah, a ranking healer in the Zimbabwean congregation. For a short period, Clement Sithole, one of Maranke's younger sons who had briefly studied in England, challenged Noah and attempted to reform the church but eventually returned to the fold with his followers. The fundamental leadership structure established by Maranke has demonstrated longevity, and the church continues to grow, with more than 500,000 members across Africa. ◆

Mason, Charles Harrison

1866–1961 ● CHURCH OF GOD IN CHRIST

Charles Harrison Mason was born to former slaves on a farm near what is now Bartlett, Tennessee. Inspired as a boy by the piety of the older ex-slaves he knew, he was converted and began to preach as a Baptist when he was 12 years old. He studied for three months in 1894 at Arkansas Baptist College in Little Rock, but left, discouraged that these Baptists were not concerned with maintaining the spirit of Christianity that sustained blacks during slavery.

Mason and a small band of followers were drawn to the Holiness movement, which maintained that sanctification was a necessary act of grace after conversion. They were ejected from the Baptist church in Conway, Ark., in 1895, where their unorthodox form of worship was not approved. That same year Mason and Charles P. Jones proceeded to found the Church of God, whose members sought sanctification in the blessing of the Holy Spirit. Their first service, held in an abandoned Mississippi cotton gin, was fired upon by hostile whites. This incident was reported in newspapers and brought fame and new followers to the church. In 1897, while in Little Rock, Mason had a vision in which God told him to call his group the Church of God in Christ (COGIC). The church continued to grow and in 1907 Mason visited Los Angeles to witness the revival of Azusa Street, which taught that speaking in tongues, or glossolalia, was evidence of baptism in the Holy Spirit. Mason returned to COGIC in Memphis, convinced of the spiritual validity of speaking in tongues. Jones disagreed, and with other worshippers thereupon left the group to form the Church of Christ (Holiness) U.S.A.

COGIC, like other holiness and Pentecostal churches, enjoyed an interracial membership until about 1913. White membership in predominantly black congregations had evaporated slowly since the church's inception. Mason had ordained ministers of all races from every region in the country, and the resulting diffusion of authority enabled white ministers to start their own churches. In 1914 a largely autonomous all-white association was formed from members of COGIC. Mason addressed the group and gave it his blessing, signifying a larger consensual parting of blacks and whites in the early Pentecostal movement.

Mason sold war bonds during World War I, but he was imprisoned in 1918 in Lexington, Miss., for advocating pacifism and aiding conscientious objectors. The Department of Justice considered him dangerous enough to investigate him and his church. Under Mason's charismatic leadership, groups for young people and Sunday schools were established. By 1926, COGIC had a foreign missionary service. In 1933 Mason was

1866 Mason is born to former slaves on a farm in Tennessee.

1894 Mason studies for three months at Arkansas Baptist College.

1895 Mason and fellow unorthodox worshippers are ejected from church.

1897 Mason has vision telling him to call group COGIC.

1907 Mason imports speaking in tongues, but some worshippers leave group.

1918 Mason is jailed for advocating pacifism during World War I.

1933 Mason is named senior bishop and chief apostle.

1958 Mason receives honorary doctor of divinity degree from Trinity Hall College.

1961 Mason dies in Detroit.

named senior bishop and chief apostle, leading the church through years of tremendous growth. In 1938 the church built the largest temple owned by African Americans, the Mason Temple in Memphis, at a cost of $2 million. (It was the site of the Rev. Dr. Martin Luther King Jr.'s final speech in 1968.) In 1958 Mason received an honorary Doctor of Divinity degree from Trinity Hall College. He died in 1961 in Detroit, when membership in the church was nearly 400,000. By the early 1990s it approached 4,000,000, making it the second largest African-American Protestant denomination in the United States, second only to the Baptists. ◆

Mohammed, W. Deen

1933– ● ISLAMIC

> "Worship to us is being of good service to mankind. Our religion has so has so many references to our relationship with people at large or to mankind, that it is impossible for us to be selfish or work for selfish ends. We must work for the global community."
>
> W. Deen Mohammed, 1993

Imam W. Deen Mohammed became the leader of the Nation of Islam, often known as the Black Muslim movement, when he succeeded his father, Elijah Muhammad, in 1975. Spelling his name differently from his father, W. Deen Mohammed has also been known as Warith Deen Mohammed or Wallace D. Mohammed.

Wallace D. was born October 30, 1933, to Clara and Elijah. Clara Evans had been born in 1899 and married Elijah Poole, in Sandersville, Georgia. The couple had six sons and two daughters. Elijah migrated north to Detroit, and Clara followed later with the children. In their neighborhood, where times were hard for African American men struggling to support families, the appealing new message of a man named Fard appeared. Clara encouraged her husband, who had been interested in the Bible, to work with Fard. Elijah and Clara both became devout followers, changing their last name to Muhammad.

W. D. Fard (or Wali Farad), a Detroit silk salesman, began the Black Muslim movement in the early 1930s. He used the Koran, the Muslim holy book, to teach that Islam, not Christianity, was the true religion of blacks. He strongly denounced the white race. After Fard mysteriously disappeared in 1934, Elijah Muhammad, his most trusted follower, succeeded him as leader of the organization that had been named the Nation of Islam. Muhammad soon established a temple in Chicago. He promoted black nationalism and separation from whites, who he called "blue-eyed devils."

The Nation of Islam was influenced by other black nationalist movements, such as the Marcus Garvey Movement of the early 1900s. Garvey taught that blacks should consider Africa their homeland and resettle there. A convert named Malcolm X became the most prominent spokesperson for the Nation of Islam in the 1950s and early 1960s. Malcolm X contributed to the Nation of Islam's greatest period of growth before he left the group in 1964 to convert to the Sunni branch of Islam, which is traditionally followed by most African Muslims. He was assassinated in 1965.

In spite of having been expelled twice for challenging the Nation of Islam's theology, on February 26, 1975, the day after his father's death, Wallace D. succeeded Elijah Muhammad as leader. He made major changes to the organization to move closer in belief and practice to orthodox Islam. He tried to shed the organization's black nationalistic characteristics. He declared that whites were not to be considered devils, and they could join the organization. W. D. Mohammed also led his followers toward the Sunni branch of Islam. The group's name changed from Nation of Islam to the World Community of Al-Islam in the West (1976–1981) and then to American Muslim Mission (1981–1985).

Following W. D. Mohammed's rise to leadership, one of the Nation of Islam's members, Louis Farrakhan, disagreed with the new direction of the organization. In 1977, Farrakhan broke away from W. D. Mohammed's group and formed his own Nation of Islam. Today, only Farrakhan's group uses the name Nation of Islam, continuing the black separatist and nationalist teachings of Elijah Muhammad.

In 1985, the American Muslim Mission dissolved. That year, W. D. Mohammed, the Chief Imam (spiritual leader), sought the approval of the Council of Imams to resign his post as leader of the American Muslim Mission and disband the movement's national structure. His followers became simply known as Muslims. The movement had a decentralized structure of independent places of prayer called masjids, another term for mosque, a public place of worship for Moslems. The new organizational structure was more in line with mainstream Islam, in which local centers are under the guidance of the Imams rather than controlled by central headquarters. News of

1933 W. Deen Mohammed is born in Georgia.

1975 W. Deen Mohammed succeeds his father as head of the Nation of Islam.

1977 Louis Farrakhan breaks away from W. Deen Mohammed's organization.

1981 W. Deen Mohammed's church takes the name American Muslim Mission.

1985 The American Muslim Mission dissolves; W. Deem Mohammed resigns his post.

1993 W. Deen Mohammed represents American Muslims at President Clinton's inauguration.

1996 W. Deen Mohammed travels to the Vatican to meet with the Pope.

1997 The followers of W. Deen Mohammed take the name Muslim American Society.

the centers is carried in the *Muslim Journal*, the weekly newspaper formerly known in the 1970s as *Mohammed Speaks*.

W. D. Mohammed continued his work as an independent Imam and lecturer. He worked to build dialogue between leaders of Islam, Christianity, and Judaism and to build respect for Islamic life in America. He has made many appearances as a speaker or participant in national and international religious gatherings. On January 20, 1993, as part of the inaugural activities for President Bill Clinton in Washington, D.C., Mohammed represented the religion of Islam in the Inaugural Interfaith Prayer Service. In March 1995, Mohammed delivered the keynote address at a Muslim-Jewish Convocation held in Illinois, a dialogue between top leaders of Islam and Reform Judaism. In October 1996, Mohammed accepted an invitation to join a small group of visitors to the Vatican to meet Pope John Paul II and to engage in dialogue with several important Vatican officials.

In 1997, the followers of Imam W. Deen Mohammed took on the name Muslim American Society, thereby distinguishing their group from the better known Nation of Islam, led by Farrakhan. The Muslim American Society hosted an Internet web site and continued publishing the *Muslim Journal* from a Chicago suburb. ◆

> In March 1995, Mohammed delivered the keynote address at a Muslim-Jewish Convocation held in Illinois, a dialogue between top leaders of Islam and Reform Judaism.

Montagu, Lily

1873–1963 ● JEWISH

Lily Montagu was the founder of the Liberal Jewish movement in England. Born in London on 22 December 1873, Lily H. Montagu was the sixth child of Ellen Cohen Montagu and Samuel Montagu. Her father was a wealthy banker and leading member of the Orthodox Anglo-Jewish community. Convinced that Orthodoxy offered her, and other women, little room for religious self-expression, she found in the works of Claude Montefiore a vision of Judaism that mirrored her own understanding of true religion as personal in nature, universal in outlook, and best revealed through daily conduct.

In the January 1899 issue of the *Jewish Quarterly Review*, Montagu published "The Spiritual Possibilities of Judaism Today," an essay in which she asked all religiously committed Jews to help her form an association aimed at strengthening the religious life of the Anglo-Jewish community through the propagation of Liberal Jewish teachings. Membership would not necessarily demonstrate allegiance to what Montefiore identified as Liberal Judaism but simply would demonstrate the recognition of its ability to awaken within many Jews a sense of spirituality and personal responsibility to God. The Jewish Religious Union (JRU), established by Lily Montagu in February 1902, instituted Sabbath afternoon worship services conducted along Liberal Jewish lines and propaganda meetings, led by Montagu, to clarify and spread its teachings. Though Montefiore agreed to serve as the group's official leader, Montagu assumed responsibility for its major activities and daily affairs.

By 1909, acknowledging the failure of its initial, all-inclusive vision, the union declared itself to be a movement specifically committed to the advancement of Liberal Judaism. During the next few decades, Lily Montagu helped form Liberal Jewish synagogues throughout Great Britain, frequently serving as their chairman or president, and became lay minister of the West Central Liberal Jewish Congregation in 1928, a position to which she was formally inducted in November, 1944. Following Montefiore's death, in 1938, she assumed the presidency of the JRU, later renamed the Union of Liberal and Progressive Synagogues. Having conceived of the idea for an international JRU as early as 1925, Montagu also helped found and eventually became president of the World Union for Progressive Judaism.

Montagu was the author of 11 books, including *Thoughts On Judaism*, a theological treatise published in 1902, and her autobiography, *The Faith of a Jewish Woman*, published in 1943. ◆

1873 Montagu is born in London, sixth child of a wealthy banker.

1899 Montagu publishes an essay seeking members for liberal Jewish group.

1902 Montagu establishes the Jewish Religious Union; publishes *Thoughts on Judaism*.

1909 Montague's group says it exists to advance Liberal Judaism.

1928 Montagu is lay minister of West Central Liberal Jewish Congregation.

1938 Montagu becomes president of the Jewish Religious Union.

1943 Montagu publishes her autobiography.

1944 Montagu is formally inducted as lay minister of WCLJC.

1963 Montagu dies.

Moses

c. 1400s B.C.E. ● JEWISH

Moses was an Israelite prophet and lawgiver and the outstanding personality in the foundation of Judaism and the emergence of the Jewish people. According to the Book of Exodus, Moses was born during a time when the burgeoning population of Hebrews in Egypt was subject to

Moses receives the
Ten Commandments

growing repression. Pharaoh, the ruler of Egypt, decreed that all newborn Israelite males should be drowned in the Nile River. Jochebed gave birth to Moses and, after hiding him for three months, secreted him in a basket which she placed among the bulrushes on the banks of the Nile, where he was found by Pharaoh's daughter, who had gone to bathe in the river. She brought him to the palace and gave the child the name Moses, explained as meaning "drawn from the water" (a folk etymology).

Moses was raised within the royal household, but when he reached manhood he still identified with the Israelites and found their suffering under slavery intolerable. When he witnessed an Egyptian taskmaster abusing an innocent slave, he killed him and, on realizing his deed was known to the authorities, fled from Egypt to Midian, in the northwest part of the Arabian peninsula. After intervening when shepherds harassed the daughters of Jethro, the priest of Midian, he became a part of Jethro's household, tending his flocks and marrying his daughter, Zipporah.

After many years, as Moses led Jethro's sheep in search of grazing land, he came to Horeb, another name for the Sinai region, and there experienced a theophany—God revealing Himself in a burning bush that was not consumed. God commanded Moses to go with the elders to demand that Pharaoh free the Jewish people for a three-day journey into the wilderness in order to sacrifice to Him, knowing that Pharaoh would not grant such a request. To aid him in convincing the children of Israel that he was sent by God, Moses was given three miraculous signs; because he stammered, his brother Aaron was to act as his spokesman.

Moses and Aaron assured the Hebrews that the time for liberation had come. But after their first meeting with Pharaoh, not only did the bondage continue, but the Israelites were denied the straw they formerly received to accomplish their task of making bricks, creating terrible hardship. The refusal of the Egyptian ruler (who has been identified with Ramses II) to set the Israelites free resulted in the series of ten plagues which proved that Moses had indeed been commissioned by God. Pharaoh remained unconvinced until the last plague, when the firstborn of Egypt were slain and the Egyptians, in panic, pressured the Israelites to leave. As Moses led the people in the Exodus out of Egypt to the shore of the "Red Sea" (the exact location is uncertain), Pharaoh changed his mind and pursued his former slaves; Moses now raised the staff that God had given him at the burning bush and split the waters, enabling the Israelites to escape. As Pharaoh and his chariots pursued them into the depths of the sea, the Israelites gained the far shore and Moses again raised his staff, drowning the Egyptian pursuers in the tumultuous waters.

From the Red Sea, Moses took the people to Mount Sinai and, on the fiftieth day after leaving Egypt, ascended to the top of the mountain, while the entire nation heard the Ten Commandments spoken by God. Coming down from Sinai later than the people expected, Moses found them worshiping a golden calf which they had created as an idol during his absence. Angered by this lapse into idolatry, Moses broke the tablets of the covenant he was carrying and destroyed the calf.

> "Now Moses kept the flock of Jethro his father in law, the priest of Midian: and he led the flock to the backside of the desert, and came to the mountain of God, even to Horeb. And the angel of the LORD appeared unto him in a flame of fire out of the midst of a bush: and he looked, and, behold, the bush burned with fire, and the bush was not consumed."
>
> Bible,
> Exodus 3:1–2

> "And Moses and Aaron came in unto Pharaoh, and said unto him, Thus saith the Lord God of the Hebrews, How long wilt thou refuse to humble thyself before me? let my people go, that they may serve me. Else, if thou refuse to let my people go, behold, to morrow will I bring the locusts into thy coast."
>
> Bible,
> Exodus 10:3–4

On Moses' order, the tribe of Levi killed the idolaters (numbering some 3,000), and a period of mourning and supplication followed. Moses asked that God forgive the people and reascended the mount to receive a second set of tablets, which he then delivered into the camp. He began to teach his disciple Joshua and the elders the divine doctrine, which was then transmitted to the people. The teachings incorporated an extensive religion-legal-ethical code to regulate all aspects of life, which became the basis of the Jewish religion. Moses also supervised the construction of a portable cult center (the Tabernacle), which accompanied the Israelites through the desert and centuries later found a permanent home in the Jerusalem Temple.

The Israelites remained in the desert region between Egypt and the Promised Land for 40 years, covering a large tract of land even though the distance to Canaan could have been traveled much more quickly by taking a direct route. During this time Moses forged them into a people with a homogenous culture and religious practices. They stopped at 42 resting places and underwent a series of tests, sometimes lacking for food and water, but for most of the period they were based in one oasis—Kadesh Barnea. Moses reprimanded the people for their protests and finally, moved to anger, struck—instead of addressing—a rock at Meriba in order to produce water, for which he was punished by not being allowed to enter the Promised Land. Because of their having idolized the golden calf, the entire generation that witnessed the revelation at Mount Sinai was condemned to die in the desert, with a few exceptions. Joshua, Moses' disciple, was one, spared because of his faith. Moses established a judicial system to distribute the burden of adjudication, which was too much for a single leader to cope with alone.

In the fields of Moab on the border of Canaan, Moses addressed the people for the last time, summarizing the Sinaitic legislation and renewing the covenant with God. He passed his leadership to Joshua when he had finished, and then ascended Mount Nebo to view the Promised Land before his death. When he died, Moses was 120 years old, and his powers had not diminished. His burial place is unknown. Joshua led the people in conquering Canaan. ◆

Mueller, Reuben Herbert

1897–1982 ● METHODIST

Reuben Herbert Mueller was a Methodist bishop and National Council of Churches official who played a key role in Protestant ecumenical and social justice activities in the 1960s.

Mueller was born in St. Paul, Minnesota. The fourth of six children born to Reinhold M. Mueller and Emma Bunse, a homemaker, he grew up in Faribault, Minnesota, where his father was a clergyman in the Evangelical Church. Reuben attended North Central College in Naperville, Illinois, a school affiliated with his denomination, and after interrupting his studies to serve in the military during World War I, he graduated in 1919; that same year, on 26 December, Mueller married C. Magdalene Stauffacher, a high school teacher. They had one daughter, Margaret, who served for a time as a missionary in Nigeria. From 1919 to 1924 Mueller taught in public high schools in Minnesota and Wisconsin, and from 1924 to 1926 he taught at North Central College.

Mueller's denomination, the Evangelical Church, was a small Protestant body with a Wesleyan (Methodist) theology and polity that had originated among German-speaking immigrants in eighteenth-century Pennsylvania. Following graduation in 1926 from the Evangelical Theological Seminary in Naperville, he served as pastor of two Evangelical churches; Grace Church in South Bend, Indiana, from 1924 to 1932, and First Church in Indianapolis from 1932 to 1937. In 1937 he began a series of administrative and executive assignments that eventually took him to the highest levels of Protestant leadership.

From 1937 to 1942 Mueller served as a superintendent of the Indiana conference of the Evangelical Church and in 1942 moved to Harrisburg, Pennsylvania, site of the denomination's headquarters, to assume the position of executive secretary of Christian education and evangelism. In 1946 the Evangelical Church merged with another small denomination with a similar theological and cultural background, the United Brethren, to form the Evangelical United Brethren Church (EUB). Mueller served as the executive secretary of Christian education in the new denomination until 1954, when he was elected

> Mueller's denomination, the Evangelical Church, was a small Protestant body with a Wesleyan (Methodist) theology and polity that had originated among German-speaking immigrants in eighteenth-century Pennsylvania.

1897 Mueller is born in Minnesota.

1919 Mueller graduates from college, gets married, and begins teaching.

1924 Mueller begins serving as pastor.

1926 Mueller graduates from the Evangelical Theological Seminary.

1942 Mueller becomes executive secretary of Christian education.

1954 Mueller is elected a bishop of Evangelical Union Brethren Church.

1963 Mueller becomes head of National Council of Churches of Christ in the USA.

1966 Mueller publishes *His Church*.

1968 Mueller becomes bishop in the new United Methodist Church.

1972 Mueller retires.

1982 Mueller dies of a heart attack.

a bishop of the EUB, assigned to the Indiana conference. He lived in Indianapolis during those years and published several books, including *Lay Leadership in the Evangelical Church* (1943) and *Christ Calls to Christian Growth* (1953).

Bishop Mueller had been active in the National Council of Churches of Christ in the U.S.A. (NCC) since its founding in 1950. This ecumenical umbrella organization was initially made up of more than 30 Protestant denominations, including the EUB, which were part of the mainline or moderate-to-liberal wing of American Protestantism. Eventually a number of Orthodox groups also joined the NCC. The NCC built on a tradition of Protestant reumenism and worked in various social, educational, and theological ways to promote Christian unity and service to society. Although Mueller represented one of the smaller member-denominations in the NCC, he served as an officer in various positions in the organization in the 1950s and 1960s more frequently than anyone else. He was the recording secretary from 1950 to 1954, a vice president (for three terms) from 1954 to 1963, and president of the NCC from 1963 to 1966. His presidency coincided with some of the NCC's most intensive activities in the areas of civil rights and race relations.

Mueller's election as president took place at the NCC's triennial convention in Philadelphia on 7 December 1963, just a few weeks after the assassination of President John F. Kennedy. The civil rights bill proposed by the late president earlier that year had languished in Congress. Two days after Mueller's election as NCC president, he joined several colleagues in a meeting at the White House with President Lyndon B. Johnson to urge action on civil rights and offer their support for the bill's passage. Civil rights had become an important priority of the NCC in 1963, in the wake of protest marches and demonstrations led by the Reverend Martin Luther King, Jr., and others. During the next three years, under Mueller's leadership, the NCC created new departments and programs and hired new staff to work for racial justice and reconciliation, especially in Mississippi through the 1964 Freedom Summer campaign and the Delta Ministry. The NCC-led grassroots lobbying and letter-writing campaign, directed primarily toward Midwestern Republican congressmen and senators, had a major impact in bringing about final passage of the Civil Rights Act of 1964. Mueller supported all of these efforts, referring to racial segregation as the "major problem" in the United States.

He also vigorously defended other aspects of the NCC's social and political agenda, including efforts toward peace and nuclear disarmament with the Soviet Union. Various critics charged that the NCC was soft on communism and betrayed the beliefs of the lay members of its denominations. On the other hand, in his 1966 book *His Church,* considered his most important work, Mueller affirmed that the NCC was opposed to communism, and especially the atheist official policy of the Soviet Union. He also expressed concern that the political involvements of the NCC, while vital to its total mission, not overshadow its religious activities in evangelism, education, and theology.

Mueller continued to serve as an EUB bishop while involved with the NCC. At the time of the formation of the EUB in 1946, Methodist bishop G. Bromley Oxnam had invited the EUB to consider merging with the much larger Methodist Church. As president of the council of EUB bishops, Mueller attended the quadrennial Methodist General Conference in 1960 as an official observer. At that meeting the Methodists authorized their representatives to begin work on a Plan of Union with the EUB, and the EUB took the same action in 1962. Thereupon Mueller and Methodist bishop Lloyd Wicke became cochairmen of the Joint Commission on Union, and by 1966 they had completed their work. Because the two denominations had essentially identical organizational structures and theological positions, the blueprint for merger did not require either side to undertake radical change in structure or program. The one exception was the EUB insistence, in which most Methodists concurred, that the last vestiges of racial segregation in the Methodist Church, in which predominantly black congregations were assigned to a separate "central jurisdiction," be abolished. In November 1966 the Methodists and EUB held simultaneous conferences in a Chicago hotel and voted to approve the plan of union. By June 1967 the necessary two-thirds of Methodist and three-fourths of EUB local conferences had given approval. When the United Methodist Church was officially proclaimed in Dallas, Texas, on 23 April 1968, Mueller became a bishop in the new denomination, continuing to serve in Indiana until his retirement in 1972. He urged United Methodists to continue to work for racial and social justice even as the political climate of the nation began to turn toward the right. Mueller lived in retirement in Franklin, Indiana, where he died of a heart attack. ◆

When the United Methodist Church was officially proclaimed in Dallas, Texas, on 23 April 1968, Mueller became a bishop in the new denomination, continuing to serve in Indiana until his retirement in 1972.

Muhammad

c. 570–632 ● MUSLIM

> "He makes the
> night seep into the
> day, and makes
> the day seep into
> the night; He has
> subordinated the
> sun and the moon,
> making each of
> them jouney to-
> wards a preor-
> dained time."
>
> Koran, 35:13

Muhammad was the founder of Islam. Muhammad was born in the city of Mecca in Arabia, to a merchant family of the Quraish tribe. Mecca was then an important religious center for the local peoples, housing the Kaaba shrine, with the maintenance of which the Quarish were involved.

Since the earliest biographies of Muhammad date from more than 100 years after his death, there is little substantial information about the prophet's life: much of the material available is of an apocryphal nature. Sources agree that Muhammad was orphaned at an early age and was raised by his uncle, Abu Talib. A successful merchant by the age of 25, he married Khadija, a widow 15 years his senior.

Contact with the many Christian and Jewish inhabitants of the region caused Muhammad to question the pagan beliefs of his tribe. He came to believe that a new religion, based on divine commandments, was needed to unite the warring Arab tribes. This idea was not unique to Muhammad; many Christian and Jewish leaders had predicted the coming of a new prophet—according to some legends, rabbis, monks, and magicians were already pointing to Muhammad as the longed-for teacher.

As Muhammad neared 40 his preoccupation with religious matters intensified. He would spend long days fasting and praying in the deserts outside Mecca. During one such vigil, later referred to as the Night of Destiny, the angel Gabriel appeared to him, telling him that God (Allah), who had "created man of a blood clot," was now calling Muhammad to be His messenger.

Muhammad later explained that he was only a channel through which God or Gabriel spoke. Khadija, who was the first to believe in the veracity of her husband's visions, encouraged him to declare himself the prophet of Allah. She is therefore considered the first convert to Islam. As Muhammad attracted a following, his revelations were transcribed. Many were later collated to form the Koran—the holy scripture of Islam, universally regarded as a masterpiece of Arabic poetry and prose—while others, known as hadiths (a record of Muhammad's words and deeds) were similarly transmitted and form the basis of much of Islamic law and tradition.

Members of Muhammad's native tribe were hostile to Muhammad's new faith. His opposition to their traditional idolatrous beliefs threatened the revenues they enjoyed from stewardship of the pagan sanctuary in the Kaaba. With the death of Abu Talib in 619, Muhammad was deprived of a powerful protector and felt increasingly insecure in Mecca. Meanwhile, small groups of Muhammad's supporters had introduced the new religion to the city of Yathrib (Medina), whose faithful now offered him sanctuary. In Mecca, the new head of the Quraish had threatened to kill him. On the evening of July 16, 622, Muhammad entered the Kaaba, smashed the idols, and began his flight to Medina, known as the *hejira*. This date marks the beginning of the Islamic calendar.

In Medina, Muhammad formalized his religion's creed, basing it on five articles of faith: belief in the One God, Allah; belief in benign and wrathful spirits (angels and *jinn*); acceptance of the Koran as the authentic word of God; acceptance of the revelations of the prophets and of Muhammad, the apostle of God; and belief in reward of the righteous, punishment of the wicked, and a future Day of Judgment. While he preached tolerance of other monotheistic religions, true believers, known as Muslims were commanded to make a profession of faith (the *shahada*, consisting of the formula, "There is no God but Allah and Muhammad is his prophet"), conduct a series of prayers and obeisance five times daily, pay the *zakat* tithe, fast during the month of Ramadan, and make the *haj* (pilgrimage to Mecca) at least once. Many of his revelations were concerned with even the most mundane secular matters, covering specific social, moral, and political issues and he enjoyed the unquestioning obedience of believers.

As converts flocked to Medina, there were severe food shortages. Raids, some under Muhammad's leadership, were conducted against the passing caravans of his Quraish rivals. One fifth of the spoils were set aside for religious and charitable purposes; raiders were promised paradise if slain.

At first, Muhammad anticipated that the local Christian and Jewish population would embrace his religion eagerly. Their reluctance to do so led to strained relations between the communities and the abandonment of many rituals (such as facing Jerusalem when praying) adopted from these rival faiths.

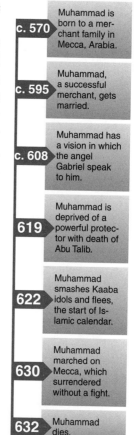

c. 570 Muhammad is born to a merchant family in Mecca, Arabia.

c. 595 Muhammad, a successful merchant, gets married.

c. 608 Muhammad has a vision in which the angel Gabriel speak to him.

619 Muhammad is deprived of a powerful protector with death of Abu Talib.

622 Muhammad smashes Kaaba idols and flees, the start of Islamic calendar.

630 Muhammad marched on Mecca, which surrendered without a fight.

632 Muhammad dies.

Great Mosque of Mecca

The Great Mosque, the world center of worship for Muslims, stands in the holy city of Mecca in Saudi Arabia. The mosque is a four-sided structure made up of arches and pillars that surround a huge courtyard, about 600 by 800 feet. The Kaaba, a 50-foot-high cube-shaped stone building, sits in the courtyard. The Kaaba contains the Black Stone, enclosed in a silver ring. According to tradition, the Kaaba was originally built by Abraham and Ishmael, and the Black Stone was given to Abraham by the angel Gabriel.

Muslims everywhere face the Kaaba during daily prayers. Each year, millions of Muslims make a pilgrimage to Mecca, either individually or for the Hajj, an annual gathering. The Hajj is held early in the 12th month of the Islamic calendar and honors the prophet Abraham, his wife Hagar, and their son Ishmael. During the Hajj, the Kaaba is draped with a black silk covering, the Kiswa, beautifully embroidered in gold and silver with texts from the holy book of Islam, the Koran. Muslims from all nationalities and classes gather peacefully for the Hajj, with rivalries put aside. Each pilgrim circles the Kaaba seven times, in a counterclockwise direction, praying and reciting verses from the Koran. Pilgrims touch or kiss the Black Stone to end the ceremony.

With a strengthened grip on the Medina area and the conversion of many influential Meccans to Islam, Muhammad was in a position to negotiate a ten-year truce with the Quraish enabling his followers to make the pilgrimage to the Kaaba. Many of his followers, however, adopted a more bellicose attitude and encouraged him to seek a pretense to take Mecca. An opportunity was provided by the Meccans in 630, when they broke the pact by abandoning their neutrality in a local dispute. Muhammad marched on the city, which surrendered without a fight. As the city's new ruler, he declared a general amnesty and swept the Kaaba clean of everything but the Black Stone, consecrating Mecca as the holy city of Islam. Soon, all of Arabia accepted Muhammad's religion and rule. For the remaining two years of his life, Muhammad governed justly, his severity leavened by frequent acts of mercy.

Even as ruler of all Arabia, Muhammad continued to practice a simple, austere lifestyle. The absence of a male heir, led many to believe that Muhammad was immortal, although he made no such claim. As news spread that the prophet was dying, the faithful crowded around his home. News of his decease was broken to them by Abu Bakr with the words: "If you are worshipers of Muhammad, know that he is dead. If you are worshipers of God, know that God is living and does not die."

Within a century of Muhammad's death, armies sweeping out of Arabia initiated the process of converting the Middle East, northwest India, North Africa, and Spain to Islam. Succeeding centuries saw Islam become the dominant religion in Malaya, Indonesia, Turkey, and the Balkans. Today it remains a vital and fast-growing religion, set to overtake Catholicism as the world's largest by the end of the century. Muhammad is now the most popular boy's name in the world. ◆

Muhammad, Elijah

1897–1975 ● NATION OF ISLAM

Elijah Muhammad was an African-American religious leader. Born Robert Poole in Sandersville, Georgia, Muhammad was one of 13 children of an itinerant Baptist preacher and share-cropper. In 1919 he married Clara Evans and they joined the black migration to Detroit, where he worked in the auto plants. In 1931 he met Master Wallace Fard (or Wali Farad), founder of the Nation of Islam, who eventually chose this devoted disciple as his chief aide. Fard named him "Minister of Islam," dropped his slave name, Poole, and restored his true Muslim name, Muhammad. As the movement

grew, a Temple of Islam was established in a Detroit storefront. It is estimated that Fard had close to 8,000 members in the Nation of Islam, consisting of poor black migrants and some former members from Marcus Garvey's United Negro Improvement Association and Noble Drew Ali's Moorish Science Temple.

After Fard mysteriously disappeared in 1934, the Nation of Islam was divided by internal schisms and Elijah Muhammad led a major faction to Chicago, where he established Temple of Islam No. 2 as the main headquarters for the Nation. He also instituted the worship of Master Fard as Allah and himself as the Messenger of Allah and head of the Nation of Islam, always addressed with the title "the Honorable." Muhammad built on the teachings of Fard and combined aspects of Islam and Christianity with the black nationalism of Marcus Garvey into a "proto-Islam," an unorthodox Islam with a strong racial slant. The Honorable Elijah Muhammad's message of racial separation focused on the recognition of true black identity and stressed economic independence. "Knowledge of self" and "do for self" were the rallying cries. The economic ethic of the Black Muslims has been described as a kind of black puritanism—hard work, frugality, the avoidance of debt, self-improvement, and a conservative lifestyle. Muhammad's followers sold the Nation's newspaper, *Muhammad Speaks*, and established their own educational system of Clara Muhammad schools and small businesses such as bakeries, grocery stores, and outlets selling fish and bean pies. More than 100 temples were founded. The disciples also followed strict dietary rules outlined in Muhammad's book *How to Eat to Live*, which enjoined one meal per day and complete abstention from pork, drugs, tobacco, and alcohol. The Nation itself owned farms in several states, a bank, trailer trucks for its fish and grocery businesses, an ultramodern printing press, and other assets.

"People strive to lose themselves among other people. This they do because of their lack of knowledge of self."

Elijah Muhammad, 1962

Muhammad's ministers of Islam found the prisons and streets of the ghetto a fertile recruiting ground. His message of self-reclamation and black manifest destiny struck a responsive chord in the thousands of black men and women whose hope and self-respect had been all but defeated by racial abuse and denigration. As a consequence of where they recruited and the militancy of their beliefs, the Black Muslims have attracted many more young black males than any other black movement.

Muhammad had an uncanny sense of the vulnerabilities of the black psyche during the social transitions brought on by two world wars; his *Message to the Black Man in America* diagnosed the problem as a confusion of identity and self-hatred caused by white racism. The cure he prescribed was radical surgery through the formation of a separate black nation. Muhammad's 120 "degrees," or lessons, and the major doctrines and beliefs of the Nation of Islam all elaborated on aspects of this central message. The white man is a "devil by nature," absolutely unredeemable and incapable of caring about or respecting anyone who is not white. He is the historic, persistent source of harm and injury to black people. The Nation of Islam's central theological myth tells of Yakub, a black mad scientist who rebelled against Allah by creating the white race, a weak, hybrid people who were permitted temporary dominance of the world. Whites achieved their power and position through devious means and "tricknology." But, according to the Black Muslim apocalyptic view, there will come a time in the not-too-distant future when the forces of good and the forces of evil—that is to say, blacks versus whites—will clash in a "Battle of Armageddon," and the blacks will emerge victorious to recreate their original hegemony under Allah throughout the world.

After spending four years in a federal prison for encouraging draft refusal during World War II, Elijah Muhammad was assisted by his chief protege, Minister Malcolm X, in building the movement and encouraging its rapid spread in the 1950s and 1960s. During its peak years, the Nation of Islam had more than half a million devoted followers, influencing millions more, and accumulated an economic empire worth an estimated $80 million. Besides his residence in Chicago, Muhammad also lived in a mansion outside of Phoenix, Arizona, since the climate helped to reduce his respiratory problems. He had eight children with his wife, Sister Clara Muhammad, but also fathered a number of illegitimate children with his secretaries,

1897 Muhammad is born, one of 13 children of poor Georgia couple.

1919 Muhammad marries and moves to Detroit, where he works in auto plant.

1931 Muhammad meets Nation of Islam founder and becomes his chief aide.

1934 Muhammad heads one faction after the founder mysteriously disappears.

1964 Malcolm X leaves the church after learning that Muhammad has fathered illegitimate children.

1975 Muhammad dies and is succeeded by his son.

a circumstance that was one of the reasons for Malcolm X's final break with the Nation of Islam in 1964.

With only a third-grade education, Elijah Muhammad was the leader of the most enduring black militant movement in the United States. He died in Chicago and was succeeded by one of his six sons, Wallace Deen Muhammad. After his death, Muhammad's estate and the property of the Nation were involved in several lawsuits over the question of support for his illegitimate children. ◆

Mukhtar, Sidi Al-

1729–1811 ● MUSLIM

Descendant of a prominent scholarly and saintly lineage, al-Mukhtar is considered by many Muslims to be the most important *mujaddid*, or rejuvenator of Islam, to appear in the central Sahara during the eighteenth century.

Sidi Al-Mukhtar, also known as Sidi al-Mukhtar al-Kunti, was a Sufi scholar and leader. Descendant of a prominent scholarly and saintly lineage, al-Mukhtar is considered by many Muslims to be the most important *mujaddid*, or rejuvenator of Islam, to appear in the central Sahara during the eighteenth century. He was a prolific scholar, authoring over 80 works, and was recognized as a *wali* ("friend of God") whose *baraka*, or spiritual grace, was said to protect all those who placed themselves under his spiritual authority. He was acclaimed as the shaikh of the Qadiriyya Sufi order in the central Sahara and was the founder of his own branch of that order, known as the Qadiriyya-Mukhtariyya. Through the expansion of this Sufi order, made possible by the renown of his scholarship and his spiritual stature, he built a network of clientage links with Muslim scholars which extended his religious authority throughout the region and into Sudanic western Africa. Al-Mukhtar was the first Muslim leader in the region to encourage a sense of exclusive identity in a Sufi order; he claimed that the Qadiriyya-Mukhtariyya was the only "pure" Muslim community that existed at the time and that the spiritual benefits it offered were superior to all others. The same mystical Islamic ideology also enabled him to extend both his political and commercial hegemony throughout the region and thus establish a voluntarist basis of social and political authority that contrasted with the Islamic statist models which were also emerging at the time, such as in the Sokoto Caliphate. ◆

Murray, Anna Pauline

1910–1985 ● EPISCOPAL

Anna Pauline ("Pauli") Murray was a clergywoman, lawyer, writer, and political activist best known for her civil rights and women's rights activities and her work as the first African-American women ordained in the Episcopal church. Murray was born in Pittsburgh, Pennsylvania, the fourth of six children. In 1914 her mother, Agnes Fitzgerald Murray, a nurse, died of a cerebral hemorrhage, and Anna's father, William Henry Murray, a former principal in the Baltimore school system, sent her to live with her aunt Pauline Fitzgerald Dame and her grandparents, Cornelia and Robert Fitzgerald, in Durham, North Carolina.

Murray graduated from Hillside High School in Durham in 1926, and after completing additional courses at Richmond Hill High School in New York City, she began studies in 1928 at Hunter College. In 1930 she was briefly married to a man she referred to only as "Billy"; the marriage was later annulled and Murray never married again. She had no children. Despite setbacks, including financial difficulties and the illness of her Aunt Pauline, Murray received her B.A. degree in English in 1933, one of only four African Americans in her Hunter College class. In 1934 she published a poem, "Song of the Highway," in a collection entitled *Color*. With Pulitzer Prize-winning poet Stephen Vincent Benet's encouragement, Murray continued to write. In 1970 she published a volume of poetry entitled *Dark Testament and Other Poems*. Benet also helped with the refinement of what became her published family history, *Proud Shoes: The Story of an American Family* (1956). Much of the work for this volume was accomplished during her residency at the MacDowell Colony for Artists, where she was one of only two African Americans (the other being James Baldwin) admitted up to that time. Her literary interests found an outlet in her acquaintance with Countee Cullen, Langston Hughes, and other writers.

After Hunter College, Murray worked for *Opportunity* magazine (1933), the Works Progress Administration (1935–1939), and the Worker's Defense League. In the process, she met and established friendships with such prominent figures as Eleanor

After Hunter College, Murray worked for *Opportunity* magazine (1933), the Works Progress Administration (1935–1939), and the Worker's Defense League.

1910	Murray is born.
1914	Murray is sent to live with relatives when her mother dies.
1933	Murray receives her B.A. degree in English.
1943	Murray graduates from Howard University Law School.
1946	Murray becomes California's first black deputy attorney general.
1960	Murray becomes senior lecturer at University of Ghana Law School.
1965	Murray is first black woman to receive Yale Law School JD degree.
1976	Murray completes a doctor of divinity degree and is ordained a deacon.
1977	Murray becomes the first woman ordained an Episcopal priest.
1985	Murray dies of cancer in Pittsburgh.

Roosevelt. These experiences inspired her to formally study the nature of race relations. She applied in 1938 to the University of North Carolina at Chapel Hill but was denied admission because of her race. Murray's work exposed the economic and political underbelly of American society including the plight of Odell Waller, a man sentenced to death in 1940 for murdering the white owner of the land he sharecropped; despite her efforts on his behalf, including raising money for defense, Waller was executed in 1942. In 1940 Murray was arrested in Petersburg, Virginia, for refusing to sit in the back of a Greyhound bus. After being jailed for three days, she was found guilty and fined. However, the nonviolent methods of protest she embraced during this time fostered attitudinal changes in prisoners and guards that captured Murray's imagination and renewed her academic interests.

In 1941 Murray enrolled in the Howard University Law School. While at Howard, Murray put her legal principle into action, for example participating in a student civil rights committee that fought for equal accommodations and an end to all forms of racial and gender discrimination. Much of what Murray and other students accomplished during these years predated similar efforts by attorneys for the National Association for the Advancement of Colored People (NAACP). Murray's experience of this period is expressed in her best-known poem, "Dark Testament," published in 1943.

Murray graduated first in her law school class in 1944, having served as class president and as a justice on the court of peers. She received a Rosenwald Fellowship but was rejected by Harvard Law School in what she saw as gender discrimination. Undaunted by Harvard's decision, Murray continued her education at the University of California at Berkeley, graduating with an L.L.M. degree in 1945. Remaining in California, Murray made history in 1946 as the first black deputy attorney general of California. She received numerous honors, including the National Council of Negro Women's Woman of the Year Award in 1946 and *Mademoiselle* magazine's selection as Woman of the Year in 1947.

Late in 1946 Murray moved to New York City, working as a law clerk because the big prestigious firms would not hire a black female attorney. In 1949 she opened her own law office, which was short-lived, and unsuccessfully ran for a seat as a city council member. In 1951 Murray published a legal text, *States' Laws on Race and Color,* which crystallized many of her legal ideas concerning Jim Crow policies. Five years later Murray became the first female associate in the law firm Paul, Weiss, Rifkind, Wharton, and Garrison. This job provided security but it did not satisfy her interest in West African independence movements.

In 1960 Murray accepted a position as a senior lecturer in the newly formed law school at the University of Ghana; while there, she co-wrote *The Constitution and Government of Ghana* (1961). She returned to the United States in 1961 to attend Yale Law School, and in 1965 she became the first African American to receive its doctor of juridical science degree. Her efforts on behalf of women and minorities, with friends such as Eleanor Holmes Norton and Marian Wright Edelman, were recognized through a 1962 appointment to the President's Commission on the Status of Women (the Committee on Civil and Political Rights). In 1965 she was appointed to the American Civil Liberties Union's board of directors; and in 1966 she became one of the founding members of the National Organization for Women (NOW). From 1966 to 1967 Murray was vice president and professor of political science at Benedict College in Columbia, South Carolina.

In 1968 Murray began teaching in Brandeis University's American studies program. During this period of civil rights activities, marked, for example, by the militancy of the **Black Panthers,** Murray's ideological stance and integrationist tactics were frequently questioned by African-American students who favored more aggressive approaches. From 1972 to 1973 Murray was the Louis Stulberg Professor of Law and Politics at Brandeis.

Black Panthers: a group of young black men organized in the 1960s in reaction to their frustration with the nonviolent stance of civil rights leaders in the United States

Disillusioned with her work and facing personal hardship—the death of her close friend Renee Barlow—Murray decided to alter the scope and direction of her life. She moved away from legal maneuvering—sociopolitical integration—and toward spiritual renewal and religious ministry. Leaving Brandeis in 1973, Murray began studies at the General Theological Seminary in New York City as the only black woman and the oldest student enrolled.

A lifelong Episcopalian, Murray openly condemned the church's discriminatory practices and sexist language, vowing to leave the church before bowing to its sexism. At one point, her discontent with the church resulted in a refusal to participate in worship. Yet Murray was fundamentally committed to transformation through confrontation and struggle. Hence, she returned to the church, and after the completion of her master of divinity degree in 1976, Murray was ordained a deacon; on 8 January 1977 she became the first black woman ordained an Episcopal priest. She spent the remainder of her life serving the Church of the Atonement in Washington, D.C., and the Church of the Holy Nativity in Baltimore. She retired from the ministry in January 1984 and moved to Pittsburgh. Murray died of cancer in Pittsburgh, Pennsylvania. Her autobiography, *Song in a Weary Throat: An American Pilgrimage*, was **posthumously** published in 1987.

posthumously: an event after the death of an individual related to that individual

In articles such as "Black, Feminist Theologies: Links, Parallels, and Tensions," published in *Christianity and Crisis* in 1980, Murray provides the early ideological and technical framework for one of the most important religious efforts of the twentieth century—liberation theology, a twentieth-century form of contextualized theological reflection that gives priority to the liberation of the oppressed. She strove to make sense of the social dynamics she encountered and extended this analysis to a larger community of the oppressed, highlighting the necessity of and potential for justice. ◆

Nanak

c. 1469–c. 1538 ● SIKH

Nanak was an Indian religious reformer and teacher (*guru*) and founder of the Sikh religion. Nanak was born in the Punjab village of Talwandi. His father, Kalu, was a member of a caste of traders and merchants. Because of Nanak's reputation as a holy man and prophet it is difficult to distinguish fact from legend about his life. It seems that at a young age he was already given to religious contemplation; his questions may have prompted one of his **libertine** school teachers to become a *sadhu*, or Hindu ascetic. Much to his parents' distress, Nanak often sat in the forest meditating. Kalu attempted to cure his son's lack of interest in worldly affairs by giving him 20 rupees with which to conduct business. Setting out to buy salt, Nanak encountered a group of *sadhus*. After spending many long hours discussing religion with them, the young man discovered that they had not eaten for four days and promptly used his money to provide them with food.

Nanak was subsequently sent to Sultanpur, where his father had arranged for him to be a storekeeper in a royal granary. There he received a good salary, married, and had two sons, but he spent most of his money on the poor, keeping only what he needed to survive. He spent most nights praying in the forest. At the time, India was torn by religious rivalries between Hindus and Muslims. Once, after spending three days secluded in prayer (during which time he was thought to have drowned),

libertine: a religious freethinker, sometimes used as a derogatory description

"In Dwapar you appeared as Krishna, slayer of Mura, and slew Kamsa, and conferring kingship on Ugrasen, rendered your devotees fear-free. In Kali Yuga you were verily Nanak, and assumed the names Angad and Amar Das; declared the Supreme Being, the reign of the holy Guru shall be immutable."

Adi Granth, Swaiyya Guru

Nanak emerged from the forest bearing a message from God that "there is no Hindu and no Muslim." Taking only one companion, he returned to the forest to become a *sadhu*. There he wrote the devotional hymns comprising the *Adi Granth*, the sacred book of the Sikh religion.

Nanak's new religion attempted to merge Hinduism and Islam. It spoke of the equality of man before God and denounced the priests and Brahmans, who presumed to be intermediaries between man and God. Despite his father's objections, Nanak set out on four missionary journeys, traveling to Benares, Gaya, Dharmasala, and Delhi. Legend states that he was imprisoned by the Mogul emperor Babur while on this expedition. The latter, however, upon hearing of Nanak's wisdom, asked to see the prisoner; after several hours of conversation, Babur granted Nanak royal protection. On his second voyage Nanak traveled south, possibly reaching Ceylon; on his third journey he went to Kashmir. Nanak's final trip took him to the west. He may have reached Mecca where, it is reported, he came into conflict with local religious officials. On being asked at a Muslim shrine how he dared put his feet in the direction of the House of God. Nanak retorted, "How can you not?"

Upon completing his voyages, Nanak settled in the town of Kartarpur, where he continued to preach but renounced the life of a *sadhu*, claiming that moderation was the true way to achieve holiness. The remainder of the *Adi Granth* was collated by his successors Baba Angad and Arjun, who continued to propagate the Sikh religion after Nanak's death.

Nanak attracted both Hindu and Muslim followers, each group promoting its own religious values in the new religion. Nanak foresaw that upon his death the two camps would be at odds over whether to cremate or bury his body and so bade them stand at opposite sides of his bier and spread flowers over both sides; they were to follow the tradition of the side whose flowers did not wither. Upon his death, the two groups remained by the body throughout the night to await the outcome. Tradition has it that they woke the next morning and found that the body had disappeared. ◆

Neolin

1760s ● NATIVE AMERICAN

Neolin, known as the Delaware Prophet, was a religious leader active among the Ohio Delaware Indians in the 1760s. Neolin (whose name means "the enlightened") was one of several Delaware prophets who arose in the latter part of the eighteenth century along the Susquehanna and Allegheny rivers in Pennsylvania and the Cuyahoga and Muskingum rivers in Ohio. The teachings of the prophet were widely known throughout the tribes of the frontier. Pontiac, the famed Ottawa chief, saw in the prophet's message divine authority for his own attempts to unite the frontier tribes. Through Pontiac, Neolin affected the policies of nearly 20 tribes from Lake Ontario to the Mississippi, including among them the Ojibwa, Ottawa, Potawatomi, Seneca, Huron, Miami, Shawnee, and Delaware. Pontiac tempered somewhat the anti-European thrust of Neolin's message by affirming the rights of the French and opposing the British. Whatever setbacks the British suffered during the 1760s west of the Alleghenies were the result not only of Pontiac's leadership but also of the appeal of the Delaware Prophet's message.

This message came from a great dream-vision journey of the prophet to the mountain home of the Master of Life, or Great Spirit. The Master instructed him to tell the people that they must give up their drunkenness, sexual promiscuity, **internecine** fighting, and medicine songs dedicated to the evil spirit. In addition, they were to cast off all of the influences of the whites and return to hunting with bow and arrow. Ritually, they were to purify themselves through sexual abstinence and the use of **emetics,** and they were to reinstitute sacrifices. These reforms would result in a revitalization of their power that would enable them to drive the whites from the continent.

The Master of Life also gave the prophet a stick on which was written a prayer, in native hieroglyphs, to be recited by all

internecine: destructive fighting and conflict within a group

emetics: agents used to induce vomiting

of his followers every morning and evening. John Heckewelder, a Moravian missionary who lived with the Delaware at this time, reports seeing a map used by the prophet in his preaching. In the center of the map was a square that represented the dwelling place of the Great Spirit. This land, full of game and forests, had been the goal of the soul's journey after death. Now, however, it was all but inaccessible because of the barriers set by the whites. Only a very few souls could now reach that land. Most fell into the hands of the evil one when attempting to overcome these barriers and were taken to his land of **emaciated** game animals and parched soil.

emaciated: very thin and sickly

East of the inner square the prophet had drawn a map of the lands formerly occupied by the Delaware but now in the control of the British. Once the Delaware had dwelt beside the ocean and in the coastal areas, where they hunted, farmed, and fished with great delight. Then they allowed the Europeans to settle, gave away or sold their land, and became dependent on the white man's goods. The result of their own follies and English acquisitiveness was migration, fragmentation, and deterioration. If they followed the instructions of the prophet, however, they could have their land and their old ways back again.

Neolin played an essential role in helping his people interpret their situation. In Neolin's image of heaven, the Delaware saw their own recently lost state. In his image of the evil spirit's land, the Delaware perceived the despoiled land of the white settlements. The entry into paradise necessitated a historical expulsion of the whites. A further dimension of Neolin's message was not always grasped by Pontiac: that is, that the Great Spirit had allowed the whites to control the land and had taken away game animals as a punishment for the immorality of the Indians.

Neolin's map depicted not only the barriers on earth and in heaven but also within the hearts of the people. They had corrupted themselves by their dependence on the whites. More importantly, the increasing dependence on the whites eroded the Indians' previous dependence on the spirit-forces of forest, field, stream, and sky. Only a spiritual purification and moral reform could give them the inner strength to cut loose from the whites and supply them with the capacity to enter again into the paradisal state they had abandoned. The prophet interpreted the social and historical situation using the religious symbolism of death and rebirth. His **paradigm** allowed for no compromise. This rite of passage from a state of degeneration

paradigm: an extremely clear example

and chaos to one of rebirth and a new order could not be entered halfheartedly. Nor could it be successful if halted before completion. The recovery of lost innocence and the regaining of lost land were intimately linked.

The prophet had faced squarely the problem that confronted his people: a problem that would continue to confront Native Americans. Namely, how does a people recover its identity and pride in the face of socioeconomic erosion and a calculatingly aggressive foe? Neolin's answer was not necessarily wrong; it came, however, too late. Nevertheless, it was a course that others followed, even when they knew it was too late, for it seemed to them the only honorable course to take. ◆

O'Connor, John

1920– ● CATHOLIC

Born to an Irish working-class family on January 15, 1920 in Philadelphia, Pennsylvania, John O'Connor grew up steeped in the values and traditions of the Irish and Italian neighborhood in which he was raised. One powerful tradition, a respect for the priesthood, had a profound influence on him, and as a youth he knew that he was destined to serve the Catholic Church. He responded to this calling to the priesthood by attending seminary school in Philadelphia and was ordained in 1945. His early goals were modest—he hoped eventually to be assigned a parish much like the community in which he grew up. Neither he nor those who knew him then could have imagined that he would one day rise to the position of the most powerful Catholic archbishop in the United States.

1920 O'Connor is born into an Irish working-class family in Philadelphia.

1945 O'Connor is ordained.

1952 O'Connor volunteers as Navy chaplain during the Korean War.

1979 O'Connor is named bishop of the armed forces of the United States.

1984 O'Connor is named Archbishop of New York.

1985 O'Connor is named Cardinal.

1999 O'Connor is hospitalized to have a tumor removed from his brain; announces plans to retire.

"Millions and millions of people, it seems to me, and the young in a very special way, are hungering for holiness. Archbishop or no archbishop, I hunger with them."

Cardinal O'Connor, 1999

Upon ordination, Father O'Connor's first assignment was to work at a school for mentally retarded children in Upper Darby, Pennsylvania. While Father O'Connor was obedient to the dictates of his church, he longed to leave the role of teacher behind and take on the challenges of ministering as a parish priest.

Along with his strong Catholic faith, O'Connor had also been raised in a tradition of intense patriotism. Therefore, in 1952, after the United States had entered into the Korean War, Father O'Connor volunteered for service as chaplain in the Navy. In the service he found that he could realize his dream of ministering to a parish. For the next 27 years he remained within the Navy, eventually receiving promotion to the rank of Captain. By the end of his career, he had become Head Chaplain of the Armed Forces and retired with the rank of rear admiral.

Throughout his career in the Navy and afterwards, Father O'Connor also pursued an academic career. He earned advanced degrees in disciplines as diverse as Ethics, Political Theory, and Clinical Psychology. In recognition of his years of service and his academic achievements, upon his retirement from the Navy in 1979 Pope John Paul II ordained him as bishop of the armed forces of the United States. Four years later, when the bishopric of Scranton, Pennsylvania, became vacant, O'Connor was given the position. A year later he was named Archbishop of New York, a diocese with 2.2 million members and comprising 10 New York counties. In 1985 he was given the title Cardinal.

The office of Cardinal in the Roman Catholic Church is one which bears great responsibilities, chief among which are providing advice in council with the Pope and providing guidance to the churches under his authority in the New York Diocese. In the event of the death of the Pope, the College of Cardinals meet to elect a successor to the highest office in the Church. John Cardinal O'Connor is the only U.S. member of the College of Cardinals eligible to vote in such elections and to serve on advisory councils to the Pope. In addition, he serves as spokesperson for Church teachings and policies. In this latter capacity, John Cardinal O'Connor has worked with the National Conference of Catholic Bishops and has served as an officer or member for numerous civic organizations.

Over the last decades of the twentieth century, the Roman Catholic Church has faced a number of controversies and challenges. Social issues such as the right to abortion, the rise in divorce, women in the priesthood, gay marriage, and other challenges to church teaching have forced representatives of the faith to take public stands. John Cardinal O'Connor built a reputation as tough and strongly conservative on these issues, often appearing confrontational in the public media. Yet in later years he has softened some of his positions. He has participated in interfaith services and has gone on record apologizing for the Church's anti-Semitism and its lack of leadership against Nazism during World War II.

In the late 1990s John Cardinal O'Connor suffered health declines, and in September of 1999 he was hospitalized in order to have a tumor removed from his brain. After weeks of radiation therapy, he returned to the pulpit of New York City's St. Patrick's Cathedral to deliver his first sermon since his hospitalization. His continuing health problems prompted him to announce the likelihood of his retirement on his 80th birthday, on January 15, 2000, touching off speculation as to who would be named his successor. In November, of 1999, however, his continuing health problems prompted him to send a farewell letter to his fellow American Catholic bishops, acknowledging the likelihood that he would not be able to fill the demands of his office for much longer. ◆

> "To choose life involves rejecting every form of violence: the violence of poverty and hunger, which afflicts so many human beings; the violence of armed conflict; the violence of criminal trafficking in drugs and arms; the violence of mindless damage to the natural environment."
>
> Cardinal John O'Connor, 1999

Saint Patrick

5TH CENTURY ● CHRISTIAN

Saint Patrick was a British Christian missionary to Ireland. Ireland's patron saint was born in Britain (the location has not been identified) into a Christian family of good standing; his father was affluent enough to own a villa, from which, at the age of 16, Patrick was carried away into slavery by Irish pirates, who pressed him into service as a herdsman for six hard years, in the area of modern Killala, County Mayo. Although previously he had not been particularly pious, Patrick's Christian devotion deepened in captivity: "In a single day I would say as many as 100 prayers, and almost as many at night," he later recalled. He also experienced dreams and visions which he took to be divinely inspired. In one of these, it was revealed to him that a ship was waiting to take him home; he duly escaped and boarded the vessel and, saving himself and the crew from starvation when his prayers for food were answered

> "Hence, how did it come to pass in Ireland that those who never had a knowledge of God, but until now always worshipped idols and things impure, have now been made a people of the Lord, and are called sons of God, that the sons and daughters of the kings of the Irish are seen to be monks and virgins of Christ?"
>
> St. Patrick, *The Confessions of St. Patrick*, 5th century

through the miraculous appearance of a herd of wild pigs, returned to his parents.

Despite his parents' protestations, Patrick was now determined to return to Ireland to carry the word of God to his heathen erstwhile captors. He dreamt that he was given a letter representing "the voice of the Irish," stating that "we beseech thee Holy Youth to come and walk once more among us." To this end, he acquired an ecclesiastical training and was duly appointed bishop for the mission to Ireland; his episcopal see was probably sited at Armagh. There, despite his self-avowed "rusticity," he was deeply beloved by the people and by the end of his life had succeeded in establishing Christianity firmly on the island; the Irish church was later to be very influential in the evangelization of Western Europe, the preservation of the monastic tradition, and, through successive waves of emigration from Ireland, in the development of Catholicism in North America.

Legends concerning the saint abound. He is reputed to have driven out the snakes from Irish shores, which have remained serpent-free to this day. He is also remembered for having used the shamrock, with its three leaves on a single stalk, to explain the mystery of the Holy Trinity as three aspects of a unity to one of his simple converts. The shamrock is now Ireland's national flower and is traditionally sported on the saint's feast day, 17 March.

Early in his career, Patrick was hindered by the jealousy and rivalry of others; he was initially refused the episcopacy when a supposed friend of his revealed to the religious authorities a sin that he was alleged to have committed. Despite his subsequent installation in the post, Patrick was deeply hurt by this evidence of treachery. In his *Confessions*, written as a vindication of his own life and conduct in the face of his ecclesiastical opponents' charges that he sought office for its own sake and was uneducated, Patrick left a moving testament which reveals his disarming honesty and modesty, his deep pastoral concern, and his sense of unworthiness for the task which God had been gracious enough to bestow upon him.

Confusion reigns over what dates can authentically be ascribed to the saint. Some scholars have suggested that he was a legendary figure, a synthetic character based on a combination of Palladius Patricius, the bishop sent by Pope Celestine to minister to the Irish between 432 and 461, and the author of the *Confessions*, whose date of death is given as 492. However,

a more likely explanation is that, given Patrick's immense proselytizing success, it was tempting to ignore the relatively feeble
attempts of his predecessor Palladius and to regard him as Ireland's first missionary. However, the actual dates of Patrick's
ministry in Ireland remain a subject of controversy. ◆

Patterson, Paige

1942– ● BAPTIST

Paige Patterson, Baptist minister and educator, was born
on October 19, 1942 in Fort Worth, Texas. Paige is the
son of Thomas Armour Patterson and Roberta Turner. In
Texas his father was a well-known fundamentalist—a believer
in the literal truth of every passage in the Bible—who served
for 14 years as executive director of the Baptist General Convention of Texas.

Raised in Beaumont, Texas, Paige Patterson at age nine
had a religious experience that committed him to a Christian
ministry and to fundamentalist, or literalist, principles. Before
going to college he did missionary work around the world. In
the early 1960s he attended attend Hardin-Simmons University in Abilene, Texas, where he was known as a maverick who
defended fundamentalism against all comers. Receiving a bachelor of arts degree from Hardin-Simmons in 1965, he moved on
to the New Orleans Baptist Theological Seminary. There Patterson obtained a master of theology degree in 1968 and a doctor of theology degree in 1973. Having served as pastor of the
First Baptist Church in Fayetteville, Arkansas, from 1970 to
1975, in the latter year he became president of The Criswell
College in Dallas, Texas, a fundamentalist stronghold. At the
same time Patterson began serving as associate pastor at the
First Baptist Church in Dallas.

Patterson was affiliated with the Southern Baptist Convention (SBC), the largest Protestant denomination in the United
States, with nearly 16 million members by the end of the twentieth century. But he believed that the SBC's leadership was
too liberal, that it had abandoned the fundamentalists' strict
belief in the infallibility of the Bible. Paul Pressler, a judge in
Houston, felt the same way, and in 1967 he visited Patterson to
discuss their common grievances. For the next ten years, they

> "Our scriptures
> should inform our
> agenda. Our agen-
> das are not to in-
> form how we view
> the scriptures."
> Paige Patterson,
> 1998

1942 Patterson is born in Texas.

1965 Patterson receives a B.A. degree from Hardin-Simmons.

1868 Patterson receives a M.A. in theology from New Orleans Theological Seminary.

1970 Patterson becomes pastor of the First Baptist Church in Fayetteville, Arkansas.

1973 Patterson earns an Ph.D. from New Orleans Theological Seminary.

1979 Patterson helps fundamentalist Adrian Rogers win the presidency of the Southern Baptist Convention.

1998 Patterson becomes president of the Southern Baptist Convention.

1999 Patterson calls for the creation of urban missions and a Baptist television station.

made unofficial contact with other Southern Baptists in order to build up support for the fundamentalist point of view.

With the presidency of the SBC expected to become vacant in 1979, Patterson and Pressler saw an opportunity to advance their cause. In 1978 they met with some 20 pastors to plan their campaign. That gathering led to meetings in 15 states, at which fundamentalist Baptists were encouraged to attend the 1979 SBC convention. At that gathering, fundamentalist candidate Adrian Rogers won the presidency, a post the fundamentalists continued to hold at century's end.

During the 1980s and 1990s, Patterson and Pressler led the fundamentalist drive to gain complete domination of the SBC by winning control of seminaries, state conventions, mission boards, and all other denominational agencies and institutions. In this battle Pressler was the chief organizer and strategist, while the articulate Patterson was the leading theological spokesmen, conducting public debates with more moderate SBC leaders, among other activities. They essentially won their struggle during the century's last two decades, although some SBC organizations remained under the control of moderates. Patterson and Pressler also pressed successfully to win endorsement from the annual SBC conventions of their conservative social views. These included the belief that a wife should obey her husband's commands, opposition to abortion, and condemnation of homosexuality. The SBC also came out against the theory of evolution because it contradicts the biblical account of creation.

Fundamentalist thinkers are absolutely certain of the truth of their beliefs, and equally sure that this truth is clearly written in the Bible for all to see. Therefore, they generally have little patience with people who disagree with the fundamentalist interpretation of scripture. In 1984 Patterson revealed that he was keeping what he called a "heresy file" on professors in SBC educational institutions whose views were at odds with fundamentalist literalism. Eight years later Patterson had the opportunity to sweep away some of these opponents when he was chosen president of the Southeastern Baptist Seminary in Wake Forest, North Carolina, which thereby became the first SBC seminary to come under fundamentalist control. Upon his selection, Patterson made it clear that while students should learn about nonfundamentalist (or what he called liberal) theology, they must also be shown that this "dog won't hunt."

Forty Southeastern faculty members resigned after Patterson became president.

In 1998 Patterson was elected president of the Southern Baptist Convention without opposition. He was reelected in 1999 in another uncontested election. As president, Patterson argued that since fundamentalist orthodoxy had triumphed within the SBC, it was time for the denomination to concentrate on increasing its membership through evangelical activity. To achieve this, he called in 1999 for the creation of urban missions and a Baptist "super" television station. With his approval, the annual conference under his presidency called for a special mission to convert Jews. This act aroused considerable anger among Jewish leaders. They were particularly disturbed by Patterson's support of groups such as Jews for Jesus, which claim that Jews can accept Jesus as their savior and still be Jews.

Along with his serious religious commitment, Patterson has said that life is meant to be enjoyed. He enjoys hunting and has pursued big game around the world; the heads and skins of animals he has killed are on display in his office at the Southeastern Baptist Seminary. True to his Texas roots, he often wears cowboy boots along with a white Stetson hat in summer and a black one in winter. ◆

> **"I think the challenge that lies before all Southern Baptists now is,** "Can we translate doctrinal correctness into evangelistic effectiveness?"
>
> Paige Patterson, 1999

Saint Paul

?–67 C.E. ● CHRISTIAN

Saint Paul, also known as Saul, was the founder of numerous early Christian communities. His letters (epistles) to these communities in the Roman empire (the Pauline Epistles), account for about one fourth of the New Testament. Born in the city of Tarsus in Cilicia, Asia Minor, the son of a Pharisee. Paul was both a Jew and a Roman citizen, and by profession a tentmaker. Surrounded by the Greek culture of the day, but educated in the Jewish tradition, he completed his studies in Jerusalem at the feet of the Jewish teacher of the law, Gamalie, becoming a thoroughgoing and zealous Pharisee, a sect that strictly adhered to the letter of the Law.

By his own admission, Paul was the most pious kind of Jew. "Circumcised on the eighth day [according to the Law of

Moses], of the stock of Israel, of the tribe of Benjamin, a Hebrew of Hebrews; as touching the law, a Pharisee; concerning zeal, persecuting the church; touching the righteousness which is the law, blameless" (Phil. 3:5–6). Paul devoted himself to seeking out and arresting those Jews who believed in Jesus, and minded the cloaks of those who stoned Stephen. So great was his hatred of these people that he obtained letters from the high priest and elders in Jerusalem to permit him to travel to Damascus in order to extradite Jews who believed in Jesus and to return them to Jerusalem for judgment.

On the road to Damascus, however, he experienced a stunning revelation. It was midday, when "suddenly there shone from heaven a great light." Saul fell to the ground and "heard a voice saying to me, 'Saul, Saul, why are you persecuting Me?' And I answered, 'Who art Thou, Lord?' And He said to me, 'I am Jesus the Nazarene, whom you are persecuting.' And those who were with me beheld the light, to be sure, but did not understand the voice of the One who was speaking to me" (Acts 22:7–9).

Saul arose from the ground but could not see and was therefore led away to Damascus. Three days later Ananias, a devout Jew and believer in the Way (as it was called), came to Saul and prayed for him, and he regained his sight. From that point on life was radically different.

His "conversion" was not well received. The Jews who already believed in Jesus were highly suspicious of Paul at first, for they knew with what purpose he had come to Damascus. In the synagogues the news was received even more violently. Jews in both Damascus and Jerusalem were so enraged that on separate occasions they sought to kill Paul. In Damascus he was forced to escape under cover of night by being lowered outside the city walls in a basket.

Paul was not deterred. The same unwavering commitment to the Law of God that had driven him to persecute the Christians now spurred him in his profession that Jesus was indeed the long-awaited Jewish messiah and had brought salvation through grace.

Paul's dramatic transformation took place about 33 C.E.. He spent some time in the Arabian desert and returned to Jerusalem three years later. He spent the next ten years in Tarsus and Antioch until he set out on his first journey—lasting some two years—to proclaim the gospel. Within approximately a 12-year period Paul completed three missionary tours of areas in the Roman Empire, bringing the Christian message of salvation. In 45 C.E. he set out from Antioch accompanied by Barnabas and John Mark, who left them after visiting Cyprus. The book of Acts records that in Cyprus and the cities of Asia Minor their preaching was often accompanied by signs and wonders, such as healing the sick and casting out demons. On Paul's third journey a young man was raised from the dead.

As was his custom, upon entering a new city Paul went first to the synagogue with his message. He and Barnabas were often well received with many, both Jews and Gentiles, accepting their teaching. However, many times those who did not believe, both Jew and Gentile, incited the city residents to chase the two out of town. In Lystra, Paul was even stoned and left for dead, but revived and completed his journey in 48 C.E.

During his second journey, which lasted for about five years, Paul was accompanied by Silas. In Lystra Timothy joined them and the three continued through Troas, Macedonia, and finally into Europe. On this trip Paul and Silas were beaten and thrown into prison.

Paul's third journey from about 54 to 57 C.E. took him mainly to Ephesus but also to Greece. During this time it is thought that Paul wrote the Epistles of I Corinthians, Galatians, II Corinthians, and Romans. Through his endeavors Christian centers were established in most cities in Asia Minor and Greece.

After the completion of his third journey, Paul went to Jerusalem. With him he carried a large offering from the Gentile Christians in the Roman Empire to the Jewish Christians in Jerusalem. He reported to the elders all that was happening among the Gentiles and was informed that there were many thousands of Jews in the city who believed and were all zealous for the Law of Moses. However, he was told that many Jews believed Paul was teaching Jews in the

"Paul, an apostle (not of men, neither by man, but by Jesus Christ, and God the Father, who raised him from the dead) and all the brethren which are with me, unto the churches of Galatia. Grace be to you and peace from God the Father, and from our Lord Jesus Christ."

Bible, Galatians 1:1–2

Diaspora to forsake the Law of Moses. In order to disprove this accusation, the elders suggested that Paul shave his head and join other Jewish Christians in the temple who were fulfilling a vow.

Near the end of the seventh day other Jews in the temple recognized Paul and accused him of preaching against the Law of Moses as well as of having brought a Gentile into the Temple. He was dragged from the temple and beaten but was rescued by Roman guards. He was arrested and through a series of appeals was granted an audience in Rome.

incarceration: imprisonment

In the spring of 61 C.E. Paul arrived as a prisoner in Rome after an eventful voyage ending in shipwreck on Malta. His **incarceration** was unusual—for two years he lived under guard in his own hired house, able to receive visitors. There he wrote the letters to the Ephesians, Philippians, Colossians, Philemon, and perhaps to the Hebrews (authorship is uncertain).

Most scholars believe he was acquitted and released from prison. He may have journeyed to Spain then but within two years he was arrested again and taken to Rome. At that time the Roman empire was ruled by Nero, who, most historians agree, set Rome alight because he wanted to rebuild a finer city. However, he needed a scapegoat on which to pin the blame for the blaze and the Christians provided the outlet. It may have been in this framework that Paul was re-arrested and beheaded in about 67 C.E.

The focus of all of Paul's writing is Jesus, through whom God has effected redemption for all people regardless of ethnic or social background. Paul's interest in Jesus is selective, taking little notice of how he lived or what he taught, focusing instead on who he was and what his death and resurrection accomplished. For Paul, Jesus is God's son in a unique and absolute sense, who by his death made possible the reconciliation of sinful man with his holy Creator and took on all the sins of the world. Once this redemption was accomplished, God set his seal on it by raising Jesus from the dead. Paul's personal revelation of the risen Jesus **permeates** his thinking. The living, ascended Jesus sent the Holy Spirit as a guarantee of the sure fulfilment of all of God's promises to the believer. Just as man fell from the image of God through sin, so Jesus took on humanity in order that men might be re-formed into the image of God's son. Paul always identifies Jesus with the church, and foresees the day when Jesus will return to take that church to himself. ◆

permeates: passing through or spreading strongly

Saint Peter

?–c. 64 b.c.e. ● Christian

S aint Peter, whose original name was Simon, was one of the Twelve Apostles of Jesus. Peter emerged as the most prominent among Jesus' disciples and was singled out for a position of leadership. After Jesus' death, Peter became the head of the Christian community in Jerusalem and in later times bishops of Rome claimed succession from Peter, proclaiming him the first pope of the Roman Catholic Church.

Peter's family originated in Bethsaida, on the northern shore of the Sea of Galilee. By the time of Jesus' ministry, Peter was married (according to later legend, with children), and lived by the Sea of Galilee in Capernaum, where he and his brother Andrew were fishermen together with two others who would become disciples, James and John, the sons of Zebedee. At the Sea of Galilee, Peter began his apostleship and was the first to proclaim Jesus as the Messiah (Matt. 16:15–16).

Peter was, with James and John, among the inner circle of Jesus's followers (termed "the pillars") permitted to accompany Jesus in his ministry. When Jesus taught the crowd at the Sea of Galilee, he stood in Peter's boat; Peter, James, and John accompanied Jesus when he raised the daughter of Jairus from the dead; the same group was also present at the Transfiguration and the critical moments in the Garden of Gethsemane. The New Testament records that it is Peter who first witnessed the Resurrection and, in the Gospel of John, Peter is told by Jesus to "tend my sheep" and "feed my lambs," references to providing spiritual instruction to the faithful in Jesus' absence. In listing the Apostles, Peter is always mentioned first and sometimes he is the only one named.

Peter's position of responsibility for the Christian community accounts for his change of name from the Hebrew, Simon, to Peter, derived from the Latin, *petros,* meaning "the rock." In the New Testament (Matt. 16:15–19), Jesus says to him, "I tell you, you are Peter, and on this rock I will build my church, and the powers of death shall not prevail against it. I will give you the keys of the kingdom of Heaven, and whatever you bind on earth shall be bound in heaven, and whatever you loose on earth shall be loosed in heaven." The church here refers to the early followers of Jesus, and Peter is given unique authority

> "So when they had dined, Jesus saith to Simon Peter, Simon, son of Jonas, lovest thou me more than these? He saith unto him, Yea, Lord; thou knowest that I love thee. He saith unto him, Feed my lambs."
>
> Bible, John 21:15

> "And Jesus saith unto them, All ye shall be offended because of me this night: for it is written, I will smite the shepherd, and the sheep shall be scattered. But after that I am risen, I will go before you into Galilee. But Peter said unto him, Although all shall be offended, yet will not I. And Jesus saith unto him, Verily I say unto thee, That this day, even in this night, before the cock crow twice, thou shalt deny me thrice."
>
> Bible,
> Mark 14:27–30

within the community, "the keys of the kingdom." The power to "bind" and "loose," indicating the authority to legislate and to determine the members of the community, was given singly to Peter as well as in common with all of Jesus' Apostles.

Despite his responsible role, Peter does not appear to have been particularly educated, either in Hebrew or Greek, and in his apostleship he erred many times. Thus, he first ate with the gentiles at Antioch but later refused, and the mission to the gentiles was taken over by Paul at that time. It was Peter who declared that he would be faithful to Jesus unto death and then denied his apostleship when confronted by the Roman authorities.

In spite of these failings, the sincerity of Peter's love for Jesus was always clear and once invested with responsibility, he carried out his role with the qualities of leadership. Indeed, Jesus prophesied that Peter's betrayal would be followed by his strengthening of the other Apostles. Thus, after Peter spoke against the Passion that Jesus foresaw, he was first severely rebuked by his master but then received a revelation and made a confession that led to his becoming the foundation of the future church. Likewise, Peter's witness of the Resurrection is said to guard the church from the possibility of future death.

After Jesus' death, Peter led the community for the next 15 years, disciplining its members, making Matthias the twelfth Apostle in place of Judas, leading the church's expansion by going to such groups as the Samaritans, performing miraculous healings, and fulfilling a pastoral role at the gatherings of the faithful. In 44 he was imprisoned by Herod Agrippa after the beheading of James, the son of Zebedee. Miraculously freed, he fled to safety and, while ceasing to play a role in the Jerusalem community he proselytized according to the instructions of James, a cousin or brother of Jesus and the new leader of the Jerusalem church. It is not clear where Peter went after his escape but possibilities include Antioch, Corinth, and Rome. The later years of Peter's life are shrouded in uncertainty; according to tradition he was 25 years in Rome as bishop, perhaps a late interpolation designed to lend credence to the claim that papal authority stemmed directly from him. It appears that Peter was martyred during the reign of Nero, somewhere between 64 and 67; traditional sources record that he was crucified upside-down. The great basilica of Saint Peter is built over the traditional site of his tomb, where human remains have been uncovered, dating from the first century C.E. ◆

Pius IX

1792–1878 ● CATHOLIC

Pope Pius IX, also known as Pio Nono, shaped the Roman Catholic church's determined opposition to liberalism from the mid-nineteenth to the mid-twentieth century. He was born Giovanni Maria Mastai-Gerretti in Senigallia, Italy. He came from an enlightened family, believed in the ideas of Catholic liberalism and until his death was popular for his extensive charity, piety, simplicity, eloquence, and sense of humor.

As archbishop of Spoleto (1827–1832) Pius helped the future Napoleon III escape to Switzerland after the failure of Romagna's 1831 revolution against papal rule. As bishop of Imola, he was out-spokenly critical of the church's failure to deal with conditions in his diocese. As a cardinal he continued to be both independent and liberal, albeit more discreetly.

Elected pope in 1846 on the basis of his liberal reputation. Pius became both spiritual head of the Roman Catholic church and temporal ruler of the central Italian Papal States. International opinion of the time displayed a rare unanimity in its condemnation of the Papal States for their inefficient undemocratic and church-administered government and judicial system, as well as for being technologically and economically backward. Pius immediately began reforming the administration of the Papal States, making it more modern, efficient, and popular. He declared a general political amnesty, established agricultural institutions, planned rail routes and street lighting, lifted censorship, revised the criminal code, reformed tariffs, and instituted limited representative government. An ardent Italian patriot he dreamed of an Italy free of Austrian dominance, of presiding over an independent federation of Italian states that would allow each state to maintain its own customs while pursing a common financial and foreign policy. He began working toward this goal by ordering the withdrawal of Austrian troops from Ferrara and negotiating the creation of an Italian customs union.

Pius was appalled when the 1848 revolutions spread throughout Europe, including Italy, with revolutionaries cheering his liberal inspiration and patronage. He did not want to be identified as a revolutionary; his reforms had been liberal, not

> "Divine revelation is imperfect, and therefore subject to a continual and indefinite progress, corresponding with the advancement of human reason."
>
> Pius, *Syllabus of Errors*, 1864

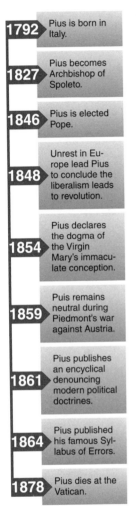

1792 — Pius is born in Italy.

1827 — Pius becomes Archbishop of Spoleto.

1846 — Pius is elected Pope.

1848 — Unrest in Europe lead Pius to conclude the liberalism leads to revolution.

1854 — Pius declares the dogma of the Virgin Mary's immaculate conception.

1859 — Puis remains neutral during Piedmont's war against Austria.

1861 — Pius publishes an encyclical denouncing modern political doctrines.

1864 — Pius published his famous Syllabus of Errors.

1878 — Pius dies at the Vatican.

radical, and he had always put the interests of the church first. Forced to grant Rome a constitution and a parliament with full legislative powers, Pius tried to remain neutral during the Italian Kingdom of Piedmont's short was with Austria; thereafter he was considered a reactionary. His prime minister was assassinated. Revolutionaries declared the end of papal rule and established a democratic republic in Rome; foreign ambassadors helped Pius escape. He then appealed to Europe's Catholic rulers for aid, and Austria and France overcame the revolutionaries, whereupon he was restored to Rome in 1850.

The events of 1848 led Pius to conclude that liberalism invariably led to revolution—which was usually anticlerical—and that political power was a necessary bulwark against attack on his spiritual power. He retained most of his initial reforms and continued to support the technological modernization of the Papal States, but for the rest of his papacy he refused to allow constitutional government, opposed nationalism, and fought any attempt to diminish his temporal power.

Liberal Piedmont's 1855 anticlerical law (closing many monasteries and nunneries) turned Pius against its expressed ideal of a free church in a free state and made him wary of Piedmont's ambition to unite Italy under its rule. Unwilling to take a stand against a Catholic ruler who had helped him return to Rome, Pius remained neutral during Piedmont's 1859 war against Austria, and as a consequence lost the Papal States to Piedmont's new kingdom of Italy. He was able to continue ruling Rome for another 10 years only because it was guarded by French troops sent by Napoleon III. When Italian troops occupied Rome during the time of the Franco-Prussian War of 1870–1871, Rome became part of an Italy in which church and state were separated. Pius refused to have anything to do with the Italian government and incarcerated himself in the Vatican until his death, losing all temporal sovereignty.

Pius was responsible for the Catholic church's 1854 declaration of the dogma of the Virgin Mary's Immaculate Conception, leading the growing movement in the church toward devotional religion and away from intellectualism and the restoration of independent Catholic hierarchies in England and Holland. He also derived conservative church doctrines from the political exigencies he faced after losing the Papal States. In 1861, he published an encyclical denouncing all modern political doctrines on the grounds that they undermined the church's authority. After France and Italy came to an agreement about withdrawing the French garrison defending Rome. Pius issued an encyclical in 1864 with his famous *Syllabus of Errors* attached listing the 80 concepts he felt were the principal errors of our times. Pius became a strong advocate of ultramonastanism (belief in the concentration of church authority in the pope's hands).

The doctrine of papal infallibility was the primary issue for the First Vatican Council (1869–1870). Pius made it quite clear to the council that he wanted that doctrine accepted. The council refused to make the syllabus official church doctrine, but it accepted the papal infallibility, allowing Pius to imprint his conservative image on the church. During the remaining eight years of his life, the church became increasingly alienated from secular political forces and anticlericalism spread throughout Western Europe. Pius was the first pope whose pontificate exceeded the 25 years traditionally ascribed to Saint Peter. ◆

> "The Church not only ought never to pass judgment on philosophy, but ought to tolerate the errors of philosophy, leaving it to correct itself."
>
> Pius, *Syllabus of Erros*, 1864

Powell, Adam Clayton

1908–1972 ● BAPTIST

Adam Clayton Powell, Jr. was a congressman, civil rights activist, and clergyman. Powell, was born in 1908 in New Haven Connecticut. Shortly thereafter his father, Adam Clayton Powell, Sr., left New Haven for New York City to assume the pastorship of the Abyssinian Baptist Church in Harlem. The elder Powell, a prominent minister, sought the best for his only son, educating him at the elite Townsend Harris High School, then sending him to Colgate University, a largely white school in Hamilton, New York. In 1932 Powell received an M.A. in religious education from Columbia University Teachers College.

By the time Powell had graduated from Colgate in 1930 and returned home, the United States was mired in the Great Depression. Young Powell was named an assistant pastor at the Abyssinian Church. Powell was not content, however, to concern himself exclusively with pastoral matters. With the depression as backdrop, young Powell rallied for help for

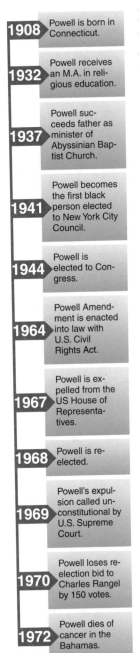

Harlemites from City Hall, and goaded the residents of Harlem to protest second-class treatment of African Americans. He declaimed from both pulpit and street corner, leading marchers not only to City Hall, but to the doorsteps of the ill-staffed and racially discriminatory Harlem Hospital. Older Abyssinian deacons considered him unpredictable, even impatient. But the younger members of the church adored him, and were eager to follow his lead. In the winter of 1937 Powell was named minister of the Abyssinian Baptist Church to succeed his father. He was 29 years old. The congregation boasted more than 10,000 members and was probably the largest Protestant Church in the United States. During the next few years, Powell, in his forceful and flamboyant manner, became the most visible leader of the boycott campaign to break the bottleneck of discrimination that existed in stores. Melding together the often factious groups that comprised the "Don't Buy Where You Can't Work" campaign, Powell's tactics were hugely successful and emulated in other cities. He pressured New York utilities, including Consolidated Edison, to hire blacks. His boycotting tactics forced the New York City private bus companies for the first time to hire black drivers. Liberals and progressives from the world of politics were invited to appear in the Abyssinian pulpit. The mix was eclectic. They were animated by the spirit of progressive reform in the manner of Robert LaFollette and Franklin D. Roosevelt, as well as black nationalist sentiments inspired by Marcus Garvey. Powell turned the church stage into a personal bully pulpit.

Powell was a natural for the political arena, and in 1941, running as an Independent, he became the first black to win election to the New York City Council. Although he would thereafter usually run as a Democrat, he always maintained his independence from the Democratic machine. Before his first term was over, he decided to run for Congress from a newly created district that would, for the first time, enable a black to be elected from Harlem. With help from the left-wing East Harlem Congressman Vito Marcantonio, the powerful Abyssinian church, and the vibrant artistic community of Harlem, Powell launched a two-year campaign that saw him elected in 1944 as the first black to Congress from the Northeast. His Washington debut was typically controversial. In fall 1945, when the Daughters of the American Revolution (DAR) refused to allow jazz pianist Hazel Scott, the second of his three wives, to perform on the stage of Constitution Hall. Powell as-

Abyssinian Baptist Church

The Abyssinian Baptist Church in New York City was founded in 1808 when the white led First Baptist Church restricted black worshippers to a segregated area of the sanctuary. The Rev. Thomas Paul, a black minister from Boston, and 18 black Baptists left and founded their own congregation on Anthony Street (now Worth Street). By 1840, the church's membership numbered more than 400, making it the largest African-American Baptist congregation outside the South. After the Civil War, the church's membership grew slowly, reaching about 1,000 by the turn of the century. In 1902, under the leadership of the Rev. Charles S. Morris, the church moved into a new building on 40th street. In 1908, a dynamic leader, the Rev. Adam Clayton Powell, Sr., was installed as pastor. Powell campaigned successfully to raise money for a church building in Harlem. In 1923, the new building opened at 132 West 138th street. Once settled in Harlem, the church immediately became active in social programs, running a senior citizens' home, a soup kitchen, a credit union, a nursery, and a school for adults. After succeeding his father as pastor in 1937, Adam Clayton Powell, Jr., led boycotts and picketing to obtain jobs for blacks in Harlem. Powell retained the pulpit of the Abyssinian Baptist Church after becoming a New York City councilman in 1941, and then a U.S. Congressman in 1945.

sailed First Lady Bess Truman in the press because of her continued connections with the DAR. President Truman was livid, and Powell was never invited to the White House while Truman was President.

Powell's talent for attracting attention and making enemies soon made him the congressional leader in the fight for civil rights legislation. Working closely with Clarence Mitchell, Jr. and the NAACP in 1950, he offered an amendment to current legislation, which came to be known as the Powell Amendment, forbidding any federal support for segregated facilities. Powell would repeatedly introduce this amendment over the next several years. Politically he was liberal, but he was also a shrewd opportunist. In 1956 Powell backed President Eisenhower's re-election bid, a move that angered Democrats. Four years later, however, Powell heartily campaigned for the Kennedy-Johnson ticket. Coinciding with Kennedy's victory. Powell had gained sufficient seniority to become chairman of the powerful House Education and Labor Committee. The influence of his powerful position, however, would not be felt until 1964, when President Johnson's heightened domestic agenda went into full action. Powell was instrumental in passage of the war on poverty legislation, on which he and Johnson collaborated. These included increased federal aid to school programs, increasing the minimum wage, and the Head Start Program for pre-school children. Billions of dollars flowed through the Powell committee. In 1964 the Civil Rights Act finally saw the core of the Powell Amendment enacted into law. From 1961 to 1967 Powell was one of the most powerful politicians in the United States, and certainly the most powerful African American. He was both an American insider and outsider, working inside the halls of Congress, and identifying with the masses who remained on the outside as one of the most riveting stump speakers in the country. He often engaged in one-upmanship with Martin Luther King, Jr. By the time his congressional career ended there would be more than 60 pieces of major legislation with his **imprimatur.**

imprimatur: mark of approval or ownership

Powell's political downfall began when, in 1960, he accused Esther James, a Harlem woman, of corruption. James successfully sued for libel. Powell refused to pay, and before he finally agreed to settle in 1966, Powell had accumulated enormous amounts of bad publicity because of his sometimes mercurial and **sybaritic** behavior. In January 1967 House members, led by southern Democrats and Republicans, refused to seat

sybaritic: luxurious

Powell until a committee could investigate his conduct, citing his indiscretions and personal lifestyle. The House committee set up to investigate Powell's conduct; the Celler Committee, chaired by New York Republican Emanuel Celler, decided to fine Powell, strip away his seniority, and have him repay money that had gone to his third wife, Yvette Diago Powell, while she had been on his payroll. The full House, however, ignored the recommendations of the Celler Committee and voted to expel Powell from Congress in March 1967. It was the first time since 1919 that the House had expelled one of its members. Powell vowed to fight the case all the way to the Supreme Court. He won a special election in March 1967 to fill his own vacant seat, and was re-elected in 1968, though he remained outside of Congress. In 1968 he barnstormed the United States, rallying black and white students on college campuses to fight for equality and end American involvement in Vietnam, peppering his defense with his catchphrase, "Keep the faith, baby." He was mentioned in 1968 as a favorite-son presidential candidate from New York. In 1969, in his last decision from the Supreme Court, Chief Justice Earl Warren ruled that Adam Clayton Powell had been unconstitutionally expelled from Congress. Back in Congress, however, Powell was without the power he had once yielded, returning as a freshman, because the Court had not ruled on the matter of his seniority and lost back pay. In 1970 he lost his last reelection bid to Charles Rangel by 150 votes. He spent the last two years of his life on the island of Bimini, in the Bahamas, where he said he was working on his memoirs, which never were published. He died of cancer in a Miami hospital on April 4, 1972, four years to the day from Martin Luther King's death. ◆

The full House, however, ignored the recommendations of the Celler Committee and voted to expel Powell from Congress in March 1967.

Rabi'a

713–714 OR 717 C.E. ● MUSLIM

Rabi'a, a Muslim Sufi woman, was born at Basra (in present-day Iraq) where she spent most of her life and where she was buried in 801 C.E. She is known as Rabi'a Basri on account of her birth-place, but also as Rabi'a Al-'Adawiyah or Al-Qaisiya because she belonged to Al-'Atik, a tribe of Qais b. 'Adi.

Rabi'a's image is shrouded in legends, including stories of miracles brought about by her intense devotion to God. But as sketchy as the historical details of her life are, they point to an extraordinary personality. Probably a fourth (*rabi'a*) daughter, she was born into extreme poverty. Orphaned at a young age, she was sold into slavery for a paltry sum. She served her master by day but spent most of her nights fasting and praying to God. Once aware of her profound piety, her master released her from bondage.

Among Rabi'a's devotees who lived a **celibate,** highly austere life were spiritual and temporal leaders of her time. But though many sought her prayers or guidance, she solicited no help from anyone, including God, despite the fact that her life was filled with **penury,** hardship, and physical afflictions. Her prayers, including the following, reflect an all-consuming passion for God that makes even Heaven and Hell irrelevant: "O my Lord, if I worship Thee from fear of Hell, burn me in Hell, and if I worship Thee from hope of Paradise, exclude me

celibate: description of an individual who abstains from sexual intercourse

penury: a state of severe poverty

315

thence, but if I worship Thee for Thine own sake then withhold not from me Thine Eternal Beauty."

Rabi'a, one of the earliest and most outstanding Sufi saints in an age of saints, whose name is used to refer to women who attain the highest spiritual station in any age, has been a source of inspiration to many mystics, including her biographer Farid ud-Din 'Attar who, in his famous poem (*The Conference of the Birds*, pays her the high compliment of being the "Crown of Men" (Taj ar-Rijal). ◆

Raiser, Konrad

1938– ● GERMAN EVANGELICAL CHURCH

The Reverend Dr. Konrad Raiser took on the top post of the World Council of Churches (WCC) in 1993, a time of great challenge for Christian churches. The WCC is a fellowship of churches that numbered more than 330 by the close of 1999. Member churches represent nearly all Christian traditions from more than 100 countries in all continents. Protestant leaders formed the World Council of Churches in 1948 to promote Christian unity. This search for unity, which grew through the 1900s, is known as the ecumenical movement.

Konrad Raiser belonged to the German Evangelical Church (EKD). He was born on January 25, 1938, in Magdeburg, Germany, about 75 miles southwest of Berlin. His father, Ludwig Raiser, a well-known law professor, served a term as president of the national synod of the EKD. Raiser spent his childhood in the towns of Schwerin, Gottingen, and Bonn-Bad Godesberg. After graduating from high school in Tubingen, a town south of Stuttgart, in 1957, Raiser worked for six months at a steel mill in Dortmund.

Following the high educational standards of his family, Raiser distinguished himself academically. He began studying theology in Tubingen in 1957, moving on to a theological school in Bethel, and later to the universities of Heidelberg and Zurich. He finished his academic theological education in Tubingen in February 1963. In 1965–66, he studied sociology and social psychology at Harvard University in Cambridge,

> "We are in search of a new language, a fresh vision. My sense is that the basic vitality of the ecumenical movement is still there. It needs to be crystalized."
>
> Konrad Raiser, quoted in *The Christian Century*, 1993.

Massachusetts. Back in Germany, he worked from 1967–69 as a university assistant in practical theology at the Protestant theological faculty in Tubingen, earning a doctorate in theology in 1970.

Raiser was ordained in May 1964. In 1965, he finished pastoral training that had included working as an assistant pastor in the Evangelical Church in Wurttemberg. In March 1967, Raiser married Elisabeth von Weizsacker. The Raisers have four sons: Martin (1967), Ulrich (1970), Simon (1974), and Christoph (1978).

Raiser's ties with the WCC began in 1969, when he joined their staff in Geneva, Switzerland, working on the Commission on Faith and Order. In 1973, he was appointed deputy general secretary, working under general secretary Philip Potter. Raiser returned to Germany in 1983 to become a professor of theology and ecumenics at the University of the Ruhr in Bochum. He also served as director of the faculty's Ecumenical Institute. Among other positions, Raiser worked on the WCC's World Convocation on Justice, Peace, and the Integrity of Creation in Seoul, South Korea, in 1990, and attended the WCC's Seventh Assembly in Canberra, Australia, in 1991 as a delegate of his church.

In August 1992, the WCC Central Committee elected Raiser as General Secretary, the organization's top post. He assumed his post in January 1993, and in September 1996 was re-elected for a second five-year term, which runs until the end of 2002. Declaring that the future of Christianity is "likely to be shaped and influenced more in Africa and Latin America than the northern regions of historical Christianity," Raiser presided over the WCC's eighth assembly in Harare, Zimbabwe, in December 1998. The assembly also marked the 50th anniversary of the founding of the WCC in Amsterdam in 1948.

By the end of the 12–day assembly, Raiser had helped prevent a major crisis within the WCC, a possible split with its Orthodox member churches. The Orthodox, who made up about half of WCC churches, had grown disillusioned with liberal trends among the council's dominant Protestant denominations. Disputed issues included homosexuality and the role of women in the church. Raiser conceded that Christian unity was "being tested severely by conflicts over moral issues, especially regarding human sexuality." In response to the Orthodox demand, the assembly created a special commission to address their complaints. "The ecumenical movement finds itself at a

1938 Raiser is born in Germany.

1957 Raiser begins studying theology in Tubingen.

1964 Raiser is ordained.

1965 Raiser begins studying at Harvard.

1967 Raiser marries Elisabeth von Weizsacker.

1969 Raiser joins the Geneva staff of the WCC.

1970 Raiser earns his Ph.D.

1973 Raiser becomes WCC deputy general secretary.

1983 Raiser becomes professor of theology at the University of the Ruhr.

1993 Raiser becomes General Secretary of the WCC.

crossroads and in urgent need of new orientation," Raiser told the assembly.

The assembly also endorsed Raiser's goal of launching a forum that would include non–WCC churches. The forum's aim was greater unity with the Roman Catholic Church, Evangelicals, Pentecostals, Charismatics, and Third World indigenous churches. Raiser called for all Christian faiths to use the year 2000 to begin working towards a universal Christian council.

In April 1999, Raiser became the highest level international church leader to officially visit communist North Korea. During the visit, Raiser met with North Korean head of state Kim Jong- Il and representatives of the Korean Christian Federation. It was the first time the government of North Korea officially welcomed the general secretary of the WCC. The WCC gave $10 million in charity to North Korea between 1995 and 1998.

Raiser is the author of four books, including *Ecumenism in Transition: A Paradigm Shift in the Ecumenical Movement* (1991). His also wrote *To Be the Church—Challenges and Hopes for a New Millennium* (1997). ◆

Ratanasara, Havanpola

1920– ● BUDDHIST

The Venerable Havanpola Ratanasara is an elder in the Theravada Buddhist tradition of Sri Lanka. Theravada, which means Way of the Elders, is the root from which other Buddhist traditions grew. Theravadans stress the importance of Buddha as a historical figure and they focus on the monastic life. Ratanasara became a leading Buddhist figure in the United States in the 1980s and 1990s.

Ratanasara was born in 1920 in Sri Lanka, the Asian country formerly called Ceylon. He entered a Buddhist order of monks at the age of 12, beginning meditation training in a 1,500-year-old cave monastery. For many years he practiced a style of meditation called Vipassana and learned Buddhist scriptures in a master-student relationship with a Buddhist master.

Ratanasara took his final vows in 1940 at the age of 20. He then entered the University of Sri Lanka, where he earned a

BA in philosophy and Pali in 1954. Pali was a language spoken in the third century B.C.E. in Magadha, a kingdom in northern India, and said to have been spoken by the Buddha. In 1957, Ratanasara entered Columbia University in New York City, where he received an M.A. in Education. He went on to the University of London, where he earned a Ph.D. in education in 1965.

Back in his own country, Ratanasara became an active force in education, and, beginning in 1970, served as advisor to the national Ministry of Education. He also served as an advisor for various Buddhist institutions of higher learning, including training colleges for Buddhist monks. From 1961 to 1976, he was Senior Lecturer in the Departments of Education and Buddhist Studies at the University of Kelaniya in Sri Lanka. He later served as the founder and director of the Post-Graduate Institute of Buddhist Studies at the University of Sri Lanka (1976–1980). In 1977, Ratanasara served as President of the National Council for Religion and Peace in Sri Lanka in 1977. His international roles included his 1957 appointment as a delegate from Sri Lanka to the United Nations. Ratanasara became a member of the Executive Committee for UNESCO's National Commission in 1966.

Ratanasara immigrated to the United States in 1980 and settled in Los Angeles. His interest in cooperation among independent American Buddhist groups led him to found the Buddhist Sangha Council of Southern California and serve as its president. A Sangha is a community of monks, and the council is an organization of Buddhist clergy. The council's purpose was to strengthen communication and reinforce ties among the ethnic branches of Buddhism in the United States. Estimates of number of Buddhists in the United States range from 1 million to 4 million. Most American Buddhists come from sects that originate in nine Asian nations—Cambodia, China, Japan, Korea, Laos, Sri Lanka, Thailand, Tibet, and Vietnam. The three main divisions are Theravada, Mahayana, and Vadrayana.

Taking advantage of the Buddhist diversity in the Los Angeles area, Ratanasara and the Council founded the College of Buddhist Studies in 1983. Serving as both a college and a seminary, the college teaches lay people about Buddhism and offers training for monks in Buddhist philosophy, history, psychology, and language, especially Pali. The college is open to any student with a serious interest in Buddhist studies. According to the college's catalogue, Los Angeles is the only place in the

1920 — Ratanasara is born in Sri Lanka.

1940 — Ratanasara takes his final vows

1954 — Ratanasara receives a B.A. from the University of Sri Lanka.

1857 — Ratanasara enters Columbia University in New York.

1965 — Ratanasara earns a Ph.D. from the University of London.

1970 — Ratanasara begins serving as advisor to Sri Lanka's Ministry of Education.

1980 — Ratanasara immigrates to the United States.

1983 — Ratanasara helps form the College of Buddhist Studies in Los Angeles.

1987 — Ratanasara helps found the American Buddhist Congress.

world where all Buddhist denominations and ethnic traditions can be found in the same area. This allows students at the school the unique opportunity to experience Buddhism in a very broad way.

Ratanasara also helped found the American Buddhist Congress in 1987, a national council of Buddhist organizations and individuals in the United States. It is a resource and information center for American Buddhists dedicated to promoting communication and cooperation among Buddhist communities of diverse traditions. The Congress promotes good will between Buddhists and other religions by actively participating within the interfaith community. Representatives from 47 Buddhist organizations from across the nation gathered at Kwan Um Sa Temple in Los Angeles to convene the first general meeting of the Congress in 1987. They adopted a constitution, elected officers, and established committees, formally inaugurating the American Buddhist Congress. The Congress established its national office permanently in the Koreatown district of Los Angeles.

Ratanasara acted as the spokesperson for Buddhism at a formal tri-faith discussion with Catholic Pope John Paul II when he visited Los Angeles in 1987. Two years later, the Council created the pioneering Los Angeles Buddhist-Catholic Dialogue to promote understanding between the two religions. Both Catholicism and Buddhism honor the **monastic** tradition. However, in his book, *Crossing the Threshold of Hope* (1994), the pope called Buddhism a "negative" system. In 1997, Ratanasara said Buddhists "are not angry" about past Vatican statements. Some Catholic officials, he said, "are guided by old, outdated writings about Buddhism that are found in Europe."

Ratanasara joined other U.S. Buddhist monks in 1997 as they took a step toward restoring opportunities for women in the Theravadan tradition. Although nuns had been ordained in Asian countries practicing Mahayana Buddhism, by the 1100s all evidence of the *bikhshuni* order of nuns had disappeared in the countries of the Theravada Buddhist tradition. The American Buddhists sought to resurrect this order when they ordained a Massachusetts woman as a **novice** in 1987. "We are taking a bold step, because it is a very controversial issue in Sri Lanka and Thailand," said Ratanasara.

A videotape of the life and work of Ratanasara was made in 1992, called *Unity Among Buddhists, Amity Among Religions: The Life and Times of Ven. Dr. Havanpola Ratanasara*. Ratana-

monastic: relating to monasteries, monks, or nuns; resembling a secluded life

novice: person newly admitted into a religious organization or community

sara also published several books on education and Buddhism and was writing *The Path to Perfection: A Buddhist Psychological View of Personality, Growth and Development* in 1999. ◆

Romero, Oscar

1917–1980 ● CATHOLIC

Oscar Arnulfo Romero was archbishop of El Salvador from 1977 to 1980. Born in Ciudad Barrios and originally apprenticed as a carpenter, Romero's early religious inclinations won him over and in 1931 he enrolled in San Miguel seminary. In 1937 he progressed to the National Seminary, then proceeded to Rome to study at the Gregorian University. He was ordained in 1942 and began a doctorate in ascetic theology, but World War II curtailed his studies. He returned to El Salvador and served his home parish until he was elevated to monsignor in 1967.

Shortly thereafter, Romero was appointed to the National Bishops' Conference and quickly earned additional responsibilities, including auxiliary bishop (1970), editor of the archdiocesan newspaper *Orientacion* (1971), bishop of Santiago de Maria (1974), and membership on the Pontifical Commission for Latin America (1975). Even at this late date, Romero still clung to a moderate, traditional interpretation of Catholic doctrines. He warned against the dangers of a politicized priesthood and instead advocated the higher ideals of brotherhood, faith, and charity. Although he frequently quoted the teachings of the Second Vatican Council, he refrained from mentioning those of the more radical conference of Catholic bishops at Medellin in 1968.

To the surprise of many, Romero was chosen over the equally qualified Arturo Rivera y Damas as archbishop of El Salvador in February 1977. The shy, retiring new archbishop faced growing tensions between church and state, and within the church itself. Shortly after his installation, Romero's close friend Father Rutilio Grande was murdered on his way to visit parishioners. When the government failed to investigate and instead stepped up its attacks on the church by expelling several priests, Archbishop Romero withdrew his support for the government and refused to attend the presidential inauguration

1917 Romero is born in El Salvador.

1931 Romero enrolls in San Miguel seminary.

1942 Romero is ordained; his post-graduate education is cut short by WWII.

1967 Romero is elevator to monsignor in El Salvador.

1970 Romero becomes auxiliary bishop.

1971 Romero becomes editor of the archdiocesan newspaper.

1974 Romero becomes Bishop of Santiago de Maria.

1977 Romero is chosen as Archbishop of El Salvador.

1980 Romero is assassinated while saying evening mass.

of Carlos Humberto Romero (no relation) in 1977. Despite the rising tide of violence, Romero still tried to distance the church from the new Liberation Theology and denied the priests permission to participate in political organizations. As the situation deteriorated, Romero's position became untenable and the moderate archbishop metamorphosed into an impassioned crusader against the violation of human rights in El Salvador. He used his sermons to preach the equality and dignity of all peoples and set up a commission to monitor and document the abuses of power by governmental authorities.

For Romero's efforts the British Parliament nominated him for the Nobel Peace Prize. In February 1980 Romero angered the Vatican by speaking out against U.S. military aid to El Salvador, which he claimed would lead to further human rights abuses. On 24 March he was assassinated while saying evening mass. His death removed a powerful voice for peace in El Salvador and contributed to the bitterness of the struggle. Archbishop Romero remains a powerful symbol of the new direction of the Catholic Church in Latin America. ◆

Russell, Charles Taze

1852–1916 ● RUSSELITE, JEHOVAH'S WITNESSES

Charles Taze Russell began the organization that in 1931 took the name Jehovah's Witnesses. Although modern members of the religion do not call Russell their founder, but rather "general organizer," his followers were long called Russellites. Russell was born on February 16, 1852, in Allegheny, Pennsylvania, now a part of Pittsburgh. His parents, Joseph L. and Ana Eliza (Birney) Russell were both of Scotch-Irish descent and raised Charles as a Presbyterian. His mother died when Charles was nine, and by his teens, Charles was working with his father in his clothing business. As a teen, Charles rebelled against the religious teachings of his youth, especially the doctrine of eternal punishment. He encountered and was inspired by Adventists, who believed in the imminent return of Jesus. He studied the Bible independently for several years, concluding that the Bible did not support the concept of eternal punishment.

In 1870, Russell formed a Bible study group and soon attracted followers in the Pittsburgh area. Russell published his ideas in a pamphlet called *The Object and Manner of Our Lord's Return* (1877). He distributed his document, which stated that Jesus had returned to earth in invisible form in 1874. In 1879, he began publishing a magazine called *The Watch Tower and Herald of Christ's Presence*, which survives today as *The Watchtower*. In 1884, Russell and his associates incorporated the forerunner of today's Watch Tower Bible and Tract Society as their governing body, with Russell as president.

Russell published *Millennial Dawn* in 1886, declaring that the Second Coming of Jesus had already occurred. True Christians were to preach judgement and wait for the final defeat of the forces of evil in a cosmic battle to come. Subtitled, "The Plan of the Ages," his book became a six-volume series of scripture studies. Russell traveled throughout the Unites States, Canada, and Europe preaching and establishing churches.

Russell met with legal adversity beginning in 1909 when his wife of 30 years, Maria Frances Ackley, sued him for divorce. She alleged that Russell had conducted himself immorally with female church members. The divorce was granted and never revoked despite five legal appeals by Russell. Following his divorce, Russell moved his headquarters to Brooklyn, New York, where he bought an old chapel under the Brooklyn Bridge. In 1911, the *Brooklyn Daily Eagle* newspaper reported on Russell's sale of "Miracle Wheat," at $60 per bushel, which was supposed to possess exceptional agricultural qualities. Russell sued the newspaper for $100,000 in damages but lost the case.

"Pastor Russell," as followers called him, traveled extensively for the rest of his life, visiting his churches all over the world. The 64-year-old Russell died suddenly of a heart attack on a train near Pampa, Texas, on October 31, 1916. According to *The Watchtower*, Russell's last words were "Please wrap me in

1831 Russell is born in Pennsylvania.

1870 Russell forms a Bible study group.

1877 Russell spreads his ideas in a pamphlet called *The Object and Manner of Our Lord's Return.*

1879 Russell begins publishing *The Watch Tower* magazine.

1884 Russell and his followers incorporate their organization.

1886 Russell publishes *Millennial Dawn.*

1909 Russell's wife sues him for divorce.

1916 Russell dies of a heart attack

a Roman toga." His request was fulfilled using sheets from the Pullman train.

Russell's primary teaching was that Jesus had returned to earth in 1874, and that since then the world was living in the "Millennial Age" or "Day of Jehovah." Jesus was to begin his invisible reign in 1914, a year that would be marked by great social upheaval and the end of the world. Upon Russell's death, his legal advisor, Joseph Franklin Rutherford, took over leadership of the group. Rutherford defended Russell's prediction of a cataclysm in 1914 by arguing that Satan had been defeated in a war that began in heaven in 1914 and afterward had been banished by God to reign on earth.

In 1931, Russell's movement took the name Jehovah's Witnesses from the Old Testament Book of Isaiah, which says "Ye are my witnesses, saith Jehovah, and I am God." The Witnesses believe in one God, called Jehovah, and use the Bible as their sole guide to belief. They obey Jesus' command to preach the "good news of the Kingdom," mainly by visiting door to door and distributing literature on street corners. The meeting places of Jehovah's Witnesses are called Kingdom Halls. *The Watchtower* is printed in more than 100 languages, and the group claims a worldwide membership of about 5.8 million. They remain headquartered in Brooklyn.

Today, Jehovah's Witnesses believe that Jesus did begin his invisible reign in 1914. They await a final battle of God, Jesus, and the angels against the forces of evil led by Satan. Evil will be defeated in that battle of Armageddon, after which Jesus will rule the earth for 1,000 years. According to Jehovah's Witnesses, the dead will rise, and all people will have a second chance to achieve salvation. At the close of the millennium, Satan will return to earth, and he and his followers will be destroyed. God's chosen people will then enjoy a perfect paradise on earth eternally. ◆

Russell, Robert John

1946– ● SCIENTIST AND THEOLOGIAN

Robert John Russell is a physicist and theologian whose desire to explore ways of relating theology and science led to the founding of The Center for Theology and the

Natural Sciences, a non-profit organization in Berkeley, California. The center sponsors public forums, graduate-level courses, and research conferences that bring together scientists, theologians, technologists, and the general public to tackle some of the most profound questions facing humankind, such as how the universe began and what the ultimate nature of human existence is. Russell has served as the center's director since its inception.

Russell was born on August 23, 1946, in Los Angeles, California. As a child he developed a passion for space and science, and at the age of eight he announced to his parents that he wanted to become a theoretical physicist. Shortly after his twelfth birthday his father died unexpectedly, leaving Russell with a deep sense of loss and sparking in him questions about the meaning of death and one's faith in God.

In 1964 Russell entered Stanford University, and although he had graduated with the highest SAT scores in the history of his high school, he suddenly found school life intensely competitive and challenging. At the same time he was tremendously stimulated by his studies and somehow still found time to take courses in the arts and humanities. Russell graduated from Stanford in 1968 with a B.S in physics and completed his M.A. in physics at the University of California at Los Angeles in 1970. An interest in religion also led him to pursue a degree in theology, and in 1972, he received his M.A. in theology from Pacific School of Religion in Berkeley, and was ordained to ministry in higher education with the United Church of Christ. While studying theology, Russell met Charlotte Stott, a seminary student at the school. Russell and Charlotte were married in 1969 and later had two children.

In 1978 Russell completed his Ph.D. in physics from the University of California at Santa Cruz. As he became more immersed in science, the theology he knew became less and less adequate as an explanation of the universe he had come to understand, and he came to feel that theological doctrines should be taken as scientific theories—open to testing and revision. At the same time, he understood that science alone did not have all the answers.

Russell began his academic career as an assistant professor of physics at Carleton College in Minnesota in 1978, where he also worked for the campus ministry, counseling students. Three years later he accepted a post as assistant professor in residence of theology and science at the Graduate Theological

> "We are at a crucial time in this dialogue when old conflicts are disappearing, retrenchment into watertight compartments has proven barren, and now both sides are eager to discover increased understanding, shared insights, and a compelling future vision of the world and its physical processes as infused with the presence of the always creating and redeeming God."
>
> Robert John Russell, 1997

> "Everywhere the spirit of God is at work bringing the physical and biological world to greater and greater degrees of complexity, even if there is no overriding directionality or explicit purpose to the overall pattern of life on earth."
>
> Robert John Russell, 1997

Union (GTU), an **ecumenical** seminary community and graduate school in religious studies in Berkeley. Russell was made full professor in residence in 1992, a post he holds to the present day. In 1981, Russell founded The Center for Theology and Natural Sciences (CTNS). Since that time, in addition to his duties as professor and director of the CTNS, he has written many articles and essays on issues related to science and religion, and has edited a number of books, including *Chaos and Complexity: Scientific Perspectives on Divine Action.* ◆

Rutherford, Joseph Franklin

1869–1942 ● Jehovah's Witnesses

Joseph Franklin Rutherford took over leadership of the Jehovah's Witnesses after the organization's founder, Charles Taze Russell, died in 1916. Jehovah's Witnesses believe that the world began as a place of happiness and peace under God's rule, but Satan rebelled and led humanity astray. After Jesus suffered his sacrificial death on earth, he began his "heavenly rule" in 1914. Witnesses believe God will take vengeance upon the wicked in our time, defeating Satan in a battle of **Armageddon.** After the battle, believers in God will remain to populate the earth with righteous people. A special group of 144,000 people (the number is based upon a passage in the New Testament Book of Revelation) will rule with Christ from heaven.

Joseph Franklin Rutherford was born of Baptist parents in Boonville, Missouri, on November 8, 1869. At age 16, Rutherford's father agreed to let him go to college if he paid his own tuition and also paid for a laborer to take his place on the farm. Rutherford studied law and became licensed as a lawyer in Missouri in 1882. Later he became a judge. In the 1900s, he converted to the beliefs of Charles T. Russell, the leader of a religious group often called Russellites. Rutherford became legal advisor to the group in 1907.

In 1916, Russell died, and Rutherford succeeded him as president of the Russellite Watch Tower Bible and Tract Society. Rutherford reorganized the religious group, introducing a system that placed greater authority in the hands of "spiritually qualified" members. In 1931, the group officially took the name

Jehovah's Witnesses. Under Rutherford, the Jehovah's Witnesses broadened the practice of door-to-door preaching and proselytizing.

The Witnesses oppose what they consider to be the three allies of Satan: churches, governments, and big business. They do not salute the flag, bear arms in war, or participate in government. This stance led to a nine-month prison confinement for Rutherford for counseling young men not to join the military in 1917, when the United States entered World War I. During World War II (1939–1945), their anti-government beliefs brought the Witnesses head-to-head with one of history's most evil leaders, German dictator Adolf Hitler. After Hitler became Germany's chancellor on January 30, 1933, thousands of German Witnesses were branded as accomplices in an alleged Communist-Jewish conspiracy and authorities began a campaign of persecution against them. The Witnesses endured threats, interrogations, and house searches.

Rutherford decided to mount a campaign to inform Hitler and the German public that Jehovah's Witnesses posed no threat. Witnesses from all over Germany gathered in Berlin on June 25, 1933, and adopted a resolution called the "Declaration of Facts" protesting the restrictions that had been placed on them. Some Witnesses were arrested and sent to labor camps.

On February 9, 1934, Rutherford sent a letter to Hitler stating, "You may successfully resist any and all men, but you cannot successfully resist Jehovah God.... In the name of Jehovah God and His anointed King, Christ Jesus, I demand that you give order to all officials and servants of your government that Jehovah's witnesses in Germany be permitted to peaceably assemble and without hindrance worship God." The Nazis stepped up abuses, sending many Jehovah's Witnesses to concentration camps. Witnesses continued to defy the German government. According to the Witnesses' written history, Hitler himself screamed, "This brood will be exterminated in Germany!"

Rutherford appeared regularly on radio, delivering lectures on the satanic nature of Nazism. On October 2, 1938, he delivered the address "Fascism or Freedom," in which he denounced Hitler in no uncertain terms. Although the American public was largely unaware of the existence of the concentration camps until 1945, according to Witness sources, detailed descriptions of them appeared often in Watch Tower publications

1869 Rutherford is born in Missouri.

1882 Rutherford becomes a licensed lawyer.

1907 Rutherford becomes legal advisor to the Russellites.

1916 Rutherford succeeds Charles Taze Russell as head of the Watch Tower Bible and Tract Society.

1931 The group takes the name Jehovah's Witnesses.

1933 Germany's Jehovah's Witnesses adopt the "Declaration of Facts" in opposition to Adolf Hitler.

1934 Rutherford sends Hitler a letter of defiance.

1938 Rutherford denounces Hitler on the radio.

1942 Rutherford dies shortly after surgery for colon cancer.

in the 1930s. There were a recorded 6,034 Jehovah's Witnesses in Germany during World War II, of which 5,911 were arrested. Many were brutally tortured, and about 2,000 were murdered.

The Witnesses also met resistance for their beliefs in the United States. Between 1940 and 1943, their refusal to perform patriotic rites led to three important civil liberties cases argued before the U.S. Supreme Court. In 1943, the court upheld their right to such refusal.

In 1942, Rutherford underwent surgery for colon cancer. He retired to his Spanish-style mansion in San Diego, built for him years earlier so he could recover from pneumonia in a dry climate. Rutherford died there on January 8, 1942. ◆

Schenirer, Sarah

1883–1935 ● JEWISH

Sarah Schenirer was a pioneer in religious education for Jewish females and founder of Bais Ya'akov educational institutions. Born to a Belzer Hasidic family in Krakow, Poland, descendant of rabbinic scholars, Schenirer was a devout Jew who worked as a seamstress by day and spent her evenings in the private study of biblical texts and rabbinic legends, a discipline begun in her youth. This was unusual for a woman in her times and even as a child she was affectionately teased as "the little pious one."

In 1914, inspired by a sermon, Schenirer conceived the idea of Jewish classes for women. Until that time, Jewish education in eastern Europe was designed exclusively for men, inasmuch as rabbinic tradition interpreted the commandment to study Torah as incumbent upon males only. But Schenirer's religious fervor and love of sacred texts, combined with her fear of the inroads of cultural assimilation, secular Zionism, and Polish feminism, led her to radical innovation: the creation of a school that would both increase the knowledge and strengthen the faith of young Jewish women.

Despite initial setbacks, Schenirer persisted. In 1918 she opened her first school in her home, with two young aides whom she sent off after a year to establish schools in other communities. In 1919, the Orthodox Agudat Yisra'el movement adopted and expanded the network of Bais Ya'akov (Yid-

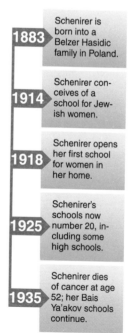

1883 ▶ Schenirer is born into a Belzer Hasidic family in Poland.

1914 ▶ Schenirer conceives of a school for Jewish women.

1918 ▶ Schenirer opens her first school for women in her home.

1925 ▶ Schenirer's schools now number 20, including some high schools.

1935 ▶ Schenirer dies of cancer at age 52; her Bais Ya'akov schools continue.

On September 5, 1866, the New Synagogue, called die Neue Synagoge in German, was opened on Oranienburger Strasse in Berlin, Germany. Built in a rich Moorish style with a gold-latticed dome, it seated 3,200 people. The New Synagogue was the second Jewish house of worship in Berlin, erected for use by liberal Jews who followed a reformed rite and abolished the traditional separation of men and women. The New Synagogue was damaged by Nazi thugs on Kristallnacht (November 9–10, 1938) but remained basically intact and was used as a synagogue until March 30, 1940, when it was taken over by the German army. On November 22, 1943, the synagogue was severely damaged by Allied bombing. In 1958 the East German government tore down what was left of the synagogue, supposedly for safety reasons. In a change of policy, however, East Germany began the reconstruction of the synagogue in 1988. On May 7, 1995 the New Synagogue reopened as a cultural institution. It serves as a museum of the history of the synagogue and of the Jews in and around Berlin, and as a Jewish community center.

dish for House of Jacob). By 1925, 20 schools were operating, including several high schools. In combining religious studies with secular and professional training, Bais Ya'akov represented a synthesis of Polish Hasidic piety and Western enlightenment.

Schenirer soon relinquished executive duties but remained a central figure in the movement, a role model and personal source of inspiration to the students. She also founded the Bais Ya'akov Teachers' Seminary and established the Bnos (Daughters) Youth Organization for religious females.

Little is known of her personal life. Her first marriage ended in divorce; a primary factor in the couple's incompatibility was that her husband was less religiously committed and observant than she. She had no children and died of cancer at the age of 52.

The Bais Ya'akov movement suffered a terrible blow in the Holocaust during World War II. Most of the students and teachers who had been involved with Basis Ya'akov between 1918 and 1939 did not survive. After the war, Basis Ya'akov and Bnos were reestablished and expanded in the United States, Israel, and Europe—with more of an eye, however, to conserving tradition than to bridging tradition and modernity, as was its aim in Schenirer's lifetime. ◆

Schuller, Robert

1926– ● REFORMED CHURCH IN AMERICA

E
vangelist Robert Schuller has reigned as one of America's most famous preachers as his *Hour of Power* became the most widely watched religious television program in the United States. By the late 1990s, his show reached about 30 million viewers worldwide.

Schuller was born September 16, 1926, in Alton, Iowa. He was the son of a farmer, Anthony Schuller, and his wife, Jennie Beltman Schuller. Robert received his Bachelor of Arts degree from Hope College in 1947 and a Master of Divinity Degree from Western Theological Seminary in 1950. Both schools are in Holland, Michigan, and are run by the Reformed Church in America, a Protestant religion in the United States and Canada comprised originally of settlers from the Netherlands. Schuller later earned a Doctorate of Divinity at Hope College in 1973.

Schuller fulfilled his lifelong dream when the Reformed Church ordained him in 1950, and he took his first post as pas-

> "This is my challenge, and the challenge of the Crystal Cathedral congregation, in the new century- to let people everywhere know that God is alive! Yes, my message in the Year 2000 A.D. is to encourage people everywhere to put a new face on their faith."
>
> Robert Schuller, 2000

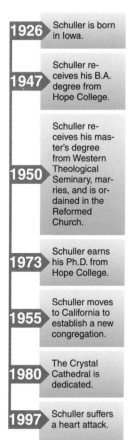

1926 Schuller is born in Iowa.

1947 Schuller receives his B.A. degree from Hope College.

1950 Schuller receives his master's degree from Western Theological Seminary, marries, and is ordained in the Reformed Church.

1973 Schuller earns his Ph.D. from Hope College.

1955 Schuller moves to California to establish a new congregation.

1980 The Crystal Cathedral is dedicated.

1997 Schuller suffers a heart attack.

"I'm popular because I bolster people up and give them hope."
Robert Schuller, 1995.

tor of the Ivanhoe Reformed Church in Chicago. Also that year, Schuller married Arvella DeHaan. During Schuller's five-year ministry at Ivanhoe, his congregation grew from 38 to about 500.

Following that success, in 1955 Schuller set out for Garden Grove, California, to found a new Reformed congregation. With just $500 and Arvella as his organist, Schuller rented the Orange Drive-in Theater near Disneyland and conducted Sunday services from the roof of the theater's snack bar. He invited folks to the new Garden Grove Community Church with the slogan, "Come as you are, in the family car." His first Easter service drew 50 people, who viewed from their cars.

Schuller broke new ground as one of the first evangelists to buy television time to preach. These televangelists, as they became known, were drawn to Southern California by the abundance of entertainment technology and the area's large base of religious conservatives. The shows often feature a television audience as congregation. Schuller's show, *Hour of Power,* became extremely popular. Arvella, always a strong part of her husband's ministry, became the executive producer of his television program. As Schuller's congregation grew, he successfully appealed to his television audience to donate over $18 million to build the Crystal Cathedral on his Garden Grove estate. The huge and flashy cathedral was dedicated in 1980.

Schuller's preaching style centered largely on the power of positive thinking. While other preachers focused on fundamentalist themes of damnation and repentance, Schuller addressed his California audiences with messages of positive possibilities and raising self-esteem.

On December 25, 1997, Schuller returned to the Crystal Cathedral after suffering a heart attack earlier that month. Before more than 3,000 celebrants at the Crystal Cathedral, Schuller, 71, delivered his Christmas sermon, as he had for 42 consecutive years. The overflow crowd filled a 500-seat tent erected next to the church, reminding visitors of the tents at old-time revival meetings.

When Robert and Arvella celebrated their 48th wedding anniversary in June 1998, their family consisted of their 5 children and 17 grandchildren. Their only son, Robert Anthony, also became an ordained minister of the Reformed Church in America and had been announced as Dr. Schuller's future successor.

By the late 1990s, Schuller had helped make Southern California the center of television evangelism. Trinity Broadcast-

Crystal Cathedral

The Crystal Cathedral in Garden Grove, California, is home to the Crystal Cathedral Ministries, which claims a congregation of over 10,000 members. It is also home to the internationally televised Sunday morning *Hour of Power,* hosted by Rev. Robert Schuller. Dedicated in 1980, the more than $18-million church was designed by architect Philip Johnson. The building's shape is a four-pointed star, with walls of more than 10,000 silver-colored panes of glass, all reflecting light at different angles. The glass is held in place by a lacy frame of white steel beams. Two 90-foot-high doors open electronically behind the pulpit to allow morning sunlight and breezes to enrich worship services. The building is longer than a football field, more than 120 feet high, and seats nearly 3,000 people. On the tenth anniversary of the cathedral, a bell tower was dedicated. The tower is comprised of polished stainless steel prisms and houses a 52-bell carillon (set of bells).

ing Network (TBN), which beamed telecasts of Schuller's Crystal Cathedral services around the world, built new world headquarters. The elaborate, state-of-the-art broadcasting complex resembled a fairy castle, featuring a sweeping marble staircase and a 15-foot statue of Michael the Archangel stomping the head of Satan. As the world's largest Christian television network, TBN was the center for more than 700 broadcast, cable, and satellite affiliates around the globe.

Being in a media capital put celebrities within easy reach, and the *Hour of Power* hosted such diverse guests as singer Naomi Judd, poet Maya Angelou, musician John Tesh, and former Los Angeles Dodgers manager Tommy Lasorda. Schuller has authored more than 30 books, including five that appeared on *The New York Times* bestseller list. Schuller's numerous honors include two Freedom Foundation Awards, the Religious Heritage of America's Clergyman of the Year, Awards of Excellence for Religion in Media, and Peacemaker Awards. His board affiliations include the Guild of Architects of the American Institute of Architects, Board of Counselors of the YMCA, and National Council of Christians and Jews. ◆

Serra, Junipero

1713–1784 ● CATHOLIC

1713 Serra is born.

1731 Serra takes his formal vows.

1744 Serra wins a teaching position at Palma's Lullian University.

1769 Serra leads the Franciscans into Alta, California.

1769 Serra establishes the first of nine missions in California.

1784 Serra dies.

1985 Serra's long canonization begins when the Pope proclaims him "Venerable."

Junipero Serra, born Miguel Serra, was known as the "apostle of California" for his missionary efforts in Alta California. He initiated the Spanish mission system that, at his death, included nine missions with 4,600 Indian residents.

Serra came from humble origins. Part of his family was descended from *conversos*, Jews who had been forcibly converted to Roman Catholicism in 1492. Perhaps because of this heritage, and because of his small stature, the Franciscans delayed in admitting him to probationary status. At the age of 16, however, he was at last admitted at the town of Palma. A year later, in 1731, he took his formal vows and the name Junipero from one of the companions of Francis of Assisi, founder of the order.

Serra flourished in the religious environment and earned a reputation for oratory, piety, and intelligence. After advanced training, he won a teaching position in moral philosophy at Palma's Lullian University in 1744. Five years later, at the age of 35, he became a missionary to the Indians of New Spain (Mexico). Serra labored tirelessly in the missions of the Sierra Gorda region of Queretaro for 20 years before leading the Franciscans into Alta California in 1769, at the age of 55.

Serra served as first Father President of the system, which established nine successful missions: San Diego (1769), San Carlos Borromeo (1770), San Antonio (1771), San Gabriel (1771), San Luis Obispo (1772), San Francisco (1776), San

Juan Capistrano (1776), Santa Clara (1777), and San Buenaventura (1782). These missions sought to bring Indians into Spanish society by converting them to Christianity and teaching them "civilized" European life styles. Indians were induced to leave their native cultures and then submerged in Spanish-Christian culture in an environment of European work and agriculture coupled with religious instruction. Serra loved the Indians but believed them to be of limited intelligence and subject to sin that necessitated correction. Legally, Franciscans stood as Spanish fathers to their Indian children, and disobedience, either civil or religious, was frequently corrected by corporal punishment, including **flogging.**

flogging: beating with a rod or whip

Because of Serra's success at mission building and his reputation for holiness, the bishop of Monterey, California, proposed him for sainthood in 1935. The slow process of canonization, the three-step sequence by which sainthood is conferred, began in 1985 when the pope proclaimed Serra "Venerable," meaning that he had lived a life of "heroic virtue" by church standards. Descendants of the Mission Indians and others protested his canonization by claiming that Serra abused Indians in the missions and destroyed native cultures. Serra's advocates pointed to his self-sacrifice and love of Indians and asked that he be judged by the standards of his day rather than by those of the present. ◆

Seton, Elizabeth Ann

1774–1821 ● CATHOLIC

Elizabeth Ann Seton (Elizabeth Ann Bayley) was a Roman Catholic saint and American religious figure. Seton was born in New York City to a wealthy and distin-

guished family. As a young woman, her concern for the sick and poor earned her the title of Protestant sister of charity. Her father was a well-known area physician who brought his children up in an Episcopal home.

In 1794 she married William M. Seton, a merchant, and in the ensuing years the couple had five children. In 1803 the family traveled to Italy to care for William's ailing health, but he failed to recuperate and died. Seton was left to mourn her husband in a foreign country, and was taken in by the Filicchi family, who were old acquaintances. The Filicchis were Roman Catholics, and it was their devotion that eventually led Seton to the Roman Catholic church. She returned to the United States and after an inner, spiritual struggle, she joined the Catholic church in 1805, becoming a member of Saint Peter's congregation in New York City. Her choice was not popular among her friends, most of whom were influenced by the anti-Catholic sentiment of that era.

In 1808 she moved to Baltimore, where she opened a grade school for girls. Several young women were placed under her care, and they soon took vows to be the Sisters of Charity of Saint Joseph. She moved the school to Emmitsburg, Maryland, in 1810 and opened the first free parochial school in the United States for both boys and girls, laying the foundation for the American parochial school system. In her work for the Sisters of Charity, as the organization was now called, Seton brought many black children into the school. She was now called Mother Seton, although she was allowed to keep legal guardianship over her natural children. Through her work with the Sisters of Charity, Seton became known as the mother of American Catholic sister-school nuns, as well as the mother of the parochial school system in the United States.

Her legacy outlived her. In 1852 the Sisters of Charity founded an orphanage, and in 1907 the case for her beatification was opened. In 1963 she was canonized by Cardinal Francis Spellman. In 1975, Pope Paul VI waived the usual requirement of four miracles for sainthood, and declared that in the case of Seton, three miracles were enough. Thus, she became the first native-born American saint of the Roman Catholic church. Her feast day is January 4. ◆

Shembe, Isaiah

c. 1870–1935 ● Zulu amaNazaretha

Isaiah Shembe was founder of the Zulu amaNazaretha church and the most outstanding figure in the independent church movement in South Africa. The large majority of the 3,000 African independent churches are either "Ethiopian" or "Zionist." The Ethiopian churches are carbon copies of mission-related churches (mainly of a Methodist or Congregational type) that have seceded from white mission churches over the issue of **apartheid** in the church. The Zionist churches, whose name implies an identification with the holy mountain of Zion in the Old Testament, are largely charismatic prophet-led healing groups. Worship in the Zionist churches is an African variant of Pentecostal spirituality. Shembe is the outstanding personality associated with a very small group of churches, often referred to as African "messianic" churches, where the leader is ascribed by his followers with supernatural powers.

apartheid: legally enforced social and economic separation of groups, usually between races of people

Fountains and mountains are the holy places where these prophets generally receive their calling. Shembe was told by a voice to climb a mountain, and it directed him to a cave where he had a dream. From this lofty position he was invited by the voice to survey the earth, and he there discovered his own putrefying corpse. The voice warned him against sexual sins, and he woke up exclaiming, "I have seen Jehovah.'" This experience on the mountain was to remain with him as a determinative factor throughout his life. By a divine call he had been set apart for a prophetic task on behalf of the Zulu.

These were turbulent times in Zulu society and South African politics, and Shembe was closely related to Meseni Qwabe, one of the militant leaders of the Zulu "reluctant rebel-

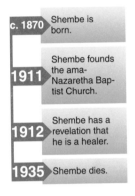

c. 1870 — Shembe is born.

1911 — Shembe founds the ama-Nazaretha Baptist Church.

1912 — Shembe has a revelation that he is a healer.

1935 — Shembe dies.

lion" of 1906. At the same time he met W. M. Leshega, a leader of a newly formed African Baptist church, who was also one of the leaders of the "Ethiopian" movement. In 1911 Shembe founded his own organization, the amaNazaretha Baptist Church, which differed from Leshega's organization on one elementary point: Saturday rather than Sunday was observed as the holy day of the week.

In 1912, Shembe once again had a revelation and was compelled to climb a particular mountain, called Inhlangakazi, located inland from the city of Durban. This mountain retreat lasted 12 days. During that time Shembe felt that he was being challenged by mysterious and supernatural powers, but he met all their temptations with the answer. "No, I am waiting for Jehovah." Angels then brought him heavenly food in the form of bread and wine; having received these gifts, he knew that he had acquired a new identity and was now a new man. When he returned to his people he also discovered that he had received a new and surprising power, one which he interpreted as the characteristic gift of Jesus of Nazareth: that of driving out demons and healing the sick. To Shembe, these were fundamental experiences: the pilgrimage to the mountain with its asceticism and its nearness to God, the identification with Moses who had climbed another mountain and was then received as the liberator of his people, and the acquisition of the power of healing. He was now ready for his task as a prophet to his people.

Compared with other African charismatic church leaders, Shembe's originality stands out on a number of points. Especially noteworthy is his creative use of traditional Zulu culture in the life of worship within the church. During church festivals the whole congregation, divided into different gender and age-groups and arrayed in traditional Zulu dress, expresses its collective religious experience in a slow-moving, dignified, and solemn dance. The annual pilgrimage to the Inhlangakazi mountain provided an opportunity for intense group cohesion of the multitude arriving from near and far.

Hymns in other independent and mission-related churches are sometimes just mechanical translations of Anglo-Saxon revival songs or ancient ecclesiastical rhymes. Shembe's hymns, on the other hand, convey the very heartbeat of Zulu religious experience from birth to death. Shembe was highly auditive;

new hymns—both lyrics and melodies combined—often came to him while he was sleeping. This was, indeed, his strongest motive for learning the art of writing. Having remained illiterate until he was roughly 40 years of age, Shembe acquired this new ability in order to commit to writing these irresistible songs that would well up from his unconscious: solemn, simple, and searching. His congregation—probably without exception—shared the feeling of being healed by the prophet, by his incisive exorcism, and his healing hand, mesmerizing the expectant crowd with his mystical black veil.

The title Shembe claimed for himself was that of "the Servant," sent by the Lord to his deprived and despised Zulu people: "But I alone come from afar, / Sent by the Lord among you." Just as Moses and Jesus had been sent to the Jews, so the Servant was sent to the Zulu. What once was biblical experience had now become a Zulu reality. "So it is also today / on the hilltops of Ohlange" (Ohlange being the place where Shembe built his church center called Ekuphakameni). In a manner that can easily be misinterpreted, he draws a comparison between himself and the biblical archetypes Moses and Jesus. One of his hymns comes close to being a creed for the Nazaretha church. It begins "I believe in the Father and the Holy Spirit / and the communion of saints of the Nazaretha." Here the Son is omitted so as to provide room for the Servant of the Spirit. But it is important to emphasize that while referring to his own role as a servant, healer, and helper, he is at the same time aware of Christ on the throne in heaven. Shembe knew that he himself, "having come with nothing and leaving with nothing," would stand before the judgment seat of God.

In order to understand Shembe's relationship to Jesus the Christ one must recall that in hierarchial Zulu society, a visitor could not directly approach the king but first had to turn to junior chiefs whose task it was to introduce the visitor to the ultimate authority. According to Nazaretha belief, this is the task of Servant Shembe in heaven, concerning the approach to the King of Kings on the throne. The Zulu prophet is seen as having a mediating role. In the words of Shembe's hymns there is ambiguity and richness of meaning. And those words, no less than the totality of Shembe's religious practice, must of course be understood in the context from which they emerged: in the worship and struggle of the Nazaretha community. ◆

> In a manner that can easily be misinterpreted, Shembe draws a comparison between himself and the biblical archetypes Moses and Jesus.

Smith, Joseph

1805–1844 ● MORMON

Joseph Smith was the founder of the Church of Jesus Christ of Latter-day Saints, popularly known as the Mormons. Joseph Smith, Jr. was perhaps the most original, most successful, and most controversial of several religious innovators—including Ellen Gould White (Seventh-day Adventists), Mary Baker Eddy (Christian Science), and Charles Taze Russell (Jehovah's Witnesses)—who created important religious movements in nineteenth-century America.

Born in Sharon, Vermont, on 23 December 1805, Smith was the third of the nine children of Joseph and Lucy Mack Smith. He grew up in the unchurched and dissenting, but God-fearing, tradition of a New England Protestant biblical culture, which attracted many of those whose economic standing in established society had been eroded. In 1816, plagued by hard times and misfortune, the sturdy, self-reliant, and closely-knit Smith family left New England for western New York in search of economic betterment; they settled in the village of Palmyra, along the route of the Erie Canal.

During the 1820s, as the Smiths continued to struggle against economic reversals, the religiously inclined young man had a number of visions and revelations. These convinced him that he was to be the divinely appointed instrument for the restoration of the gospel, which in the opinion of many of his contemporaries had been corrupted. Under the guidance of an angel he unearthed a set of golden plates from a hill near his parents' farm. He translated these golden plates with divine aid and published the result in 1830 as the *Book of Mormon*. Smith claimed that this book, named after its ancient American author and compiler, was the sacred history of the pre-Columbian inhabitants of

America, migrants from the Near East, some of whom were the ancestors of the American Indians. In 1829, divine messengers had conferred the priesthood—the authority to baptize and act in the name of God—on Smith and his associate Oliver Cowdery. Shortly after the publication of the *Book of Mormon*, Smith and Cowdery officially organized the Church of Christ in Fayette, New York, on 6 April 1830. In 1838, the name was changed to the Church of Jesus Christ of Latter-day Saints.

Prominent among those attracted to Smith's teachings was Sidney Rigdon, erstwhile associate of Alexander Campbell. Rigdon invited Smith and his New York followers to establish a Mormon settlement in Kirtland, Ohio. It was there that Smith greatly amplified and broadened his theological and organizational principles in a series of revelations (first published in 1833 as the *Book of Commandments,* and later enlarged into the current, canonical *Doctrine and Covenants*). The Saints were enjoined to gather in communities as God's chosen people under an egalitarian economic system called the Law of Consecration and Stewardship. They were also directed to build a temple as the sacred center of the community. These revelations initiated a patriarchal order that harkened back to Old Testament traditions.

In the meantime, Smith also established settlements in Missouri, which he regarded as the center of a future Zion. In 1838, economic difficulties and internal dissension forced Smith to give up the Kirtland settlement. His intention of gathering all the Saints in Missouri, however, had to be deferred after the Mormons were ruthlessly driven from the state in 1839. It was in Nauvoo, a settlement founded in 1839 on the Mississippi River, that Smith further expanded his ambitious vision of a Mormon empire that was to be both spiritual and temporal. By 1844, Nauvoo had become the largest city in Illinois, with a population of about 11,000. This city was under the full religious, social, economic, and political control of the Mormon kingdom, with Joseph Smith as its charismatic leader.

Some historians suggest that he may have become touched by megalomania; he assumed leadership of the Mormon militia in the resplendent uniform of a lieutenant general and announced his candidacy for the presidency of the United States. Smith ostensibly made his gesture toward the presidency in order to avoid making a politically difficult choice between the two major parties, but he was also imbued with the millennial belief that if God wanted him to be president and establish

"Behold I say unto you that this thing shall ye teach—repentance and baptism unto those who are accountable and capable of committing sin; yea, teach parents that they must repent and be baptized, and humble themselves as their little children, and they shall all be saved with their little children."

The Book of Mormon, 1830

1805 Smith is born the third of nine children to a Vermont couple.

1816 Smith moves with his family to western New York.

1829 Smith is made a priest by divine messengers.

1830 Smith becomes co-founder of the Church of Christ in Fayette, New York.

1833 Smith publishes what is now called *Doctrine and Covenants.*

1838 Smith's church becomes the Church of Jesus Christ of Latter-Day Saints.

1844 Smith and his brother are killed by a group of anti-Mormons.

Mormon dominion in the United States, no one could hinder him. Innovative ordinances, such as baptism for the dead, and especially plural marriage—with Smith and his closest associates secretly taking numerous wives—offended the religious sensibilities of many Mormons. Likewise, controversial doctrines such as pre-existence, metaphysical materialism, eternal progression, the plurality of gods, and man's ability to become divine through the principles of Mormonism, failed to gain universal acceptance among the Saints. A group of alarmed anti-Mormons effectively capitalized on internal dissent and were able to organize a mob that killed Smith and his brother Hyrum on 27 June 1844.

History has shown the killers of the Mormon prophet wrong in thinking that they had delivered a mortal blow to Mormonism, although their crime was an implicit recognition of Smith's crucial role in creating and sustaining the new religion. It was his spirituality, imagination, ego, drive, and charisma that not only started Mormonism but kept it going in the face of nearly insurmountable internal and external opposition. At the same time, these were the very characteristics that had generated much of that opposition. Smith's was a multifaceted and contradictory personality. Reports of encounters with him by both non-Mormons and believers give the impression of a tall, well-built, handsome man whose visionary side was tempered by Yankee practicality, geniality, and a sense of humor that engendered loyalty in willing followers. Though after his death his followers could not all agree on precisely what he had taught and split into several factions, they all accepted Smith's central messages of the restoration of the gospel and the divine status of the *Book of Mormon*, continuing revelation by prophets, and the establishment of the kingdom of God with Christ as its head. ◆

Snake, Reuben, Jr.

1937–1993 ● NATIVE AMERICAN

Reuben Snake, Jr., a greatly admired spiritual leader and political activist, was known for his wisdom, humor, and diplomacy as he fought for Native American rights.

Snake was born in Winnebago, Nebraska, in 1937. He belonged to the tribe called Winnebago by whites and Hochunk amongst tribe members themselves. Snake's tribe had earlier been forced to leave their Wisconsin homeland and to resettle in the Nebraska area. Snake grew up near the Omaha Indian Reservation, which bordered the Winnebago Indian Reservation. In 1939, his great-grandfather baptized Snake into the Native American Church (NAC) and gave him the name *Kikawunga*, his traditional clan name. Although Snake attended the University of Nebraska in Lincoln (1964–1965) and Peru State College (1968–1969), he never completed a college degree.

As an adult, Snake became active in the NAC, a religious movement that combines Christianity with Native American philosophy. One of the central sacraments of the church includes the use of peyote, which practitioners consider a sacred herb and which they call "Medicine." The peyote cactus grows in parts of the southwestern United States and northern Mexico. For more than 1,000 years, Indians around that region have ingested a portion of the cactus for ceremonial purposes. In 1918, some practitioners of the peyote religion officially incorporated as the Native American Church in order to obtain a legal charter to protect their religious freedom. Ceremonies of the NAC consist of all-night vigils in a teepee or other traditional Indian structure, during which participants pray and take peyote. The use of peyote is meant to heighten awareness of God. Snake became trained as a Roadman, the ceremony leader, and believed that peyote was a gift from God who "endowed it with his love and compassion."

In the early 1990s, the U.S. Supreme Court ruled that the "free exercise of religion" guaranteed in the Constitution did not include the NAC's use of peyote. Snake created the Native American Religious Freedom Project to challenge the ruling. During a four-year-battle, Snake made tireless speeches and appearances. Finally, Congress passed the American Indian Religious Freedom Act Amendments of 1994 (which President Clinton signed into law) allowing the 250,000 members of the NAC to pray with peyote.

The fight over peyote was not Snake's first encounter with the nation's highest political levels. In 1972, Snake became national chairman of the American Indian Movement (AIM). In November of that year, AIM organized a group that traveled in

1937 Snake is born in Nebraska.

1964 Snake enrolls in the University of Nebraska, but never gets his degree.

1972 Snake becomes national chairman of the American Indian Movement.

1975 Snake is elected chairman of the Winnebago tribe.

1985 Snake begins heading the National Congress of American Indians.

1993 Snake returns to Nebraska and dies surrounded by friends and family.

1996 Snake's autobiography *Your Humble Serpent: Indian Visionary and Activist* is published.

caravans from around the country to focus attention on the Indian struggle for equal rights. The caravans met at the offices of the Bureau of Indian Affairs in Washington, D.C., and presented a 20-point list of demands for President Richard Nixon. Snake emerged as an outspoken leader during the event.

In 1975, Snake was elected as chairman of the Winnebago tribe and held the position for more than a dozen years. In addition to his continuing role as a spiritual leader, he spoke publicly on such subjects as Indian education and Native American religious rights. He worked as a conflict resolution manager and as a teacher at the Winnebago Community College. From 1985 to 1987, Snake headed the National Congress of American Indians, speaking out on treaty obligations of the U.S. government to Indians. Snake served as a consultant to the Americans for Indian Opportunity, headed by Comanche activist LaDonna Harris.

In his later years, Snake served as an instructor and cultural resource person for the Institute of American Indian Arts in Santa Fe, New Mexico. However, when his health began to fail, Snake returned to Nebraska. Surrounded by many friends and family members, Snake died peacefully there in 1993.

Snake co-wrote *One Nation Under God: The Triumph of the Native American Church* (published in 1996) with Huston Smith about the use of peyote in their church. *Reuben Snake, Your Humble Serpent: Indian Visionary and Activist* (1996) is Snake's autobiography as told to Jay C. Fikes. Snake often signed letters humorously with the closing, "Your Faithful Serpent."

Near the end of his life, Snake warned that many tribal people had drifted from their culture and uncritically accepted the teachings of the larger society. "When you put these footprints down, be very careful because your children are going to follow along," he said. "They're not going to do what you say, they're going to do what you do." ◆

> "When you put these footprints down, be very careful because your children are going to follow along," he said. "They're not going to do what you say, they're going to do what you do."

Suzuki, D. T.

1870–1966 ● Buddhist

D. T. Suzuki was the westernized name of Suzuki Daisetsu Teitaro a Japanese lay Buddhist, author, and lecturer, known in Europe and America primarily for his expositions of Zen. Born on 18 October 1870 in Kanazawa in north central Japan, Suzuki was the youngest of five children. He attended local schools until age 17, when it became financially impossible for him to continue. Proficient at English, he taught it in primary schools for a few years and in 1891 moved to Tokyo, where he became a special student at what is now Waseda University. He then also began to frequent the Engakuji, a Zen monastery in Kamakura. His relationship there with the abbot Shaku Soyen (1856–1919) was of critical importance for his later life. This was both because it was the basis for his knowledge of Zen and because Shaku Soyen was chosen to represent Zen Buddhism at the World's Parliament of Religions in Chicago in 1893 and would later arrange for Suzuki to become the assistant to the Illinois industrialist and amateur Orientalist Paul Carus (1852–1919), who was keenly interested in the translation and interpretation of Asian religious and philosophical texts.

Suzuki went to America in 1897 and lived in LaSalle, Illinois, working as cotranslator with Carus until 1908. During these years he made the first English translations of a number of important Buddhist texts and published his own *Outlines of Mahayana Buddhism* (1907).

In 1908 Suzuki traveled to Europe and in Paris copied important materials on Chinese Buddhism newly discovered among the Tun-huang manuscripts. He returned to Japan in 1909 to teach English at the Peers' School (Gakushu-in) until 1921, at which time he accepted a chair in Buddhist philosophy at Otani University, a post held until his retirement. In 1911 he married Beatrice Erskine Lane, an American who frequently was his co-editor until her death in 1939. Although he made journeys to England, China, Korea, and America, Suzuki resided in Japan until 1950 and published voluminously both in Japanese and in English during these four decades. At the age of 80 Suzuki moved to New York. There, under the auspices of the Rockefeller Foundation, he began to lecture on Buddhism and Zen at a number of American campuses, especially at Columbia University, where he later became a visiting professor and until 1958 held lectures that were open to the general public. Most of his remaining years were spent in extensive travel and interaction with Westerners. He died in Tokyo on 12 July 1966.

Suzuki lived large portions of his long life both in Japan and in the West, and he pursued his work in both worlds. In

1870 Suzuki is born in north central Japan, the youngest of five children.

1891 Suzuki moves to Tokyo to continue his studies.

1897 Suzuki moves to Illinois to work as a translator.

1907 Suzuki publishes *Outlines of Mahayana Buddhism*.

1908 Suzuki goes to Paris and copies Chinese Buddhism materials.

1911 Suzuki marries an American who becomes his co-editor.

1921 Suzuki accepts a chair in Buddhist philosophy at Otani University.

1966 Suzuki dies in Tokyo.

> "However incomparable the Buddha-truth is, I vow to attain it."
> T. D. Suzuki,
> *Manual of Zen Buddhism*, 1950

Japan his career began differently from that of most academics, and for some years he was outside the mainstream there. Nevertheless his collected works in Japanese number 32 volumes, including many essays that contributed to a rekindling of scholarly and public interest in Buddhist subjects at a time when these were generally ignored by most of his Japanese contemporaries. Many of his essays in Japanese comprise a sustained insistence upon the formative importance of Buddhism—specially of its Zen and Pure Land forms—in the history of Japanese culture, a topic often less than popular in Japan during the first half of the twentieth century.

Suzuki's voluminous writings in English include *Essays in Zen Buddhism, An Introduction to Zen Buddhism* (1934), *Zen and Japanese Culture* (1959), and *The Training of a Zen Buddhist Monk* (1934). Certainly his facility with English, his extensive lecturing in America and Europe, and his participation in conferences all over the world brought Buddhism and Zen in particular to the attention of many who would otherwise have been totally unfamiliar with these topics.

Concerning Suzuki's influence in the West, it is often said that he made Zen into an English word; certainly he helped to make Zen a topic of great public interest, especially in the 1960s and 1970s. His scholarship made basic Asian texts available in English, and although he has been criticized for being insufficiently sensitive to history, he clearly stimulated a dramatic surge of interest in East Asia among American scholars. Through his lifelong dialogue with Western theologians and religionists, he contributed greatly to an awareness of the Buddhist tradition. Sometimes dismissed as merely a popularizer of Zen, he has also been hailed by the distinguished historian Lynn White, Jr., as someone whose writings broke through the "shell of the **Occident**" and made our thinking global. His influence upon twentieth-century Japan has also become increasingly clear: he championed Japan's inheritance of continental Buddhism during decades when nationalism focused upon Shinto. Moreover, his writings in Japanese and his obvious ability to make a credible presentation of Buddhism in the West have contributed to what some have called a twentieth-century renaissance of interest—at least an intellectual interest—in Buddhism on the part of the Japanese. ◆

occident: description of ideas and places relating to the Western hemisphere

Swedenborg, Emanuel

1688–1772 ● CHRISTIAN

Emanuel Swedenborg was a Swedish scientist, mystic, philosopher and theologian. A man of massive erudition, Swedenborg created a comprehensive, if bizarre, theology in his later years, and it is for this that he is best known; it has offended the prudish through its frank detailing of explicit sexual dreams while inspiring the spiritual seeker with its resonant and complex symbolism. However, it was not until he was nearly 60 that Swedenborg abandoned secular concerns; prior to this, he had already produced a significant body of work on the natural sciences. Much of this material received little attention until long after his death, by which time its findings had been largely superceded by subsequent developments; nonetheless, though unacknowledged, its originality testifies to his quality as a thinker.

Swedenborg's father was the bishop of Skara and a believer in guardian spirits and angels. However, young Swedenborg did not enter the clergy; rather, his interest was in mathematics and the natural sciences, which took him abroad for five years after his graduation from Uppsala University. He benefitted from the patronage of Charles XII on his return, and worked with the foremost mechanical minds in the country to produce Sweden's first scientific journal in 1715. Charles's death in 1718 led to a decline in Swedenborg's influence; he published nothing further for 15 years.

After another European journey in 1733, his quiet labors were crowned by the publication, in 1734, of his *Principles of Natural*

1688 Swedenborg is born in Sweden, son of a bishop.

1715 Swedenborg helps produce Sweden's first scientific journal.

1734 Swedenborg publishes *Principals of Natural Things.*

1743 Swedenborg writes of traveling in the realms of spirits and angels.

1772 Swedenborg dies.

"Real charity is dealing fairly and faithfully in whatever position, business, or work one is engaged in, and with those with whom one comes into contact."

Emanuel Swedenborg, *The True Christian Religion,* 1771

Things, parts of which anticipated Immanuel Kant and Laplace's nebular theory. A two-year sojourn in Amsterdam produced *The Economy of the Animal Kingdom,* in which the "animal kingdom" is the human body—the kingdom of the animal, or soul. Swedenborg believed the soul to be located in the cellular cortex, and his researches to confirm this end led him to many useful and significant conclusions in the field of psycho-physics.

The period 1743–1744 was a critical one in Swedenborg's life, chronicled in his *Journal of Dreams;* he experienced prolonged, intense, and repeated spiritual visions and was moved to a painful reevaluation of himself and his faith. He details his travels among the realms of spirits and angels and his climactic vision of Jesus. Swedenborg guiltily realized the extent of his own spiritual pride and desire to be recognized as a great man of science and, repentant, abandoned his secular writings forthwith, leaving a projected synthesis of his scientific writings unfinished. The remainder of his long life was devoted to the exegesis of his religious vision.

His doctrines, as summarized in his work *True Christian Religion,* clearly borrow many structural notions from his scientific theories. Thus his doctrine of correspondence suggests that everything outward and visible in nature has an inward spiritual cause; Swedenborg's earlier search for a universal language (a problem that had also interested French philosopher Rene Descartes) led him to believe that his doctrine enabled one to uncover the hidden, inner, spiritual meaning of sacred scriptures. Further, he envisaged the contents of the cosmos as forming an ordered hierarchical series culminating in man, while he attributed the rise of evil in the world to man's selfish desires, which divert his love from its appropriate object, God. Swedenborg's God has his essence in love and wisdom; furthermore he rejected the conventional notion of the Trinity and asserted that Christ was not the son of God.

The range of people influenced by Swedenborg is considerable and sometimes surprising. Kant was one of only four purchasers of the original published version of his mystical system and pronounced it "very sublime", while William Blake's rich and complex symbolic universe is of an undeniably Swedenborgian character; he even annotated sections from Swedenborg for posterity. Although Swedenborg never preached his doctrines, the Church of the New Jerusalem was founded on the basis of his teachings after his death. His emphasis on a divine landscape mappable through observation of the workings of the microcosm that is man also attracted creative talents such as Honore Balzac, Baudelaire, Ralph Waldo Emerson, Strindberg, and W. B. Yeats. He is fashionable again today among those who see parallels between his cosmology and esoteric Eastern religious doctrines, which also stress introspection as a means to revelation. ◆

Szold, Henrietta

1860–1945 ● JEWISH

Henrietta Szold was a Zionist leader and founding president of Hadassah, the leading women's Zionist organization in the United States. Born in Baltimore, Maryland, the eldest child of Benjamin Szold and Sophia (Schaar) Szold, she was educated by her father, a rabbi, and in local schools, graduating first in her high school class. She subsequently taught, wrote articles in the Jewish press, and organized night classes for east European Jewish immigrants in Baltimore before leaving for Philadelphia in 1893 to work for the Jewish Publication Society of America (founded 1888). There, she edited and translated important volumes of Judaica, indexed Heinrich Graetz's *History of the Jews,* and for a time compiled the *American Jewish Year Book.* In 1903 she attended classes at Jewish Theological Seminary of America in New York.

In 1909, after her first love, Louis Ginzberg, professor at the seminary, married another woman, she traveled to Palestine, where her Zionist commitments were renewed. In 1910, she became secretary of the Federation of American Zionists, and two years later joined

> "There is a vast storehouse filled with treasures. The key, the Hebrew language, is in our guardianship. Have we a right to throw the key into the ocean of oblivion?"
>
> Henrietta Szold, 1896

rapproachment: the establishment of good relations between previously disagreeing parties

with other women to found Hadassah on a nationwide basis. After 1916, she devoted her full attention to the organization and spent considerable time in Palestine involved in its medical and educational endeavors as well as broader Zionist affairs. She spent her last years directing the efforts of Youth Aliyah, the movement established to save Jewish youngsters in Nazi-occupied Europe by bringing them to Palestine.

Henrietta Szold espoused a Jewish way of life that was at once deeply religious, strongly ethical, and broadly tolerant. Her religious practices and outlook were shaped by Conservative Judaism, but she followed an independent course, evinced considerable interest in Jewish religious writings by women, and insisted on her right to recite the Qaddish prayer in memory of her mother, as well as to fulfill other Jewish religious obligations traditionally restricted to men. Impelled by her religious values as well as her lifelong pacifism, she associated during her last years with Jewish thinkers in Palestine who sought Arab-Jewish **rapprochement** and advocated a binational state. Her example of Jewish social activism coupled with her fostering of traditional Jewish ideals has inspired Jewish women throughout the world, particularly those associated with Hadassah. ◆

Tai-hsu

1890–1947 ● BUDDHIST

Tai-hsu was a Chinese Buddhist reformer, founder of the Wu-ch'ang Buddhist Institute and active participant in various Buddhist movements. T'ai-hsu's lay name was Lu P'ei-lin. Born in Hai-ning in Chekiang, he became a monk of the Lin-chi school of Ch'an Buddhism at the age of 16.

Buddhist scriptures as well as radical political writings by other Buddhist leaders inspired him to act for the reformation of Chinese Buddhism. He tried to put his reform programs into practice by founding the Association for the Advancement of Buddhism in 1912, but the association was short-lived owing to opposition from conservative Buddhists. In 1917 T'ai-hsu visited Taiwan and Japan. Later, he established the Enlightenment Society at Shanghai with the help of some **eminent** Chinese. The society organized public lectures and disseminated knowledge of Buddhism through its own publications. T'ai-hsu next made a preaching tour of several cities in China and in Malaya (in present-day Malaysia). In 1920 he founded the Buddhist periodical *Hai-ch'ao-yin*. He established the Wu-ch'ang Buddhist Institute in 1922, the first modern Buddhist seminary in China. In 1923, T'ai-hsu and a few followers founded the World Buddhist Federation. Two years later he led the Chinese Buddhist delegation to the Tokyo Conference of East Asian Buddhists. In 1927 he became the head of the Min-nan Buddhist Institute. During that year, he associated with the Chinese Nationalist leader Chiang Kai-shek, who financed

eminent: conspicuous; standing out so as to be noted

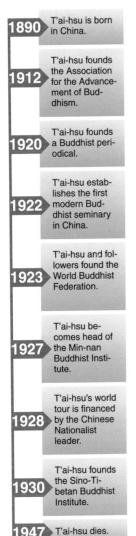

T'ai-hsu is born in China. — **1890**

T'ai-hsu founds the Association for the Advancement of Buddhism. — **1912**

T'ai-hsu founds a Buddhist periodical. — **1920**

T'ai-hsu establishes the first modern Buddhist seminary in China. — **1922**

T'ai-hsu and followers found the World Buddhist Federation. — **1923**

T'ai-hsu becomes head of the Min-nan Buddhist Institute. — **1927**

T'ai-hsu's world tour is financed by the Chinese Nationalist leader. — **1928**

T'ai-hsu founds the Sino-Tibetan Buddhist Institute. — **1930**

T'ai-hsu dies. — **1947**

T'ai-hsu's world tour in 1928. The Chinese Buddhist Association was founded by Reverend Yuan-ying (1878–1953) at Shanghai in 1929, but T'ai-hsu's early relation with it was not cordial, though he was on its standing committee. In 1930 he founded the Sino-Tibetan Buddhist Institute in Chungking. During the World War II, T'ai-hsu led a Chinese Buddhist mission of goodwill to Burma, India, Ceylon, and Malaya to win support and sympathy for China, and he was awarded a medal by the Chinese government for his contributions to the war effort. His influence on Nationalist leaders declined after the war, and he died on 12 March 1947. His writings were published posthumously in 33 volumes.

Since the late nineteenth century, Chinese Buddhism has been under constant pressure from the government and from intellectuals. In 1898 a high official proposed that 70 percent of monastic buildings and their income should be taken over to finance the public school system. Although this was not put into practice, and although the Buddhists managed at times to put off or soften anti-Buddhist threats, the idea of using Buddhist property to finance education arose again in 1928 and 1942. T'ai-hsu's suggestions for reform were part of the Buddhist reaction to public pressure. As a compromise, T'ai-hsu suggested in 1942 that 40 percent of monastic income be used for educational and charitable institutions run by the Buddhists in exchange for government protection of monastic property, but his suggestion had no effect on either side.

T'ai-hsu's attempts to reform and modernize Chinese Buddhism were to some extent successful. A number of prominent scholars and religious leaders were trained at the academies and libraries that he founded, and his lectures and writings helped create a more positive public attitude toward Buddhism. But his larger dream of a worldwide Buddhist movement, and his plan for reorganizing Buddhist institutions throughout China never materialized during his lifetime. His ideas were often viewed by the conservative Buddhist establishment as radical and unacceptable. They cooperated with him reluctantly in times of crisis but were always opposed to his ideas on monastic affairs. Yet, viewed from a historical perspective, his program of reform and modernization (the establishment of Buddhist academies, journals, foreign contacts, and so forth) can be seen to have created new patterns for Chinese Buddhism.

The religious thought of T'ai-hsu falls in the mainstream of Chinese Buddhism. It recognizes that all sentient beings possess the Buddha nature and are subject to the law of causation. The operation of cause and conditions is universal and incessant, and all worldly phenomena are based on that operation. If one follows the five Buddhist precepts, a happy life in this world is achievable. This happy life is, however, not lasting; it is subject to change. One must therefore strive for a higher wisdom and thus attain *nirvana*. When one realizes that there is neither self nor object and that only the mind is universal and unlimited, one will work for the salvation of all **sentient** beings so that they too may become Buddhas. T'ai-hsu's contribution is his adoption of a new terminology and a modern style of writing, thus tuning the old philosophy to the new thought in China. He often used words like *revolution, evolution, science, democracy, philosophy,* and *freedom,* as well as other concepts popular in his time. Although he may not always have used these terms with a clear understanding of their modern meaning, by incorporating them into the context of Buddhism he made the tradition continue to appeal to young people at the beginning of the century. ◆

sentient: aware; conscious or responsive to certain stimuli or thought

Taylor, Gardner

1918– ● BAPTIST

Gardner Calvin Taylor was an African American Baptist minister. Gardner Taylor was born in Baton Rouge, Louisiana. He received his B.A. degree from Leland College in 1937. Taylor aspired to be a lawyer and was accepted to the University of Michigan law school. Before he was to leave for Ann Arbor, however, he narrowly survived a traffic accident; after this incident, he decided to devote his life to religion.

Taylor attended Oberlin Theological Seminary in Oberlin, Ohio, and was ordained a Baptist minister in 1939. During his studies he served the pastorate at nearby Elyria, from 1938 to 1940. After earning his B.D. in 1940, he moved back to Louisiana and headed congregations at New Orleans and Baton Rouge. In 1948, Taylor accepted the pastorate of the Concord Baptist Church of Christ in Brooklyn's Bedford-Stuyvesant neighborhood in New York.

"You must never succumb to the notion that Christianity in its earliest and purest expression was addressed to the affluent…. The Christian faith has been appropriated and tailored by the privileged."

Gardner Taylor, quoted in *Christianity Today,* 1999

Gardner Taylor
preaching

After the Concord Church burned down in 1952, Taylor helped to raise nearly $2 million for a large new church. Dedicated in 1956, the church expanded to include a nursing home and a clothing exchange. Taylor and his wife, Laura S. Taylor, a teacher educated at Oberlin, opened the Concord Elementary Day School in 1961 as an alternative to public schools. Laura Taylor developed much of the curriculum, which emphasized black history and culture and used innovative teaching methods. Appointed by Mayor Robert F. Wagner to the New York City Board of Education in 1958, Gardner Taylor campaigned for equity in funding for predominantly minority school districts. He often disagreed with the other six members of the board over cases like the 1958–1959 Harlem Nine controversy, in which parents of African-American and Puerto Rican students withdrew their children from school, protesting the substandard conditions of the schools that poor and minority students were compelled by the state to attend. Taylor sided with the parents in their call for a citywide boycott. He was also active in the Citywide Committee for Integrated Schools and worked for employment opportunities for African Americans with the Urban League of Greater New York throughout the 1950s and 1960s.

By the early 1960s, Taylor was a respected leader in the civil rights movement. He was active in the top echelons of the Congress on Racial Equality (CORE) and instrumental in the selection of James Farmer as the organization's national director in 1961. Taylor was a close friend of the Rev. Dr. Martin Luther King, Jr. Taylor and several like-minded Baptist ministers challenged the autocratic, conservative leadership of Joseph H. Jackson of the National Baptist Convention, USA, Inc., the governing board of the National Baptists. Jackson, who was lukewarm at best toward the civil rights activism of King, was challenged by a slate headed by Taylor. A power struggle already in progress over the legitimacy of Jackson's presidency erupted in 1961 between Taylor's supporters, who included King, Ralph Abernathy, and Adam Clayton Powell, Jr.,and the faction led by Jackson. At the Philadelphia convention, the Taylor team protested the reelection of Jackson, whereupon Jackson's partisans adjourned the meeting. The Taylor team nevertheless remained, elected Taylor, and organized a sit-in to enforce the election. When the controversy was decided in Jackson's favor in court. Taylor and his supporters formed the Progressive National Baptist Convention, which openly supported activist organizations, especially the Southern Christian Leadership Conference (SCLC) and CORE. Taylor was president of the PNBC from 1967 to 1968, when the convention became the first predominantly black religious body to denounce the Vietnam War.

In 1962, Taylor served a term as president of the Protestant Council of New York City, the first African American and Baptist to hold that position. Under his leadership, the Concord Baptist Church grew to 12,000 members, 5,000 of them active. It became the largest Protestant congregation in the United States. Known as the "dean of black pastors," Taylor was acknowledged to be one of the most effective preachers in American history. He delivered Yale University's prestigious Lyman Beecher Lectures in 1977, published in *How Shall They Preach?* A book of sermons, *The Scarlet Thread*, was published in 1981. Taylor received an honorary degree from Brooklyn's Long Island University in 1984. Shortly before he retired in 1990, Taylor introduced Nelson Mandela at New York City's Riverside Church on the occasion of the South African leader's

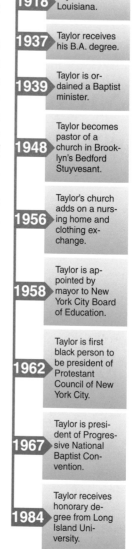

1918 Taylor is born in Louisiana.

1937 Taylor receives his B.A. degree.

1939 Taylor is ordained a Baptist minister.

1948 Taylor becomes pastor of a church in Brooklyn's Bedford Stuyvesant.

1956 Taylor's church adds on a nursing home and clothing exchange.

1958 Taylor is appointed by mayor to New York City Board of Education.

1962 Taylor is first black person to be president of Protestant Council of New York City.

1967 Taylor is president of Progressive National Baptist Convention.

1984 Taylor receives honorary degree from Long Island University.

historic visit to the United States. In the 1990s, Taylor continued to live in Bedford-Stuyvesant and delivered lectures and sermons in podiums and pulpits across the country. ◆

Saint Teresa of Avila

1515–1582 ● CATHOLIC

S aint Teresa of Avila (Teresa de Cepeda y Ahumada) was a Spanish religious leader. Author of three celebrated works of spiritual autobiography and two about stages of mystical prayer, Teresa also initiated the reform of the Carmelite order in the face of vast opposition and her own failing health.

Teresa was born in Avila, Spain, daughter of an affluent merchant family. Her relationship with her mother was particularly close. At a very young age, Teresa's devoutness evidenced itself. At seven she left home with her brother to journey to the Moorish part of Spain in order to die a martyr's death by decapitation, hoping to thus come to see God. The two children were discovered on the way by their uncle, and thereafter Teresa's father kept a watchful eye on his daughter's enthusiasm.

On reaching her teen years, Teresa's interest in religion waned as her beauty increased. She read chivalric tales that were popular at the time and was involved romantically with her cousin. However, her mother's death when Teresa was 15 turned her back to her religious foundations, as she sought comfort through a relationship with the Virgin Mary to fill the void.

In 1531 her father entrusted her education to Augustinian nuns and in 1535 she ran away from home and entered the Carmelite Monastery of the Incarnation at Avila, finally donning the habit of a nun, an act to which her father ultimately became resigned. Teresa committed herself to a life of prayer and penitence but she soon became ill, her condition being perhaps of psychological origin; nevertheless, her health degenerated seriously over the next year. By 1539 she lapsed into a coma and when she regained consciousness she had lost the use of her legs, a paralysis that lasted for three years.

During her convalescence she developed her mental prayer but she remained split between her need for approval by

> "Just so contemplatives have to bear aloft the standard of humility and must suffer all the blows which are aimed at them without striking any themselves. Their duty is to suffer as Christ did, to raise the Cross on high, not to allow it to leave their hands, whatever the perils in which they find themselves, and not to let themselves be found backward in suffering."
>
> Teresa of Avila, *Interior Castle*, 1527

friends, family, and religious fellows and her inner spiritual life. Finally, at age 39, she experienced a vision of Christ wounded that enabled her to decisively break with outer concerns. From this point on she frequently experienced ecstatic mystical states. Her inner turmoil and religious triumph are recorded in her autobiography, usually called *The Life of Teresa of Avila*, composed in the years 1562–1565.

Three years after her spiritual awakening she initiated a reform movement within the Carmelite order, the thrust of which was to return the Carmelite movement to its original austere values, isolating the nuns from the world in chastity and poverty, completely dependent on the alms of the community so as to allow them to concentrate on God, penitence, and reparation for man's sins. Teresa's single-mindedness earned her the opposition of the Carmelite order and the community around her, which did not want an unsupported convent in their midst.

Nevertheless, in 1562 Pope Pius IV approved Teresa's reform and the same year she opened her first convent, Saint Joseph's of the Carmelite Reform. During the next five years of relative peace, she wrote her autobiography and another work, *Meditations of the Canticles*. In 1567 John Baptist Rossi arrived in Avila from Rome, giving the papal stamp to Teresa's work and directing her to establish more monasteries. It was at this time that she met Juan de Yepes (later to become Saint John of the Cross) and encouraged him to institute reforms in the Carmelite men's order parallel to her reforms for women. The men's reforms were instituted while Teresa opened another 16 more convents throughout Spain, her reform order becoming known as the "discalced" or unshod (Primitive) Carmelites as opposed to the "calced" or shod Carmelites. The division within the order reached a crisis in 1575, when Teresa was commanded by her superiors in the Carmelite order to go to Castile and to cease founding new monasteries.

In 1579 a solution to the Carmelite impasse was worked out with the aid of King Philip II of Spain, an admirer of Teresa's accomplishments. Teresa's Carmelites of the Primitive Rule were to have independent jurisdiction from this point on, a decision confirmed by Pope Gregory XIII in 1580. Once this was granted, Teresa, now in poor health, resumed her vocation, traveling throughout Spain to the sites of the Carmelite Reform convents, giving spiritual guidance and solving administrative problems. On her way home from Burgos to Avila in

1515 Teresa is born in Spain to an affluent merchant family.

1531 Teresa is sent by her recently widowed father to be taught by nuns.

1535 Teresa runs away and becomes a nun at the Carmelite monastery.

1539 Teresa lapses into a coma, later losing use of her legs for three years.

1562 Teresa's reforms are approved by Pope Pius IV; Teresa opens her first convent.

1575 Teresa is commanded to stop opening monasteries.

1582 Teresa collapses and dies.

1582 Teresa collapsed and died. She was buried at Alba, a town 60 miles from her birthplace.

The prayer life written about in Teresa's autobiography is further developed in her work *The Interior Castle*. Here, the beginnings of prayer are compared to entering a palace composed of six concentric rings, each ring made up of separate mansions or apartments. The three outer rings describe the admirable life of a virtuous believer, consisting of humility, meditation, and exemplary conduct. The inner three represent the depths of contemplation as the soul begins to find union in God. The center or sixth circle is called the holy of holies where the soul is betrothed to God, overcome by divine light in direct communion with the Creator.

Teresa's writings, though banned by the Inquisition, enjoyed widespread subsequent influence. In 1622 Teresa was canonized by Pope Gregory XV, and in 1970 Pope Paul made her a doctor of the church. She is also the patron saint of Spain. ◆

Mother Teresa

1910–1997 ● Catholic

"I am like a little pencil in his hand. That is all. He does the thinking. He does the writing. The pencil has nothing to do with it."

Mother Teresa, quoted in *Time*, 1989

OPPOSITE:
Mother Teresa

Mother Teresa was a Roman Catholic nun who founded a religious order called Missionaries of Charity. She was born Agnes Gonxha Bojaxhiu in Skopje, capital of present-day Macedonia. At the age of 18 Agnes joined the Order of the Sisters of Loreto in Ireland, later taking the name Teresa in honor of Therese of Lisieux, the patron saint of missionaries. Mother Teresa came to embrace suffering as the primary means of salvation and based her life's work on that ideal.

As a result of an inner calling to serve the poor, in 1950 Mother Teresa established the Order of the Missionaries of Charity in Calcutta, India. The Missionaries of Charity was designed to provide education to disadvantaged children, shelter for the homeless, and care for the sick. Within three years of its founding a home for the dying and an orphanage were opened. The Missionaries of Charity now operate over 500 missions worldwide.

Mother Teresa received the 1979 Nobel Peace Prize, among several other awards, for her charitable accomplishments. She

1910 Mother Teresa is born in the capital of present-day Macedonia.

1929 Mother Teresa takes her vows as a nun with the Sisters of Loreto.

1950 Mother Teresa establishes the Order of the Missionaries of Charity.

1979 Mother Teresa is awarded the Nobel Peace Prize.

1982 Mother Teresa gets 37 captive children released from Beirut Hospital.

1997 Mother Teresa dies.

became well known for her work among victims of leprosy and AIDS. Although Mother Teresa received three esteemed awards from India, natives of West Bengal expressed concern over western perceptions of Calcutta created by the emphasis on the poor and destitute. In 1982 Mother Teresa was credited with negotiating the release of 37 children held captive in a Beirut hospital.

During her career Mother Teresa met with many world leaders and high-profile figures, including some of controversial reputation. Both her fundraising efforts and the use of funds came into question. There was criticism of the methods in which the Missionaries of Charity were run and issues were raised about the quality of care provided in the homes.

Controversy also surrounded Mother Teresa's stance on women's role in society. She maintained a strong pro-life, pro-family position, speaking against the use of birth control and abortion; women were encouraged to have many children—including women of impoverished developing-world societies. It has also been noted that the nuns in the Missionaries of Charity order lead an obsequious life with minimal emphasis on education.

Beyond the criticism, Mother Teresa's charitable efforts and unwavering dedication were difficult to ignore. She made a significant impact on many lives and seemed to embody the Indian concept of karma yoga, yoga in action and service. Throughout her life, the energetic, strong-willed nun remained determined to spread her simple message of love. She died after a long illness in 1997. ◆

Theodosius

1933– ● Orthodox Church in America

Metropolitan Theodosius became head of the Orthodox Church in America (OCA) when he became Bishop of Washington, D.C. His full title was The Most Blessed Theodosius Archbishop of Washington, Metropolitan of All America and Canada, Primate, Orthodox Church in America. The OCA is one among the federation of independent churches that make up the Eastern Orthodox religion that grew from a split in the Christian church that occurred in

1054. Each area church is governed by its own head bishop, who may be called patriarch, metropolitan, or archbishop. However, in the United States, the many separate ethnic communities within the Orthodox religion have changed its traditional structure and administrative organization. Some American metropolitan areas have several Orthodox bishops and many Orthodox parishes of different ethnic groups.

Theodosius oversees bishops, who administer each of the archdiocese's 10 districts. District headquarters are located in eight large American cities as well as Toronto, Canada, and Buenos Aires, Argentina. Supervising Theodosius is the Ecumenical Patriarch of the Eastern Orthodox Church, based in Istanbul, Turkey.

Theodosius was born in Canonsburg, Pennsylvania, near Pittsburgh, in 1933. He studied at Washington and Jefferson College in Washington, Pennsylvania, and then graduated from Saint Vladimir's Seminary in Crestwood, New York, in 1960. He then studied for a year at the Ecumenical Institute, Bossey, Switzerland.

Back in the United States, Theodosius took monastic vows in 1961 and then was ordained as a deacon and then priest. Deacons are the first of the three main orders of Orthodox clergy, followed by priests and bishops. Although married men may become priests, bishops are elected from among celibate or widowed clergy. From 1961 until 1966, Theodosius served as rector of the Nativity of the Holy Virgin Church, Madison, Illinois, and as an assistant military chaplain.

Theodosius was elected Bishop of the Diocese of Alaska, the OCA's oldest diocese, in 1967. The Orthodox religion in America began when a small group of Russian missionaries landed on Kodiak Island, Alaska, in 1794. In 1970, Theodosius headed a delegation to Moscow to formally accept the Tomos of Autocephaly (decree of self-governance) from the Russian Orthodox Church. As Bishop of Alaska, he hosted one of the first official acts of the new self-governing church: the canonization of Father Herman of Spruce Island, one of the original missionaries who began their ministry on Kodiak Island in 1794.

The church leadership transferred Bishop Theodosius to the Diocese of Pittsburgh in 1972. Bishop Theodosius was elected Archbishop of New York and Metropolitan of All America and Canada in October 1977. When church leaders decided in 1980 to establish a new diocese as the seat of the

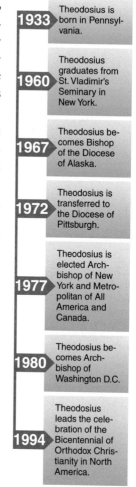

1933 Theodosius is born in Pennsylvania.

1960 Theodosius graduates from St. Vladimir's Seminary in New York.

1967 Theodosius becomes Bishop of the Diocese of Alaska.

1972 Theodosius is transferred to the Diocese of Pittsburgh.

1977 Theodosius is elected Archbishop of New York and Metropolitan of All America and Canada.

1980 Theodosius becomes Archbishop of Washington D.C.

1994 Theodosius leads the celebration of the Bicentennial of Orthodox Christianity in North America.

American Primate, Theodosius took on the title of Archbishop of Washington, D.C. He had became the longest ruling Primate of the Orthodox Church in America by the end of the 1990s.

In his role as a top religious leader, Theodosius met with numerous religious and political leaders. He was a frequent guest at the White House, and Presidents George Bush and Bill Clinton sought his advice on religious and political affairs in Eastern Europe. In September 1994, he attended the Library of Congress opening of an exhibit on the contribution of the Orthodox Church and native Alaskan cultures to North America. Both Clinton and Russian President Boris Yeltsin attended. Also in 1994, Theodosius led the celebration of the Bicentennial of Orthodox Christianity in North America. ◆

Saint Therese De Lisieux

1873–1897 ● CATHOLIC

> "What is this little way which you would teach souls? It is the way of spiritual childhood, the way of trust and absolute surrender."
>
> Therese of Lisieux,
> *Novissima Verba,*
> 1898

Saint Therese De Lisieux was a French Carmelite nun, popularly known as the Little Flower. Originally named Marie Francoise Therese Martin, she was youngest of nine children of a devout watchmaker in Alencon, France. Her mother died when she was four years old and the family moved to Lisieux, where Therese attended the Benedictine convent as a day student. From an early age she was drawn to religious perfection, and when she was 15 obtained permission to enter the convent of the Discalced Carmelites in Lisieux, where two of her older sisters had already been admitted.

It was in the convent that she spent the remaining nine years of her life before dying of tuberculosis. Her years at the convent were spent practicing and teaching her doctrine of the "Little Way"—a way of spiritual childhood, trust and absolute surrender, holy life that, in the words of Pope Pius XI, "did not go beyond the common order of things." It was this outlook that she taught to the novices whom she was appointed acting mistress of novices in 1893. She exemplified the Little Way, achieving goodness by performing the humblest of tasks. Six months before her death, her tubercular condition forced her to retire to the convent's infirmary.

The story of Therese's spiritual development, *L'Histoire d'une ame* (*Story of a Soul*), was written at the command of her superiors. Before her death she asked her sister, Mother Agnes of Jesus, to edit these memoirs which, published as her autobiography, have become one of the most widely read religious autobiographies. It is filled, as are her letters, with her message of seeking good with childlike simplicity, and greatly appealed to the ordinary people attracted by the message that sanctity could be attained not only through mortification but through ongoing renunciation in small matters, and her grave became a place of worship and pilgrimage, and a basilica in her name was built there. She was canonized in 1925 and throughout the Roman Catholic world many churches were dedicated to her. Meditations from her writings are also read by many of the devout. She is often represented in art carrying an armful of roses, because of her promise that "After my death I will let fall a shower of roses." She is the patron saint of aviators and foreign missionaries and was proclaimed by Pope Pius XI, "the greatest saint of modern times." In 1947 she joined Joan of Arc as patroness of France. ◆

> Therese was canonized in 1925 and throughout the Roman Catholic world many churches were dedicated to her.

Thomas à Kempis

c. 1380–1471 ● CHRISTIAN

Thomas à Kempis was a Dutch theologian. Born in Kempen near Cologne (hence his name), Thomas was sent to Deventer when he was 13 to study at the school conducted by Florentius Radewijns and the Brethren of the Common Life; this community, founded by the Dutch mystic Gerard Groote, stressed and sought to emulate the simplicity and sincerity of the early Christians. Thomas wholeheartedly adopted the teachings of the Brethren, and was later to write biographies of both Radewijns and Groote.

In 1399 Thomas entered the Augustinian monastery of Mount Saint Agnes, near Zwolle in The Netherlands, where his elder brother John was prior; he remained there for the rest of his long life. Ordained in 1414, he held a succession of administrative posts within the monastic community, and was a prolific writer of sermons, hymns, popular spiritual treatises, contemporary chronicles and biographies.

> "Now, there are many who hear the Gospel often but care little for it because they have not the spirit of Christ. Yet whoever wishes to understand fully the words of Christ must try to pattern his whole life on that of Christ."
>
> Thomas à Kempis,
> *The Imitation of Christ*, c. 1424

Thomas à Kempis is credited with writing of *The Imitation of Christ*, one of the most famous and influential works of Christian literature. A complete Latin manuscript of the work became available in 1427; subsequently, some 20 persons were proposed as possible authors, but Thomas's right to be regarded as author of the definitive edition is now uniformly acknowledged, although many ascribe the basic composition to Gerard Groote himself. In the days before printing, it was relatively common for devotional works to pass through several hands, being modified along the way, while many authors were content to remain anonymous.

The *Imitation* marks a reaction against what many perceived as the excessive intellectualism of theological scholasticism and recommends simple piety, devotion, and renunciation as the foundations of a true Christian life. Consisting of aphoristic reflections and counsels written in a straightforward and familiar style, it comprises four books: the first looks at ways of liberating oneself from worldly concerns and preparing for the spiritual life; the second offers advice and admonitions concerning the life of devotion; the third discusses the consolation offered by Christ to those who earnestly follow him; and the fourth gives recommendations for receiving Holy Communion in a devout manner.

As the author of the *Imitation* Thomas is probably the outstanding representative of "Devotia Moderna" (Modern Devotion). This late medieval religious movement sought to make religion intelligible in the context of the attitudes arising in the Netherlands at the end of the fourteenth century, and heralded the beginnings of an emphasis on personal Christian witness as a reaction against the spiritual shortcomings and materialistic pomp of the Catholic establishment. It laid great stress on education and achieved notable successes in capturing the imagination of young people who came to study at schools subscribed to the movement's views.

Both the movement generally and *Imitation of Christ* specifically had a profound impact upon the church; Martin Luther and Deiderius Erasmus, central figures in the massive religious upheavals of the sixteenth century, were influenced at an early age by Modern Devotion, while the *Imitation* was the favorite book of Ignatius of Loyola, founder of the Jesuits, who spearheaded the Catholic Counter-Reformation. Subsequently, the *Imitation* affected individuals as diverse as the lexicographer and wit Samuel Johnson and the religious reformer

John Wesley. Thus, its impact on the evolution of Protestantism in England and Germany during the eighteenth century was substantial. ◆

Saint Thomas Aquinas

1225–1274 ● CHRISTIAN

Saint Thomas Aquinas was a Christian philosopher and political thinker. He was born to a noble family near Aquino, Italy, and educated at Monte Cassino, home of the Benedictine order. In 1243, however, while still a youth, he joined the Dominican order. To his family of feudal lords such a change of allegiance was a disgrace which would bring no honor to the family. In an attempt to dissuade him they confined him to the family castle for almost two years, but to no avail. His family released him in 1245 and he went to Paris to serve his novitiate. There he studied with the German philosopher Albertus Magnus, whom he followed to Cologne in 1248. As Aquinas was heavyset and quiet, his fellow novices called him Dumb Ox, but Magnus, who knew his student better, is said to have predicted that "this ox would one day fill the world with his bellowing."

Aquinas was ordained c. 1250 and in 1252 returned to Paris, where he began to teach at the university. His first major work, *Commentaries on the Sentences of Peter Lombard*, appeared in about 1256. That year he received a doctorate in theology and was appointed professor of philosophy at the University of Paris. He gained fame rapidly and was highly regarded because of his method of using Aristotelian philosophy for theological purposes—

later called the Thomist system of study. Thanks to him Aristotelianism rather than Platonism became the foundation of Christian thought. In 1259 he was summoned to Rome by Pope Alexander IV, and enjoyed great favor there. He was offered the archbishopric of Naples but turned down this and other preferred ecclesiastical positions. Upon his return he was plunged into controversy with the Averroists, who based themselves on a different variation of Aristotelianism from Aquinas's own and threatened to destroy the positions he had built up so carefully with Magnus. In the contest between Aquinas and the Averroist representative, Siger de Brabant, Aquinas outlined his position in the treatise *On the Unity of the Intellect against the Averroists* (1270); he was victorious but the victory was hard-won and wearying. In 1272 he went to Italy to organize a new Dominican school and devoted himself to a life of prayer and contemplation. He died while traveling to the Second Council of Lyons, called by Pope Gregory X to attempt the union of the Greek and Latin churches. Rulers, religious orders, and universities vied for Aquinas's body, which was eventually given by the pope to Toulouse. He was canonized by Pope John XXII in 1323 and proclaimed a Doctor of the Church by Pope Pius V in 1567.

Aquinas is regarded as an outstanding theologian and philosopher of the Catholic church. He was a prolific author and is credited with some 80 works. His *Summa theologica* (written 1266–1273), one of the earliest and longest essays dealing with the whole of Christian theology, was highly regarded by his contemporaries and successors. *Summa contra gentiles*, a treatise for Catholic missionaries, offered a brief presentation of Christian faith intended to persuade intellectual Muslims of the truth of Christianity. He also presented a new rationalist basis for many Christian doctrines, notably transubstantiation. In 1879 Pope Leo XIII decreed that Aquinas's system be the basis of all philosophy reading in Catholic institutions.

Aquinas's political ideas were expressed in *De regimine principum*, where he distinguished between laws of nature, divine law, and human law and concluded that the social establishment of his age was necessary in a Christian state. He also developed the concept that a monarchy should be bound by law and allowed full authority only within a legal framework. The latter idea led to his distinguishing between king and tyrant—a tyrant being a king who has lost the grace of God and who therefore could justifiably be condemned to death. ◆

"If there existed in our souls a perfect image of God, as the Son is the perfect image of the Father, our mind would know God at once. But the image in our mind is imperfect; hence the argument does not prove."

Thomas Aquinas,
Summa Theologica,
1273

Tutu, Desmond

1931– ● ANGLICAN

Desmond Tutu was Anglican archbishop of Cape Town, South Africa, and metropolitan of the Church of the Province of Southern Africa. Born in Klerksdorp in the Transvaal, Tutu became a high school teacher in 1955 after having graduated from the Pretoria Bantu College in 1953. He obtained a bachelor of arts degree from the University of South Africa in 1958. After a serious illness, and under the influence of Father Trevor Huddleston of the Community of the Resurrection, Tutu studied for the priesthood at Saint Peter's College, Johannesburg. He was ordained deacon in 1960 and priest the following year. From 1962 to 1965 he studied at King's College, University of London, obtaining a bachelor's degree in divinity and a master's degree in theology. From 1967 to 1969 he lectured at the Federal Theological Seminary in Alice, Cape, and from 1970 to 1972, at the universities of Botswana, Lesotho, and Swaziland (in Roma, Lesotho). From 1972 to 1975 he was associate director of the Theological Education Fund of the World Council of Churches, based in England.

> "We dream of a new society that will be truly non-nracial, truly democratic, in which people count because they are created in the image of God."
>
> Desmund Tutu, 1984

Having been elected dean of Johannesburg in 1975, he returned to South Africa. In 1976 he was consecrated bishop of Lesotho, but two years later he accepted appointment as the general secretary of the South African Council of Churches. During his tenure in this office he became an international spokesperson in the struggle against apartheid and was awarded the Nobel Peace Prize in 1984. The same year he was elected bishop of Johannesburg, and in 1986 he became archbishop of Cape Town. He retired from this office in June 1996. In January 1996 he was appointed the chairperson of the Commission on Truth and Rec-

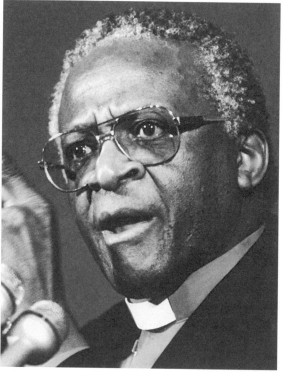

"I said to myself: I'm doing God's job, so God had jolly well better look after me if he wants me to do it."

Desmund Tutu, 1993

onciliation by President Nelson Mandela. Recipient of many honorary doctorates and other awards, Tutu was elected president of the All Africa Conference of Churches in 1987, and re-elected to that office in 1993. After the unbanning of the liberation movements in South Africa in February 1990, Tutu played a major role in facilitating peace, reconciliation, and national reconstruction in South Africa. Tutu is married to Leah Nomalizo Shenxane; the couple has four children. ◆

'Umar Ibn Sa'id Tal

c. 1794–1864 ● MUSLIM

'Umar Ibn Sa'id Tal was a Muslim cleric who exerted a profound influence on the spread of Islam and one of its brotherhoods, the Tijaniyya, across a broad swath of West Africa. Through his writing, charisma, and military achievements, and through his descendants, he remains a prominent figure for Muslims in Senegal, Guinea, Mali, and other parts of West Africa.

'Umar was born in the valley of the Senegal River at Halwar, near the town of Podor (1794 and 1797 are the dates of birth most frequently advanced). He was the son of a local cleric and teacher in a Muslim society dominated by the Fulani (Fulbe) people, who played a leading role in the spread of Islam across West Africa in the eighteenth and nineteenth centuries.

'Umar showed a strong aptitude for learning as he pursued his clerical training in the conventional peripatetic pattern. In addition to his studies in Islamic law, theology, and literature, he accepted initiation into the Sufi brotherhood called the Tijaniyya, which had begun in Algeria and Morocco in the late eighteenth century. 'Umar then made the pilgrimage to Mecca and Medina; in fact, he fulfilled this obligation in three successive years (1828–1830). During this time his initiation into the Tijaniyya was reaffirmed, and he was authorized to spread the brotherhood in West Africa.

During his studies and his pilgrimage, 'Umar spent significant time in most of the main Muslim centers of West Africa,

> 'Umar remains a prominent figure for Muslims in Senegal, Guinea, Mali, and other parts of West Africa.

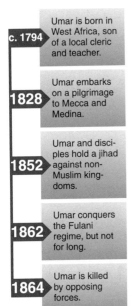

c. 1794 Umar is born in West Africa, son of a local cleric and teacher.

1828 Umar embarks on a pilgrimage to Mecca and Medina.

1852 Umar and disciples hold a jihad against non-Muslim kingdoms.

1862 Umar conquers the Fulani regime, but not for long.

1864 Umar is killed by opposing forces.

particularly in the areas where Fulani Muslims had taken power through the jihad or "holy war": the imamate of Futa Jalon, the caliphate of Hamdullahi or Masina, and the Sokoto caliphate. 'Umar spent the 1840s in Futa

Jalon developing a very loyal group of disciples. During this period he wrote his major work, *Al-Rimah*, an important resource for Tijaniyya today.

Between 1852 and his death in 1864, 'Umar enlisted his disciples and many other Muslims in a jihad against some predominantly non-Muslim kingdoms in the upper Senegal and middle Niger river valleys. Most of his recruits were Fulani from the area of Futa Jalon, Futa Toro, and Senegambia; most of his opponents were Mandinka and Bambara living in the western part of what is today Mali.

In 1862 'Umar went beyond his mission of destroying the structures of "paganism" when he issued an ultimatum to Hamdullahi to cease support of the Bambara regime of Segu. He conquered this Fulani Muslim regime, but its inhabitants soon joined forces with an influential Timbuktu cleric, Ahmad al-Bakkay, overturned the new regime, and brought 'Umar's life to an end in 1864.

'Umar has left his imprint on the societies of Senegal, Guinea, and Mali in particular. His works, especially *Al-Rimah*, are widely used in Tijaniyya teaching. Many of his descendants are well placed in the elite political and religious classes today. In Senegal he is remembered as a hero of Islamic expansion and resistance to the French, whereas many in Mali see him as an invader who destroyed indigenous states and weakened their social structures. ◆

Vivekananda

1863–1902 ● HINDU

Vivekananda was the religious name of Narendranath Datta, or Dutt, a leading spokesman for modern Hinduism in the late nineteenth century and founder of the Vedanta Society in the West and the Ramakrishna Mission in India. *Vivekananda* is the westernized form of the Sanskrit name *Vivekānanda* ("bliss of discerning knowledge").

Narendranath came from a Bengali family, *kayastha* by caste, which consisted of scribes, clerks, and government officials. Since the early nineteenth century his family had raised its status through the process of westernization. Narendranath's grandfather had abandoned his wife and young son to become a traditional Hindu *samnyasin* ("renunciant"), but his son, Bisvanath Dutt, had become a prosperous lawyer in the Calcutta High Court. It was assumed that Narendranath would follow his father's profession. He entered college in Calcutta in 1878 and received his

> "Here I stand and if I shut my eyes, and try to conceive my existence, I, I, I, what is the idea before me? The idea of a body. Am I, then, nothing but a combination of material substances? The Vedas declare, "No." I am a spirit living in a body. I am not the body. The body will die, but I shall not die."
>
> Vivekananda, 1893

bachelor's degree in 1884, but when his father died shortly thereafter he turned from the law to a personal religious quest.

In 1881 he met Ramakrishna (1836–1886), a celibate devotee of the goddess Kali, a man unlearned in a formal sense but wise in religious experience. Although impressed by the depth of Ramakrishna's renunciation and spiritual attainments, Narendranath was disturbed by Ramakrishna's image-oriented worship of Kali and his lack of social concern. As an intellectual Brahmo, Narendranath believed in the formlessness of God; Ramakrishna urged him to meet God in person by worshiping Kali. Narendranath was deeply committed to social reform; Ramakrishna was concerned about individual spiritual transformation.

Unable to come to terms with Ramakrishna's views, Narendranath withdrew periodically during his college years to immerse himself in Western philosophy and science and in Indian music, for he excelled as a singer. Ramakrishna pursued him, seeing in Narendranath not only a youth whose singing touched his emotions but one who had the potential for greatness. It was only after Narendranath finished college and after his father died that he yielded to Ramakrishna's appeal. In 1885 Narendranath accepted Ramakrishna as his guru and began a period of intensive religious training that lasted until Ramakrishna's death in August 1886.

Before he died, Ramakrishna brought Narendranath to a personal experience of Kali that he considered his pupil's final test and appointed him to guide his other disciples after his death. Narendranath accepted the responsibility, became a *samnyasin*, and taught the disciples as best he could for several years, but by 1889 he had lost confidence in his previous religious views. He left his fellow disciples in 1890 for an extended pilgrimage throughout India, during which he gradually developed a position that combined the devotional insights of Ramakrishna with the social concerns that he identified with both the Buddha and modern reformers. When he heard that the World's Parliament of Religions was to be held in Chicago in 1893, he conceived a plan to seek Western material support for the revitalization of Hinduism and to share in return Hindu spiritual insights. After obtaining travel funds from the maharaja of Khetri and adopting the name *Vivekananda*, suggested by his patron, he left for America.

Vivekananda was not the only Hindu representative at the World's Parliament of Religions in Chicago in the autumn of 1893, but he was the most dynamic. In contrast to the learned dissertations by other Hindu speakers, Vivekananda gave a powerful argument for the universal truth of Hinduism that brought him widespread attention in the press and numerous speaking engagements. He soon began to attract a dedicated group of Western followers, and gradually shifted his plans from raising money for India to creating a worldwide religious movement based on the eternal truths of Hinduism. With that purpose, and with his new Western disciples as the core, he founded the Vedanta Society in New York in 1895. He soon had chapters in London and Boston, for which he summoned two swamis (Sanskrit for "teachers") from India to help direct their work. The mission to the West was well under way by the end of 1896 when Vivekananda left for India to begin the second phase of his program.

Vivekananda's arrival in India early in 1897 with a group of Western disciples was treated by the Indian press as a triumphal return, but not all Hindus were happy with his aggressive proselytizing of Westerners or with his unorthodox ideas. Ramakrishna's former disciples, whom Narendranath had left seven years earlier, were themselves uncertain how to respond to Narendranath-turned-Vivekananda and his Western disciples.

Vivekananda's dynamism and persuasive powers, however, carried the day, just as they had in the West. His orthodox critics were not all silenced, but the disciples were won over to his program of work in the world. To implement this program, Vivekananda founded the Ramakrishna Mission on 1 May 1897, and organized the disciples as monks in the Ramakrishna Order to carry out its work of education and service. In 1898, with money from Western disciples, he purchased a site near Calcutta for a center to house the Mission and Order. A worldwide organization was established by 1899, when Vivekananda turned over the active work to his Indian and Western disciples.

After visiting friends in America and Europe from 1899 to 1900, Vivekananda returned to India in semi-retirement and died on 4 July 1902. In less than 40 years of life, and in less than 10 years of intensive effort, he had created a permanent link between Hinduism and the West in which Hinduism for the first time was the dominant influence. Vivekananda's teaching was not the Hinduism of the orthodox, however, or even that of Ramakrishna, but what Vivekananda called "practical Vedanta," a universal Hinduism that combined devotion and practical work for the world with the ultimate goal of union with the One. ◆

1863 Vivekananda is born into a Bengali family.

1884 Vivekananda receives his bachelor's degree.

1885 Vivekananda accepts Ramakrishna as his guru.

1890 Vivekananda leads his disciples on an extended pilgrimage.

1893 Vivekananda attends Chicago's World Parliament of Religions.

1895 Vivekananda founds the Vedanta Society in New York.

1897 Vivekananda founds the Ramakrishna mission.

1899 Vivekananda establishes a worldwide organization.

1902 Vivekananda dies.

Wesley, John

1703–1791 ● METHODIST

John Wesley was an English evangelical preacher and founder of the Methodist Society. He was born in Lincolnshire, the fifteenth of 19 children, less than half of whom survived infancy.

His formal education, by his mother, began at the age of five. She was particularly fond of John, probably because of an event that occurred in 1708. He had been trapped in the nursery of the Epworth rectory as it was engulfed by fire but, exhibiting extraordinary presence of mind for a five-year-old, he pushed a chest to a window, stood on it, and attracted the attention of rescuers below. This was regarded by witnesses, and later by the Methodist church, as an indication of special divine interest in the boy.

At the age of ten Wesley went to the Charterhouse School in London and after six years there obtained a scholarship to Christ-

church College, Oxford; in 1725 he was ordained as a deacon and, shortly after, a fellow of Lincoln College. At Oxford in 1728, his brother Charles had gathered together a group of young men with the intention of studying the Bible and books of divinity. Wesley soon emerged as their leader and began to promote other activities, such as visiting the sick. The group became known derisively as "The Bible Moths," "The Holy Club," and, notably, "The Methodists," because of the curiously methodical religion they prescribed. Yet at this stage Wesley's "Methodism" was still concerned with personal holiness through inward searching rather than outward benevolence.

In 1735 the numbers in the club dwindled, and both John and Charles were searching for a new challenge. A chance meeting with General James Edward Oglethorpe, the founder of the American colony of Georgia, led to an invitation for John to become pastor at the new settlement of Savannah, and for Charles to be the general's personal secretary. John was captivated by the notion of preaching Christianity to the "noble American savages," and with their mother's encouragement they accepted the positions.

In December 1735 the Wesley brothers set sail for the colony. On board their ship was a party of 26 Moravian settlers. John was awed by the simple faith of these Christians when, during a violent Atlantic storm that shattered the ship's mast, they calmly and courageously sang hymns while he nervously contemplated his imminent demise. On their arrival in Georgia, the Moravians were met by their own minister, August Spangenberg, whom Wesley approached for counsel. Spangenberg, who later remarked of Wesley "that true grace dwelt and reigned in him," stressed in their brief conversation the two themes that were later to dominate Wesley's preachings—the inward witness of the Spirit and the knowledge of personal salvation.

Despite this inspirational beginning his time in Georgia proved a failure. His new parishioners were not pious Oxford students but a motley collection, mostly ex-convicts, who had no time for the strictures of Wesley's methods. The climactic event that ended his time in Georgia involved a young woman whom he considered marrying, but while he prevaricated, the woman married another suitor. Wesley, shocked by her behavior and perhaps harboring certain resentments, refused her communion, an action which resulted in his being sued for defamation of character. Not waiting for the issue to be resolved, Wesley left for England.

On his arrival in early 1738, the dejected Wesley sought out the small Moravian community that was on its way to America. He saw that he had been ineffectual because he had lacked a firm personal faith until, in his words, on May 24, 1738, while attending a Bible society meeting "the peace was granted." This marked a turning point in his religion and his life. His formidable personal energy and intellect, no longer focused on his own personal salvation, were directed outward.

In 1739 Wesley was invited to become pastor to a poor community of colliers in Kingswood Chase. At first he was reluctant to preach to people who in all likelihood would be uneducated and unwilling recipients, but he realized that this was a mission necessitated by his new convictions.

Wesley continued the pervious pastor's habit of preaching in fields and on street corners. Soon, with his sincere and penetrating message of personal salvation, he was drawing crowds; people yelled and convulsed in religious fervor as he spoke. His own reputation grew rapidly as he traveled to preach in prisons and other towns. Religious societies sprang up that drew their character from Wesley's teachings and were regarded as distinctly Methodist.

Many in England, however, believed that Wesley's teachings might stir up rebellious sentiments and others were apparently jealous of his remarkable success. The Church of England opposed his "enthusiastic" style and eventually banned him from their pulpits. He continued to travel throughout Britain, mostly on horseback, preaching in the open, usually four or five times a day. Occasionally he and his lay preachers encountered mobs organized to break up his meetings. His role was always to stand up to a mob, despite sometimes barely escaping death.

Wesley was endowed with an extraordinary gift for organization. By 1745, through all the persecution, this small, intense man had established a nationwide network and held the first gathering of his clerical supporters. Recognizing that for the most part, his parishioners were from the lower classes, he determined a need to establish schools for the poor. In 1774 he was perhaps the first notable voice in England to speak out against slavery. He campaigned for improving the conditions in prisons and moved to establish clinics for the poor. His compassion for humanity and sense of social justice were in many ways

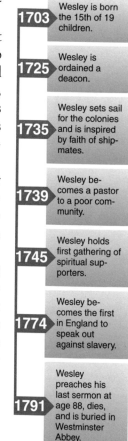

1703 Wesley is born the 15th of 19 children.

1725 Wesley is ordained a deacon.

1735 Wesley sets sail for the colonies and is inspired by faith of shipmates.

1739 Wesley becomes a pastor to a poor community.

1745 Wesley holds first gathering of spiritual supporters.

1774 Wesley becomes the first in England to speak out against slavery.

1791 Wesley preaches his last sermon at age 88, dies, and is buried in Westminster Abbey.

generations ahead of their time. He preached his last sermon in 1791, at 88, and was buried in Westminster Abbey. ◆

White, Ellen Gould

1826–1915 ● SEVENTH-DAY ADVENTIST

> "In the hearts of all mankind, of whatever race or station in life, there are inexpressible longings for something they do not now possess."
>
> Ellen Gould White, *The Desire of Ages*, 1898

Ellen Gould White was the cofounder of the Seventh-day Adventist church. Ellen Gould Harmon was born 26 November 1827 on a farm near Gorham, Maine. As a child she moved with her family to Portland. When she was nine or ten, an angry schoolmate hit her in the face with a rock, knocking her unconscious for several weeks. The accident left her a semi-invalid, unable to continue her schooling (except for a brief period at the Westbrook Seminary and Female College) and unlikely to fulfill her ambition of becoming a scholar.

Raised a Methodist, Ellen in 1840 joined the Millerites, who believed that Christ would return to earth in 1843 or 1844. When he failed to appear on 22 October 1844, the date finally agreed upon, disappointment and confusion swept through the Millerite camp. In December, while praying with friends for guidance, 17-year-old Ellen went into a trance, the first of many visions during which she claimed to receive divine illumination. In this state God assured her that the Millerites' only mistake lay in confusing the second coming of Christ with the beginning of the heavenly judgment, which had indeed begun on 22 October. In 1846 Ellen was shown the importance of observing the seventh-day sabbath. In both instances her visions supported doctrines that others were already teaching, a pattern that came to characterize her role as a religious leader.

In 1846 Ellen married James White, who became her editor, publisher, and manager. For several years they traveled throughout the Northeast preaching. When children began arriving, Ellen reluctantly left them with friends. In 1852 the weary, impoverished couple settled in Rochester, New York, where they collected their children about them and James acquired a printing press. After three discouraging years, the Whites moved to Battle Creek, Michigan, where in the early

1860s they formally created the Seventh-day Adventist church, then numbering about 3,500 members.

Health concerns dominated Ellen White's life during the 1860s. Since her childhood accident she had suffered almost constantly from an array of illnesses: heart, lung, and stomach ailments, frequent "fainting fits" (sometimes once or twice a day), paralytic attacks, pressure on the brain, breathing difficulties, and bouts of anxiety and depression. At times she feared that Satan and his evil angels were trying to kill her. In 1863, only months after using water treatments to nurse her children through a diphtheria epidemic, she received a special vision on health. Adventists, she learned, were to give up eating meat and other stimulating foods, shun alcohol and tobacco, and avoid drug-dispensing doctors. When sick, they were to rely solely on nature's remedies: fresh air, sunshine, rest, exercise, proper diet, and, above all, water. A second vision on health led her in 1866 to establish the Western Health Reform Institute in Battle Creek, the first of a worldwide chain of Adventist sanitariums.

During the 1870s the Whites spent considerable time proselytizing on the West Coast. In 1881, James died. Following a year-long depression, Ellen White resumed her ministry through missions to Europe (1885–1887) and to Australia and New Zealand (1891–1900). Upon returning to the United States in 1900, she purchased a farmhouse near Saint Helena, California, from whence she continued to guide her growing church. Although she never assumed formal leadership of the Adventist organization, White wielded enormous influence, especially late in her career, in matters relating to both doctrine and policy. While in semi-retirement, she directed a major campaign to build an Adventist sanitarium "near every large city" and to open a medical school, the College of Medical Evangelists (now Loma Linda University), in southern California. She died on 16 July 1915, at age 87; over 136,000 Seventh-day Adventists mourned her passing.

Although better at speaking than writing—her modest reputation among non-Adventists derived largely from her lectures on temperance—Ellen White enjoyed her greatest success as an author. Between the late 1840s, when her first broadsides appeared, and 1915, she published over 100 books and pamphlets and contributed thousands of articles to church periodicals. Since her death the Ellen G. White Estate has

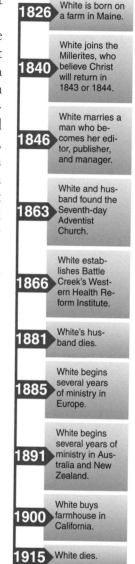

1826 White is born on a farm in Maine.

1840 White joins the Millerites, who believe Christ will return in 1843 or 1844.

1846 White marries a man who becomes her editor, publisher, and manager.

1863 White and husband found the Seventh-day Adventist Church.

1866 White establishes Battle Creek's Western Health Reform Institute.

1881 White's husband dies.

1885 White begins several years of ministry in Europe.

1891 White begins several years of ministry in Australia and New Zealand.

1900 White buys farmhouse in California.

1915 White dies.

brought out dozens of additional books, compiled from her letters, sermons, and articles. Few subjects escaped her attention. Among her most notable works were three sets of books on biblical history and eschatology: *Spiritual Gifts* (1858–1864), *Spirit of Prophecy* (1870–1884), and the "Conflict of the Ages Series" (1888–1917), which included *The Great Controversy between Christ and Satan.* Her health writings culminated with the widely circulated *Ministry of Healing* (1905). In *Education* (1903), she emphasizes "the harmonious development of the physical, the mental, and the spiritual powers." Between 1855 and 1909 she published 37 volumes of *Testimonies for the Church,* in which she relayed counsel that she had received in visions. The most popular of her books was *Steps to Christ* (1892), a brief devotional work that sold in the millions.

Since early in Ellen White's career critics have alleged that she sometimes contradicted herself, failed to acknowledge— and on occasion denied—her indebtedness to other authors, and allowed her testimonies to be manipulated by interested parties close to her. In response, she insisted on the consistency, originality, and independence of her inspired writings. "I do not write one article in the paper expressing merely my own ideas. They are what God has opened before me in vision—the precious rays of light shining from the throne." In recent years scholars have uncovered evidence that she borrowed extensively from other authors and that her literary assistants provided more than routine editorial and secretarial services.

Although Ellen White preferred to style herself as "the Lord's messenger" rather than as a prophetess, she classed herself with the biblical writers. "In ancient times God spoke to men by the mouth of prophets and apostles," she wrote in 1876. "In these days he speaks to them by the Testimonies of his Spirit" an unambiguous reference to her own work. Many early Adventists, including her own husband, resisted efforts to equate her writings with the Bible and to make acceptance of her inspiration a "test of fellowship." Nevertheless, by the early twentieth century Adventist churches were "disfellowshipping" members who questioned her gift, and were relying on her views to determine the correct reading of scripture. Among the faithful the very phrase "Spirit of Prophecy" became synonymous with Ellen White and her writings, which they regarded as authoritative not only in theology but in science, medicine, and history as well. ◆

Wise, Stephen Samuel

1874–1949 ● JEWISH

Stephen Samuel Wise left his mark as a religious leader, a founder of and activist in the Zionist movement in the United States, and a spokesman for the cause of civic betterment. Wise was born in Budapest, Hungary, in 1874, the eldest son on Sabine and Aaron Weiss, a rabbi. The Weiss family immigrated to the United States the following year settled in New York, and changed their family name to Wise.

Stephen Wise graduated from Columbia University in 1891 and was ordained a rabbi in 1893, becoming assistant rabbi of New York City's Congregation B'nai Jeshurun. In 1900, he became rabbi of Temple Beth Israel in Portland, Oregon, where he remained for six years. He returned to New York in 1907 and founded the Free Synagogue remaining its spiritual leader until his death. In 1922 he established the Jewish Institute of Religion (JIR), an academy for training Reform rabbis, and was its president until its merger with the Hebrew Union College of Cincinnati in 1948. Wise was a crusader for social causes. His sermons and speeches focused on every civic cause of the 1920s and 1930s, including municipal corruption and labor's right to organize. It was his campaign to compel the corrupt James Walker, mayor of New York, to resign that brought him into conflict with Franklin D. Roosevelt, who was governor of New York from 1928 to 1932. This rupture lasted until the presidential election of 1936, when Wise became a staunch supporter of the administration.

Wise played a key role in establishing the American Zionist movement. In 1897 he helped found the New York Federation of Zionists,

> "Israel has a mission still: Truth-seeking in the world of thought, and right-doing in the world of action!"
>
> Stephen Wise, *Sermons and Addresses*, 1905

1874 Wise is born in Hungary.

1875 Wise and family emigrate to the U.S.

1893 Wise is ordained a rabbi, becoming assistant rabbi at a New York temple.

1897 Wise helps found the New York Federation of Zionists.

1900 Wise becomes a rabbi at a temple in Portland, Oregon.

1907 Wise founds the Free Synagogue in New York.

1920 Wise helps organize of the American Jewish Congress.

1922 Wise establishes the Jewish Institute of Religion.

1933 Wise enlists American Jewish Congress support for German boycott.

1936 Wise establishes the World Jewish Congress.

1949 Wise dies; his autobiography is published.

which became the Federation of American Zionists a year later. Together with Louis D. Brandeis, he helped convince President Woodrow Wilson to support the Balfour Declaration. He was a spokesman for the Zionist cause at the Paris Peace Conference of 1919–1920 and assumed the presidency of the Zionist Organization of America that same year, heading it from 1918 to 1920 and again from 1936 to 1938. Wise was among the organizers of the American Jewish Congress, founded in 1920, and in 1936 he established the World Jewish Congress, of which he was president until his death. The leadership role that Wise sought to fill proved increasingly difficult after 1933, when the Nazis came to power in Germany. American Jewry was weak and divided. In 1933, Wise enlisted the support of the American Jewish Congress for the movement to boycott German products, seeing this as the morally correct thing to do. At the same time, he wavered in his support for the Haavara Agreement that existed between Germany and the Yishuv, the organized Jewish community in Palestine.

Abba Hillel Silver, a fellow Reform rabbi and Zionist but a Republican supporter, had been radicalized by the events in Europe. He had made an agreement with the more moderate Wise (who was under Roosevelt's influence) to avoid confronting the administration publicly. In 1943 Silver broke the agreement by arousing American public opinion on behalf of Zionism. The aging Wise was at the same time confronted by the Revisionist Zionists, whose cause (aiding the Irgun Tseva'i Le'ummi) had been considerably strengthened by a group of Palestinian Jews headed by Peter Bergson (alias of Hillel Kook). Wise came into open conflict with the Revisionist Bergson Group, which, he was convinced, was intending to take over the American Zionist movement. At the same time, he faced opposition from the newly organized anti-Zionist constituency within the Jewish community. Clearly, the American Jewish community had, in the crucial year of 1943, become more fragmented than ever. Wise's attempt to play the role of conciliator came to naught. The divisions within the community were too great, as was the gap between what the Jewish rescue advocates sought and what the Roosevelt administration was willing to give during wartime.

By 1943, some felt Wise's leadership to be inconsistent and weak. He found it difficult to plead the special case for the rescue of European Jewry before the Roosevelt administration at a time when the nation faced such awesome dangers. He agreed that Under Secretary of State Sumner Welles should corroborate the news of the "Final Solution" contained in the Riegner cable before making it public, lest Jews be accused of atrocity-mongering. By 1944, Wise had become deeply disillusioned. The establishment of the Jewish state a year before his death gave him considerable gratification, but as the radical losses suffered by European Jewry became known, his despair intensified. His autobiography, *The Challenging Years: The Autobiography of Stephen Wise*, was published in 1949. ◆

> "Every Jew, Atlas-like, bears upon his shoulders the burden of the whole world's Jewry."
> Stephen Wise,
> *Sermons and Addresses*, 1905

Wovoka

c. 1856/8–1932 ● NATIVE AMERICAN

Wovoka was a Paiute Indian religious prophet and messiah of the Ghost Dance of 1890. He was called Jack Wilson by white settlers. Although he often referred to himself as Kwohitsauq ("big rumbling belly"), after his paternal grandfather, he was given the name Wovoka (or Wuvoka, "cutter") by his father, Tavibo ("white man"), who was reported to have trained his son in Paiute shamanistic practices. Tavibo had been an active participant in the 1870 Ghost Dance led by the Paiute shaman-prophet Wodziwob. Central tenets of this earlier Ghost Dance were related to the later teachings of Wovoka, which in turn led to the Ghost Dance movement of 1890. Among these earlier revelations was the prediction of the return of the ancestral dead. This imminent return was to be assisted through the practice of a round dance, which would also effect an earthly cataclysm and so result in the removal of white men

In addition to Paiute shamanic practices and the Ghost Dance of 1870, Wovoka was influenced by his contact with Skokomish Shakers, Mormons, and other Christians. The Puget Sound Shaker religion of the Skokomish leader Squsacht-un (called John Slocum by whites) was primarily concerned with healing. It combined native shamanistic and Christian religious practices. These Shakers produced twitching-ecstasies and trances that sometimes lasted for days. Wovoka's later teachings were also similar to Mormon doctrines regarding the rejuvenation of the American Indians, the radical transformations in the earth's terrain, and the return of the

> "I want you to dance every six weeks. Make a feast at the dance and have food that everybody may eat. Then bathe in the water. That is all. You will receive good words from me again some time. Do not tell lies."
> Wovoka,
> *The Messiah Letter*,
> transcribed by James Mooney, 1891

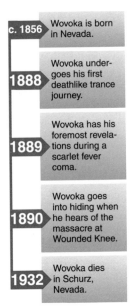

c. 1856 ▸ Wovoka is born in Nevada.

1888 ▸ Wovoka undergoes his first deathlike trance journey.

1889 ▸ Wovoka has his foremost revelations during a scarlet fever coma.

1890 ▸ Wovoka goes into hiding when he hears of the massacre at Wounded Knee.

1932 ▸ Wovoka dies in Schurz, Nevada.

Messiah. Moreover, Paul Bailey indicates in his biography of Wovoka (1957) that the famous Plains Ghost Dance shirt bears a resemblance to Mormon holy garments. Finally, after his father died, Wovoka was hired by a white family named Wilson. This position brought him into close contact with Presbyterian Christianity, which involved Bible reading, moral exhortations, and pietistic stories about Jesus.

Around 1888 Wovoka is reported to have undergone his first deathlike trance-journey to heaven. From this point his teachings were derived from conversations with the ghosts of the dead. Wovoka's oral revelations were associated with the ritual performance of the round dance, which promoted moral and spiritual renewal. His teachings were transmitted by means of a syncretic mythology and dramatized through the skillful use of his personal power symbols.

Wovoka's foremost revelations came in a deathlike coma experienced while he was suffering from scarlet fever during the solar eclipse of 1889. During this trance-coma Wovoka related that he saw God on a transformed earth where Indians and game animals abounded. Wovoka's messages increasingly focused on the presence of the Messiah, a role he himself gradually assumed. His mythology centered on the imminent revival of deceased Indians, who would be reunited with their living kin in an earthly paradise. His description of the fate of whites varied. He predicted that they would be either swept away by the cataclysm or amalgamated into the restored humanity. Many of these doctrines, such as the transformed earth, were more fully explicated by Wovoka's disciples, who disseminated the Ghost Dance in the years following 1889.

The later Ghost Dance, similar to that of the Ghost Dance of 1870, was a kind of round dance that lasted for five nights. Men and women, their fingers intertwined, shuffled sideways around a fire, dancing to the songs that Wovoka received from the dead. While the Paiute participants themselves did not go into a trance, Wovoka did occasionally journey in a trance state to the ghosts, who assured him that Jesus was already on the earth with the dead, moving about as in a cloud. Moreover, along with their remonstrations against lying, drinking, and fighting, the dead said that Indians should work for the whites and have no more trouble with them.

Wovoka's personal power-symbols were typical of native shamanic practices. Along with his sombrero he used eagle, magpie, and crow feathers and red ocher paint from the traditional Paiute holy mountain (now called Mount Grant). As with so many visionary symbol systems, their meaning is not fully known, but Wovoka often incorporated these symbols into his teaching so as to foster belief in his messianic role among his followers.

Wovoka went somewhat into hiding when news of the Wounded Knee massacre of 1890 reached him. He vigorously condemned the misunderstanding of his teachings, especially as reflected in the Lakota armed resistance. He also denied any influence in the development of the Ghost Dance shirts. He later reemerged as the countinuing leader of the much diminished Ghost Dance. He readjusted his predictions of imminent earthly transformation, explaining that Indian ritual and ethical behavior had not conformed properly to his visions. Wovoka died on 20 September 1932 in Schurz, Nevada; his death was preceded a month earlier by that of his wife, Mary, his companion for over 50 years.

More is known of Wovoka than of other similar religious figures, but he can be seen as part of a larger revivalistic movement of the period. Various tribal groups, caught in the death throes of their traditional cultures and the inescapable morass of governmental reservation policy, responded to Wovoka's revelations from a variety of motivations that mediated between their present distress and their future hopes. Wovoka's injunctions against warfare, immoral behavior, and some traditional medicine practices enabled many who participated in the Ghost Dance to begin the psychic transitions needed to respond to the changing circumstances of life. Most important in this connection was Wovoka's orientation away from exclusive tribal recognition toward a pan-Indian identity. ◆

"The dead are still alive again. I do not know when they will be here; maybe this fall or in the spring. When the time comes there will be no more sickness and everyone will be young again."
Wovoka,
The Messiah Letter,
transcribed by
James Mooney,
1891

Xavier, Francis

1506–1552 ● CATHOLIC

Francis Xavier was a Spanish Roman Catholic missionary. Born into a noble family in Navarre in northern Spain, in 1525 Xavier traveled to Paris, then the academic center of Europe, to continue his studies, earning his philosophy degree at the university there in 1530. He remained at the university as a lecturer in philosophy until 1534, when he transferred to theological studies.

It was in Paris that, in 1529, he met the man who was to conclusively shape his future life's course; Ignatius Loyola, an ex-soldier 15 years Xavier's senior, became his roommate and persuaded him to pledge his allegiance to the religious vision Loyola was developing. Xavier's original skepticism toward Loyola's plans abated, and he was one of the seven men who, on August 15, 1534, took a vow of poverty, celibacy, and devotion to the salvation of others. He had previously pursued the 30 days of "spiritual exercises" that Loyola had devised; the mystical insights they prompted were to remain an important influence on him for the rest of his life.

Xavier and his colleagues were ordained in Venice in 1537 and then moved to Rome, where they founded the Society of Jesus under Loyola's command. Until 1540 Xavier was secretary of the new organization, later known as the Jesuits; then, Loyola chose him to lead the mission to those eastern regions that had become colonies of King John III's Portuguese empire. Xavier left for Goa on the Indian subcontinent, arriving there in 1542.

> "As to the numbers who become Christians, you may understand them from this, that it often happens to me to be hardly able to use my hands from the fatigue of baptizing: often in a single day I have baptized whole villages."
>
> Francix Xavier, letter from India, 1543

387

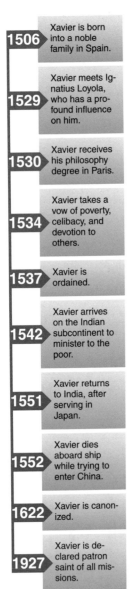

1506 — Xavier is born into a noble family in Spain.

1529 — Xavier meets Ignatius Loyola, who has a profound influence on him.

1530 — Xavier receives his philosophy degree in Paris.

1534 — Xavier takes a vow of poverty, celibacy, and devotion to others.

1537 — Xavier is ordained.

1542 — Xavier arrives on the Indian subcontinent to minister to the poor.

1551 — Xavier returns to India, after serving in Japan.

1552 — Xavier dies aboard ship while trying to enter China.

1622 — Xavier is canonized.

1927 — Xavier is declared patron saint of all missions.

He commenced a painstaking village-to-village ministry among the Paravas, poor pearl fishers of the southeast coast who had converted to Catholicism seven years earlier in the hope of winning Portuguese aid against their tribal enemies.

The villagers had received little pastoral care subsequent to their conversion, so Xavier concentrated on educating them in the tenets of their new faith. His missionary efforts bore fruit throughout the coastal area and into Ceylon; Xavier recorded baptizing over 10,000 villagers in one month alone. The converts he won during his mission to the islands of the Malayas and among the ferocious headhunters of the Mollucas were later forced to renounce their Christian faith as a result of persecution in the seventeenth century, but only after thousands had been martyred. On his return to India, Xavier took control of the diocese of Goa, stretching from the Cape of Good Hope on the southern tip of Africa, to China. The College of Holy Faith in Goa came under Jesuit control and trained native missionaries for continuing the proselytizing work.

Ever keen to spread the Christian gospel to new regions, Xavier was greatly excited by the possibility of converting the Japanese, whom he considered "the best people yet discovered." Reaching Japan in 1549, he was the first westerner to send reports of this mysterious new country and its culture back to Europe. Always able to communicate with people effectively, regardless of their age, race, or belief, he abandoned his poverty for a strategy of studied display, which was more impressive to the Japanese. Returning to India in 1551, he left behind him 2,000 Japanese Christians in five communities. Xavier's hopes of proselytizing China, which was then closed to foreigners, were never realized: he died aboard ship while attempting to enter the country. His body was taken back to Goa, where it was enshrined and remains an object of veneration to this day. Through his ministrations, 30,000 people were baptized and Christianity was permanently installed in India.

Xavier's efforts were a key factor in promoting the importance of the Jesuits within the missionary and educational arm of the Roman Catholic church. He was also instrumental in determining the method, character, and approach of future Catholic missionary activity; he stressed the need for a missionary to learn the native customs and language of a country, and to promote the training of dedicated native evangelists to ensure continuing pastoral support for nascent Christian communities. Canonized in 1622, he was declared patron saint of all missions in 1927. ◆

Young, Brigham

1801–1877 ● MORMON

Brigham Young was an American religious and pioneer leader, businessman, and second president of the Church of Jesus Christ of Latter-day Saints. He was born in Whitingham, Vermont, the ninth of 11 children of a Revolutionary War veteran. When he was three, his family moved to central New York state, then almost virgin land, settling at Sherburne when Young was ten. There, he had a vigorously physical upbringing, clearing land for agriculture, farming, and hunting. The family was a poor one and, especially after his mother's death in 1814, Young often knew hunger.

His father soon remarried and Young left home not long after. He worked successfully as a carpenter, painter, and glazier, married in 1824, and settled in Port Byron, New York, where he and his wife joined the Methodist church. It was through his brother Phineas, a traveling preacher, that he first received a

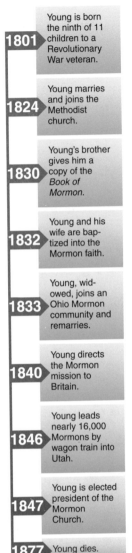

1801 Young is born the ninth of 11 children to a Revolutionary War veteran.

1824 Young marries and joins the Methodist church.

1830 Young's brother gives him a copy of the *Book of Mormon*.

1832 Young and his wife are baptized into the Mormon faith.

1833 Young, widowed, joins an Ohio Mormon community and remarries.

1840 Young directs the Mormon mission to Britain.

1846 Young leads nearly 16,000 Mormons by wagon train into Utah.

1847 Young is elected president of the Mormon Church.

1877 Young dies.

copy of Joseph Smith's *Book of Mormon* in 1830; he, his wife, and immediate family were baptized into the Mormon faith in 1832, and Young began his preaching mission soon after. Well-built, of greater than average height, sandy-haired, and with penetrating blue-gray eyes, Young was a charismatic individual and persuasive speaker responsible for the decision of many to embrace the Mormonism to which he devoted himself wholeheartedly.

In 1833, soon after his wife's death from tuberculosis, Young moved to Kirtland, Ohio, to join the nascent Mormon community under Joseph Smith's leadership. There he married a fellow Mormon. His dedication and potential led to his election to the church's Quorum of the Twelve Apostles, a traveling high council charged with spreading the Mormon gospel. In this capacity he undertook missionary trips east each summer, returning to Kirtland in the winter to help build up the Mormon community.

When disputes over Smith's leadership divided the Kirtland community, Young's support of the prophet prompted him to flee Kirtland. In 1838, he and others among the Kirtland faithful moved to Caldwell County, Missouri. The Mormons alienated veteran settlers there, who feared their bloc power, and they were dispossessed and violently driven from the state; with the senior Mormon leadership, including Smith, imprisoned, it was Young who organized the group's evacuation to Commerce (later renamed Nauvoo), Illinois.

Now quorum president, Young, despite illness exacerbated by the many hardships he had endured, directed the Mormon mission to Britain in 1840; this won 8,000 converts, nearly 1,000 of whom emigrated to Nauvoo. Back in the United States, it was Young who took responsibility for the purchase of lands on which to settle the immigrant faithful.

Smith's teachings on plural marriage were only reluctantly accepted by Young, who feared the ammunition this practice might provide to the church's opponents. However, he went on to embrace the custom wholeheartedly, marrying 26 women by whom he had a total of 57 children.

In Nauvoo, too, the Mormons' autonomy aroused the fear and suspicion of the non-Mormon citizenry. Shortly before his death while in custody, Smith advised the quorum to move to the Rocky Mountains. After Smith's death, Young led his followers on the great westward trek he deemed necessary to fulfill Smith's prophecies, escape persecution, and find a place suited for the creation of a new theocracy.

Under his inspirational leadership, nearly 16,000 Mormons set out in February 1846 on the pioneering journey by wagon train into unknown territory, with the more affluent helping those less fortunate than themselves so that none might be denied the opportunity to migrate. Upon first seeing the Salt Lake Valley, Utah, in July 1847, Young identified it as a place of appropriate harshness and isolation to "make Saints." Elected president of the church in December 1847 (a position he held until his death), he went on to supervise the organization and construction of Salt Lake City, directing cooperative efforts in building and clearing land for agricultural use. A perpetual emigrating fund was created to assist the emigration of Mormon converts from Britain and Europe. As the number of immigrants increased, so too did the number of colonies established to accommodate them; in all, Young was responsible for founding nearly 400 colonies, making him one of America's great colonizers.

Poor relations between the Mormons and outside federal appointees led to rumors that they were flouting U.S. laws, and in 1857 U.S. president Millard Fillmore authorized the dispatch of federal troops to pacify what he had been led to believe was a self-declared Mormon state in rebellion. A violent confrontation was narrowly avoided, although the troops remained to occupy Camp Floyd, a post some 40 miles from Salt Lake City.

A canny businessman who believed in adopting the newest technology to benefit his followers, Young contracted to build telegraphs and railroads in the Utah region and beyond, which served to connect Mormon communities to communication networks worldwide. In an effort to preserve Mormon identity in the face of the resultant increased exposure to outside influences, he also set up local manufacturing and merchandising cooperatives and promoted the development of local resources. His commercial activities made him a rich man, to the benefit of both his family and community.

Bearded and prophet-like in his later years, Young remained active in his capacity as the social architect and guiding light of the community of Mormon faithful up until his death. ◆

Upon first seeing the Salt Lake Valley, Utah, in July 1847, Young identified it as a place of appropriate harshness and isolation to "make Saints."

Zoroaster

Zoroaster, also known as Zarathushtra or Zardust, was a Persian religious leader and reputed founder of Zoroastrianism. Zoroaster was a priest, poet, prophetic seer, and original religious thinker. Virtually nothing is known about the historical figure of Zarathushtra (Zoroaster is the Greek rendition of his name); historical facts have been obscured by legend. Even the historical period in which he lived is the subject of considerable debate; according to some, he was born around 7000 B.C.E. Most scholars reject this date; much of what is known about his life would be **anachronistic.** The site of his birth also remains uncertain; a variety of locations, ranging from the Aral Sea to central India, have been suggested.

Zoroaster's name, meaning, "he who manages camels," perhaps indicates his birth to a wealthy family. Most accounts agree that he was the middle of five sons. According to legend, his birth was foretold in several ancient oracles. According to legend, Zoroaster was the only person in history to laugh rather than cry upon being born. The house filled with light, causing his father to think that the child was possessed by demons. On three occasions, a priest attempted to kill the frightening infant. At first, Zoroaster was placed in front of stampeding cattle. When these failed to kill him, he was cast in a fire, but escaped unscathed. Finally he was put in the den of a she-wolf, but was again miraculously preserved.

> "This I ask Thee, tell me truly, Ahura. Who upholds the earth beneath and the firmament from falling? Who the waters and the plants? Who yoked swiftness to winds and clouds? Who is, O Mazda, creator of Good Thought?"
>
> Avesta Yasna

Brought up in polytheism, at 15 Zoroaster studied for the priesthood. Unsatisfied, he left home at 20 to seek out the truth. For ten years he wandered through the countryside, often spending lengthy periods meditating in a cave. When he was 30, he walked down to the river to draw water for ablutions. There, the Holy Immortal Vehu Manah appeared to him, clothed in light so bright that Zoroaster was unable to see his own shadow. Vehu Manah summoned him to the court of Ahura Mazda, Lord of Wisdom. In the ensuing conversation, Zoroaster asked and Ahura Mazda answered those questions that had plagued him for so many years. He asked about the three perfections and was told that they are: good thoughts, good words, and good deeds. Ahura Mazda also explained about the duality of the universe, and of his conflict with the evil spirit Ahriman. Only through man's actions would Ahura Mazda finally emerge victorious.

For ten years, Zoroaster wandered the countryside preaching his new belief in one eternal uncreated Being, Ahura Mazda, wholly wise, just, and good. Opposed to him is Angra Mainyu, the Evil Spirit, with a host of wicked forces. In this dualism, man must fight on the side of his creator. At that time, Zoroaster won only one convert, a cousin. Chased from his home, Zoroaster arrived at the court of Vishtaspa, king of Chorasmia. Queen Hutaosa was impressed by the prophet, but evil priests convinced the king to throw him in prison. At the time, the king's favorite horse suddenly became lame. Zoroaster agreed to cure the horse in return for a favor for each leg healed. For the first leg, he asked that Vishtaspa accept the new religion; for the second, that his son champion it; for the third he asked that the queen also accept the new faith, and for the fourth, that his enemies be put to death.

With Zoroastrianism as the official religion of Chorasmia, Zoroaster now prospered. Some accounts claim that he remained celibate. References to a daughter in one of the "Gathas," five hymns he allegedly composed, are understood to be an allegory. According to another account, he had one wife, Hvovi. Most Zoroastrians, however, believe that Hvovi was his third wife, who conceived three sons to be born by virgins at 1000-year intervals: Ukhshyatereta (he who makes righteousness grow), Ukhshyatnem (he who makes reverence grow), and Astvatereta (he who embodies righteousness).

Zoroaster, was killed at age 77, by a jealous priest. His religion, however, survives until today in Iran and India. It was adopted as the official state religion by the Persian Achaemenid (550–330 B.C.E.) and Sassanian (226–640 C.E.) dynasties, but was overthrown by Islam in the seventh century. The descendants of Persian religious refugees who fled to India are known as the Parsees. Through Gnosticism, Zoroastrian doctrines also influenced Judaism and Christianity. ◆

> **"The teacher of evil destroys the lore, he by his teaching destroys the design of life, he prevents the possession of Good Thought from being prized. These words of my spirit I wail unto you, O Mazda, and to the Right."**
> Avesta Yasna

Zwingli, Ulrich

1484–1531 ● PROTESTANT

Ulrich Zwingli was a Swiss religious reformer. Born of pious Catholic parents in Wildhaus, he attended the universities of Vienna and Basel, graduating in 1504; he was ordained in 1506, by which time he was already a confirmed humanist. He studied Greek and Hebrew, and corresponded with the influential Dutch humanist scholar Desiderius Erasmus, of whom he considered himself a follower.

Zwingli was a pastor in the parish of Glarus from 1506, but left in 1516 when he became unpopular due to his opposition to Pope Leo X's recruitment of Swiss mercenaries. Moving to Einsiedeln, he began to criticize clerical abuses in his sermons; however, he remained doctrinally orthodox and, in 1518, was appointed to the position of People's Preacher at the Old Minster in Zurich, despite opposition from those who mistrusted his humanistic tendencies. In that capacity, and influenced by his exposure to the writings of Martin Luther, he launched on a series of sermons on the New Testament liberally leavened with topical applications.

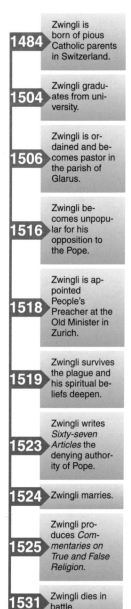

1484 — Zwingli is born of pious Catholic parents in Switzerland.

1504 — Zwingli graduates from university.

1506 — Zwingli is ordained and becomes pastor in the parish of Glarus.

1516 — Zwingli becomes unpopular for his opposition to the Pope.

1518 — Zwingli is appointed People's Preacher at the Old Minister in Zurich.

1519 — Zwingli survives the plague and his spiritual beliefs deepen.

1523 — Zwingli writes *Sixty-seven Articles* the denying authority of Pope.

1524 — Zwingli marries.

1525 — Zwingli produces *Commentaries on True and False Religion.*

1531 — Zwingli dies in battle.

The plague that struck Zurich in 1519 marked an important turning point in Zwingli's life. While he contracted the disease but recovered, his brother died from it, and the experience led to the ripening of those dissident spiritual and theological elements in his thinking which had hitherto been overshadowed by humanistic concerns. The city council of Zurich supported him in his championing of the reform movement initiated by Luther: in 1520 they ordered that Holy Scripture should be taught "without human additions." Zwingli was now in open revolt against the established church, and his increasingly subversive sermons helped prompt revolts against fasting and clerical celibacy in 1522, making Zurich the second center of the Reformation after Wittenburg.

In 1523 Zwingli wrote the *Sixty-seven Articles;* they denied the authority of the pope, the doctrine of transubstantiation (the transformation of the bread and wine to the actual body and blood of Jesus Christ during Mass), the veneration of saints, the state of purgatory, and fasting. Basing his arguments on them, he defeated papal representatives in two disputations that year; the outcome signaled the end of Catholicism in Zurich, and marked the beginning of liturgical reform there. Soon the local cathedral school was also functioning as a theological seminary training reform pastors.

Zwingli incisively elucidated the main tenets of the reformers. These rested on the fundamental belief in the supremacy of scripture over any worldly injunction, including that of the pope. Mass was rejected as an affront to the sacrifice and death of Christ, and images and pictures were banished from places of worship. Marriage was considered lawful for all and Zwingli himself married in Zurich Cathedral in 1524.

Zwingli continued to be the most influential figure in the Swiss reform movement. His *Commentaries on True and False Religion,* produced in 1525, helped spread the reforming doctrines from Zurich to other Swiss cantons, and soon a Christian civic alliance was formed among those cantons where the reform movement held sway.

In his *On Baptism* and *Tricks of the Catabaptists*, Zwingli was ruthless in his advocacy of the need to suppress the Anabaptists, who rejected his policy of accommodation between church and state, and advocated the creation of a pure church of true believers and an end to infant baptism: their leaders were later executed. Zwingli's own vision was of the preacher as the people's tribune before the civil rulers, reminding them of the views of those who legitimized their government while being prepared to accept some civil jurisdiction over church life.

Zwingli fell out with Luther over the latter's assertion that Christ was present in some form in the elements of the Mass. In *On the Lord's Supper*, Zwingli argued against any such real presence, choosing to interpret Christ's words "This is my body" and "This is my blood" figuratively rather than literally. The Marburg Colloquy of 1529 was convened to ameliorate disputes within the reform movement, but no agreement was achieved on this sensitive subject.

In 1529 the First War of Capel broke out, in which the Christian civic alliance of reform Swiss cantons launched a pre-emptive attack against the Catholic forest cantons (the five oldest Swiss cantons) who threatened them. This conflict ended inconclusively but hostilities soon broke out again. Accompanying the reform forces as chaplain carrying the banner, Zwingli fell in battle. His writings, often criticized as disjointed and over-intellectual, remained important. ◆

Zwingli fell out with Luther over the latter's assertion that Christ was present in some form in the elements of the Mass.

Article Sources

The following articles in **Macmillan Profiles:** *Religious Leaders of the World* were newly written for this volume.

ARTICLE	AUTHOR
Alexy II	Mary Carvlin
Anderson, H. George	John Jones
Barbour, Ian	Patty Ohlenroth
Bartholomew	Mary Carvlin
Bernardin, Joseph	Mary Carvlin
Campbell, Joan Brown	Mary Carvlin
Lee, Chung Ok	Mary Carvlin
Dalai Lama	Patty Ohlenroth
Demetrious	Mary Carvlin
Essrog, Seymour	Michael Levine
Fools Crow, Frank	Mary Carvlin
Forbes, James A.	John Jones
Gomes, Peter	Mary Carvlin
Graham, Billy	Mary Carvlin
Griswold, Frank	Mary Carvlin
Kroloff, Charles	Michael Levine
Mohammed, W. Deen	Mary Carvlin
O'Connor, John	Nancy Gratton
Patterson, Paige	Michael Levine
Raiser, Konrad	Mary Carvlin
Ratanasara, Havanpola	Mary Carvlin
Russell, Charles Taze	Mary Carvlin
Russell, Robert John	Patty Ohlenroth
Rutherford, Joseph F.	Mary Carvlin
Schuller, Robert	Mary Carvlin
Snake, Reuben	Mary Carvlin

The following articles were adapted from the *Encyclopedia of Religion,* published by Macmillan Library Reference in 1987.

ARTICLE	AUTHOR
Abduh, Muhammad	Ali E. Hillal Dessouki
Akiva ben Joseph	Gary G. Porton
Ambedkar, B. R.	Eleanor Zelliot
Asbury, Francis	Frank Baker
Aurobindo Ghose	June O'Connor
Baha'ullah	Alessandro Bausani
Barth, Karl	James B. Torrance
Besant, Annie	Dora Kunz
Besht	Joseph Dan
Bhave, Vinoba	Ishwar C. Harris
Blavatsky, H. P.	Emily Sellon
Bonheiffer, Dietrich	Eberhard Bethge
Booth, William	Edward H. McKinely
Bukhari, Al-	R. Marston Speight
Campbell, Alexander	David Edwin Harrell, Jr.
Channing, William Ellergy	John C. Godbey
Cranmer, Thomas	Massey H. Shepherd, Jr.
Dan Fodio, Usuman	Mervyn Hiskett
Day, Dorothy	William D. Miller
Dayananda Sarasvati	Thomas J. Hopkins
Eddy, Mary Baker	Stephen Gottschalk
Gandhi, Mohandas	Mark Juergensmeyer
Ghazali, Abu Hamid al-	W. Montgomery Watt
Handsome Lake	Donald P. St. John
Harris, William Wade	Sheila S. Walker
Hasan Al-Basri	Hasan Qasim Murad
Hillel	Stuart S. Miller
Hooker, Thomas	Frank Shuffelton
Kang Yu-Wei	Hao Chang
Kimbangu, Simon	Bennetta Jules-Rosette
Knox, John	John H. Leith
Krishnamurti, Jiddu	Charles S. White
Lee, Ann	Lawrence Foster
Lenshina, Alice	George Clement Bond
Montagu, Lily	Ellen M. Umansky
Neolin	Donald P. St. John
Schenirer, Sarah	Blu Greenberg
Shembe, Isaiah	Bengt Sundkler
Smith, Joseph	Klaus J. Hansen
Suzuki, D. T.	William R. LaFleur
Szold, Henrietta	Jonathan D. Sarna
Tai-Hsu	Jan Yun-Hua
Vivekananda	Thomas J. Hopkins
White, Ellen Gould	Ronald L. Numbers
Wovoka	John A. Grim

The following articles were extracted from the *Encyclopedia of African American Culture and History*, published by Macmillan Library Reference in 1996.

ARTICLE	AUTHOR
Allen, Richard	Gary B. Nash
Elaw, Zilpha	Allison X. Miller
Farrakahn, Louis	Lawrence H. Mamiya
Father Divine	Jill M. Watts
Grimke, Francis James	Henry J. Ferry
Harris, Barbara	Debi Broome
Horn, Rosa Artimus	Harold Dean Trulear
Jones, Absalom	Gary B. Nash
Mason, Charles Harrison	Lydia McNeill and Allison X. Miller
Muhammad, Elijah	Lawrence H. Mamiya
Powell, Adam Clayton	Wil Haygood
Taylor, Gardner	Allison X. Miller

The following articles were extracted from the *Scribner Encyclopedia of American Lives*, published by Charles Scribner's Sons in 1998 (vol. 1) and 1999 (vol. 2).

ARTICLE	AUTHOR
Abernathy, Ralph David	Irvin D. Solomon
Armstrong, Herbert W.	Theodore N. Thomas
Blake, Eugene	John B. Weaver
Bowman, Thea	Alison M. Parker
Kelman, Wolfe	Sharona A. Levy
Lord, John Wesley	Bernard Hirschhorn
Mueller, Reuben Herbert	John B. Weaver
Murray, Anna Pauline	Anthony Bernard Pinn

The following articles were extracted from the *Encyclopedia of Latin American History and Culture*, published by Charles Scribner's Sons in 1996.

ARTICLE	AUTHOR
Gutierrez, Gustavo	Matthew J. O'Meagher
Las Casas, Bartolome de	William Donovan
Romero, Oscar	Karen Racine

The following articles were reprinted from the *Encyclopedia of Women and World Religion*, edited by Serinity Young and published in 1999 by Macmillan Reference USA.

ARTICLE	AUTHOR
Alinesitoue	Robert M. Baum
Anandamayi Ma	Karen Pechilis Prentiss
Cabrini, Frances Xavier	Leonard Norman Primiano
Jonas, Regina	Rachel Monika Herweg

Rabi'a

Teresa, Mother

Riffat Hassan

Vanessa Nash

The following articles were extracted from the *Encyclopedia of Africa South of the Sahara*, published by Charles Scribner's Sons in 1997.

ARTICLE	AUTHOR
Braide, Garrick Sokari	Lamin Sanneh
Crowther, Samuel Ajayi	J. F. Ade Ajayi
Kiwanuka, Joseph	Adrian Hastings
Maranke, John	Bennetta Jules-Rosette
Mukhtar, Sidi Al-	Louis Brenner
Tutu, Desmond	John W. De Gruchy

The article on Abraham Joshua Heschel by Theodore N. Thomas was extracted from the *Dictionary of American Biography, Supplement 9*, published by Charles Scribner's Sons in 1994.

The article on Jonathan Edwards was adapted from *North America in Colonial Times: An Encyclopedia for Students*, published by Charles Scribner's Sons in 1998.

The remaining articles were extracted from *They Made History: A Biographical Dictionary*, published by Macmillan Reference USA in 1993.

Photo Credits

Photographs appearing in *Religious Leaders of the World* are from the following sources:

Ralph David Abernathy (page 3): CORBIS/Bettman
Richard Allen (page 14): Public Domain
B. R. Ambdedkar (page 17): The Library of Congress
Saint Anthony (page 23): CORBIS/Bettman
Herbert W. Armstrong (page 25): Unknown source
Francis Asbury (page 28): The Library of Congress
Saint Augustine (page 29): The Library of Congress
Karl Barth (page 42): The Library of Congress
Saint Thomas Becket (page 50): Public Domain
Saint Benedict (page 53): The Library of Congress
Saint Bernard (page 55): The Library of Congress
Vinoba Bhave (page 62): Archive Photos, Inc.
Black Elk (page 64): AP/Wide World Photos
William Booth (page 74): The Library of Congress
John Calvin (page 88): The Library of Congress
Alexander Campbell (page 91): The Library of Congress
William Ellergy Channing (page 95): The Library of Congress
Confucius (page 97): Public Domain
Dalai Lama (page 108): AP/Wide World Photos
Dorothy Day (page 113): Public Domain
Father Divine (page 132): The Library of Congress
George Fox (page 138): Public Domain
Saint Francis of Assisi (page 140): The Library of Congress
Mohandas Ghandi (page 146): The Library of Congress
Peter Gomes (page 153): Jerry Bauer

Handsome Lake (page 166): The Library of Congress
Barbara Harris (page 169): AP/Wide World
Thomas Hooker (page 180): Archive Photos, Inc.
L. Ron Hubbard (page 184): AP/Wide World Photos
Saint Jerome (page 188): The Library of Congress
Jesus Christ (page 191): Archive Photos, Inc.
Kang Yu-Wei (page 205): The Library of Congress
Mordecai Kaplan (page 208): The Library of Congress
Martin Luther King, Jr. (page 218): National Archives/Betsy G. Rayneau
John Knox (page 224): The Library of Congress
Jiddu Krishnamurti (page 227): The Library of Congress
Lao-Tzu (page 233): Unknown source
Bartolome de Las Casas (page 236): The Library of Congress
Alice Lenshina (page 244): Archive Photos, Inc.
Saint Ignatius of Loyola (page 250): Public Domain
Martin Luther (page 253): Unknown source
Moses Maimonides (page 261): Public Domain
Moses (page 270): Archive Photos, Inc.
Elijah Muhammad (page 280): AP/Wide World Photos
John O'Connor (page 293): Archive Photos
Saint Patrick (page 297): CORBIS/Bettman
Saint Paul (page 302): CORBIS/Bettman
Charles Taze Russell (page 323): The Library of Congress
Robert Schuller (page 331): AP/Wide World Photos
Junipero Serra (page 335): The Library of Congress
Elizabeth Ann Seton (page 336): Archive Photos, Inc.
Joseph Smith (page 340): The Library of Congress
Emanuel Swedenborg (page 347): Public Domain
Henrietta Szold (page 349): The Library of Congress
Gardner Taylor (page 354): AP/Wide World Photos
Mother Teresa (page 359): AP/Wide World Photos
Saint Thomas Aquinas (page 365): Public Domain
Desmond Tutu (page 367): CORBIS/Bettman
Vivekananda (page 371): The Library of Congress
John Wesley (page 375): The Library of Congress
Stephen Samuel Wise (page 381): The Library of Congress
Brigham Young (page 389): The Library of Congress
Zoroaster (page 394): CORBIS/Bettman

Additional Resources

BOOKS

Bentley, James. *A Calendar of Saints: The Lives of the Principal Saints of the Christian Year*. Facts on File, 1986.

Bonvillain, Nancy. *Native American Religion*. Chelsea House, 1996.

The Cambridge Illustrated History of the Islamic World. Cambridge University Press, 1999.

Carson, Clayborne, et al. *The Eyes on the Prize Civil Rights Reader*. Viking, 1991.

Eliade, Mircea, et al., eds. *The Encyclopedia of Religion*. Macmillan, 1987.

Ellwood, Robert S., ed. *The Encyclopedia of World Religions*. Facts on File, 1998.

Goldman, Elizabeth. *Believers: Spiritual Leaders of the World*. Oxford University Press, 1995.

Knappert, Jan. *The Encyclopaedia of Middle Eastern Mythology and Religion*. Element, 1993.

Lugira, Aloysius Muzzanganda. *African Religion*. Facts on File, 1999.

Macmillan Information Now Encyclopedia: World Religions. Simon and Schuster, 1998.

Martell, Hazel. *The World of Islam Before 1700*. Raintree Steck-Vaughn, 1999.

Mbiti, John S. *African Religions and Philosophy*. 2nd ed. Heinemann, 1990.

Melton, J. Gordon. *Encyclopedia of American Religions*. 5th ed. Gale Research, 1996.

Tobias, Michael, Jane Morrison, and Bettina Gray, eds. *A Parliament of Souls: In Search of Global Spirituality: Interviews with 28 Spiritual Leaders from Around the World*. KQED Books, 1995.

Walker, Paul Robert. *Spiritual Leaders: American Indian Lives*. Facts on File, 1994.

Young, Henry J. *Major Black Religious Leaders, 1755–1940*. Abingdon, 1977.

Young, Serenity, ed. *Encyclopedia of Women and World Religion*. Macmillan Reference USA, 1999.

VIDEORECORDINGS (*See also:* individual entries.)

Eyes on the Prize: America's Civil Rights Years, 1954–1965. PBS Video, 1987; and *Eyes on the Prize: America at the Racial Crossroads.* PBS Video, 1989.

Roman Catholicism. Films for the Humanities and Sciences, 1996.

Smithsonian World: Islam. PBS Video, 1991.

WEBSITES (*See also:* individual entries.)

The Catholic Encyclopedia. http://www.newadvent.org/cathen/

Catholic Online Saints Index. http://saints.catholic.org/stsindex.html

Rabbinic Wisdom. http://religion.rutgers.edu/iho/sages.html

Religion and the Founding of the American Republic (Library of Congress online exhibit). http://lcweb.loc.gov/exhibits/religion/religion.html

Virtual Religion Index. http://religion.rutgers.edu/vri/index.html

ABDUH, MUHAMMAD

Kedourie, Elie. *Afghani and Abduh: An Essay on Religious Unbelief and Political Activism in Modern Islam.* Frank Cass, 1997.

Kerr, Malcolm H. *Islamic Reform: The Political and Legal Theories of Muhammad 'Abduh and Rashid Rida.* University of California Press, 1966.

"Islam in the Modern World." *USC Muslim Students Association Islamic Server.* http://www.usc.edu/dept/MSA/introduction/woi_modernera.html

ABERNATHY, RALPH

Abernathy, Donzaleigh. *Partners to History: Martin Luther King, Jr., Ralph David Abernathy, and the Civil Rights Movement.* General Publishing, 1998.

Abernathy, Ralph. *And the Walls Came Tumbling Down: An Autobiography.* Harper and Row, 1989.

Applebome, Peter. "Rights Leaders Denouncing New Book by Ex-King Aide." *New York Times,* Oct. 13, 1989.

Reef, Catherine. *Ralph David Abernathy.* Dillon Press, 1995.

Severo, Richard. "Ralph D. Abernathy, 64, Rights Pioneer." *New York Times,* Apr. 18, 1990 (obituary).

ABU BAKR (*See also:* MUHAMMAD.)

Ahmad, Fazl. *Abu Bakr, the First Caliph of Islam.* Muhammad Ashraf, 1987.

Madelung, Wilfred. *The Succession to Muhammad: A Study of the Early Caliphate.* Cambridge University Press, 1997.

Martell, Hazel. *The World of Islam Before 1700.* Raintree Steck-Vaughn, 1999.

AKIVA BEN JOSEPH

Finkelstein, Louis. *Akiba, Scholar, Saint and Martyr.* Atheneum, 1981.

Nadich, Judah. *Rabbi Akiba and His Contemporaries*. Jason Aronson, 1998.

Neusner, Jacob, ed. *History of the Jews in the Second Century of the Common Era*. Garland, 1991.

Neusner, Jacob. *The Oral Torah: The Sacred Books of Judaism*. Harper and Row, 1986.

ALEXY II

Davis, Nathaniel. *A Long Walk to Church: A Contemporary History of Russian Orthodoxy*. Westview Press, 1995.

"Don't Bless My Souls." *The Economist*, June 21, 1997.

Gordon, Michael R. "Russians Pass Bill Sharply Favoring Orthodox Church; Other Christians Hurt." *New York Times*, Sept. 20, 1997.

"Patriarch Alexy II of Moscow and All Russia." *Russian Orthodox Church (Moscow Patriarchate)*. http://www.russian-orthodox-church.org.ru/pa2_e.htm

ALINESITOUE

Ford, Clyde W. *The Hero with an African Face: Mythic Wisdom of Traditional Africa*. Bantam Books, 1999.

Lugira, Aloysius Muzzanganda. *African Religion*. Facts on File, 1999.

Mbiti, John S. *African Religions and Philosophy*. 2nd ed. Heinemann, 1990.

Parrinder, Edward Geoffrey. *African Traditional Religion*. Greenwood Press, 1976.

ALLEN, RICHARD

Campbell, James T. *Songs of Zion: The African Methodist Episcopal Church in the United States and South Africa*. Oxford University Press, 1995.

Klots, Steve, and Nathan I. Huggins. *Richard Allen*. Chelsea House, 1991.

Payne, Daniel Alexander. *History of the African Methodist Episcopal Church*. Arno Press, 1969.

"The African Methodist Episcopal Church: An Historical Note." *African Methodist Episcopal Church*. http://www.ame-church.org/

AMBEDKAR, B.R.

Gokhale, Jayashre B. "Castaways of Caste." *Natural History*, Oct. 1986.

Hutton, J.H. *Caste in India: Its Nature, Function, and Origins*. 4th ed. Oxford University Press, 1963.

Iyer, V.R. Krishna. *Ambedkar Centenary*. South Asia Books, 1992.

"Dr. B.R. Ambedkar." *FreeIndia.Org*. http://freeindia.org/biographies/ambedkar/

ANANDAMAYI MA (ANANDA MA)

Hallstrom, Lisa Lassell. *Mother of Bliss: Anandamayi Ma (1896–1982)*. Oxford University Press, 1999.

Lannoy, Richard. *Anandamayi: Her Life and Wisdom*. Element, 1996.

Lipski, Alexander. *Life and Teachings of Sri Anandamayi Ma*. Vedams Books, 1998.

Shree Shree Anandamayi Ma's Darshan. http://www.anandamayi.org/

ANDERSON, H. GEORGE

Anderson, H. George. *A Good Time to Be the Church, A Conversation with Bishop H. George Anderson*. Augsburg Books, 1997.

Anderson, H. George. "Pray for Jerusalem." *The Lutheran*, Mar. 1998. http://www.thelutheran.org/9803/page53.html

"The Rev. H. George Anderson." *Evangelical Lutheran Church in America*. http://www.elca.org/ob/Anderson.html

SAINT ANTHONY

Fulop-Miller, Rene. *Saints That Moved the World: Anthony, Augustine, Francis, Ignatius, Theresa*. Ayer Book, reprint 1972.

Kerry, Margaret Charles. *Saint Anthony of Padua: Fire and Light*. Pauline Books and Media, 1999.

Ling, Sheila Ward. *St. Anthony of Padua: Friend of All the World*. Alba House, reissue 1996.

"St. Anthony of Padua." *Catholic Online Saints Index*. http://saints.catholic.org/saints/anthonypadua.html

ARMSTRONG, HERBERT W.

Armstrong, Herbert W. *Mystery of the Ages*. Dodd, Mead, 1985.

"Herbert Armstrong, 93, Dies; Evangelist and Broadcaster." *New York Times*, Jan. 17, 1986.

Hopkins, Joseph Martin. *The Armstrong Empire; A Look at the Worldwide Church of God*. Eerdmans, 1974.

Worldwide Church of God. http://www.wcg.org/

ASBURY, FRANCIS

Ludwig, Charles. *Francis Asbury: God's Circuit Rider*. Out of print. "Mr. Wesley's Preachers: Francis Asbury."

Methodist Archives and Research Centre. http://rylibweb.man.ac.uk/data1/dg/methodist/asbury.html

Religion in Eighteenth-Century America (Library of Congress online exhibit). http://lcweb.loc.gov/exhibits/religion/rel02.html

AUGUSTINE, SAINT

Augustine, Saint, Bishop of Hippo. *The Confessions*. Vintage Books, 1998.

Fitzgerald, Allan, et al., eds. *Augustine Through The Ages: An Encyclopedia*. Eerdmans, 1999.

Fulop-Miller, Rene. *Saints That Moved the World: Anthony, Augustine, Francis, Ignatius, Theresa*. Ayer Book, reprint 1972.

Wills, Garry. *Saint Augustine*. Viking, 1999.

"St. Augustine of Hippo." *Catholic Online Saints Index*. http://saints.catholic.org/saints/augustinehippo.html

AUROBINDO GHOSE

Bruteau, Beatrice. *Worthy Is the World: The Hindu Philosophy of Sri Aurobindo*. Fairleigh Dickinson University Press, 1972.

Ghose, Aurobindo. *The Essential Writings of Sri Aurobindo*. Oxford University Press, 1998.

Sri Aurobindo Society. http://www.sriaurobindosociety.org.in/index.htm

THE BAB

Bab, Ali Muhammad Shirazi. *Selections from the Writings of the Bab*. Baha'i Pub. Trust, 1976.

Martyrdom of the Bab: A Compilation. Kalimat Press, 1992.

Smith, Peter. *A Short History of the Baha'i Faith*. Oneworld Publications, 1996.

BAHA'ULLAH

Esslemont, J. E. *Baha'u'llah and the New Era: An Introduction to the Baha'i Faith*. Baha'i Pub. Trust, 1980.

Hatcher, William S. *The Baha'i Faith: The Emerging Global Religion*. Harper and Row, 1984.

Smith, Peter. *A Short History of the Baha'i Faith*. Oneworld Publications, 1996.

Baha'i Texts on the Internet. http://www.bcca.org/services/srb/texts.html

BARBOUR, IAN G.

Barbour, Ian G. *Religion in an Age of Science*. HarperCollins, 1990.

Barbour, Ian G. *Technology, Environment, and Human Values*. Praeger, 1989.

Kiernan, Vincent. "Physicist and Templeton Prizewinner Strives to Reconcile Science and Religion." *Chronicle of Higher Education*, Apr. 30, 1999.

Niebuhr, Gustav. "$1 Million Religion Prize for Physicist-Theologian." *New York Times*, Mar. 11, 1999.

BARTH, KARL

Barth, Karl. *Humanity of God*. Westminster Press, 1960.

Busch, Eberhard. *Karl Barth: His Life from Letters and Autobiographical Texts*. Fortress Press, 1976.

Green, Clifford, ed. *Karl Barth: Theologian of Freedom*. Fortress Press, reprint 1991.

BARTHOLOMEW

Niebuhr, Gustav. "Patriarch's Visit Bolsters Orthodox Church." *New York Times*, Oct. 19, 1997.

Steinfels, Peter. "Eastern Orthodox Prelates Name Ecumenical Patriarch." *New York Times*, Oct. 24, 1991.

"Biography of Bartholomew, Archbishop of Constantinople, New Rome and Ecumenical Patriarch." *Ecumenical Patriarchate of Constantinople*. http://www.patriarchate.org/visit/html/biography.html

SAINT THOMAS BECKET

Anouilh, Jean. *Becket or The Honor of God*. Riverhead Books, 1996.

Becket. MPI Home Video, 1989 (videorecording).

Eliot, T. S. *Murder in the Cathedral*. Harcourt Brace, 1963 (play).

"St. Thomas Becket." *Catholic Online Saints Index*. http://saints.catholic.org/saints/thomasbecket.html

SAINT BENEDICT

Vest, Norvene, et al. *Benedict: Stories of the Great Saint*. Source Books, 1997.

The Order of Saint Benedict. http://www.osb.org/ "St. Benedict."

Catholic Online Saints Index. http://saints.catholic.org/saints/benedict.html

SAINT BERNARD

McGuire, Brian Patrick. *The Difficult Saint: Bernard of Clairvaux and His Tradition*. Cistercian Publications, 1992.

Merton, Thomas. *The Last of the Fathers*. Harcourt Brace, 1982.

"St. Bernard of Clairvaux." *Catholic Encyclopedia*. http://www.knight.org/advent/cathen/02498d.htm

"St. Bernard of Clairvaux." *Catholic Online Saints Index*. http://saints.catholic.org/saints/bernardclairvaux.html

BERNARDIN, JOSEPH

Bernardin, Joseph Cardinal. *The Gift of Peace: Personal Reflections*. Loyola Press, 1997.

Bernardin, Joseph Cardinal. *A Moral Vision for America*. Georgetown University Press, 1998.

Kennedy, Eugene C. *My Brother Joseph: The Life and Spirit of Cardinal Bernardin*. St. Martins Press, 1997.

Steinfels, Peter. "Cardinal Bernardin Dies at 68; Reconciling Voice in Church." *New York Times*, Nov. 15, 1996.

BESANT, ANNIE

Besant, Annie Wood. *The Ancient Wisdom: An Outline of Theosophical Teachings.* Quest Books, 1999.

Dinnage, Rosemary. *Annie Besant.* Penguin Books, 1986.

Oppenheim, Janet. "The Odyssey of Annie Besant." *History Today,* Sept. 1989.

Wessinger, Catherine. *Annie Besant and Progressive Messianism: 1847–1933.* Edwin Mellen Press, 1988.

BESHT (BA'AL SHEM TOV; ISRAEL BEN ELIEZER)

Ben-Amos, Dan, and Jerome R. Mintz, eds. *In Praise of the Baal Shem Tov (Shivhei Ha-Besht: The Earliest Collection of Legends About the Founder of Hasidism).* Jason Aronson, 1994.

Buber, Martin. *The Legend of the Baal-Shem.* Princeton University Press, 1995.

Klein, Eliahu. *Meetings With Remarkable Souls: Legends of the Baal Shem Tov.* Jason Aronson, 1995.

Rosman, Moshe. *Founder of Hasidism: A Quest for the Historical Ba'Al Shem Tov.* University of California Press, 1996.

Singer, Isaac Bashevis. *Reaches of Heaven: A Story of the Baal Shem Tov.* Farrar, Straus, Giroux, 1980.

BHAVE, VINOBA

"Bhave, Vinoba." *Current Biography* Jan. 1983 (obituary).

Bhave, Vinoba. *Moved By Love: The Memoirs of Vinoba Bhave.* Green Books, 1994.

Lanza del Vasto, Joseph Jean. *Gandhi to Vinoba; The New Pilgrimage.* Schocken Books, 1974.

Sonnleitner, Michael W. *Vinoba Bhave on Self-Rule and Representative Democracy.* South Asia Books, 1989.

BLACK ELK

Black Elk. *Black Elk Speaks: Being the Life Story of a Holy Man of the Oglala Sioux.* University of Nebraska Press, reprint 1988.

Black Elk, Wallace. *Black Elk: The Sacred Ways of a Lakota.* Harper, reprint 1991.

Rice, Julian. *Lakota Storytelling: Black Elk, Ella Deloria, and Frank Fools Crow.* Peter Lang, 1989.

Steltenkamp, Michael F. *Black Elk, Holy Man of the Oglala.* University of Oklahoma Press, 1993.

Walker, Paul Robert. *Spiritual Leaders: American Indian Lives.* Facts on File, 1994.

"Black Elk." *American Indian Heritage Foundation.*
http://www.indians.org/welker/blackelk.htm

BLAKE, EUGENE

"Blake, Eugene Carson." *Current Biography*, Oct. 1985 (obituary).

Brackenridge, R. Douglas. *Eugene Carson Blake, Prophet with Portfolio.* Seabury Press, 1978.

Cunningham, Sarah. "Pastors' Conference on Legacy of Eugene Carson Blake Offers Clues for Church Leadership in the 21st Century." *World Council of Churches.* http://www.wcc-coe.org/wcc/news/press/98/nyfeat.html (press release, Feb. 1998)

BLAVATSKY, H. P.

Cranston, S.L. *HPB: The Extraordinary Life and Influence of Helena Blavatsky, Founder of the Modern Theosophical Movement.* Putnam, 1992.

Hanson, Virginia, ed. *H.P. Blavatsky and the Secret Doctrine.* Theosophical Publishing House, 1988.

Washington, Peter. *Madame Blavatsky's Baboon: A History of the Mystics, Mediums, and Misfits Who Brought Spiritualism to America.* Schocken Books, 1995.

BONHOEFFER, DIETRICH

Bethge, Eberhard. *Dietrich Bonhoeffer: A Biography.* Revised ed. Fortress Press, 1999.

Bonhoeffer, Dietrich. *Letters and Papers from Prison.* Macmillan, 1997.

Hanged on a Twisted Cross: The Life, Convictions, and Martyrdom of Dietrich Bonhoeffer. Gateway Films/Vision Video, 1996 (videorecording).

Robertson, Edwin Hanton. *The Shame and the Sacrifice: The Life and Martyrdom of Dietrich Bonhoeffer.* Macmillan, 1988.

Wind, Renate. *A Spoke in the Wheel: The Life of Dietrich Bonhoeffer.* Eerdmans, 1992.

BOOTH, WILLIAM

Bennett, David. *William Booth.* Bethany House, reissue 1994.

Fellows, Lawrence. *A Gentle War: The Story of the Salvation Army.* Macmillan, 1979.

Winston, Diane H. *Red-Hot and Righteous: The Urban Religion of the Salvation Army.* Harvard University Press, 1999.

The Salvation Army International Headquarters. http://www.salvationarmy.org/

BOWMAN, THEA

"Nun Provides Young Blacks with 'A Way out of the Helplessness'". *New York Times,* Oct. 21, 1989.

Steinfels, Peter. "A Memorable Woman Who Wove the Rich Threads of the Black Experience in the Catholic Cloth." *New York Times,* May 26, 1990.

Sr. Thea, Her Own Story: A Video Autobiography. United States Catholic Conference, 1992 (videorecording).

"Tribute to Sister Thea Bowman." *Thea Bowman Center (Boston College).* http://www.bc.edu/bc_org/svp/ahana/Thea.html

BRAIDE, GARRICK SOKARI

Barnes, Sandra T., ed. *Africa's Ogun: Old World and New.* 2nd ed. Indiana University Press, 1997.

"Christianity in Sub-Saharan Africa," in Eliade, Mircea, et al., eds. *The Encyclopedia of Religion.* Macmillan, 1987.

Mbiti, John S. *African Religions and Philosophy.* 2nd ed. Heinemann, 1990.

BUDDHA, GAUTAMA

Chodzin, Sherab. *The Awakened One: A Life of the Buddha.* Shambhala/Random House, 1994.

Lowenstein, Tom. *The Vision of the Buddha.* Little, Brown, 1996.

Parrinder, Geoffrey. *The Sayings of the Buddha.* Ecco Press, 1998.

Rhys-Davids, Caroline. *Stories of the Buddha: Being Selections from the Jataka.* Dover Publications, 1990.

Saddhatissa, Hammalawa. *Before He Was Buddha.* Ulysses Press, 1998.

Schumann, Hans Wolfgang. *The Historical Buddha: The Times, Life, and Teachings of the Founder of Buddhism.* Arkana, 1989.

AL-BUKHARI

Bukhari, Imam. *Sahih Al-Bukhari.* Kazi Publications, 1993.

Khan, M. Muhsin. "Translation of Sahih Bukhari." *USC Muslim Students Association Islamic Server.* http://www.bukhari.com/ or http://www.usc.edu/dept/MSA/fundamentals/hadithsunnah/bukhar i/

CABRINI, FRANCES XAVIER

Keyes, Frances Parkinson. *Mother Cabrini: Missionary to the World.* Ignatius Press, 1997.

Sullivan, Mary Louise. *Mother Cabrini: Italian Immigrant of the Century.* Center for Migration Studies, 1992.

Saint Frances Xavier Cabrini. http://www.fordham.edu/halsall/medny/mccabe.html

"St. Frances Xavier Cabrini." *Catholic Online Saints Index.* http://saints.catholic.org/saints/francesxaviercabrini.html

CALVIN, JOHN

Bouwsma, William James. *John Calvin: A Sixteenth-Century Portrait.* Oxford University Press, 1988.

Ganoczy, Alexandre. *The Young Calvin.* Westminster Press, 1987.

McGrath, Alister E. *A Life of John Calvin: A Study of the Shaping of Western Culture.* Basil Blackwell, 1990.

Stepanek, Sally. *John Calvin.* Chelsea House, 1986.

CAMPBELL, ALEXANDER

Cochran, Louis, and Bess White Cochran. *Captives of the Word.* Doubleday, 1969.

McAllister, Lester G., ed. *An Alexander Campbell Reader.* Chalice Press, 1988.

"Alexander Campbell." *Central Christian Church (Disciples of Christ).* http://www.cccdisciples.org/ACampbell.html

CAMPBELL, JOAN BROWN

"Ecumenical Climb: An Interview with Joan Brown Campbell." *Christian Century,* Nov. 8, 1995.

Goldman, Ari L. "Ecumenist in Charge: Joan B. Campbell." *New York Times,* Nov. 18, 1990.

"NCC General Secretary The Rev. Dr. Joan Brown Campbell." *National Council of Churches of Christ in the USA.* http://ncccusa.org/welcome/campbell_bio.htm

CHANNING, WILLIAM ELLERGY

Mendelsohn, Jack. *Channing, the Reluctant Radical: A Biography.* 2nd ed. Skinner House, 1984.

Robinson, David, ed. *William Ellergy Channing: Selected Writings.* Paulist Press, 1985.

Unitarian Universalist Association. http://www.uua.org/

William Ellergy Channing Center. http://www.athens.net/~wells/indexwec.htm

CONFUCIUS

Chung, Tsai Chih. *Confucius Speaks: Words to Live By.* Anchor Books, 1996.

Confucius: Words of Wisdom. A&E Home Video, 1997 (videorecording).

Hoobler, Thomas. *Confucianism.* Facts on File, 1993.

Sargent, Claudia, ed. *Confucius: The Wisdom.* Bulfinch Press, 1995.

Wilker, Josh. *Confucius: Philosopher and Teacher.* Franklin Watts, 1999 (juvenile).

CRANMER, THOMAS

Ayris, Paul, and David Selwyn, eds. *Thomas Cranmer: Churchman and Scholar.* Boydell and Brewer, 1999.

MacCulloch, Diarmaid. *Thomas Cranmer: A Life.* Yale University Press, 1996.

Thompson, Stephen P., ed. *The Reformation.* Greenhaven Press, 1999.

Cranmer, Thomas. *Necessary Doctrine* (excerpts). http://www.markers.com/ink/tcdoctrine.htm

CROWTHER, SAMUEL ADJAYI

Page, Jesse. *The Black Bishop: Samuel Adjayi Crowther.* Reprint of 1908 edition. Greenwood Press, 1999? Rogers, J. A., ed.

World's Great Men of Color. Touchstone Books, reissue 1996.

"World Missions and the Social Gospel." *Society of Archbishop Justus.* http://justus.anglican.org/resources/timeline/14missions.html

DALAI LAMA

Bstan-'dzin-rgya-mtsho, Dalai Lama XIV. *Freedom in Exile: The Autobiography of the Dalai Lama.* HarperCollins, 1990.

Bstan-'dzin-rgya-mtsho, Dalai Lama XIV. *My Land and My People: The Original Autobiography of His Holiness the Dalai Lama of Tibet.* Warner Books, 1997.

Dalai Lama: The Soul of Tibet. A&E Home Video, 1998.

Hicks, Roger. *Great Ocean: An Authorized Biography of the Buddhist Monk Tenzin Gyatso, His Holiness the Fourteenth Dalai Lama.* Penguin Books, 1990.

Piburn, Sidney, ed. *The Dalai Lama, a Policy of Kindness: An Anthology of Writings By and About the Dalai Lama.* Snow Lion Publications, 1990.

The Tibetan Government in Exile. http://www.tibet.com/

DAN FODIO, USUMAN

Hiskett, Mervyn. *Sword Of Truth; The Life And Times Of The Shehu Usuman Dan Fodio.* Northwestern University Press, 1994.

"Fulani People." *Art and Life in Africa Project (University of Iowa).* http://www.uiowa.edu/~africart/toc/people/Fulani.html

"Usman dan Fodio and the Sokoto Caliphate." *Nigeria—A Country Study (Library of Congress).* http://lcweb2.loc.gov/frd/cs/ngtoc.html

DAY, DOROTHY

Coles, Robert. *Dorothy Day: A Radical Devotion.* Addison-Wesley, 1987.

Day, Dorothy. *Loaves and Fishes.* Orbis Books, reprint 1997.

Day, Dorothy. *The Long Loneliness.* HarperSanFrancisco, 1997.

Entertaining Angels: the Dorothy Day Story. Warner Brothers Home Video, 1996 (videorecording).

Kent, Deborah. *Dorothy Day: Friend to the Forgotten.* Eerdmans, 1996.

DAYANANDA SARASVATI

Jordens, J. T. F. *Dayananda Sarasvati: His Life and Ideas.* Oxford University Press, 1998.

Lata, Prem. *Swami Dayananda Sarasvati.* South Asia Books, 1990.

Arya Pratinidhi Sabha America. http://www.aryasamaj.com/

DEMETRIOS

Brozan, Nadine. "Greek Orthodox Archbishop Resigns in Face of Dissent." *New York Times,* Aug. 20, 1999.

Niebuhr, Gus. "Greek Orthodoxy in U.S. Is on the Cusp of Change." *New York Times,* Sept. 18, 1999.

"His Eminence Archbishop Demetrios of America." *Greek Orthodox Archdiocese of America.* http://www.goarch.org/goa/archbishop/

SAINT DOMINIC

Woods, Richard. *Mysticism and Prophecy: The Dominican Tradition.* Orbis Books, 1998.

"Dominic de Guzman." *Catholic Community Forum.* http://www.catholic-forum.com/saints/saintd02.htm

Order of Preachers - Dominicans. http://www.op.org/english/

"St. Dominic." *Catholic Online Saints Index.* http://saints.catholic.org/saints/dominic.html

EDDY, MARY BAKER

Eddy, Mary Baker. *Christian Healing and Other Writings on Christian Science.* Bookmark, 1992.

Gardner, Martin. *The Healing Revelations of Mary Baker Eddy: The Rise and Fall of Christian Science.* Prometheus Books, 1993.

Gill, Gillian. *Mary Baker Eddy.* Perseus Books, 1998.

Soul of a Woman: The Life and Times of Mary Baker Eddy. New Hampshire Public Television, 1994 (videorecording).

Thomas, Robert David. *With Bleeding Footsteps: Mary Baker Eddy's Path to Religious Leadership.* Knopf, 1994.

EDWARDS, JONATHAN

Edwards, Jonathan. *The Surprising Work of God.* Whitaker House, 1997.

Hatch, Nathan O., and Harry S. Stout, eds. *Jonathan Edwards and the American Experience.* Oxford University Press, 1988.

Miller, Perry. *Jonathan Edwards.* Greenwood Press, 1973.

Yarbrough, Stephen R., et al. *Delightful Conviction.* Greenwood Publishing Group, 1993.

ELAW, ZILPHA

Andrews, William L. *Sisters of the Spirit: Three Black Women's Autobiographies of the Nineteenth Century.* Indiana University Press, 1986.

ESSROG, SEYMOUR

Gillman, Neil. *Conservative Judaism: The New Century.* Behrman House, 1996.

The Rabbinical Assembly. http://www.rabassembly.org/

FARRAKHAN, LOUIS

Alexander, Amy. *The Farrakhan Factor: African- American Writers on Leadership, Nationhood, and Minister Louis Farrakhan.* Grove Press, 1998.

Cottman, Michael H. *Million Man March*. Crown, 1995.

Levinsohn, Florence Hamlish. *Looking for Farrakhan*. Ivan R. Dee, 1997.

Magida, Arthur J. *Prophet of Rage: A Life of Louis Farrakhan and His Nation*. Basic Books, 1996.

Singh, Robert. *The Farrakhan Phenomenon: Race, Reaction, and the Paranoid Style in American Politics*. Georgetown University Press, 1997.

FATHER DIVINE

Smith, Jessie Carney, ed. *Black Heroes of the 20th Century*. Visible Ink Press, 1998.

Watts, Jill. *God, Harlem U.S.A.: The Father Divine Story*. University of California Press, 1992.

Weisbrot, Robert. *Father Divine and the Struggle for Racial Equality*. University of Illinois Press, 1983.

FOOLS CROW, FRANK

Fools Crow, Frank. *Fools Crow*. Doubleday, 1979.

Fools Crow, Frank. *Wisdom and Power*. Council Oak Books, 1991.

Rice, Julian. *Lakota Storytelling: Black Elk, Ella Deloria, and Frank Fools Crow*. Peter Lang, 1989.

Welch, James. *Fools Crow*. Viking, 1986 (fiction).

"Chief Frank Fools Crow." *American Indian Heritage Foundation*.

http://www.indians.org/welker/foolcrow.htm

FORBES, JAMES A.

Goldman, Ari L. "Members Elect a New Pastor at Riverside." *New York Times*, Feb. 6, 1989.

Goldman, Ari L. "Riverside's Pastor at Center of Turmoil." *New York Times*, May 18, 1992.

Woodward, Kenneth L. "Heard Any Good Sermons Lately?" *Newsweek*, Mar. 4, 1996.

"The Senior Minister: The Rev. Dr. James A. Forbes, Jr." *Riverside Church*.
http://www.theriversidechurchny.org/minister.html

FOX, GEORGE

Bailey, Richard. *New Light on George Fox and Early Quakerism*. Edwin Mellen Press, 1992.

Gwyn, Douglas. *Apocalypse of the Word: The Life and Message of George Fox*. Friends United Press, 1986.

Jones, Rufus M. *Journal of George Fox*. Friends United Press, 1976.

Kolp, Alan. *Fresh Winds of the Spirit*. Friends United Press, 1991.

SAINT FRANCIS OF ASSISI

Frugoni, Chiara. *Francis of Assisi: A Life*. Continuum, 1998.

Fulop-Miller, Rene. *Saints That Moved the World: Anthony, Augustine, Francis, Ignatius, Theresa*. Ayer Book, reprint 1972.

Nerburn, Kent. *Make Me an Instrument of Your Peace: Living in the Spirit of the Prayer of Saint Francis*. HarperSanFrancisco, 1999.

Ugolino, di Monte Santa Maria. *The Little Flowers of St. Francis of Assisi*. Vintage Books, 1998.

"St. Francis of Assisi." *Catholic Online Saints Index*. http://saints.catholic.org/saints/francisassisi.html

GANDHI, MOHANDAS

Brown, Judith M. *Gandhi: Prisoner of Hope*. Yale University Press, 1989.

Dalton, Dennis. *Mahatma Gandhi: Nonviolent Power in Action*. Columbia University Press, 1993.

Fischer, Louis, ed. *The Essential Gandhi: His Life, Work, and Ideas*. Vintage Books, 1983.

Fischer, Louis. *Gandhi, His Life and Message for the World*. New American Library, reissue 1991.

Gandhi. Columbia TriStar Home Video, 1990 (videorecording).

Gandhi, Mahatma. *All Men Are Brothers: Autobiographical Reflections*. Continuum, 1995.

AL-GHAZALI, ABU HAMID

Ghazali. *The Alchemy of Happiness*. Octagon, 1980.

Ghazzali. *On the Duties of Brotherhood*. Overlook Press, 1976.

Ghazzali. "The Niche of Lights: The Mishkat of al-Ghazzali," in *Four Sufi Classics*. Octagon, 1980.

GOMES, PETER

"God and Harvard: Harvard's Peter Gomes Is a Conservative Clergyman Who Says That the Religious Right Is Wrong, and the Bible Is His Evidence." *The New Yorker*, Nov. 11, 1996.

Gomes, Peter J. *The Good Book: Reading the Bible With Mind and Heart*. W. Morrow, 1996.

Gomes, Peter J. *Sermons: Biblical Wisdom for Daily Living*. W. Morrow, 1998.

Lively, Kit. "Harvard's Powerful Preacher." *Chronicle of Higher Education*, Jan. 10, 1997.

GRAHAM, BILLY

Cornwell, Patricia Daniels. *Ruth, a Portrait: The Story of Ruth Bell Graham*. Doubleday, 1997.

Crusade: The Life of Billy Graham. A&E Home Video, 1993 (videorecording).

Graham, Billy. *Just As I Am: The Autobiography of Billy Graham.* HarperSanFrancisco, 1997.

Martin, William C. *A Prophet with Honor: The Billy Graham Story.* W. Morrow, 1991.

Billy Graham Online. http://www.billygraham.org/

GRIMKE, FRANCIS JAMES

Trimiew, Darryl M. *Voices of the Silenced.* Pilgrim Press, 1993.

Woodson, Carter Godwin. *The History of the Negro Church.* 3d ed. Associated Publishers, 1972.

Young, Henry J. *Major Black Religious Leaders, 1755–1940.* Abingdon, 1977.

GRISWOLD, FRANK

Niebuhr, Gustav. "Divided Episcopalians Install Leader Who Urges 'a Compassionate Heart' in Members." *New York Times,* Jan. 11, 1998.

Niebuhr, Gustav. "Moderate Bishop Elected to Lead Episcopal Church." *New York Times,* July 22, 1997.

"Church Leader Knocks 'Denominational Idols.'" *Christian Century,* Oct. 21, 1998.

GUTIERREZ, GUSTAVO

Brown, Robert McAfee. *Gustavo Gutierrez: An Introduction to Liberation Theology.* Orbis Books, 1990.

Gutierrez, Gustavo. *On Job: God-Talk and the Suffering of the Innocent.* Orbis Books, 1987.

Gutierrez, Gustavo. *We Drink From Our Own Wells: The Spiritual Journey of a People.* Orbis Books, 1990.

Steinfels, Peter. "New Liberation Faith: Social Conflict Is Muted." *New York Times,* July 27, 1988.

HANDSOME LAKE

Bonvillain, Nancy. *Native American Religion.* Chelsea House, 1996.

Walker, Paul Robert. *Spiritual Leaders: American Indian Lives.* Facts on File, 1994.

Wallace, Anthony F.C. *The Death and Rebirth of the Seneca.* Vintage Books, 1972.

HARRIS, BARBARA

Goodrich, Lawrence. "Pact Smooths Over Controversy." *Christian Science Monitor,* Oct. 6, 1989.

Niebuhr, Gustav. "Barbara Harris: 1989, the First Female Bishop of the Episcopal Church." *Working Woman,* Nov.-Dec. 1996.

Steinfels, Peter. "Woman Is Consecrated as Episcopal Bishop." *New York Times,* Feb. 13, 1989.

HARRIS, WILLIAM WADE

Eliade, Mircea, et al., eds. *The Encyclopedia of Religion*. Macmillan, 1987.

Haliburton, Gordon MacKay. *The Prophet Harris: A Study of an African Prophet and His Mass Movement in the Ivory Coast and the Gold Coast*. Oxford University Press, 1973.

Walker, Sheila S. *The Revolution in the Ivory Coast: The Prophet Harris and the Harrist Church*. University of North Carolina Press, 1975.

HASAN AL-BASRI

"Al Hasan Al Basri." *Universal League of Islamic Literature*. http://www.interlog.com/~ulil/albasri.html

"On Tasawwuf: al-Hasan al-Basri." *As-Sunna Foundation of America*. http://sunnah.org/tasawwuf/scholar1.htm

HESCHEL, ABRAHAM JOSHUA

Heschel, Abraham Joshua. *God In Search of Man*. Noonday Press, reprint 1997.

Heschel, Abraham Joshua. *Man's Quest for God*. Aurora Press, 1998.

Heschel, Abraham Joshua. *The Wisdom of Heschel*. Noonday Press, 1986.

Heschel, Abraham Joshua. *Who Is Man?* Stanford University Press, 1965.

Lester, Julius. *The Thought of Rabbi Abraham Joshua Heschel*. http://www.congregationbeth-el.org/heschel.html

HILLEL

Buxbaum, Yitzhak. *The Life and Teachings of Hillel*. Jason Aronson, 1994.

Charlesworth, James H., and Loren L. Johns, eds. *Hillel and Jesus: Comparisons of Two Major Religious Leaders*. Fortress Press, 1997.

Neusner, Jacob. *Judaism in the Beginning of Christianity*. Fortress Press, 1984.

Rabbinic Wisdom. http://religion.rutgers.edu/iho/sages.html

HOOKER, THOMAS

Ball, John H. *Chronicling the Soul's Windings: Thomas Hooker and His Morphology of Conversion*. University Press of America, 1992.

Hart, Benjamin. *Faith and Freedom: The Christian Roots of American Liberty*. Lewis and Stanley, reprint 1990.

Shuffelton, Frank. *Thomas Hooker, 1586–1647*. Princeton University Press, 1977.

HORN, ROSA ARTIMUS

Erickson, Hal. *Religious Radio and Television in the United States, 1921–1991: The Programs and Personalities*. McFarland, 1992.

Hill, George H. *Airwaves to the Soul: The Influence and Growth of Religious Broadcasting in America*. R and E Publishers, 1983.

Wright, J. Elwin. *The Old Fashioned Revival Hour and the Broadcasters*. Garland, reprint 1988.

HUBBARD, L. RON

Corydon, Bent. *L. Ron Hubbard, Messiah or Madman?* L. Stuart, 1987.

Hubbard, L. Ron. *Battlefield Earth: A Saga of the Year 3000*. St. Martins Press, 1982.

Miller, Russell. *Bare-Faced Messiah: The True Story of L. Ron Hubbard*. H. Holt, 1988.

Scientology Home Page. http://www.scientology.org/

SAINT JEROME

Hodges, Margaret. *St. Jerome and the Lion*. Orchard Books, 1991.

"St. Jerome." *Catholic Encyclopedia*. http://www.newadvent.org/cathen/08341a.htm

"St. Jerome." *Catholic Online Saints Index*.

http://saints.catholic.org/saints/jerome.html

JESUS CHRIST

Charlesworth, James H. *Jesus Within Judaism: New Light from Exciting Archaeological Discoveries*. Doubleday, 1988.

Crossan, John Dominic. *Jesus: A Revolutionary Biography*. HarperSanFrancisco, 1994.

From Jesus to Christ: The First Christians. PBS Home Video, 1998 (videorecording).

Grant, Michael. *Jesus: An Historian's Review of the Gospels*. Scribner, 1977.

Sanders, E. P. *The Historical Figure of Jesus*. Penguin Press, 1993.

Sheehan, Thomas. *The First Coming: How the Kingdom of God Became Christianity*. Random House, 1986.

Wilson, A. N. *Jesus*. W. W.. Norton, 1992.

JOHN XXIII

Coppa, Frank J., ed. *Encyclopedia of the Vatican and Papacy*. Greenwood Press, 1999.

Hebblethwaite, Peter. *Pope John XXIII, Shepherd of the Modern World*. Doubleday, 1985.

McBrien, Richard P. *Lives of the Popes: The Pontiffs from St. Peter to John Paul II*. HarperSanFrancisco, 1997.

Wynn, Wilton. *Keepers of the Keys: John XXIII, Paul VI, and John Paul II, Three Who Changed the Church*. Random House, 1988.

JONAS, REGINA

Nadell, Pamela S. *Women Who Would Be Rabbis: A History of Women's Ordination, 1889–1985*. Beacon Press, 1998.

Taitz, Emily. *Remarkable Jewish Women: Rebels, Rabbis, and Other Women from Biblical Times to the Present*. Jewish Publication Society, 1996.

"Regina Jonas." *Jewish Women in Berlin*.
http://hagalil.com/brd/berlin/rabbiner/jonas.htm

JONES, ABSALOM

"Absalom Jones." *Biographical Sketches of Memorable Christians of the Past*. http://justus.anglican.org/resources/bio/98.html

"Absalom Jones." *The Lectionary*.
http://www.satucket.com/lectionary/Absalom_Jones.htm

KANG YU-WEI

Chang, Hao. *Chinese Intellectuals in Crisis: Search for Order and Meaning (1890–1911)*. University of California Press, 1987.

"Kang Youwei (K'ang Yu-Wei)." *Ralph's World Civilizations*.
http://www.wwnorton.com/college/history/ralph/resource/33kan g.htm

KAPLAN, MORDECAI

Gurock, Jeffrey S. *A Modern Heretic and a Traditional Community: Mordecai M. Kaplan, Orthodoxy, and American Judaism*. Columbia University Press, 1997.

Kaplan, Mordecai Menahem. *Dynamic Judaism: The Essential Writings of Mordecai M. Kaplan*. Schocken Books, 1985.

The New American Haggadah. Behrman House, 1999.

Scult, Mel. *Judaism Faces the Twentieth Century: A Biography of Mordecai M. Kaplan*. Wayne State University Press, 1993.

KELLY, LEONTINE

Briggs, Kenneth A. "Methodists Choose 19 New Bishops." *New York Times*, July 29, 1984.

Lanker, Brian, and Maya Angelou. "I Dream a World." *National Geographic*, Aug. 1989.

"Leontine T.C. Kelly." *U.S. News & World Report*. Feb. 13, 1989.

KELMAN, WOLFE

Goldman, Ari L. "Innovators Redefine Role of Rabbis." *New York Times*, Aug. 20, 1989.

Goldman, Ari L. "Rabbi Wolfe Kelman, 66, Dies; Leader in Conservative Judaism." *New York Times*, June 28, 1990.

KIMBANGU, SIMON

Kaufman, Michael T. "Zaire's 2 Worlds: Twain Rarely Meet." *New York Times*, Oct. 25, 1983.

Martin, Marie-Louise. *Kimbangu: An African Prophet and His Church*. Out of print.

Mufson, Steve. "A Once-Banned Religion Thrives in Zaire." *Wall Street Journal,* Sept. 11, 1984.

KING, MARTIN LUTHER, JR.

Abernathy, Donzaleigh. *Partners to History: Martin Luther King, Jr., Ralph David Abernathy, and the Civil Rights Movement.* General Publishing, 1998.

Branch, Taylor. *Parting the Waters: America in the King Years, 1954–63.* Schuster, 1988.

Carson, Clayborne, et al. *The Eyes on the Prize Civil Rights Reader.* Viking, 1991.

Eyes on the Prize: America's Civil Rights Years, 1954–1965. PBS Video, 1987; and *Eyes on the Prize: America at the Racial Crossroads.* PBS Video, 1989 (videorecordings).

King, Martin Luther, Jr. *Strength to Love.* Harper and Row, 1963.

King, Martin Luther, Jr. *Stride Toward Freedom.* Harper and Row, 1958.

The Martin Luther King, Jr. Center for Nonviolent Social Change.

http://www.thekingcenter.com/

Martin Luther King, Jr. National Historic Site. http://www.nps.gov/malu/

Martin Luther King, Jr., Papers Project at Stanford University. http://www.stanford.edu/group/King/

KINJIKITILE

Lugira, Aloysius Muzzanganda. *African Religion.* Facts on File, 1999.

Pakenham, Thomas. *The Scramble for Africa: White Man's Conquest of the Dark Continent from 1876 to 1912.* Avon Books, 1992.

Petraitis, Richard. "Bullets into Water: The Sorcerers of Africa." *Reall News.* http://www.reall.org/newsletter/v06/n06/bullets-into-wat er.html

KIWANUKA, JOSEPH

"Christianity in Sub-Saharan Africa," in Eliade, Mircea, et al., eds. *The Encyclopedia of Religion.* Macmillan, 1987.

"From the Book of Numbers." *U.S. Catholic,* Aug. 1999.

KNOX, JOHN

Cowan, Henry. *John Knox: The Hero of the Scottish Reformation.* AMS Press, 1970.

Knox, John. *On Rebellion.* Cambridge University Press, 1994.

Knox, John. *The Political Writings of John Knox: The First Blast of the Trumpet Against the Monstrous Regiment of Women and Other Selected Works.* Folger Shakespeare Library, 1985.

Mason, Roger A., ed. *John Knox and the British Reformations.* Ashgate Publishing, 1999.

KRISHNAMURTI, JIDDU

Field, Sidney. *Krishnamurti: The Reluctant Messiah*. Paragon House, 1989.

Krishnamurti, J. *The Limits of Thought*. Routledge, 1998.

Krishnamurti, J. *This Light in Oneself: True Meditation*. Shambala, 1999.

Lutyens, Mary. *Krishnamurti, His Life and Death*. St. Martins Press, 1990.

Transformation of Man: Conversations with J. Krishnamurti, David Bohm, David Shainberg. Mystic Fire Video, 1995 (videorecording).

KROLOFF, CHARLES

Brozan, Nadine. "New Leader of Conference of Rabbis Sets Agenda." *New York Times*, May 18, 1999.

Kroloff, Charles A. *54 Ways You Can Help the Homeless*. Behrman House, 1993.

Kroloff, Charles A. *When Elijah Knocks; A Religious Response To Homelessness*. Behrman House, 1996.

LAO-TZU

Cleary, Thomas F. *The Essential Tao: An Initiation into the Heart of Taoism Through the Authentic Tao Te Ching and the Inner Teachings of Chuang Tzu*. HarperSanFrancisco, 1992.

Lao-Tzu. *Lao-tzu's Taoteching, with Selected Commentaries of the Past 2000 Years*. Mercury House, 1996.

Lao-tzu. *Te-tao Ching: A New Translation Based on the Recently Discovered Ma-wang-tui Texts*. Modern Library, 1993.

Robinet, Isabelle. *Taoism: Growth of a Religion*. Stanford University Press, 1997.

LAS CASAS, BARTOLOME DE

Casas, Bartolome de las. *The Devastation of the Indies: A Brief Account*. Johns Hopkins Paperbacks, 1992.

Casas, Bartolome de las. *Indian Freedom: The Cause of Bartolome de las Casas, 1484–1566: A Reader*. Sheed and Ward, 1995.

Gutierrez, Gustavo. *Las Casas: In Search of the Poor of Jesus Christ*. Orbis Books, 1993.

Stopsky, Fred. *Bartolome de las Casas: Champion of Indian Rights*. Discovery Enterprises, 1992.

LEE, ANN

Joy, A. F. *We Are the Shakers: Mother Ann's Story*. Apollo Books, 1985.

Peters, Robert Louis. *The Gift to Be Simple: A Garland for Ann Lee*. W. W. Norton, 1975.

The Shakers. Goldhil Video, 1998 (videorecording). "History and Origin of the Shakers." *Shaker Heritage Society*.

http://www.crisny.org/not-for-profit/shakerwv/history.htm

LEE, CHUNG OK

Chong, Key Ray. *Won Buddhism: A History and Theology of Korea's New Religion*. Edwin Mellen Press, 1997.

United Religions Initiative 2000. http://www.tcsn.net/fbchurch/fbcunite.htm

Won Buddhism. http://www.egr.msu.edu/~leek/won/won_cont.htm

LENSHINA, ALICE

Lugira, Aloysius Muzzanganda. *African Religion*. Facts on File, 1999.

Wills, A. J. *An Introduction to the History of Central Africa: Zambia, Malawi, and Zimbabwe*. 4th ed. Oxford University Press, 1985.

"A Time to Mourn." *Lusaka Lowdown* (Zambia). http://www.lowdown.co.zm/may99/book.htm

LORD, JOHN WESLEY

"Lord, John Wesley." *Current Biography*, Jan. 1990 (obituary).

"United Methodist Bishops." *Church Library - United Methodist Bishops*. http://www.umc.org/churchlibrary/discipline/bishops/

SAINT IGNATIUS OF LOYOLA

Caraman, Philip. *Ignatius Loyola: A Biography of the Founder of the Jesuits*. Harper and Row, 1990.

Fulop-Miller, Rene. *Saints That Moved the World: Anthony, Augustine, Francis, Ignatius, Theresa*. Ayer Book, reprint 1972.

Ignatius of Loyola, Saint. *Personal Writings: Reminiscences, Spiritual Diary, Select Letters*. Penguin Books, 1996.

"St. Ignatius Loyola." *Catholic Encyclopedia*.

http://www.knight.org/advent/cathen/07639c.htm

"The Society of Jesus." *Catholic Encyclopedia*.

http://www.knight.org/advent/cathen/14081a.htm

LUTHER, MARTIN

Bainton, Roland Herbert. *Here I Stand: A Life of Martin Luther*. Penguin USA, reprint 1995.

Erikson, Erik. *Young Man Luther*. W. W. Norton, reissue 1993.

Manns, Peter. *Martin Luther: An Illustrated Biography*. Crossroad, 1983.

Marius, Richard. *Martin Luther: The Christian Between God and Death*. Belknap Press, 1999.

Todd, John Murray. *Luther, A Life*. Crossroad, 1982.

MAHAVIRA

Dundas, Paul. *The Jains*. Routledge, 1992.

Tobias, Michael. *Life Force: The World of Jainism*. Asian Humanities Press, 1991.

Beck, Sanderson. "Mahavira and Jainism." *Ethics of Civilization*. http://www.san.beck.org/EC8-Mahavira.html

MAIMONIDES, MOSES

Heschel, Abraham Joshua. *Maimonides: A Biography*. Farrar, Straus, Giroux, 1982.

Kellner, Menachem Marc. *Maimonides on Judaism and the Jewish People*. State University of New York Press, 1991.

Maimonides, Moses. *Guide for the Perplexed*. Dover Publications, 1950.

Twersky, Isadore. *Introduction to the Code of Maimonides*. Yale University Press, 1982.

MARANKE, JOHN

Beckwith, Carol, and Angela Fisher. *African Ceremonies*. Harry N. Abrams, 1999.

Cox, Harvey. "Healers and Ecologists: Pentecostalism in Africa." *The Christian Century*, Nov. 9, 1994.

Jules-Rosette, Bennetta. *African Apostles: Ritual and Conversion in the Church of John Maranke*. Cornell University Press, 1975.

MASON, CHARLES HARRISON

Maxwell, Joe. "Building the Church of God in Christ." *Christianity Today*, Apr. 8, 1996.

The Church of God in Christ. http://www.cogic.com/

MOHAMMED, W. DEEN

"Farrakhan Berated by W. Deen Mohammed." *Christian Century*, Nov. 22, 1995.

"In the Muslim Mainstream." *Christian Century*, Oct. 26, 1994.

Ministry of Imam W. Deen Mohammed. http://www.worldforum.com/ministry/abmnstry/mission.htm

Rivera, Elaine. "Islam's Positive Face." *Articles Drum*.

http://drum.ncat.edu/~drwww/deen.html

MONTAGU, LILY

Montagu, Lily (Lilian Helen). *Lily Montagu: Sermons, Addresses, Letters, and Prayers*. Edwin Mellen Press, 1985.

Montagu, Lily (Lilian Helen). "The Girl in the Background." Reproduced from Urwick, *Studies of Boy Life in Our Cities* (1904).

http://www.users.globalnet.co.uk/~infed/e-texts/e-mont.h tm *Lily Montagu and West Central*. http://www.infed.org/walking/wa-monta.htm

MOSES

Fleg, Edmond. *The Life of Moses*. Hope Publishing House, 1995.

Freud, Sigmund. *Moses and Monotheism*. Random House, 1987.

Hurston, Zora Neal. *Moses, Man of the Mountain*. HarperCollins, reprint 1991.

Kirsch, Jonathan. *Moses: A Life*. Ballantine Books, 1998.

Wiesel, Elie. *Messengers of God: Biblical Portraits and Legends*. Summit Books, 1985.

MUELLER, REUBEN HERBERT

"Mueller, Reuben Herbert." *Current Biography*, Sept. 1982 (obituary).

"Historical Statement." *United Methodist Church*.

http://www.umc.org/churchlibrary/discipline/history/default. htm

National Council of Churches [of Christ]. http://ncccusa.org/

MUHAMMAD

Armstrong, Karen. *Muhammad: A Biography of the Prophet*. HarperSanFrancisco, 1993.

Bennett, Clinton. *In Search of Muhammad*. Cassell, 1999.

Cook, Michael. *Muhammad*. Oxford University Press, 1984.

Okine, Abdul Hamid. *And God Speaks to Muhammad*. Vantage Press, 1998.

Poonawala, Ismail K., ed. *The History of Al-Tabari*. State Uniuversity of New York Press, 1988.

MUHAMMAD, ELIJAH

Clegg, Claude Andrew. *An Original Man: The Life and Times of Elijah Muhammad*. St. Martins Press, 1997.

Elijah Muhammad: Religious Leader. Schlessinger Video Productions, 1994 (video-recording).

Evanzz, Karl. *The Messenger: The Rise and Fall of Elijah Muhammad*. Pantheon Books, 1999.

Halasa, Malu. *Elijah Muhammad: Religious Leader*. Chelsea House, 1990.

MUKHTAR, SIDI AL-

Atterbury, Anson Phelps. *Islam in Africa*. Greenwood Publishing, 1999.

Holt, P. M., ed. *Cambridge History of Islam: The Indian Sub-Continent, Southeast Asia, Africa and the Muslim West*. Cambridge University Press, 1977.

"The Legacy of Muslim Slaves." *Islamic Forum*.

http://www.islamic-forum.org/livingislam/i2article3.htm

MURRAY, ANNA PAULINE

Murray, Pauli. *Pauli Murray: The Autobiography of a Black Activist, Feminist, Lawyer, Priest and Poet*. University of Tennessee Press, 1989.

Murray, Pauli. *Proud Shoes: The Story of an American Family*. Harper and Row, 1987.

Murray, Pauli. *Song in a Weary Throat: An American Pilgrimage*. Harper and Row, 1987.

NANAK

Sagu, Harbans Kaur. *Guru Nanak and the Indian Society*. South Asia Books, 1993.

Sikhism: The Golden Temple. Films for the Humanities and Sciences, 1996 (video-recording).

"The First Master, Guru Nanak Dev (1469–1539)." *Sikhism*. http://www.sikhs.org/guru1.htm

NEOLIN

Walker, Paul Robert. *Spiritual Leaders (American Indian Lives)*. Facts on File, 1994.

"The Lenape and the Moravian Missions." *Marist College Academic Web*. http://www.academic.marist.edu/papers/lenape/moravian.htm

O'CONNOR, JOHN

Brozan, Nadine. "Cardinal's Health Is Topic of Concern and Prayers." *New York Times*, Sept. 6, 1999.

Elie, Paul. "The Next Cardinal." *New York Times Magazine*, Oct. 10, 1999.

Hentoff, Nat. *John Cardinal O'Connor: At the Storm Center of a Changing American Catholic Church*. Scribner, 1988.

"Cardinal O'Connor's Letter to a Jewish Friend." *National Christian Leadership Conference for Israel*. http://www.nclci.org/Articles/cardinal_oconnor.htm

PATRICK, SAINT

Hanson, R. P. C . *The Life and Writings of the Historical Saint Patrick*. Seabury Press, 1983.

Hopkin, Alannah. *The Living Legend of St. Patrick*. St. Martins Press, 1990.

Patrick, Saint. *The Confession of Saint Patrick*. Triumph Books, 1996.

Proudfoot, Alice-Boyd, ed. *Patrick: Sixteen Centuries with Ireland's Patron Saint*. Macmillan, 1983.

"St. Patrick." *Catholic Online Saints Index*. http://saints.catholic.org/saints/patrick.html

PATTERSON, PAIGE

Kennedy, John W. "Patterson's Election Seals Conservative Control." *Christianity Today*, July 13, 1998.

"Ousted College Leader Reinstated by Baptists." *New York Times*, Nov. 14, 1991.

Steinfels, Peter. "The Southern Baptists' Declaration That Wives Should 'Submit' Touches off a Debate Among Christians on How the Relevant Scripture Evolved." *New York Times*, June 13, 1998.

"Paige Patterson Q and A." *The Conservative Record*. http://www.ncbaptist.com/June98/Patterson.htm

SAINT PAUL

Caldwell, Taylor. *Great Lion of God*. Doubleday, 1970 (fiction).

Maccoby, Hyam. *The Mythmaker: Paul and the Invention of Christianity*. Harper and Row, 1987.

Wallace, Richard. *The Three Worlds of Paul of Tarsus*. Routledge, 1998.

Wilson, A. N. *Paul: The Mind of the Apostle*. W. W.. Norton, 1998.

"St. Paul." *Catholic Online Saints Index*. http://saints.catholic.org/saints/paul.html

SAINT PETER

Grant, Michael. *Saint Peter: A Biography*. Scribner, 1995.

McBrien, Richard P. *Lives of the Popes: The Pontiffs from St. Peter to John Paul II*. HarperSanFrancisco, 1997.

Murphy, Walter F. *Upon This Rock*. Macmillan, 1987 (fiction). Walsh, John Evangelist. *The Bones of St. Peter: The First Full Account of the Search for the Apostle's Body*. Doubleday, 1982.

"St. Peter." *Catholic Online Saints Index*.
http://saints.catholic.org/saints/peterchains.html

PIUS IX

Coppa, Frank J., ed. *Encyclopedia of the Vatican and Papacy*. Greenwood Press, 1999.

Hasler, August. *How the Pope Became Infallible: Pius IX and the Politics of Persuasion*. Doubleday, 1981.

McBrien, Richard P. *Lives of the Popes: The Pontiffs from St. Peter to John Paul II*. HarperSanFrancisco, 1997.

"Pope Pius IX," in Brusher, S. J. *Popes Through the Ages*. Van Nostrand, 1959.

Reproduced at http://www.knight.org/advent/Popes/pppi09.htm

"Pope Pius IX." *Catholic Encyclopedia*.
http://www.newadvent.org/cathen/12134b.htm

POWELL, ADAM CLAYTON

Haskins, James S. *Adam Clayton Powell: Portrait of a Marching Black*. Africa World Press, 1993.

Haygood, Will. *King of the Cats: The Life and Times of Adam Clayton Powell, Jr.* Houghton Mifflin, 1994.

Powell, Adam Clayton. *Adam by Adam: The Autobiography of Adam Clayton Powell, Jr.* Citadel Press, 1994.

Powell, Adam Clayton. *Against the Tide: An Autobiography*. Ayer, 1980.

RABI'A

Renard, John, ed. *Windows on the House of Islam: Muslim Sources on Spirituality and Religious Life*. University of California Press, 1998.

Smith, Margaret. *Rabi'a: The Life and Work of Rabi'a and Other Women Mystics in Islam*. Oneworld Publications, 1995.

Smith, Margaret. *Rabi'a the Mystic*. Kazi Publications, 1996.

RAISER, KONRAD

"Rearticulating an Ecumenical Vision: An Interview with Konrad Raiser." *Christian Century*, May 12, 1993.

"World Church Group Names a German Scholar as Leader." *New York Times*, Aug. 25, 1992.

World Council of Churches. http://www.wcc-coe.org/wcc/english.html

RATANASARA, HAVANPOLA

Learning, Jeremy. "County Denies Buddhists' Request to Build Monastery in California Town." *Freedom Forum*.
http://www.freedomforum.org/religion/1998/7/13monastery.asp

"The Story of the American Buddhist Congress." *American Buddhist Congress*.
http://www.wgn.net/~abc/history.html

ROMERO, OSCAR

Brockman, James R. *Romero: A Life*. Orbis Books, 1989.

Romero, Oscar. *Voice of the Voiceless: The Four Pastoral Letters and Other Statements*. Orbis Books, 1985.

Sobrino, Jon. *Archbishop Romero: Memories and Reflections*. Orbis Books, 1990.

Romero. Vidmark Entertainment, 1992 (videorecording).

RUSSELL, CHARLES TAZE

Harrison, Barbara Grizzuti. *Visions of Glory: A History and a Memory of Jehovah's Witnesses*. Simon and Schuster, 1978.

Penton, James. *Apocalypse Delayed: The Story of Jehovah's Witnesses*. 2nd ed. University of Toronto Press, 1998.

Jehovah's Witnesses: Watchtower Bible and Tract Society. http://www.watchtower.org/

RUSSELL, ROBERT JOHN

Russell, Robert John. "Bridging Science and Religion: Why It Must Be Done." *Center for Theology and the Natural Sciences*. http://www.ctns.org/

Russell, Robert John, et al., eds. *Chaos and Complexity: Scientific Perspectives on Divine Action*. University of Notre Dame Press, 1997.

Russell, Robert John. "Christian Discipleship and the Challenge of Physics: Formation, Flux, and Focus," in *Perspectives on Science and Christian Faith* (1990). Reproduced at http://asa.calvin.edu/ASA/PSCF/1990/PSCF9–90Russell.html

Russell, Robert John, et al., eds. *Quantum Cosmology and the Laws of Nature: Scientific Perspectives on Divine Action*. Center for Theology and the Natural Sciences, 1993.

RUTHERFORD, JOSEPH FRANKLIN

Harrison, Barbara Grizzuti. *Visions of Glory: A History and a Memory of Jehovah's Witnesses*. Simon and Schuster, 1978.

Penton, James. *Apocalypse Delayed: The Story of Jehovah's Witnesses*. 2nd ed. University of Toronto Press, 1998.

Jehovah's Witnesses: Watchtower Bible and Tract Society. http://www.watchtower.org/

SCHENIRER, SARAH

Grossman, Naomi. "Orthodox Feminism: A Movement Whose Time Has Come." *Tikkun*, May-June 1997.

Zolty, Shoshana Pantel. *And All Your Children Shall Be Learned: Women and the Study of Torah in Jewish Law and History*. Jason Aronson, 1997.

SCHULLER, ROBERT

Penner, James. *Goliath: The Life of Robert Schuller*. HarperPaperbacks, 1993.

Schuller, Robert. Prayer: My Soul's Adventure With God. T. Nelson, 1995.

Steinfels, Peter. "Behind the Feel-Good Religion of Robert Schuller Is a Missionary Zeal." New York Times, Sept. 26, 1992.

Voskuil, Dennis. Mountains Into Goldmines: Robert Schuller and the Gospel of Success. Eerdmans, 1983.

Woodward, Kenneth L. "From the Glass House to the White House: Bill Clinton May Have Found a Soul Brother in His New Friend the Rev. Robert Schuller." Newsweek, Mar. 3, 1997.

SERRA, JUNIPERO

Dolan, Sean. *Junipero Serra*. Chelsea House, 1991.

Genet, Donna. *Father Junipero Serra: Founder of California Missions*. Enslow Publishers, 1996.

Rawls, James J. *Never Turn Back: Father Serra's Mission*. Raintree, 1993.

"Junipero Serra." *People in The West*.
http://www.pbs.org/weta/thewest/wpages/wpgs400/w4serra.htm

SETON, ELIZABETH ANN

Dirvin, Joseph I. *The Soul of Elizabeth Seton*. Ignatius Press, 1990.

Feeney, Leonard. *Mother Seton: Saint Elizabeth of New York*. Ravengate Press, 1975.

Power-Waters, Alma. *Mother Seton: First American-Born Saint*. Pocket Books, 1976.

"St. Elizabeth Ann Seton." *Catholic Online Saints Index*.
http://saints.catholic.org/saints/elizabethannseton.html

SHEMBE, ISAIAH

Eliade, Mircea, et al., eds. *The Encyclopedia of Religion*. Macmillan, 1987.

Hexham, Irving, ed. *The Story of Isaiah Shembe: History and Traditions Centered on Ekuphakameni and Mount Nhlangakazi*. Edwin Mellen Press, 1997.

Kitshoff, M. C. "Isaiah Shembe's Views on the Ancestors in Biblical Perspective." *Faculty of Theology, University of Zululand*. http://www.uzulu.ac.za/the/bibs/sys-kit2.html

SMITH, JOSEPH

Brodie, Fawn McKay. *No Man Knows My History: The Life of Joseph Smith the Mormon Prophet*. 2nd ed. Vintage Books, 1995.

Bushman, Richard L. *Joseph Smith and the Beginnings of Mormonism*. University of Illinois Press, reprint 1988.

Faulring, Scott H., ed. *An American Prophet's Record: The Diaries and Journals of Joseph Smith*. Signature Books, 1989.

Hill, Donna. *Joseph Smith, the First Mormon*. Signature Books, 1999.

"The Prophet Joseph Smith." *All About Mormons*. http://www.mormons.org/daily/history/people/joseph_smith/

SNAKE, REUBEN, JR.

Fikes, Jay C., and Reuben Snake. *Reuben Snake, Your Humble Serpent: Indian Visionary and Activist*. Clear Light Publishers, 1996.

Smith, Huston, and Reuben Snake, eds. *One Nation Under God: The Triumph of the Native American Church*. Clear Light Publishers, 1996.

"Founding Trustee: Reuben A. Snake, Jr." *American Indian Ritual Object Repatriation Foundation*. http://www.repatriationfoundation.org/snake.html (obituary).

SUZUKI, D. T.

Abe, Masao, ed. *A Zen Life: D. T. Suzuki Remembered*. Weatherhill, 1986.

Suzuki, Daisetz Teitaro. *Essays in Zen Buddhism*. C. E. Tuttle, 1994.

Suzuki, Daisetz Teitaro. *An Introduction to Zen Buddhism*. Grove Wiedenfeld, 1991.

Suzuki, Daisetz Teitaro. *Selected Writings of D. T. Suzuki*. Doubleday, 1996.

SWEDENBORG, EMANUEL

Dole, George F. *A Scientist Explores Spirit: A Biography of Emanuel Swedenborg with Key Concepts of His Theology*. Chrysalis Books, 1997.

Larsen, Robin, ed. *Emanuel Swedenborg: A Continuing Vision; A Pictorial Biography and Anthology of Essays and Poetry*. Swedenborg Foundation, 1988.

Sigstedt, Cyriel Sigrid. *The Swedenborg Epic: The Life and Works of Emanuel Swedenborg*. The Swedenborg Society, 1981.

Swedenborg, Emanuel. *Angelic Wisdom Concerning Divine Love and Wisdom*. Swedenborg Foundation, 1995.

SZOLD, HENRIETTA

Gidal, Tim. *Henrietta Szold: A Documentation in Photos and Text.* Gefen Books, 1997.

Krantz, Hazel. *Daughter of My People: Henrietta Szold and Hadassah.* Dutton, 1987.

Kustanowitz, Shulamit E. *Henrietta Szold: Israel's Helping Hand.* Viking, 1990.

Szold, Henrietta. *Lost Love: The Untold Story of Henrietta Szold: Unpublished Diary and Letters.* Jewish Publication Society, 1997.

Brody, Seymour. "Henrietta Szold: A Role Model Who Helped To Found Hadassah." *Jewish Heroes and Heroines in America.* http://www.fau.edu/library/bro48.htm

TAI-HSU

Eliade, Mircea, et al., eds. *The Encyclopedia of Religion.* Macmillan, 1987.

Welch, Holmes. *The Buddhist Revival in China.* Harvard University Press, 1968.

TAYLOR, GARDNER

Dyson, Michael Eric. "Gardner Taylor: Poet Laureate of the Pulpit." *The Christian Century,* Jan. 4, 1995.

Lorch, Donatella. "Cleric of Quiet Activism Retires After 42 Years." *New York Times,* July 1, 1990.

Taylor, Gardner, and Samuel Proctor. *We Have This Ministry: The Heart of the Pastor's Vocation.* Judson Press, 1996.

SAINT TERESA OF AVILA

Fulop-Miller, Rene. *Saints That Moved the World: Anthony, Augustine, Francis, Ignatius, Theresa.* Ayer Book, reprint 1972.

Lincoln, Victoria. *Teresa, a Woman: A Biography of Teresa of Avila.* State University of New York Press, 1984.

Medwick, Cathleen. *Teresa of Avila: The Progress of a Soul.* Knopf, 1999.

"St. Teresa of Avila." *Catholic Online Saints Index.* http://saints.catholic.org/saints/teresaavila.html

MOTHER TERESA

Muggeridge, Malcolm. *Something Beautiful for God: Mother Teresa of Calcutta.* Harper and Row, 1986.

Spink, Kathryn. *Mother Teresa: A Complete Authorized Biography.* HarperSanFrancisco, 1997.

Teresa, Mother. *My Life for the Poor.* Harper and Row, 1985.

Teresa, Mother. *No Greater Love.* New World Library, 1997.

"Mother Teresa 1910–1997." *Catholic Information Center on the Internet.* http://www.catholic.net/RCC/people/mother/teresa/teresa.html

THEODOSIUS

Genet, Harry. "Westernizing the Eastern Church: Two Models." *Christianity Today*, Apr. 10, 1981.

"OCA Primate Celebrates 30th Anniversary of Episcopal Consecration." *Orthodox Church in America*. http://www.oca.org/OCA/Press-Releases/OCA-pr-1997–0506.html

SAINT THERESE DE LISIEUX

Furlong, Monica. *Therese of Lisieux*. Pantheon Books, 1987.

Gaucher, Guy. *The Story of a Life: St. Therese of Lisieux*. Harper and Row, 1987.

Therese de Lisieux, Saint. *Story of a Soul: The Autobiography of Saint Therese of Lisieux*. 3rd ed. ICS Publications, 1996.

"St. Therese of Lisieux." *Catholic Online Saints Index*. http://saints.catholic.org/saints/thereselisieux.html

THOMAS A KEMPIS

The Imitation of Christ by Thomas a Kempis; a Modern Version. Doubleday, 1989.

The Imitation of Christ in Four Books. Vintage Books, 1998.

"Thomas à Kempis." *Catholic Encyclopedia*. http://www.knight.org/advent/cathen/14661a.htm

THOMAS AQUINAS, SAINT

Gilson, Etienne. *The Christian Philosophy of St. Thomas Aquinas*. Octagon Books, 1983.

Kenny, Anthony. *Aquinas*. Oxford University Press, 1984.

Pieper, Josef. *Living the Truth: The Truth of All Things and Reality and the Good*. Ignatius Press, 1989.

"St. Thomas Aquinas." *Catholic Online Saints Index*. http://saints.catholic.org/saints/thomasaquinas.html

TUTU, DESMOND

Bentley, Judith. *Archbishop Tutu of South Africa*. Enslow Publishers, 1988.

Du Boulay, Shirley. *Tutu: Voice of the Voiceless*. Eerdmans, 1988.

Tutu, Desmond. *No Future Without Forgiveness*. Doubleday, 1999.

Tutu, Desmond. *The Rainbow People of God: The Making of a Peaceful Revolution*. Doubleday, 1994.

"Desmond Mpilo Tutu: The Nobel Prize in Peace 1984." *Nobel Foundation*. http://www.nobel.se/laureates/peace-1984.html

'UMAR IBN SA'ID TAL (AL HAJJ)

Hanson, John H. *Migration, Jihad, and Muslim Authority in West Africa: The Futanke Colonies in Karta*. Indiana University Press, 1996.

Robinson, David. *The Holy War of Umar Tal: The Western Sudan in the Mid-Nineteenth Century.* Oxford University Press, 1985.

Willis, Frank Ralph. *In the Path of Allah: The Passion of Al-Hajj 'Umar.* Frank Cass, 1990.

VIVEKANANDA

Myren, Ann, ed. *Living at the Source; Yoga Teachings of Vivekananda.* Shambala, 1993.

Niebuhr, Gustav. "Honoring Sensational Swami of 1893." *New York Times,* July 11, 1998.

Nikhilananda, Swami. *Vivekananda: A Biography.* Ramakrishna Vivekanada Center, 1989.

Vivekananda, Swami. *Complete Works of Swami Vivekananda.* Vedanta Press, 1947.

WESLEY, JOHN

Collins, Kenneth J. *A Real Christian: The Life of John Wesley.* Abingdon Press, 1999.

Wellman, Sam. *John Wesley: Founder of the Methodist Church.* Chelsea House, 1998.

Wesley, John. *The Works of John Wesley.* Abingdon Press, 1988.

Yrigoyen, Charles. *John Wesley: Holiness of Heart and Life.* Abingdon Press, 1999.

"John Wesley: An On-line Exhibition." *Methodist Archives and Research Centre.* http://rylibweb.man.ac.uk/data1/dg/methodist/jwol1.html

WHITE, ELLEN GOULD

Jordan, Anne Devereaux. *The Seventh-Day Adventists: A History.* Hippocrene Books, 1988.

Seventh-Day Adventists Believe: A Biblical Exposition of 27 Fundamental Doctrines. Ministerial Association, General Conference of Seventh-Day Adventists, 1988.

White, Ellen Gould Harmon. *America in Prophecy [Spirit of Prophecy].* IBE, 1988.

Adventist World Church. http://www.adventist.org/

WISE, STEPHEN SAMUEL

Urofsky, Melvin I. *A Voice That Spoke for Justice: The Life and Times of Stephen S. Wise.* State University of New York Press, 1982.

Wise, Stephen Samuel. *Challenging Years: The Autobiography of Stephen Wise.* Putnam, 1949. Out of print.

Stephen Wise Free Synagogue: The First Ninety Years. http://swsf.org/History.htm

WOVOKA

Hittman, Michael, and Don Lynch, eds. *Wovoka and the Ghost Dance.* University of Nebraska Press, 1998.

Walker, Paul Robert. *Spiritual Leaders: American Indian Lives.* Facts on File, 1994.

"Wovoka." *American Indian Heritage Foundation*. http://www.indians.org/welker/wovoka.htm

"Wovoka." *People in THE WEST*. http://www.pbs.org/weta/thewest/

XAVIER, FRANCIS

Byrne, Lavinia. *Life and Wisdom of Francis Xavier*. Hodder and Stoughton, 1998.

De Wohl, Louis. *Set All Afire*. Ignatius Press, reprint 1991 (fiction).

Nevins, Albert J. *St. Francis of the Seven Seas*. Ignatius Press, 1995.

"St. Francis Xavier." *Catholic Online Saints Index*.
http://saints.catholic.org/saints/francisxavier.html

YOUNG, BRIGHAM

Arrington, Leonard J. *Brigham Young: American Moses*. Knopf, 1985.

Brigham Young, Frontiersman. Fox Video, 1995 (videorecording).

Bringhurst, Newell G. *Brigham Young and the Expanding American Frontier*. Little, Brown, 1986.

Sanford, William R. *Brigham Young: Pioneer and Mormon Leader*. Enslow Publishers, 1996.

The Church of Jesus Christ of Latter-Day Saints. http://www.lds.org/

ZOROASTER

Hartz, Paula R. *Zoroastrianism*. Facts on File, 1999.

Nietzsche, Friedrich. *Thus Spoke Zarathustra*. Modern Library, 1995.

Zoroaster: Life and Work of the Forerunner in Persia. 2nd ed. Grail Foundation Press, 1996.

World of Traditional Zoroastrianism. http://www.Zoroastrianism.com

ZWINGLI, ULRICH

Gabler, Ulrich. *Huldrych Zwingli: His Life and Work*. T and T Clark, 1999.

Jackson, Samuel M. *Huldrych Zwingli: The Reformer of German Switzerland*. AMS Press, 1988.

Pipkin, H. Wayne, ed. *Prophet, Pastor, Protestant: The Work of Huldrych Zwingli After Five Hundred Years*. Pickwick Publications, 1984.

"Ulrich Zwingli." *Catholic Encyclopedia*.
http://www.knight.org/advent/cathen/15772a.htm

caliph Arabic term for deputy.

cantons States of the Swiss confederation.

celibate Description of an individual who abstains from sexual intercourse, or, to abstain from sexual intercourse.

chun-tzu Confucian term meaning "noble man."

collier Coal miner.

colloquy A serious or high-level conversation.

ducat Gold coin used in European nations around the fourteenth century.

ecumenical Representing an entire body of churches; general in religious influence.

emaciated Very thin and sickly.

emetics Agents used to induce vomiting.

eminent Conspicuous; standing out so as to be noted.

encomendero Land grantee, usually a European beneficiary of colonial expeditions.

Evensong An evening prayer.

exegesis Critical interpretation of biblical text.

flogging Beating with a rod or whip.

gaiwiio Native American word representing the "good word" of Native American leaders.

gnostic One who believes that matter is evil and that salvation comes through esoteric knowledge of a spiritual truth.

hadith Narrative record of the sayings and customs of Muhammad and the collective body of Muslim traditions relating to him and his associates.

hegira Arabic word for the Islamic prophet Muhammad's migration from Mecca to Medina in 622.

heyoka Native American word for "sacred clown."

imams Shiite Muslim leaders.

imprimatur Mark of approval or ownership.

incarceration Imprisonment.

internecine Destructive fighting and conflict within a group.

jen Confucian virtue translated as humanity and benevolence; a moral and social philosophy.

jihad Arabic word for holy war against non-believers on behalf of Islam.

keuala-Jnana Indian word meaning "the highest knowledge."

kheyal Word signifying the conscious intent to enter into a spiritual discipline in Hindu religion.

kirtana Devotional Hindu songs.

libertine A religious freethinker, sometimes used as a derogatory description.

mahar A caste in India, made up of village menial workers— a so-called "untouchable" cast.

mahdi Arabic word for messiah; the Bab claimed to be the mahdi.

matin Relating to the early morning.

abbot The highest ranking individual in a monastery for men.

ahimsa Indian word meaning reverence for all life and the avoidance of injury to any ing thing.

alwah Arabic word for letters; Baha'ullah sent alwah to sovereign nations to invite port for his prophetic mission in the 1860s.

amulets Charms that were believed to ward off evil such as disease or witchcraft.

anandamayi Word meaning the embodiment of Bliss; taken from the Hindu spi leader Anandamayi Ma.

anachronistic Description of someone or something that is out of chronological

apartheid Legally enforced social and economic separation of groups, usually bet races of people.

apostasy Abandonment or renunciation of a religious faith.

Arians Individuals who believe that Jesus Christ was created as an agent for the cre of the world, and not of the same substance as God.

Armageddon Scene where the Bible predicts the final battle between good and ev be waged.

ascetics Group of people practicing strict austerity measures in relation to their rel faith.

awqaf Arabic word representing Islamic religious endowments.

bania A merchant caste in India into which Mohandas Ghandi was born.

bar mitsvah Rite of passage for young Jewish men, usually at about 13 years of age religious responsibilities are asusmed.

baraka Arabic word for spiritual grace.

bat mitsvah Rite of passage for young Jewish women, usually at about 13 years when religious responsibilities are assumed.

Black Panthers A group of young black men organized in the 1960s in reaction t frustration with the nonviolent stance of civil rights leaders in the United States.

bull A papal letter with the imprint of the bulla (a round seal).

minyan Hebrew word for prayer quorum.

monastic Relating to monasteries, monks, or nuns; resembling a secluded life.

mufti Arabic word signifying an individual recognized as the highest authority in the interpretation of Muslim law.

mujaddid Arabic word meaning "rejuvenator of Islam."

mutumwa Arabic word representing holy messenger and interpreter of Christian doctrines.

namajapa Chanting of God's name in Hindu religion.

nascent New; having recently come into existence.

ngunza Zambian word meaning "prophet" or "preacher."

novice Person newly admitted into a religious organization or community.

novitiate A place where novices or newcomers to a particular skill or belief are trained by experts.

obeisance Bowing or moving in such a way as to show religious devotion and respect.

occident Description of ideas and places relating to the Western hemisphere.

panegyric Formal and often elaborate religious praise.

paradigm An extremely clear example.

penitent Expressing regret or sorrow; repenting for sins.

penury A state of severe poverty.

permeates Passing through or spreading strongly.

pietist A person displaying overly emotional or exaggerated religious devotion.

polytheism Belief in and worship of more than one religion or god.

posthumously An event after the death of an individual related to that individual.

prelate An ecclesiastic of higher rank, such as an abbot or bishop.

prevaricate To stretch the truth or tell an outright lie. Also, to act in collusion with another, or to straddle.

qadar Arabic word meaning free will.

rapprochement The establishment of good relations between previously disagreeing parties.

rood A cross or crucifix symbolic of the cross on which Jesus Christ is said to have died.

sachchidananda Word for the highest level of being, consciousness, and bliss in the Hindu religion.

sachem Native American chief or leader; chief of the Algonquin confederation of tribes of the North Atlantic coast.

sadhana Word for the spiritual discipline in Hindu religion.

Samnyasians Order of Hindu religious scholars.

satyagraha Indian word referring to a "truth force."

sentient Aware; conscious or responsive to certain stimuli or thought.

seraphic Angelic saint—another name ascribed to St. Francis of Assisi.

shahada Profession of faith in Islam.

shibboleth Common custom or methodology.

simony Buying or selling of an ecclesiastical office or position of influence.

sunnah Arabic word which represents the traditions of the Prophet.

sybaritic Luxurious.

syncretism Combination of two or more different forms of belief or religious practice.

synod Episcopalian governing assembly.

taqqanot Hebrew word meaning enactments.

taqlid Arabic word referring to a blind acceptance of tradition or philosophy.

ta-t'ung Great unity.

theophany Visible manifestation of God—as when Moses encountered a burning bush that was not consumed by the fire.

tikkun olam Hebrew for "the improvement of the world."

tirthankars Indian word meaning "finders of the path."

transubstantiation Roman Catholic and Eastern Orthodox belief that the elements of communion transform into the body and blood of Jesus Christ while keeping the appearance of bread and wine.

vihars Buddhist temple compounds.

vizier High-ranking executive officers in some Muslim nations.

wali Arabic word meaning "friend of God."

wu wei Non-doing.

zakat A tithe in the Islamic faith.

Index